REST ASSURED

REST ASSURED

SWAMIJI SRI IRAIANBAN

GenNext Publication

First Published, 2019

Published by

GenNext Publication
5, Ansari Road
Daryaganj, New Delhi-110002
Phone: 9811692060
E-mail: gennextpublication@hotmail.com

Printed at: G. Print Process, Delhi.

Cataloging in Publication Data—DK
Courtesy: D.K. Agencies (P) Ltd. <docinfo@dkagencies.com>

Iraianban, ***Swami*****, author.**
Rest assured / Swamiji Sri Iraianban.
pages cm
ISBN 9789380223568

1. Spiritual life. 2. Religion and science. I. Title.

LCC BL624.I73 2019 | DDC 204.4 23

Contents

Preface

"Rest Assured" is our own personal experiences which have been registered in print for mankind, to uplift themselves to attain liberation. Life is for living, how to live it in this mundane world filled with a wide range of amusements, entertainments, fun and frolic, distractions, recreational delights etc., and achieve salvation, and how to lead life with spiritualism so as to live in this materialistic world with shanthi and peace. This book has been given in **8** chapters, each chapter shows the different procedures and directions to saturate with the Almighty.

Chapter 1 - "The Science of the Cosmos - its influence" makes us to know about "Sri Nataraja's Cosmic Dance", and if we realise the cosmic dance, we can know all else with ease and care. Our curiosity to know more (though nothing is yet known even now) about cosmic science, astrology and cosmic energy is kindled, so as to produce solar energy for the development of our nation and other nations can follow suit. Realisation is the best way to know all the wisdom of this universe, by which one can go beyond the earth's conclusions and all sciences of the structural and physical resemblances, can be easily known by our own senses. If the VI sense is projected, everything will be possible to attain and reasonable for having such maintenance of this universe by atomic power and its branches of sciences.

Then there is the Astro - chemical science by which we can make many trips to all over the world to spell about this Astro - chemical prospectiveness and this can be made public. It is absorbing to know about a new process that is Astro-psychological science - an analysis by which we can easily understand the facts of this component which are in proportion, they have form of structure neutrality and naturality of this article. Astro chemical process philosophy is hard to understand, existing, which is in the brain comes out of it and expels its greatness and thus, we can touch the tip of the ether or sky. This philosophy can be learned by training or experiments, thereby we can easily understand another's intellect. The whole universal science is not at all known by our scientists, so to say knowledge is not sufficient, as we say, we must use our intellectual wisdom, through which we can upgrade ourselves to the extreme plane of science.

Science is valueless in some occasions and thus, mankind can go some distance through the cosmic and solar science, but he cannot penetrate the Horizon of Cosmic science. And yet some super power nations boast of having gone, landed and walked on the moon which is really a humbug, a tall story. It is adviced that we should be aware of the happenings and how mankind is everything for passion, love and affection. Love alone can spread love over the cosmic space. This is emphasised by Shri Natarajamurthy's non - stop dance. He is dancing, we call Him the king of dance; there are many processes, beyond these, one can dance, dance comes out of the pure heart and mind. So our heart is filled with everlasting peace and Budhi may teach good, bad and evil things and they do not make us calm and silent.

We may be of divine birth, come for a divine proposal, which is going to be done through Himself, thus, we have descended to this earth and we will be an ever glittering star in the space dance of Sri Natarajamurthy which can also be explained, if it is identified then the Chidambaram secret is nothing but very easily adored by the human race and this is the supreme stage of spirituality.

Chapter 2 - "The Ins and Outs" deals with the concept of the Guru who is a universal teacher and has attained perfection through his own efforts, by which he has the ability to make us pure, and it is the way to attain eternal salvation. We have highlighted, if we spend our whole life with confidence and truthfulness, God, Himself will visit our residence, our epics emphasise this truth, as we are not aware to wake up from the slumber of maya and our whole strength will be focused to make necessary modes to attain 'Samadhi', while we are living this materialistic life and its consequences will not disturb us in any way. So we must have a Guru, will automatically come in search of us and he comes to make us pure, divine in nature of creation, and we can practice all yogic sadhanas which are karmic for Gnana sadhanas.

This moment onwards, we should make ourselves ready to surrender to such a Guru and thereby make our whole life meaningful by this golden opportunity. He is the most supreme of all beings. According to His judgement, the entire universe is rotating in an orbit and we should realise His extreme greatness and entire powerful sovereignty also. He is the unchangeable being of all the universal beings. He is a mighty powerful Emperor of this mighty creation and He can do anything and everything in a fine manner. One who has lived and is living a chaste life alright then he is considered to be a Gnani and so, he can be established as a boon to mankind. Such horizons will come and set at that time and his entire life is for dedicating his life. Haves and have - nots should be erased and the best actions are to be included within the cost of knowledge and wisdom oriented people, that is why our scriptures specify a chaste life otherwise everything will be a waste, thus, truthfulness is admired by all and this is considered to be the signal of a bonafide one man army.

Bharat or India are the twin names of our nation, marvelous things will happen if any one name is used. So we have to either call Bharat or India. When generally we call India, our ancestral genesis is grasped'; if we call Bharat, we can realise the ancestral code of our nation, 'so, this collusion should be eradicated.

We openly declare to strengthen our Army Force, Navy Force and Air Force to ward off our enemies on all; sides. We make a dig at the government on advertisements given by it, concerning the matter on ladies. If we concentratingly note this point - This is wearable, no chance of Aids? We question whether this is the way to stop prostitution? According to myself this advertisement only encourages and flourishes the habit of prostitution by humanity, but we insisit on being a role model for the citizens, and so the advertisement should be - 'If you have domestic conjugation with your wife, wife wishes to conjugate with her husband at all times, it is acknowledged and advisable, other advertisements may cause us cancer or urinal infection and sexual diseases, they are not curable; so be chaste citizens of India. If this is the advertisement it will transform India as Ramarajyam. We are all wishing to establish Ramarajyam, but in those advertisements, you may have connection with anybody but for safety, use our products; is this a progressive nation? Nothing. Even if 10,000 Gandhis and 20,000 Jesus, 1000000 Nabis come again to this earth, they will at the next moment desire to return to their abode and curse our culture and instructional life's atrocities and we never can stand erectly at all so, if each man/woman is chaste then what is the work for condoms and the likes of these kinds of advertisements.

There is more to it in this chapter which makes one get involved in the book. This chapter wholly deals with my life's experiences, activities, ideals and thoughts on various subjects and topics.

We prevail upon the fact that a conducive, lovable atmosphere should persist in the family by all means, in every way and in every situation and this is stressed' upon in **Chapter 3** - "Go Home To Live". Parents receive a secret order to keep us from time of birth until their last breath; but we? so we should be ready to do service to them physically and mentally. The service to our nation, universe gives us peace and harmony throughout our life. So, like patriotism, we should have enough directorship to render service to the aged.

Female gender is on the whole of turbulent character; they wish to over rule the male gender. That is why this kind of transferable to untransferable; we can earn and how to earn and learn to be ready to do whatever kind of work there is; their fundamental loop holes are found in our general political life. Whoever may be, everybody is struggling to preserve their ancestral fame and name, this is because they wish to establish good fame for our ancestors. Thus, the females are existing satisfactorily and sophistically leading their lives.

'Parents carefully maintain their whole family with care and they protect their son's wife and children, but at the same time when parents are old enough, their children are grown up, but nobody is willingly to look after their parents safely. They are not secure in their old age as children think they are a burden to them in their old age session, in which they will search for humility support and at least they need the security of their children. But in most homes they are only houses but not homes.

We are anxious so as to speak on the new trend that has arisen. Each 2 year old child is pushed into school. Whether he/she gets education or not, he/she should not bother parents. This kind of mentality is rampant, in course of time, how can we expect a loyal real helpful son / daughter to be thriving. Like the parents they too simply act as if they are looking after their parents. We may say, within a hut, a man and female as wife - husband make themselves as Father/Mother and look after their parents. We simply have the Brahma's Shrusti in order to look after them kindly and smoothly, we just put children in school and we leave as parents. Parental care, without this, our sons and daughters and so on go in a mischievous way of life.

We reckon that our nation, India is among all countries the one which is a karmic bhoomi and those who have done penance, can be having birth in India. If the world is a home, the pooja room is considered to be a boon for us, where we will not do any untoward action. We may have 36500000 crores of money or American dollars, but hunger, thirst and appetite and whenever we are sleeping He should make us awake, otherwise, we are not men and women; others simply neglect our names and simply call us corpse. Such an impermanent life, that we own. Within 365 days plus, worldly days, make us to live in this world; we can earn more than 3650000 dollars, but it is not easy to live such and such days, when we count it, our nature of life is based upon our inhalation and exhalation of air. Such jeevan point is fixed in our body and that is why, we are speaking and talking.

God alone gives and forgives; man gets and forgets, that is why their fate is in action and as a result they are very much afraid of married life and so, we should be careful in choosing a bride or a bridegroom. Our knowledge and wisdom is having certain limitations. Apart from these, we have to rejoice or trouble ourselves and so we must have faith upon the Almighty, we can assimilate anything whether it is positive or negative and its repulsions too. A unit is a home. We can build beautiful houses but not a home. Home means, all the members living under one roof, such united family alone can win the race. But, today, after marriage, son/daughter with their relations set themselves a magical family and thus, we are troubling ourselves so much. So we should cultivate what is needed in order to live for all, for all creatures' well being.

True friendship does what is what and it identifies ourselves true love, so friendship with male / female will convince and their main balance is only love and affection and friendship cannot be explained by each other; now we are having so many friends, but only for fulfilling some desires. If he is our friend, we can marry his sister who is so beautiful; such theme is basically taken and cinemas are coming out. Truthful friendship always convinces and consoles our heart with full of contentment and it forgives all means of acts without punishment. There is no tension, untoward doings in connecting with pure friendship. Mainly if we pray God for a good friendship, He, Himself descends for us to be in friendship with Him. Example, Sri Sundarar and Sri Parameswaran; their unity is exemplified by one word 'friendship'.

Chapter 4 - In this Chapter, we lay bear what is life and how to attain the aim and goal of life. Thus, it is an "Intellectual Search for Divinity" as, this confused life is full of ananda; as such several people are thinking and hoping to live without leaving it and they are very much fond of having all facilities. We can live a comfortable life without any doubt. But with enough experience, we start to realise the worthlessness of the whole world. There is no change of permanent choice of happiness, and these sorrows seem to be our foresight and we falsely acknowledge this life is full of Ananda. In any corner of this earth, there is nothing, particularly Ananda is not in pursuit because of maya or illusionary sight, in different angles, some happiness is in all activities and this is false. When we come around the incidents and actions, there is nothing which is having permanent happiness or sorrow, which are identified falsely, when we look, these objects are the orientation of happiness. Naturally we believe there is only happiness in each and every action in full, but there is only sorrow, when we search for it in the earth. There is nothing, filtered as happiness and nothing can be segmented as sorrows. Everything is the illusionary appearance, because of our parachemical view and that is why, it seems to be sorrow or happiness.

Thus sorrow and happiness are rolling over us. What we think as sorrow, there is something which repels as success. So both feelings are actually available, but we weigh these facts because of our creation of those sensual assessments. Senses with mind have oneness period, its illusionary perception is exhibition of happiness and are involving in those exercises, have the exhibition of happiness and sorrowful activities. Though the activity is done by us, we are not responsible for our activity and hence, nothing in this world will include us as a member of the action or inaction.

May be our thoughts and deeds differentiate one from another but desire is ever not changeable; such crimes can be pardoned in the name and recommended by those men and women because of their own circumstances.— Men's desires are uncountable, So we have to suffer a lot, if we obey and fear God, then our life will be a satisfied one and everything which given to us is the mighty boon of His grace and mercy. Karunyam is the best stage of the humanitarian race and so our life will be entirely blossomed with divine nectar and scents, because there He is in His mighty residence and where is His residence, it is as simple as the pure Heart.

According to our circumstances and time factor, we believe everything is done by us; this is the failure fact, because our do's and don'ts trail, will give us no confirmed solution, everything is altered as an altar, He remains controlling everything in our favour or otherwise. If we realise it we will be saints on one side of the coin. If we keep silence and patience, we will one day achieve our aim and goal, which is derived by God and He expects at all times, our characteristic phenomena of peace and brotherhood harmony. We speak and lecture in a hall of fame, trying to earn and learn how to make money; but by mere accumulation of money, we cannot buy our inner conscious' contentment and satisfaction.

Godliness, cannot be attained within one minute or one hour, whole span of life is not enough to establish our mind with gurgitations. Exercises and their implementational footsteps over the plane of mind to establish this, we first, should have patience, thus, we can attain peace which is ever present in ourselves. Those who have won the outer world are respected very much, but at the same time, we have to win over our senses, they have to naturally stand still, so we have to control it by our mind. If mental equilibrium is kept then all will be easy to make things normal. This is the universal fact. If we are ready to cause in the midst of all, first we have to stop our talking and should give preference to our best thoughts, deeds by realising the uncertainty of all. Nothing in this universe is stable it is the natural fact and we should adhere to the rules without mistake. We shall attain our originality within a second or fraction of a second.

Mind is to be on the plane of peace and harmony not by doing yogic exercises, but whatever we do, if we do them with true pious dedicated significances, we can attain even jeevasamadhi. Here, we quote for example saint Thiagaraja Swamy, Sri Ramakrishna Paramahamshar or even Sri Ramalingar who all did not do any thanthric modes or any specific yogic exercises but purely by their piety and dedication they attained their deities simply.

Divinity what does it mean? Everybody has his own conclusion about this term divinity. It is nothing but purity of mind and action and goodness of our deeds and thoughts, also to be with full of purity and shanthiful confidence upon the Almighty, then only we can realise the full meaning of the divinity of everything. We question the genuineness of the many rishis and munis and peedams all over the world. Just this one question is put to them, that is what was their last birth? Where did they live and who were their parents, and how many brothers and sisters they had? What was his/her educational qualifications in that birth? and how many years he/she lived in that birth? Is there any sage or swamiji in India or all around the world to answer these questions? They know something about epics and truths from books. They learn some basic tricks and simply cheat humanity, earning more and more recognition, medals and money and lastly they live their life in jail and die as orphans. We caution the forthcoming generations to beware of such duplicates and also before entering into this spiritual world.

Chapter 5- "It is Now or Never" is a thought provoking chapter to make us realise that this human birth is given to us now in order to attain liberation and saturate with the Almighty. If it is not now, in this human birth, then, we cannot be sure that we will be given a human birth in our next cycle of birth. May be we will born as some creature or so. We are having a golden, excellent chance to live as a human being in this birth, we must utilise this chance to do good deeds and attain personal salvation, otherwise if it is wrongfully lived for the name sake of life there is nothing to be blessed by Him and we cannot get rid of births and deaths. So doing our prompt deeds salvation will be a sure one. Whatever we do, we should start as a dedication to Himself and begin our deed, nothing will be a failure and everything will be without delay and the final result will be a 1st: class end. So, now, we should be living with thoughts of Himself alone and this will give us all benefits and gains. Wherever we are, but, we should be with His thoughts and chanting the holy name of God. Chanting will give us permanent shanthi to make our mind go in the path of His way and thereby we will get our deed successfully done. Most probably, all are to attain success in all of their deeds, we should fix an attachment with him always then our deeds will be Himself and so victory will be the end of the courses. So, chanting his name with divine mood we have success in all our deeds and His presence will do quite good to all creatures. That is. why, God Himself is born in this earth for doing good to all, but we never understand His deeds, and we blame His deeds, after knowing that He is Universal, we fall in love with Him, at that time, He will be seated in our heart and the ones searching His place attain nothing.

Wherever and whenever we have time, we should utilise it and express our ideas with proper understanding of the audience. If we set a bulletin, it is to screwing their mind and are perfectly doing the proper handling of the public audiences' expressions and their impulses, Therefore, when we have a chance to give an idea elaborately explain our ideas and conclusions, by which we will be an eminent lecturer and orator and demonstrator about any event. Thus, if we are not able to express our ideas and regulations, for the next time, we have to wait, or at that time which will be the modern trend and the ideas will change altogether. Thus, our ideas will not be considered, that is why, our chance of expressing should be delivered without any hesitation and objections, we can boldly express the impressions of the ideas...

So also we should play any game and in one chance we gain victory in two ways, one is playing the game and another is trying to promote the game's introduction too. As such so many fantastic players life is wasted because they are not given opportunity to exhibit their skills. Politics and money are playing a hand in the selection and the play is hand transferring, so if we choose basket ball icons, are here, football experts and geniuses are more in number but we are not at all selecting the dispensed players; if we identify them, all the cups in sports and games will be for us Indians. Such trained experts are here, but we are not having the sense to identify and make a good team. We challenge the government also. Therefore, steadily and without desire for money and recommendation, if we select some eleven boys they can win even the world cup in all games and sports.

As according to life's rules and regulations, their insistence may differ, but the main embryo sac is only one which is meant to be realised by all. If it is in day-to-day life, there will be quarrels with each other, and all are having right to walk in the streets with hands swinging front and backwards, but it would disturb others. Likewise, we should maintain even other religion's regulations, and they can pray whoever they may be, our Bhakthi is universal, God alone will come to invite us to His divine hall---

Economically, one may be weak, but humanity's sight, the Guru, is a gem among all and has character and thayai and grace. Such persons are in need in today's political and social life, if we practice our children everywhere, all sects and creeds, beyond sex and religions we can establish a new era in our lively situation of the Universe. Today, we are in need of forgiveness, tolerance, anti- corruption. All are willingly and wishing to have divine life, but we are not knowing the path how to make up our answer to this question, then we will be the genius among all fools.

Chapter 6 - 'Wisdom for Elevation'. India is a karmic bhoomi, where there is no time for mankind to spend even a second or its fraction without proper renunciation of life. Those who are willing to attain eternal liberation have to follow our rules and regulations and thereby they can be peaceful and lead a peaceful co-ordinated life. Maybe we are educated and learning to earn a lot of paper currencies, gold, silver and platinum ornaments, lots of designed clothes, but these never come with us to the court of God. So, we can be always aware of our thoughts and deeds, that is why, prayer and lovable heart towards others is needful; we can cheat our consciousness but not God, the Almighty.

Motivation of life should not be disturbed; but life's vibrations will certainly attack us is the essence, is quite essential, otherwise we will not be energetic. If we have belief and total surrender, are only for having a good result in our life, by showing bhakthi and worshipping sharply without any bilateral assignments, we can have the best felicitation which is given to us. If we want to attain from all, we have to respect first, and then show it to others, it will return 50 percent above the range of our respect which we show towards others. Nobody will be fond of our words and they will never be taken into consideration and nothing can be achieved with fulfillment.

Those who are willing to lead a noble life, they must be ready to get rid of evil thoughts and deeds, because our body and soul are dispensed by God, and they are to be utilised for the divine purpose only. A proverb is in our language-- "The fear of God is the beginning of knowledge", there is nothing in this world is stable. All things and activities are unstable and nothing is permanent. Our life's ambition, the basic principle of human life is to saturate with Eternal Bliss. That, is why God created this marvellous body and all inner and outer organs through which we should predominantly thrive with Civilisation and Self-Realisation and thus, we will be free from births and deaths.

India is the biggest democratic country and it is honoured by all nations because of its holy principles. Unity, maybe, diversity between Religions, Creeds, Sects and Languages, they are all together when nation wide thought arises. This nation is a Karmic Bhoomi, where God, Himself descends to the plane of earth and lives according to the mundane principles and regulations and they emphasise what is Dharma, how it is operating everything and itself too.

What is mediation? Even our masters, so called for acquiring mental stamina to race through any problems in the midst of this materialistic burdens were very much confident that yoga will eradicate all our sins and give us ideology of subject and art of living. So they spent money for yoga, but this is not at all the way to keep body and mind, and then they simply have confidence with characteristic phenomena of the Art of Living. In this present period nothing can be fruitful by doing some breathing exercises in the name of yogic exercises; and it is very different to keep clean both our mind and body. Apart from these simply to say that by these practical efforts we cannot attain anything by which we spend more money and thereby only ruin our body and meditation and there is nothing to do so; it is the simplest way to get rid of the burdens; we simply spoil others too, by spending time in the morning and evening hours, we cannot attain anything of ecstasy. So if we do namashmarana of Holy God alone we can make us pure and clean; thus, we can simply attain our inner conscious mental equilibrium. If our thoughts and deeds are on the right procedure to attain salvation, Bhakthi yoga in this kaliyuga period is very easily fruitful to be saturated with Divine honey and thus, our human birth will bloom to the highest pedestal/plane of ecstasy.

Chapter - **7** Every single second, we are getting old and expecting death; this valuable human birth is not sure to be dispensed once again to us with the sense of bhakthi and Athma Vichara. If this is possible, the only way, He must dispense Himself to us, whole heartedly approve of us as His Bhakthas; otherwise, we cannot even have a single thought of Him whether He is present or not; and we cannot at all have a permanent solution for this puzzle, and thus, we plan this life for about 365 days (it is not at all sure that we can have 100 years of life) so within this stipulated period, have to overcome all of our materialistic worries, miseries and losses. We have to be obedient, sincere and polite and patiently search our own selves. Thus, we can identify us and can realise our inner self is full of His own and nothing else. These are not imagination or money making efforts. It is sathyam on Himself. So, have belief upon these holy words. They are universal truths, they cannot be changed in any circumstance by these materialistic creatures. We should have such brain and mind to realise, then only we can be known by ourselves first and then by others as a true Gnani. He Himself comes to show His full infrastructural phenomenon of deeds and thoughts to us. He is ever ready to contact us, but we have not the thinking about the Holiest Paramathama to the entire upliftment of our materialistic and spiritual lives.

All are willing to live with wealth and health for a long time, but we have to know our fate. For all of us our time of death is mentioned herewith when we come to this earth. God fixed it, each respiration is counting in and out and how many respirations are to him, that is his span of life. We are thinking that through astrology, we can come to know all about our life and date of death. This is not known by anybody even Yamadharma Rajan does not know it, it is the intuition by Sivam at that time, the incident will happen and the soul will be free from all worthless life.---- This is the sad situation for the longest life. So, everything is having one and only, stage of rest, each and every being needs rest of mind and body, otherwise the whole body will be easily decayed to the bottom of the heart and become diffused, in a sense we become mad and nothing can be done forever, so death is nothing but, an interval pattern for the passage of mind and soul. So, we have to live whole heartedly and earn and learn each and everything.

Human beings have the privilege to get rid of births and deaths. How?! This is elaborately discussed in this chapter. First 'I' and You' what does it mean? we have to identify 'I' and you' what do they mean? This is a favourite question.--- As scheduled by the Almighty every single second of time can be utilised in a proper manner by which we can attain the abode of God.

Whatever we earn, whatever we learn, whatever we accumulate whether it is gold or platinum etc., our honours convocation certificates will be got rid of. Nothing can be done, after death occurs. So daily we have to spend a single second to think about death; here in this world all and everything is impermanent. What we see and study are only due to Maya illusions, because of maya, it seems to be real and permanent, so we have to realise the full truthfulness and illusions and realise that which is permanent is God alone; nothing is permanent other than Him, we must realise our truthfulness and destruction and we are day by day marching towards destruction of this body, but nobody can even touch the soul, this is the supremacy of the Supreme Truth.

This chapter 'Why Life and Death Occur' is spell binding, fascinating for it educates man not to have fear about Death. Death is only an incident, occurrence between Life and Death. As we read on we come to realise that Yama Dharma comes to snatch away the soul of the sinful ones; but the elevated souls, who have attained salvation, liberation, are on the pedestal of Ecstasy, they go into Samadhi and even while in Samadhi they perform miracles, and do good to the whole of humanity. This chapter simmers down or rather totally banishes our fear of death and we will learn that it is meaningless to mourn or weep or lament at the death of even our own kith and kin, relatives, friends and parents too. This chapter enlightens the reader and trains his mind to be fearless about Death. Each and everyone is willingly eager to live a good healthy and most probably wealthy life and it should be a long one. Nobody wants to die, if one comes to realise about DEATH it is so sweet, sweeter than any other of these mundane Honey experiences.

Chapter- 8 This chapter "Rest Assured" means nothing but tolerance, which is held by anyone, he will always be happy and he will not effectively bother about anything. Another elucidation of "Rest Assured" is to emphasise that what is said is true or will definitely happen. We emphatically stress to be bold, as we can execute, and exercises can uplift us to the highest pedestal of Eternity. Often we are stressing, this is the human birth's motto.

Everybody, they always have fear about anything and everything; fear complex is always a dangerous one, and it should be erased by the heart itself from the sapling stage; if it grows, it will uproot us without any kind of worthfulness and value of our dispensed life. But fear of God is the beginning of knowledge. Therefore, we have to be out of fear complex and thus, we can boldly face any kind of problems throughout our entire life. If we have fear upon God, it will always, keep us to lead a beautiful life which is registered and He will dispense Himself through Himself; thus, our ancestors like Karaikalammaiyar, Theresa, Kamarajar, lived a very calm life, without name and fame, and today we are trying to live that kind of life. This is Tapas and Penance. This is the one and only way to attain His grace and mercy, by which we can set up our self- betterment life very easily. So we also emphasise that if we have belief upon God Himself, He is, ready at all times and circumstances to come to our assistance throughout our life span. If we also are ready to trust Himself, to entertain our life with fullest satisfaction and contentment, He will fulfill all our needs---, Rest Assured.

We are nothing but God Himself, His will and pressure pushes through curses, boons; and dispensations, we are here to resolve all of our credits. If there is no income and expenses automatically, He will definitely release us from this births and deaths' cycle. This is the juice of all Religions Epics, Puranas and whole spiritualism's goal and will.

If anyone is in an angry mood, he is supposed to be an animal; if he discusses whether it is correct or not, he is in a manual mood; if he is in the mood of speaking and thinking about God's prosperity and values, he is considered to be in a divine mood. Thus, we must identify and in this way we should live our own life. If it is possible, God will come to us without any rituals and ceremonies. He is the utter slave for Bhakthi only. Do bear this in mind and Rest Assured.

Kaliyuga is considered to be the very miserable yuga, with all the evils, all destructions on the fullflow and very difficult to live according to Dharma. Adharma will be demolished by God, thus, He, Himself comes as the Mightiest man and destroys all the evils to construct the pillar of Dharma.

Up to this day, all illusions, unbelievable, unexpectable happenings will happen and thus, the whole universe will be in the grip of Adharma. Those who are leading a shanthi and peaceful life will suffer a lot, but illegal persons will be crowned as the first class men and women in this kaliyuga. The pure Educationalists, will not be honoured; the rulers and their rulership modes are not honoured and accepted by God, but according to Yuga Dharma, they also acknowledge the happenings and this kaliyuga honours each and every rowdy element. Even the educationalists too are the slaves of money and they give ideas to the wicked to earn money and they make them to be the major donors to construct temples and the welfare of normal peace. These wicked and money minded people construct many universities, schools in order to acquire more and more money---But God is the witness; whenever His turn comes, these bloody rascals will be out of the frame; if they realise this truth the world itself will be very fine as God dispenses all---. Rest Assured.

This chapter illustrates what is soul? What is Paramathma the connection between the two aspects, the dharsan of our true Acharya and Acharyas, the role they play in the common man's life. They stress on the Vairagya that should be divine, for vairagya for others comes through dejection and unfulfilled desires. When we expound our views on the subject, though all human beings are seeming to be one by only infrastructural appearance, there are crores and crores of Gunas (habits, characteristics) and all in all they are having many more differences that is, God's mighty creation. --- The book explicitly illustrates the tech- constructional Engineering of God. Some may seem to be Gnanies and yogis, but they are not able to control their outer and inner organic systems and their evolutions and how they suffer a lot. On the other hand, True yogis are up and up in the evolutions and up in the elevation point of Mukthi, thus, their vairagya stimulates day by day and they surely attain the lotus feet of God. This chapter also elucidates the mode of prayer and thankful adorations. It expounds the salient features of the Guru who is divinely character - oriented and his equanimity. It further goes on to state the realisation of the inhidden universal truth, that is, everything is operated by the Almighty and we are only puppets in His hands. The Almighty only proposes, and He also disposes of all. He has a hand in everything we do or say. He insists on cultivating mental and will power to face the force of the Athman, that is our inner strength of the soul.

We have not at all written this book for name and fame and particularly not for money, He insisted and gave "Rest Assured"---. and He Himself has imprinted all the words. Hence, it is not our work. He has made us an instrument and this is delivering as His wish and pleasure. He gave us the job, and we have done it. Rest will be His will and pleasure. On the whole, the readers can delve deep into the depths of this vast ocean of wide experiences and emerge with materialistic and spiritual thoughts, deliberations, contemplations to be enlightened. Each chapter gives ounces of pure spiritual knowledge and true wisdom to cultivate with an open mind so as to attain the highest learning by which we know God, all else a mere waste, and also to tune our own life to the path of spiritual journey in order to reach our original abode the Lotus Feet of the Almighty.

Chapter - 1

Science of the Cosmos-Its Influence

"Rest Assured" is the topic of this book, Which deals with our ancient sidhars' marvellous service to the Universal beings. They have done service not only to human beings; the whole universe would learn a lesson as they had emphasised according to their age of period, language and situations. Hinduism emphasises all its ceremonies and customs which are to be analysed. They are pure vedantha and nature of chemical integrations are foolish and childish in nature and so all are not able to understand, and by grasping those Universal Truths we come to realise the nature of human beings' livelihood nature. Our civilisation is the forerunner of all medical science; even, they have touched astrological point through "Sri Nataraja's cosmic dance".

If we realise the cosmic dance, we can know all else with ease and care. Our science is day by day developing and constructing during the phenomena of such innumerable constitutions; but we are not as patient as the other animals keep their times to reach their goal; so the entire cosmic energy is lost by losing our energy in some mundane exercise.

The whole humanity is willing to know about solar energy and its significances and is trying to use it for the development of their commitments, and each nation wants to be a super power among all nations. That is why, they are very eagerly sending so many rockets to know about the cosmic insistence and its' energetic world. But how to do this, is not known properly by them. That is why, they are not knowing what to do? If anyone lights one candle, automatically they will light all the candles by their earnestness and by their conscious inner subtle efficiencies. They have some knowledge and wisdom; but they are not suitable to go forward in this field, and though they are unable to do, they are always trying their best to clip one of the tiny drops of water and make it an ocean. So if one film is caught, then they will be able to make their foot prints to the planet or star sometimes, they publish in magazines and newspapers about cosmic energy that they know their longitude and latitude, there should be no place to organise it to discover a new point through their activities. Some times they fail; some times, they give them some lesson to the level of consciousness of the Almighty.

If the VI sense is projected, everything will be possible to attain and reasonable. for having such maintenance of this universe by atomic power and its branches of sciences. Though we have enough power of realising and doing the processes of atomical science in a comparable way, we do not have such ability to reproduce it into remarks of huge quality and quantity. Our epics, Idhikasas emphasise several Arrows namely devasthras; they can be utilised in person but not asthmas which are not seen, they make the valid into invalid. Our ancestors, through severe penance got several asthras from various deities for use in battles; as such all are doing Tapas to get some asthras (arrows and bows) through God's dispensable disciples, and they won the races verily. But today's world, we cannot do such Tapas or penance and get God's grace directly, because this is Kaliyuga, so we have to introduce our scientific knowledge to compensate such instruments and should win the races. Likewise, we are having abundance of knowledge to analyse about today's needs and fulfill them and keep the nation very safely. Such power is natural. We got it in birth, and this is the supreme truth and therefore, we can be one of the super forces among all other nations.

First, we have to win over our fear over all things; whether it is lively, or not we have such fear to touch even the portrait or statue of a tiger; we all have fear over such kinds of animals, instruments, even shadows; if we are fearless first, we will win the race first step. Then we can win the battle in some armed ways and use our weapons with tactics; we shall show our courage. Thus, we can win the second stage of the battle, for we can win the battle with strength and unity, and we can win it very easily. Like it, this World is on ...!

Realisation is the best way to know all the wisdom of this Universe, by which one can go beyond the earth's conclusions and all Sciences of the structural and physical resemblances, can be easily known by our own sense. Though these five elements are going on revolving around each other, there is no proof of embracing even one another. This is the best science which is the natural situation of the cosmic power. Though they produce para-electrical sense they stimulate the cosmic science to be known by everyone of us, because it is very interesting to realise the cosmopolitant surroundings of these planets and stars. This cosmic science kindles mankind to know about the scientific truth which is behind the stars and planets, and their contents. Is there any chance of pressurising and sailing over them, the opportunities to survive a normal life there and science gives us the supreme power by which we can go beyond this science and learn about their vast knowledge and their ingredients in these mandalas and through which, man can feel and realise the senses of the solar science. Through this we can come to a conclusion to fulfill the fullest recall of this exclamatory appraisal of these claiming up the decisions, and by which we can understand the development of the science of this solar scientific naturalism. By proposing this attitude, we can have a clear cut idea of solar energy its existence, its naturality, its density and their systems of power production can be known thoroughly. Thus, we can come to a conclusion to do what is necessary, or nothing at all, if it is useful for the development of humanity to grow with or by this science. If there is any possibility from this solar science to humanity it is well and good to utilise it by using this energy. We can grow up and up the level of some plane by which solar can be utilised for the development of natural and synthetic sciences. Throughout this entire humanity may increase its energy power to the upgrade mark of such production of something whether they are chemical of physical sciences. These both predominantly occupy the energical circumference and such ways, we can progress to save the energy and use it for our scientific development. Such developments may encourage us to do so many achievements in the fields of physics and chemistry, even we can go to the mark of atomic plantation. Thus, the plantation can be spilt into electron and neutrons and we can have much more uncountable quantity of solar energy through which we can do the level best for agriculture, physical and chemical developments and introduce new formulae for the development of this physio-chemical atomic sciences. And this is to be centered and all the humanity will be benefitted to the mark of existence of all creatures and these scientific fields should be common to all mankind. Otherwise, the powerful nations will make them as its royalty combined ownership and other nations will not know about this. Is there any justice?

The whole universal science is not at all known by our scientists; we have some knowledge about something in some ways with some creations, but if our desire to know and realise the part and parcel of those who are responsible for the scientific principles as such as we desire to have pure science, then only we can really realise the truth of true knowledge, so to say, knowledge is not sufficient; we must use our intellectual wisdom, through which we can upgrade ourselves to the extreme plane of science. Science is valueless in some occasions and thus, mankind can go some distance through the cosmic and solar science, but he cannot penetrate the Horizon of cosmic science. We are producing so many cinema type wars and warriors through which all our desire is to accumulate huge money and felicitations. And their desires are fulfilled, but they cannot know the science of solar and cosmic science, there are many more scientific fields, the wisdom of a human being cannot penetrate this cosmic technology so, therefore, we should be ready to estimate scientific mythological survey, then only we can go into the deepest atom of science. Thus, we can penetrate the cosmic science towards analysis of its hard and smoothness beyond doubts. Through our continuous efforts, we have some scientific clarification of truth (science) and each subject has its own final result of its own. We have to fulfill all the knowledge of the whole science, how is it possible? In dreams, we can achieve a step, but not in the state of reality.

We can imagine; and all should be original from one and all will merge with that point of every spot; because there is no other point of saturation with oneness of the scientific departments. There are many, more, most divisions in the field of Science, but all cannot be realised upto the mark. Because it is natural, one can be fluent in one only, not in all points. Nobody can be a lawyer, doctor, engineer, businessman, speaker, clerk, manager, director, film actor and as all at the same time. Thus, there are so many, innumerous departments in science but we can specialise in only one department, at one time. We can manage to understand it and have some good conclusion; but all will not be possible. So these discoveries are one among all the uncountable departments. But, in one point, we can be a genius to the highest level, through which some truth can be established in the world and thus, we can be honoured to the highest mark. We may be a genius in physics or chemistry, if you for example, cannot be mastering two or three departments of chemical studies. As such, no one can achieve this kind of super knowledge. That is why our proverbs trumpet that ours is accountable; but those who are not knowing are abnormal and abundant in number. Likewise, we can be a master of one period of field. No field is known thoroughly and though we should be knowing our inability and its natural phenomenon of this life's innocence and inability to uncover all dusts of our physical world.

We are struggling and quarreling with nature, to win over it. It is an utter foolish action, first, we have to assimilate this universal truth; all our thoughts, deeds and results will be reflections and refractions of our past, present and future livelihood. So, we should be aware of the happenings and how mankind is everything for passion love and affection. Love alone can spread love over the cosmic space. This is emphasised by shri Natarajamurthy's non-stop dance. He is dancing, we call Him the king of dance, there are many processes, beyond those, one can dance; dance comes out of the pure heart and mind, so our heart is filled with everlasting peace; and Budhi may teach good, bad and evil things and they do not make us calm and silent.

All our scientists and astrologers are handy enough to produce power when they know how to break an atom and how much yield is gotten. Frankly they are lying that this power will be utilised only for agricultural and chemical development; but other nations calculate the number of such bombs and how they react; when WAR is declared all are well equipped with such weapons, and they will certainly use their bombs with fiery attack. Then, what will be our words; we are assuring one, but, so to say, we react in another way. Thus, we lack strength and valour. Such courage, is essential, but not this way. Peace, truthfulness, patriotism, giving respect to all; then we establish such a blossoming human life; we are not animals, but our behaviors are nothing but resemblance of animals, we should be cautious, there is no choice at all. But non-violence is the one and only way to establish Ramarajyam.

If we derail from this theme, we have to face more untoward happenings. I am saying that we react as cowards; but the war, of frustrations, we have to be patient to provide peace and shanthi. Moreover, our activities are not at all equalised to zoological studies; husband quarrels with wife. They quarrel with each other and come to court for divorce, Is this civilisation? Animals are far better than us; if a cow is pregnant the male will not go nearby, by the smell it discovers that the cow is pregnant but our human beings, from the womb the child is facing the world, he or she is willing to have copulation, so, we are in the form of man and woman, but our habits are lower than animals; so, we have first of all to modernise as human beings typically.

Philosophy. is described as the formula of a concept and it explains the classification of these materialistic concepts. Theoretically it is nothing but the test of a truth. If we understand about philosophy, this means that only these concepts are described about whatever the field is. Truly, philosophy is the customs of the trials by which we understand the circumstances and situations, which is conceived into an embryo sac of the truths and this is nothing but the consequences of the mundane circumstances and other fields. So, it is considered that it is the acceptance of the concrete substance which brings the natural, truth, ever pervading of the fact, and full of truths are subjected to the emphasis of our own trials. Such circumstances will be very rare and they are very important to capture the department that chooses to analyse about all and some truths and these are nothing but the ever living philosophical societies and this is the main subject of one's full truthfulness, it can be available in public and make the people to apply it in their own propositions and innocence and in accordance of the essence of truthfulness. So, philosophy can be described as the pure Truth.

As per Astro-chemical science is illustrating the students, about the formation of hills and sand, they are universally doctorates, even though they conclude this aspect, how can we have its illustrations. Whether it is called philosophy, it should be indefinitely analysing these facts and opinions would enter into the laboratory and which is truth and which is wrong, we have to adhere to the pathway of science, we can get some of the truths as they are especially essential to the felicitation of concepts. If we thoroughly analyse these concepts slowly but steadily we can examine their truthful nature and their assistance in an environment of situations, if they note down and explain those books can solve our doubts, therefore we can be a genius in astro-chemical field. According to the prachnam (prophetic words) it is, we will know all the subjects theoretically but not in experience, we will be honoured by being given cups, medals and so on. Many trips to all over the world to spell about this Astro-chemical prospectiveness will be brought about on the dias by us - therefore, we will be honoured by all pundits thereof.

Astro-chemical industry is on one side. We come to a new process that is Astro-psychological analysis, we can easily, understand the facts of this component which are in proportion, they have form of this structure neutrality and naturality of this article, so, we can study the subject elaborately and understandingly. We have to explain this truth by our means of life, and then come to explain the subject, when it is analysed it is very much understandable, the Astro-Chemical process is again hard to understand its philosophy, existing, which is in the brain comes out of it and expels its greatness, and thus, we can touch the tip of the ether or sky. Whoever may be this is the process only, you can learn this philosophy, through training or experiments you can easily understand somebody's intellect may begin to work and then they will be a genius and a doctorate will, come easily, and automatically.

And therefore, they quote; some quotations will be told to telecast these facts so, we the students do not go to other professors to get rid of these mistakes, totally, one self is dependable is very hard, if they spread around all, most of the pupils will determine, that all their doubts can be resolved, so keep balance and equilibrium of mind, otherwise, they have to lose this world ultimately.

The culture and civilisation and contemporary companions sort out our life sketch to the agreeable factor, and they are twins and they work as a vasthu, but in two ways, it will help us towards the gateway of possession of this mundane world and thus, they will be out of delay and hence, aid when a man both idiotically, and ideologically, they are lazy but due to their uncomfortable moods, they simply propose without any kind of intervention such as doing and their modes of demonstration. Thus, they provide their cause of him and he remains to the pedestal of all organic systems. So, our sole metabolism is equaled between mind their speed and recovery of those prepositions which is already classified into several parts and they can minimise them in order to prevent diseases and mental depression, they cannot withstand and wither all of their leaves, then where are the fruits, nothing else, will be apart from non-sensual accumulations and thereby we have to face the problems. It will kindle you to tackle in this way; we must be cautions, do this procedure and thus, everyone is naturally quite enjoyable and at the most rejoice through all channels of the world. Normally, the gap between ours is not an establishment and instrumental so, what we can ask it will not be done through any formulae and thus, they accompany us to do the same task. This kind of risky task taken into consideration, it will be a great boon to all of us. Through this period, we should be prepared to offer anything we wish is an essential mode of Meditation or yogic exercise. Therefore, there will be no mistakes and thus, we were helpless, but now like yours so many people are taking part of our damages and illustrations wrong and we should elevate the signals of the procedure of customs, which are present by all means.

Those who are interested in yoga or yogic exercises, should continue those exercises daily. Our physical body will be shaped sizably and mental strength grows day by day to a certain measurement and, physical, intellectual body also combine altogether and run on their own ways. Thus, our body and soul get strength to be in an extraordinary wisdom which will be in one line and we have to finish and understand the formulae without any mistakes and there will be no chance to have doubts of life and its style and mode of life. In modern times we join one of the so many yoga classes and trumpet this as a rare being and these are not sufficient to realise first, who am "I". If it is finally realised through myself then, it will be the final stage and one can attain Astama sidhies and he is crowned by all beings as a respectful being and it very much difficult and rare to identify him. He is supposed to be the part and parcel of all things. He is ever living and everlasting, capable of grasping anything from the five elements, and he can estimate and create an astral body and marvelous and excellent activities are done without publicity. When his time comes, he is ready to pull out this fleshy body and remove His soul separately and saturate with the Almighty. All the stars, human beings are drawn to these divine twinklings and they serve the universal beings in all planets which they control and govern and the normal materialistic world of the people, by the people; for the people; thus, the star which is up graded by God, it showers the mighty boons to this universe, thus, all beings are doing all activities. They are in normal stage to the prime state by doing soul-oriented courtesy, they all become stars of the grade of the Almighty and hence, we too try to accelerate the doings in the appropriate ways and attain divine possessions and positions. Thus, it has a primary stage as star, which is twinkling ever and the ambrosia or nectar will be dropped by drops and they are all nothing but what the catalyst (chemistry) does for the betterment of the world. Therefore, first we would think about ourselves, as the divine birth and for a divine proposal, which is going to be done through myself, thus, I am descending to this earth and, I will be an ever glittering star in the space dance of Sri Natarajamurthy which can also be explained, if it is identified, then the Chidambaram secret is nothing but very easily adored by the human race and this is the supreme stage of spirituality. This is the experimental stage for soul and its operation is strong and strength oriented one which can survive these particles in this universe's combinations and they clearly understand the process of these natural beings and do or die, which comes first. If these questions will be traced out and they will be even minded and those start its way and when time comes, according to its presence as the star, the final stage of this incarnation is to be verified and established by several serious happenings, thus, we can go around this Holy university. Therefore, this human birth is not at all a waste, we do not say frequently and thus, we make this period for the orientation of space and many discoveries and inventions can be known by humanity and they can be well established and thus, make money from this electricity department.

These various methods of investigation and calculus and some circumstances make man to invent a new article and so, the whole human beings are well to do and comfortable standing in a stage of peace and shanthi. This is the procedure by which we have come to this earth, definitely they will be achieved by God and other catalysts. Whatever education we have this will make us to prefer the stage of human being as the present situation is not at all favourable, and then this stage comes, then the next stage if working hard and earning a lot to the entire satisfaction of all of you. All of our earnings will help us go upwards to the upliftment of humanity, and if it is in day-to-day life, nothing wrong will be caused through anything. All are ever holy and the holiest; if they say that it is a suggestible one but not practicable; thus, they declare but, through regular processes and formations will lead our way without any kind of failures.

The whole universe is His creation and He is the sole proprietor of this Universe and He has the authority to do anything. But according to Dharma, He is operating this universe. So rules and regulations are His will and pleasure. He can do as per His thoughts and during His rulership it is His operation and He is the sole controller of all the deeds and creatures, whatever we witness, is a part and parcel of His own ideal preparations. So, He cannot be explained and we have to implicitly feel and sense it to know it. He Himself reveals His creation and Himself, we can have the mighty power of Himself. There is nothing apart from Him, if we realise this universal truth, there will be no mental depression and no more puzzles and loads to the mind. Because, everything is in His creation, everything is sathyam and moral things and concepts are the basement of His own. Therefore, we praise Him, because He is the Mighty Father of this universe and His grace is unlimited; His form is shown to us according to His will and pleasure. Whenever we think about this philosophy, all the deeds are seeming to be the gracious look of His sight. So, we cannot even think, without Himself. So, our epics stress to do good. We must treat all as the creation of God, as I am the creation of Himself. This is the supreme truth of all truths. Whatever we do, everything is His valuable mighty doing and He spends each second as a valuable one. We should search Him, when times is ripening, His dharsan can be visible and His dominance is nothing but His representation to us. Those who are doing true penance on God, Himself, he can attain His Lotus Feet and realise the philosophy of His whole creation as a Mighty one. Such constructional power is His own and He plans all the creation. The various planets and stars can be set up by His own pleasure. He is never sorrowful, but is ever blissful. Thus, His correspondence with us should be worshipped. If this is happening in our daily life, we can attain His Kingdom and pleasure for all times. Each one is struggling for various things in several ways, some succeed and others fail in dejection. If we have deep faith on His Feet, everything can be successfully attained and we will be able to meditate in the process of His Mighty creation, we can attain supremacy. That, is why we have been given this birth, through which we should chant His holy name always and through chanting, we can attain peace and shanthi forever. These are emphasised by God's mighty action whenever needed, He presents Himself as a doer and shows His mightiness. Thus, His Eminence is showered on all of us, we do not feel this happening and that is why, we think these are in value of Maya of this earth. Though we cannot understand His greatness of mercy, He never punishes anyone, but He teaches all of us His grace and mercy and thus, we can live like independent citizens of Himself. If we are obedient to Himself ever, all our efforts are successfully looked after with victory. There is nothing possible by us for us and from us, but they are His mightiness. Sometimes we would not have thought that we should have been born then to this couple about this colour, the number of our brothers and sisters, our life span and soul, likewise, we can only think about these things but can only think and we cannot set up these. These are in the Mighty Hands of Himself the One and only one so we must be free from a life of desires.

He is to be adored this should be conducted as daily time table of the Grand Master, God. Thus, He Himself creates everything as according to His pleasure and His creation and destruction are due to His eminent scholarship. On the whole, if our life span is surely certain, His blessings are essential, and He has the ability ever to transfer our fate, and forgive us everything and make us saints. Therefore, if we chant His holy names daily, without any doubts, He will dispense everything and He will be always with us and our deeds will have victory by all means. Whatever may be the final result, this result will be transferred into success ever. So, we should have the strength of His assistance, there is no necessity to be afraid of anything; all will end with pure bhakthi and dedication, that is needed. To call our own as per experience, there is nothing in this world, when we are born, we do not come with anything; at death, we do not take our own, nothing is cabled. This is the universal truth; all are completely knowing this truth; but due to maya, we in between our birth and death, live with something which are what He has granted and think that they are our ownselves. No, if we come out of this false appearance, they are not attached to us, we will be true saints and will have clarity about life and we are tenants only, not at all our own. We should realise the presence of God and who is I'? We represent when one can identify the self as 'I' but we do not know anything about 'I'. But if we realise His real features, we will get true nature of 'I'. If it is realised by spiritual exercises, we can realise it surely. Hence, we should perfectly live with honour and majesty. If we please God by our moral activities, He will dispense all to our entire satisfaction of our life and its present position. Therefore, what we think and do, everything must be truthful to Him. If this happens, God's representation will be our wealth and all of our needs will be fulfilled and the thought of ownership will be erased. But we are aiming to have the target of attaching our whole life with others and these kinds of activities may yield sins, but He, the Almighty graciously erases all our sins and gifts us with contentment throughout our life. This is life's GOAL.

The solar exercises of the Sun privately teaches so many experiences, if we go on practicing immense concentration with proper manthras, after getting these Truths, our experience is one and only the realisation of Astra-geological concentration of the mixture. What is this? This is not only a broad form of science, some Astronomical mind is enough to discover our consciousness and the whole institute, thus, we analysed and got a sum as result? As such, they both are different persons, who are interestingly searching the result of this mathematical puzzle, but, those who are going to profit and benefit, they are pinned with sleep, very good, these are the eminent ones to create phonographic INDIA with 100 dynamic persons under the age of 25, thus, Vivekananda called up....! Is it possible? Just as a cinema posture, we are recruiting something on the posture and they do compromise their idleness and failures. In our astronomical period, we have discovered a concept which is having only in this period and this is the source of liquid atom bomb which can be in our hand with 75 grams of weight and it, splits and blasts, the whole 2500 square feet. This disaster can be known by all the countries,. Now, without doubt at all, INDIA is the one and only supreme force among the nations, 'if anybody wishes to have sensation and seeing through our own ideas, make arrangements, and fix a point we are ready to battle with whoever may be let us know who is who?' In this present world, INDIA alone is the supreme force which does not voluntarily wish to wage war with anybody else thus, we have dreamt so many years may be 44 years. Now, by God's co-ordinators' sole co-operation we have achieved this best article and through fear all nations should be giving respect to INDIA and continue their relationship with most caution. If we wish to initiate our progression in this field, we are the right person, because we are having such brain and its circumstances will not be enough to understand the formula of the highest sum of this bomb. So, whenever, we are here, come personally, we will make you to know the formula of this bomb. But you cannot make it in future in numerous numbers and by sale of these, you cannot be fleshy monetarily! If you are in this mentality, our secret force will destroy into ashes within 3 minutes. So, be cautious by all means. It is common to all those who are such culprits. When we travel through out our one and only way if you ask me, I will explain the truth, thinking of your confidence and your patriotism, I will clearly make you to understand the idea. So whoever it may be alert and afraid of INDIA when you hear about it. And throughout our experiences,! we can trumpet that INDIA is not beatable in anyway and it is the superforce and thus, we can do our services to the development of our nation only, and we should not call off India, by any means. This is the best statement of our Prime Minister to all the nations. One who wishes to examine this super power, we can put a riddle, who will win, let us wait for 12 seconds and then we can come to a conclusion. Destruction is not our policy at all; but construction of all degrees, this is our motto; but you, all the other nations make us to bring this idea into action. We do try to develop in agriculture and thus, nobody should not even touch the border stone of INDIA. Uncountable times, we had spent our time for the welfare of the nation; as such Pakistan and Srilanka are attacking surrounding our fishermen on all sides and about katcha Island's problems are not acceptable. On the whole, they had attacked Indian Parliament, what courage they have, an end should be put to this.

Hereafter, if they begin to think of India, the thinking itself should be an action which they should be afraid of. According to them they must not pronounce India even in their dreams. India is a very majestic gentleman; those who are having relationship, if you are enemies, we are your true enemies and whatever your thoughts and deeds be, it will cease to exist within 2 minutes and there will be nothing to identify your nation; so mind it and have friendship with us. For all opportunities, we serve you and in all circumstances we will assist you normally, if something goes wrong, destruction will automatically be caused by you surely. Up to this second, we are nothing but citizens of India, if you treat India as an enemy, you can realise its power of atomic energy and how it can give you destruction and then, if you spread any lies on the criminal side, we are not responsible for those statements. The most sacred concept is by God's that is, truth always wins all. Therefore, if we adhere to Dharmam and Sathyam they alone win all the races; such of these, no controversies and therefore we should not plan in a damaged way to have fruitful result in any action at all. Whether it is the materialistic or spiritualistic paths, we should create a path of our own, and thus, walk through this way to our residence and turning aside to other places, we must try to continue our traditional realities and thus, we will be in peace and shanthi ever. Those who are trying truly to attain Divine ecstasy ever, should try to know the TRUTH, which is the cemetery concrete as the basement of spiritual life, and through this, sadhanas which are done by us will be ever truthful and easily we attain the Truth itself. If we know what is truth, theoretically we can speak more than one hour, but the truth is ever the same in all verses. Those who are trained with truth in all their duties, discharged through truth, shall attain Moksha through adhering to truth by all means. So we should make others to realise the Truth's significance. Its validity and significance must be told without doubts and they will come to be truthful persons in future. Whatever is going on, all will be for the welfare of the citizens of this universe, as such, our prayer must be for all creations, and thus, we will be truly significant in all the ways.

History of the scientific society is to be known, not in pleasing words, but they discuss with two or more physicians and M.S. degree holders too. Both women and men are present in this normal way to analyse the bookish knowledge thus, without studying medicine practically, but they silently analyse their deeds and publish to the world by conducting big seminars, praising all and giving the author a distinguished style of appreciation and he is praised by all who are having correspondence with medical line. Thus, everything is set grandly, and all the professors and the deans will also speak about this author and give him a momento and with currencies also as prize. Thus, he is introduced through all the scientists and they praise his patience from 7 A.M to, 4.00 P.M. Still there is nobody who is going to introduce him and serve something to him. But his wants, to eat or drink, even water is not given to him. Therefore, the manual life has some systematic stages to live comprehensively and thus, we can get rid of some of our possibilities and therefore we can manage the financial situation.

The entire Prapancha's creation, is an accentric science and the definition of this analysis is nothing but our Darwin's theory. Just naturally, Man got the formula and after thousands of years, Darwin invented them around 6 O' clock. So, we should not be holding anything apart from God; but we can keep the shop open, and the shop, keeps you — like this old saying, our life has more symbolic theories and realistic formations are very, very cheap. The essential is love and its effects are nothing but pure Gnana. By this we can live a divine life and thus, our normal oneness minded tendency will always be kept on. If this is capitalised on our materialistic life, will be water on Lotus flower, touch and blank it. Therefore, if we acknowledge the occurrence of any type of incidents, we cannot exercise our life without sensual control. If these are normally on oneness of one spot, then, it is the appropriate centre of kundalini and thus, we can elevate us to the pedestal of divinity without any support. So the best convocation is nothing but liberation. Whether they are Doctorate holders in cytology or microbiological science they cannot find out the disease's natural occurrence, how long it is proceeding into this fleshy body. After we perish with five elements, our life is still prolonged. It is a pure, entirely new metabolism; through this procedure, everything is installed due to this brightest metabolism. So, God, alone creates and has the power to protect and make us to leave this world and beyond this process. He will give a new era for this fleshy body through which we have to furnish our life with all relations and neighbours, consequences will also go throughout the journey to their entire shelter. But, they never drop it and have pure, normal body and thus, its soul also goes into the fire or mud, will be fabricated by nature and finally they will be without care, then we, also will be with this miniatures of this universal university which is mentioned as all of the land and seas as well as ourselves too. These general principles are not at all effective with any so-called effects but consciousness does not sleep, it should be ever in awaking mode, otherwise, we will hand over our independence which will be barred.

If we can understand the cosmic dance of Sri Chidhambara Nataraja every thing will be understood and the theme for this contest with kali is nothing but illusionary and magically predicted manthras will be spelt 1000 times, at the end of this Holy Yagna, we had spent lots of money, because, if we spend some money by doing rituals, ceremonies, we can reproduce a stable amount of three or four crores, thus, our thoughts are processed until the end of the yagna. But, there is no possible result thus, we have met a heavy loss. If we do yagnas, we should propose a positive thought of welfare of all, we should start the ritual and we will gain good benefits; otherwise, our vibrations will be violent, and there is no possibility of succeeding our life with any favours only. According to one's fate the level of that attainment of those cases, they will be shared out, otherwise, whatever may be, in front of us, nothing can be achieved and all such things will be an utter waste; if this truth is understood, we all will proceed to that class of life which will give us a lot of money. If one who is stable and united in mind and physically, they will accumulate health and wealth ever. Due to our greedy mind we cannot wait for some more time and our efforts are in vain. Such people who are fully greedy will not at all get these kinds of wealth. One, who worships Goddess Mahalaxmi, adoring money is due to our process that the conditions is not successful, he successfully married in this Kulathevatha's temple according to all the relations and peoples. So, this is a great success during the life's journey of a lady and a young man. Thus, they had married, and hence during this truthful's density, they will live with lovely and smoothly line of successes and they all should realise the truth of human life. All the creatures take food, excrete and produce their offsprings, lastly when time comes, they perish, if these are common to man also, then he is considered to be as an animal, but man is dispensed with the sixth sense and we must be aware of doing good things and they all should come as natural habits, and they are not alone, but all the people will survive the best approach to the end of life. After our demise, a single paise is not at all taken from this earth and everything is a meaningless activity. So, we should realise the impermanence of wealth, youth, properties and even his name is transformed into dead body(savam) so, nothing in this world is stable everything is an illusion and we are full of honesty like thriving sanjeevi herbs, will be steady and in time, it grows, the trees and thriving in a good state, now.

We are not blaming anybody particularly and society, we are all responsible for this uncultivable landslide, and because of our foolishness that is fools do foolish actions and the result will be foolishness at its worst. If we are learned and experienced enough we will not make land unfertile and sell our lands to money minting people, and building so many buildings. We are in name genius; we call ourselves Geniuses; no only fools, to find our end by our ownselves and thus, we are quarrelling each other department to department, man to man and such things are only the brutal range of actions, by which our human culture is only in the books which do not often come in the practical way. Do see our roads and exhibitions; the truth within my concept can be understood crystal clearly. Our ancient and the holiest Vedas are the oldest literary and spiritualised monuments of this whole Universe. Even foreign authors and scholars permit that the RIG VEDIC is atleast 12,000 years old and that an oldest script does not exist in the libraries of the world. The same Rig Veda tells us that darkness prevailed everywhere before the creation of this Universe. In the midst of this darkness even beyond it subsisted, all by the Almighty, one glorious Being (Almighty) consisting of nothing but intelligence and having no origin other than the Almighty 'Himself. It evolved itself out of the darkness and created the whole Brahmanda, Universe out of the darkness and created the universal creatures, and herbs and plants. It revolved Himself out of the darkness and created the universal beings by the dint of His penance that is His knowledge power. Thus, Rig Veda says, this very idea has been echoed by Lord Manu, who says that before its evolution this universe consisted of nothing but darkness only. Everything was lying dormant, as it was. Out of that darkness, arose that intelligence, effulgent Being, the Originator, who Himself does not depend on any other power or shakthi to reveal Himself and who subsists forever in His own grandeur and supports Himself on His own power.

The veil of darkness was lifted as soon as He revealed Himself. Such as the time of Universal destruction, this whole universe had merged as it were, in darkness. It was in a chaotic condition, indistinguishable, indefinable, inconceivable and incomprehensible; it was lying dormant, as it were, at the end of this period that Glorious Being, who is the original originator of Himself, evolved this manifest universe through Himself though Himself unmanifest and having thus, unfolded His creative energy, revealed Himself after lifting the veil of darkness. He who is beyond the ken of the senses, subtle, unmanifest, eternal and incognito nay, who is the very soul of all the beings thus, shone Himself by Himself. "At the beginning of creation, I alone subsisted, the one beyond the manifest and unmanifest, and nothing else. And it is I alone who survives and nothing else and it is I alone, who survives the creation. This phenomenal world is nothing but Myself, and whatever remains after that is also Myself. At that moment of time it was Rudra alone who created. It was that which protected the Universe who first created it and in the end dissolved it. He has eyes all round, faces on all sides and hands and feet in every direction. Lord Maheswara is the sole creator of heaven and earth; He is the undoubted origin and source of all deities. He is the seer without eyes and hears without ears. He knows all though no one knows Him. He is known as the Supreme Being. He alone is the Supreme Soul, the Eternal Being; real self-luminous, infinite, the primordial cause of all that is constant, or imperishable, always happy, untainted by illusions, self-sufficient, peerless, unequalled and immortal. This idea, which is common to the Vedas, the Smritis and the Puranas, has been succulently expressed by the immortal Saintpoet Thulasidas who has given detailed descriptions. Paramathma is only one, all-pervading, imperishable, all existent mass of Spiritual and spirituality and an embodiment of a mass of Bliss; no one has been able to find out His beginning or end. Even the vedic concepts have sung in praise of Him according to their limited capacity. He walks without feet; hears without ears, and performs various activities, even though devoid of hands. He relishes all flavours even without a palate, and is a master-orator even though He has got notongue. He touches without a body, sees without eyes and smells everything without a nose; in this way, all His activities are highly excellent and marvellous. In no way all His activities can be described. No one can ever describe His excellence and greatness?

This Earth is one part of the Universe, in this Brahmandam there are 11000 Suns likewise 11000 Brahmanandas ever rotating by themselves and their Suns. On the earth, each and every various creatures are created and they live their life, and all towards liberation finally. One who attains Mukthi he becomes part and parcel of one star or planet, and through them, he exhibits his Dharmic consequences like rays which help the jeevans in all Brahmandams. This is the secret, Death occurs to every one of us and by this death each gets promotion in his following births, and they, according to their efficiency, they do moralistic activities, and they save their gains as punyas. The sum total of Punyas, totally high enough, will make others to live a divine life and he becomes a Guru. This Guru has some disciples, and he makes them suitable to attain oneness with divinity, they in all Brahmandam. Many Gurus are trying to their extent to make their disciples to attain final and Eternal saturation with God. Therefore, we have to live a moralised life, and thus, we should get punya in total. It should be raised to its highest point, by this, the holy soul can elevate their disciples towards final saturation. This kind of rotation or cycle is going on continuously. It is a never ending process which goes on and on. Nothing cannot be destroyed, but we can make another one. So, try to understand the fatal aspect of these Brahmandas. If once this has happened in one's experience, he will be sworn as God. Everything is equal to God, He can finalise anything in favour of the sin-holders. His mere eye sight is enough to change one's fate. Thus, His greatness will be high enough and astamasidhis will be ready to act according to His will. Therefore, He is considered to be the very next to Godliness. He is ever in thoughtless position. His greatness can do anything to all, He has no have's and have-not's this type of thought will not be his Era. So, we can approach Him directly without any kind of fear, so it is REST ASSURED. Thus, He has enough and more measure of strength by the will His own efforts, He is, can be and is one among us. He is one of our neighbours who blesses all for their betterment and development of their selves to be on the plane of goodness in all their efforts and purity of mind. If they have purity of mind by all means, in all situations, they will be blessed and they will come into the shelter of this blessed one. He then takes them in His custody and resolves them of all their sins and blesses with divine sight. If this happens, nothing more is required to anyone personally. Everybody is suitable for this happening but purity of heart is surely necessary and readiness to trust themselves to Him.

If such. mentalities are their own, they will not bother about anything. They will be contented with peace and shanthi, if this position is realised a bit, then the whole Maya will automatically disappear and the Eternal Truth will be realised to its full measurement. This stage is to be attained; this is order of God for all the creatures. Likewise from L.K.G to their fate, they study and earn money and save a bit for future life; in between their life, they have to see to their children's study, marriage etc, after their duties, they live calmly without expecting anything from their own children. If in turn the children are ready to serve them, they generously say, God gives and He is helping us in all times. Likewise, the Divinely honoured ones will not expect anything from others. They dispense what they have to those who are in need realising their expectations, whichever is good enough, they give them as dispensations according to their karmas. But they will be the best dispensation, for which they prayed and expected. This is God's dispensation, if we realise God's will, then there will be no more to worry about anything. Whether we are awake or not, nothing horrible happens in our daily life. At all times, He guides and guards us with His mightiest hands. Such grace and mercy is the structural embodiment of Godliness.

Why does God create this Universe? What is the reason, behind creation, presenting and destruction and why does He destruct all? These questions are asked by most of the people, but, nobody can give a proper answer, because they cannot know or realise the maya or illusionary screen of the creation, which is the most powerful unit of God. That is why, we can ask questions but not all these questions are still as questions. This creation is an illusionary one, first of all we must have this confident belief, then we can analyse the answers for these questions very easily. In our day-to-day life, we come across many births and deaths, some disturb us, some are not causing any kind of impression of gain or loss, so this type mind, if one has, it is a boon to him/her. Do mind this....! With this explanation, if we analyse, about the creation, it is not at all a creation, it is beyond mind and we cannot imagine how many years, have been taken for the first creation on the earth? If we ask this question, that is Athmavisaram by which we can realise implicitly the reason of creation and keeping for some period, and at the second round, the jeevan releases itself from the body and then, the body is worthless, He at that time is then allowing ourselves to digest the loss, maybe, gain, we return to our normal state. Even when we have so much affection on a dog or anybody else, when we lose them, we are getting depressed for some hours or some days or some years, but nobody is ready to give up their jeevan in order to keep him, therefore, everything in this earth are illusionary scenes only, and our capacity to digest some universal truths, because, our mental concentration has not sakthi to penetrate the curtain of Maya. Many of us do not torture or investigate the scene, and go beyond it, within the period death occurs. So we are born, grow, walk, run, and educate ourselves, doing various jobs for money for our expenses, and finally one day we perish, so, they are illusionary scenes only. For example, see our just born baby's photo till the old age, maybe even after death, our bodily size is focused in so many styles, likewise, the illusions seem to be permanent; there is nothing permanent on this earth. So, these questions are out of illusion only, but nothing is answerable; we can know and realise the answers implicitly. So, in tamil, those who see, do not expose it to the outer world, those who tell, do not at all see anything. This is, common verse which means nothing is permanent, not destructable it will be modified into another thing and when death occurs, it will be automatically, we forget all, and its illusions, and shadows too. Therefore, questioning in any subject is very easy, but to answer will be the most difficult and that is why, we should not publicly question. We can question anybody, but someone may answer. This is the sacred, but illusionary creation and so on.

Therefore, the core of universal scientific knowledge is nothing but stands on the base of God, the creator's mahasakthi until then there will be no reason of birth, preservation and destruction; these are going on rotating as a cycle, and in this way, this whole Brahmanda keeps going on its own way, each and every action, custom is in the practical way. For our discussion, we suppose, if there is no God, then who is the creator, preserver and destructor; what is the answer for this question? If there is a particle, it must have a creator, without a creator, how can a thing be presented here, if we find the answer to this question, automatically we can discover the creator without puzzles and riddles. Such sathsangams are developing us to be right royal to lead a moral life and thus, we will not lose our normal temperament in any course of situations. Therefore, if we have a clarification about this question, we can lead a peaceful life ever and ever. This doubt makes us to come to a conclusion to find out what is the cause by which we are suffering and some are living with the richest things, what is the reason behind it, if we wish to know the differenciation, Unity among diversity, is possible, if we find the answer to this interrogation only. Only we Gnanies are able to discover the truth of the existence of God, others may have various decisions and opinions of their own, and they satisfy themselves as they feel that there is nothing more to think and conclude about the existence of God. In this situation only, we can conclude one conclusion finally, whether God exists or not. Each and every normal human being is having the right to understand the secret of his/her births and deaths. Many people are not at all worrying about this, and they do not have any process of accommodation in their mind, even a space to conclude about this matter. Because their birth concludes such thoughts and beyond this, they can be illustrated by anything. If there is one who is a post-graduate and the same doctor is an Engineer (post-gratduate) nobody can attempt to do this. Thus, the Universal presence of Godliness can be realised only through the dispensed souls only, others can speak and discuss, but in the end, they will quarrel among themselves and will not be able to come to a pure suitable decision. This must be dispensed by God alone.

Chapter - 2

The Ins and Outs

Today's trend is accumulating wealth and for diseases, to have rescue from them, we are ready to spend crores of money, and this is not the way to attain perfection. Perfection is that we should accumulate good health, and money to meet out our daily needs and a good moral life. If we spend our whole life with confidence and truthfulness, God, Himself will visit our residence, our epics emphasise this truth and thus, we are not aware to wake up from slumber of maya and whole strength will be focused to make necessary modes to attain Samadhi, while we are living this materlistic life and its consequences will not disturb us in anyway. So, we must have a Guru; we do not want to search for a well-oriented Guru. If we pray God intensively and truthfully, Guru, will automatically come in search of us and he comes to make us pure, divine in nature of creation and thus, we can practice all yogic sadhanas which are karmic for Gnana sadhanas. So, we should discharge our duties to the entire satisfaction of God, then He Himself descends as a guru one day. Good patience and penance are needed to attain a guru.

When guru comes, the Almighty Himself identifies Guru, and He makes us a proper disciple unto him and he will in due course of time make us a Guru. We, ourselves should to be ready to be a Guru in this world and we can show our eminence and scholarship of our studies through our intensive penance, that is why should do whatever the matter is, we have to discharge our whole duties, should be neat and clear and it will reach all our 720000 nadis. This is supposed to be Thanthric sadhana through which in kaliyuga it is so difficult to practice and note it. We should practice Bhakti yoga and thus, attain Eternal salvation. So, first we should believe that we are human beings and our thoughts and mind should be on an equilibrium and if it is possible, we can attain Eternal perfection. This human life is given to us only to attain natural perfection and thus, our life will be meaningful.

This Bharat or India, are the twin names, marvelous things will happen if any one name is used. So we have to either call Bharat or India, then, see, how long it is going to take for the development of our nation. When, generally we call India our ancestral genesis is grasped; if we call Bharat, we can realise the ancestral code of our nation, so this collusion should be eradicated. And we have to carry on. The NAVY force is still not developed. We have to fulfill our needs to protect the coastal area of about 3000 kms. So, we can have, sincerely, education from our old scripts and thereby we can stand on our own legs. This is the first puzzle in front of us. Our nation is originally in the cups of our own people; if it is in day-to-day life, India will not be developed in accordance to the development of the nation.

We are all concentrating to build up our Armed forces and planes squad; Ok, It is alright; if our navy is in full strength, we will not be easily dominated over by many nations in the whole world. Whatever the problem is, one brilliant man can solve it and be free from tension. Thus, we can easily solve India-Pakistan problem and Indo-Chinese and India-Srilanka's political or whetever the problems are; we can easily solve them by having peace and shanthi only, if the sitting representatives are accumulating such kind of peace and shanthi. If, violent minded people are in the squad, nothing will be fruitful. So, we should be very careful in solving our problems, but our politicians are firing and drop petrol, to light them with heat and water. So it is necessary to be confident on sathyagraha as well as peace and shanthi.

Thus, we started the family procedures without any kind of possessions, we understand one another, they, too live sensibly and usefully to all in all---. They are all saying a few words about this family's excellence and they take this mode of life, as lessons to all beyond sects, creeds and religions. Only love is the vedic base of this cleared life. Then all will finish towards profit and loss. Get rid of the assets of mischievous thoughts and deeds, and needs will be fulfilled, they realised this supreme truth until their last breath, and whatever happens here, everything will blossom with purity and clarity and therefore, we have to wash our mind with punishments of the organs system. Thus, if we treat our organs, it will realise and get pure and clean.

There is no necessity to have a lot of disciples and cheat them and us by means of having done so many fraudulent activities throughout our life, because one day whether this human court punishes or not we have to stand before the court of divinity and there, there is no way to escape from the consequences of the judgement of God. It is very cruel according to human perception; while living, we have to be diseased with a lot illnesses, ever no food for our hunger and no water for our thirst and no digestion process and the eyes will lose their sight; the ears, kidneys and so many inner organs do not co-operate to lead life peacefully. In total while living, every second of life will be with full of, lots of, implicit, discomforts may cause and make us not fit to lead a fine life. Then there will be no meaning of our life at all. We are just living for name sake; but there is no peaceful and harmonious mind with excellence and co-operation of Godly support. We have no respiration discipline also and thus, our life will be full of miseries and discomforts; so we have to chant the Holy Name of God, whether we do this or not, we have to have fear of God, then we do good deeds and thus, make our life so divine and meaningful; and thus, we can lead a disciplined life, have a normal death, when death occurs. Therefore, we have to have much fear and bhakthi upon God, otherwise miserable unexpected activities will demoralise our life entirely and there will be no sense of living this life. Our whole life should be meaningful, it is only possible through the realisation of God and surrender of oneself to Him with full of trust in Him. If it is possible, then we can succeed in all events and circumstances in our entire life.

This moment onwards, we should make ourselves ready to surrender to such persons and thereby we can make our whole life meaningful by this golden opportunity. If we entrust our entire and whole life at the lotus feet of the Lord Himself, like Brahma gives His spouse Goddess Saraswathi on Her tongue (full of Vedic chanting), Lord Vishnu gives His spouse His heart, Lord Parameswara, kirupanithi of all deities, Santha Bava is the only one auspicious prospect of Himself to give His half side to His spouse Goddess Parvathi. But He is ready always to give us Himself for the welfare and upliftment of us; our entire life will be transferred into peaceful, ever harmonious and ecstatic one. Nothing can be compared with this stage, He is the most Supreme of all supreme beings. On the whole, He Himself gives us Himself for the penance and sadhanas which are done by His grace and mercy only. He gives all credit to our efforts by verses. This supreme truth is emphasised by all vedas in different modes, styles according to the guru's nationality, language and culture, so that, all credit of the operation of creation of this entire universe for us is to lead a shanthiful life which is entirely dispensed by Him only. This kind of life only is meaningful, we have to achieve this through our pure Bhakthi and devotion only. No recommendation or bribe can have a sway in His Holy kingdom. He is the lawyer, the prosecutor and also the supreme judge. What is His judgement?

According to His judgment, the entire universe is rotating in an orbit and we should realise His extreme greatness and entire powerful sovereignty also. He is the unchangeable being of all the universal beings. He is a mighty powerful emperor of this mighty creation; and He can do anything and everything in a fine manner; but we due to our irresponsible moods of life, we become selfish and proud. We do unnecessary activities and also go beyond the rules and regulations of His contentment; that is why, we are suffering a lot. Though we are leading our ecstatic life into a miserable one, we are entirely responsible for this destruction. We ourselves ruin our body and mind because of the day-to-day life's style. If we go along with God's creation of nature no harm will be available in His Holy kingdom. He Himself embraces us if we do good things but He punishes also because of our entire mode of life style. That is why, He is now in a mood of unpleasant and unsatisfactory application of Himself. He loses His temperament of Shanthi and Anantha because of the life style of these creatures. According to regulations of Dharma and the Epics any man/ woman can, adhere to the principles that are particularly for the betterment of our mind and Budhi. Gnanam if it is in sidhi, we can easily quote these holy principles; we can have Dharsan of the Lord and be with Him, we can speak spontaneously and liberally and thus, we will be blessed by the Lord to the best of our life. What is the best boon which is dispensed by God? they are a very constructive body and good health. As per our truthful penance, we get wealth, but one point is to be learnt by rote. We must realise the truthful, Universal concept; "If wealth is lost, nothing is lost, if health is lost something is lost, if character is lost everything is lost", we have to realise the inner, hidden universal concept of this truth. We can be free from all of this worldly burdens, agonies and nothing can disturb us and we can learn and elevate our development and betterment in our whole and entire spiritual life.

One who has lived and is living a chaste life alright then he is considered to be the Gnani and so, he can be established as a boon to mankind. Such horizons will come and set at that time, and our entire life is for dedicating our life. Haves and have nots should be erased and the best actions are to be included within the cost of knowledge and wisdom oriented people, that is why, our old scriptures specify a chaste life otherwise everything will be a waste, thus, truthfulness is admired by all and this is considered to be the signal of a bonafied one man army. Our ancestor's life style is considered and like wise, we have to omit those who are not equal to keep others. In this world, everything is dubious, for example, several marriages are done in an auspicious day, but how many are blessed by God and others, but we have to mention, thus, our human life is too rare to be dispensed by god, and so, we have to be certified as a saint. The whole universe will be normal under His restrictions and rules. Therefore, what we deliver, that is truthful in nature and we are made with fire and while living, our character is fire, everything is noble and wide hearted, one whose Excellency cannot be under estimated. So, man should have rules of life by which we gain a lot of ecstatic philosophy and therefore, we have to go with his nature's nature. The matured mind is always noble and fine; because there is nobody who can enter into ugly undignified ponds. Therefore, they have to revise their route towards the pleasant, incomparably neatness is seen and we live a solitary full-fledged life herewith and so on. This is the one and only way to maintain our heart with pure and dignified thoughts which is ruled by God and this is the manner of which, His entire creation should be ready to saturate with the oneness of liberation. There will be slavery status to nobody and thus, they will retain their position with allegoric mood and grasped by all devathas, and they will dispense our needs and thus, our deeds will be comfortable while we work or not. It is His duty to discharge food materials so that we should thrive through the paths of other doctrines. So, we have to always be free from agonies and struggles. Then there will be no use for rockets and missiles. This is Ramarajya and hence, Lord Ram will associate with us to do good, the best deeds, thus, the whole world will be full of shanthi and peace. When death occurs, it is also divineful and sanctioned with all facilities in this world of heaven. After tasting this ambrosia which is coming from Mighty God it will not be compared to this mundane limitless creations. It is nothing but creation of Almighty itself. Each and every personality is willingly going up to elevate themselves, and thus, they are very much suitable of his agonizing and painful diseases. So, his body is full of strength and valour, we have to beg to retain this mood of situations. In these ways, we can obtain an honourable seat in God's situation, and therefore they are all asking about the character's strength and its experiments. If we win over this competition, maya's illusions, we have to keep them to the mark of pass and go to higher classes. So we have to be fully alive with enriched good qualities.

All of our allegations, supporting our habits and our manifestation of privilege are only the symbols of our civilisation. The government is encouraging all the current businesses with licence No, and why have we stopped our traditional mark of drinking liquors, lahahiri vasthu's usual accordance, ladies matter for the advertisements; in this, if we concentratingly note this point. This is wearable, no chance of Aids. Is this the way to stop prostitution? According to me this advertisement means, it encourages, and flourishes the habit of prostitution of humanity, but we want to be a role model for the citizens, we should give the advertisement like this:- If you have domestic conjugation with your wife, wife wishes to conjugate with her husband at all times, it is acknowledgeable and advisable, other advertisements may cause us cancer or urinal and sexual diseases, they are not at all curable; so, be chaste citizens of INDIA. IF this is the advertisement, it will transform India as RamaRajyam. We are all wishing to establish RamaRajyam, but in those advertisements, you may have connection with anybody but for safety, use our products, is this a progressive nation? Nothing; 10000 Gandhis and 20000 Jesus 1000000 Nabis come again to this earth, they will at the next moment, desire to return to their abode and curse our culture and instructional life's atrocities and we never can stand erectly at all. If each man/woman is chaste then what is the work for condoms and the likes of these kinds of advertisements. It is enough to trumpet our Nation's literal and cultural development of construction of our contribution to the welfare, in total, nothing will be the answer. So, we should not give any respect to these advertisements; if you advertise this matter as in the second, there is some benefit for the public and the government too. Just 50 years before the citizens were having fear over doing evils and they had salient respect for each other and patriotism was very much celebrated by donating a lot of funds for the expenses of military jawans at war times, and the public co-operated nation wide, in every kind of good events. But we are just spending our time. I am not elaborately signifying anything, this everybody knows very well.., so, these are to be changed and a new generation should flourish with National integration. We are working, and within 5th of every month, the government gives good salary to all the workers, then, they are probably begging for bribe? Is this an an encouraging factor? Before 1960's may be 25 paise, how it goes upto crores and crores, if in this way, India travels to future welfare, there will be no nation and no culture and no welfare. Do mind it.

Silence is the best language by which we can win anybody and have a fine result. Thus, all our riddles will end with God's Ecstasy. In this world, nothing is fully injured and nothing is fully good, so we have to identify and choose the better one, we can lead our life quietly without any problems, probably with the Eternal blessings. If we really uplift our Highness among the society, we must educate ourselves with wisdom and consider to be the respiratory system for all creatures. You should believe that education is totally equal to God, it moralises us without any expectation, and thus, we can hoist our wisdom flag everywhere. We are all having abundant knowledge, but we do not know how to bring it out and for the whole society's welfare, we must use this rare wisdom. Thus, we can uplift INDIA in all prospects and we never expect anything from the nations; we have to serve the nation and thus, we can be a proud member in the crowd or squad at the time when the clapping in a mass of people. Thus, all influential orators form and they become best tellers in the society and earn more and they live in a posh house, car and good bank balance, such life is awaiting us. But we are not in belief of this concept. If we download our fullest concentration in our analysis, we can win the race. We can be a professor in this same Anna university. So have belief and thus, try to achieve it in action.

Whenever our parents had tears in their eyes, hearing that their son is speaking a lecture, more than 10000 people are listening to his ardent speech, such mere combination of words make our parents into the swargham and there is nothing more they need. So do bear it in your mind and try in all ways to achieve this goal. I also will meet you with this rare designation. God bless you, by all means.

Though we are in samadi we will show response to everyone's classical and sincere prayers and such persons, while living, have attained the holiness or majesty; these titles can be given, they are pure-minded and wherever they are in all the circumstances, they will serve the universe for its betterment. They are never steadfast to unsatisfied programmes and their subsequent guidance will serve for the universal university and thus, everybody will be satisfied by their service oriented deeds. These may be felt in their attempts and there is only one caution to them. Do not hesitate to work hard and struggle for non-sensical ideas and deeds. They prevent us to go through rough ways, everything will be erased by their scholarships. So, without doubt, He is considered to be, a part and parcel of the Almighty and the suffering and non-sufferings will not show their huge variation in or out of the situation and their major self-identification, is to serve all nation wide annonists. They cannot be identified by all, but some persons can realise their value as in Mahabaratha, Krishnan is identified only by 5 persons, the remaining persons could not identify Him. In the Gita itself, Bhagavan illustrated that "I am not identified by anyone; but some persons will easily identify Myself as one of them. In every incarnation, I am doing only the best to all. But, the foolish cannot understand our birth and death, how will they be identified by the Almighty". Ok this is identified as MAYA. If it is opened through Almighty's wish, the Athmasadhahan will-realise about himself, who is ‘I’?. Then there is no necessity for guides and even realising these aspects still according to this human births, attachment and our attitudes, we do not omit the happenings are natural, nothing can transfer the concepts to the entire satisfaction of the purest Athma. Whenever we humbly understand and realise the fact He is our father, and that is why, without, beyond identification or attention He is considered to be our father. Likewise, everything is only our confidence, and such confidence is the only need to identify the classical harmony of Annonists.

Some thirty per cent of people of the world’s population are going on and they blame others to take risks and they cannot win the race. These people are gambling in a duplicate name and as such they make themselves rich or poor. So, our epics and puranas express golden words to the welfare of the whole family and, nobody is trying to go back to these principles, if they are going, India will be one of the richest nations among the many richest nations. We are now-a-days becoming a rich nation. But our wealth is under one roof of bucketing into the sand and riches are deposited in various banks; many of the richest are putting their wealth and riches in unloaded lorries and these lorries are ever travelling all over India, and thus, they are in many ways, not identified. If they are caught, everything, will be the nations, now think overleaf. India is the one and only richest nation in the world. The rich and poor can be identified only on the basis of their business, media and share market. It is known that India is the first country to standby at the nook and corner of all claiming and posturing this world’s components to fix the rate of a share. Thus, India is placed, its participation is exemplary to hold the key. India is considered to be in the placement of 1st class in the first row of share market.

Do bear in mind, many families are sinking like our nation is sinking because of Sri Lankas’s Pakistan’s and Chinese refugees are more than 5 lacs when they are taken in counting; who will give food and medicine and fulfill their wants; who is going to fulfill their needs through their deeds. They are not at all our citizens, then how can we expect pure sense of our own Indians undertakings. We have undertaken these people it shows our generosity but they think that we (Indians) are easily cheatable and we nicely push and pull life with new rails and leave the world as a nice refugee. In India, that is why we are suffering. If the situation is like this, how can we upgrade India’s progress in all branches of civilisation. Sowing producing various creatures and even trees.

If we commit any mistake in the family, Guru can get rid us of our karma, but if guru curses, three Moorthies and even the Istha devies, cannot rescue us from that curse. So Hindu Dharma emphasizes that Guru should bless us. If His blessings are with us nothing will go right or wrong and nothing will touch us by any means. God's grace should be always with us. Then there is nothing to worry. Therefore, we should be calm, speak slowly and humbly, and stop and encroach kasta mouna, it will give us many peoples' instructional friendship to lift our progress to touch the Himalayan's richest peak, that is Manosover, very good go on. The human goal, ambition is to be reached by all of us. Do penance to achieve the greatness more than others by Sri Meenakshi's grace.

Our Hindu gurumars are honoured by the Almighty, and they are recognised by the public people, for they are fundamentally having no single paise with them but they are very energetic to guide the society to the highest seat of all worlds. They do anything, even they can give the dead body soul. Thus, they do exercises, they are not slaves to money and other luxurious things, but they will be very, very simple and live on a meal a day. They will survive in the midst of heat and rain; and they will not be restful. Their life is entirely dedicated towards the betterment of this humanity and they too attain this stage of Godliness. First, they weep that they cannot attain His Holiness. "Now I got this position with your mercy and blessings, the whole universe should be like me". What a gracious heart they are having, This is the magnimous position of the learned and the sidhimans. And they never consider rain, hunger, draught, heat etc, everything, all will be obtained in a normal and equal way, they are not irresponsible about the betterment of the universe this is because, whatever the cause is, if the Guru minds it, the agony, itself goes out of us and we can lead a good life. According to their problems, the public come and obtain their blessings, and the Gurus through their yogic dispensation, the public get well versed with peace and satisfaction. If we wish to have this experience, not reading, and observing the miraculous activities, done by them, will not be enough; we have to be like the pupils and then it is very easy to have oneness with the mighty Guru. For this, we must do rigourous penance and then we will be considered by God Himself. These holy people are lanterns to the world and the light will be a light in the night and this proceeds as doing like a prophet. The Guru's considered to be the cosmic man and he identifies himself makes others to be fine and in a fabulous state. So, when we go to have darshan of Maharishis, we should offer some fruits and flowers, and obediently pray to them to give peace of mind, divine wisdom. If we ask them they will be very well pleased they will bestow us that kind of life within matter of seconds. Even we may be poor, so we can offer even a single flower, it is enough to have dharsan of the guru, because they need nothing from the visitors, they have the ever giving kamadhenu along with them; this divine cow offers all to the world and himself, so they can allot alertness and they never expect anything as alms. By giving money they give us a bill, this type of behaviour will not be found in a true Guru. So with pure boldness, with our full courage we can go and have dharsan of such Gurus and get blessings.

True Gurus are ever divine, because their activities are only for the welfare of the society and they on their part are also trying to make humanity ever blissful; but we are not ready to look after them. Their mouna or silence, reveals such thousands of moral points to us. They in a very simple manner arrange their life simply and do what they can through their pandithyam. They lecture to the people and explain the value of Dharma. They explain why we do dharma, these will be energetic pulses to you. In any situation, (by God's grace and penance) they do not lose their consciousness and valour. Whatever happens they will not be nervous to do classical service to the society, that is their achievement, by this type, we can live with shanthi and have a life with full peace, health, wealth etc. Such saints are there to have their dharsan, we must politely request them to bless us; if guru blesses us wholeheartedly then, divine blessings are with us. So there is nothing to be afraid of. If we happen to have a chance, we should not miss the chance; we should be ever cautious and wakeful to set eyes on a Guru. We are pitiable ones and we have to do penance without delay and failure, if we proceed in our offerings along with Gurubhakti, then we can obtain good marks and ranks and be well educated, attain a good job and live a happy married life. These are the dispensations of God through these divine sidhars. So we should look after their needs and thus, we should be perfect in our deeds. This is considered to be the Gurukanikkai for all Gurus. Therefore, we must be crystal clear for our mind is registered in their diaries and they recommend to God, to be blessed for His dharsan and much to His own entire satisfaction and contentment. This is their gracious overall deeds.

Man's mind is always thinking and needing something; this is its procedure. It goes where it likes and when it likes, but we should not make it go as it likes and must keep it under our control itself. We have not retained our original faculty which is peace. This life is to live as He gives us the limitation, and thus, we never give up our life time, it is not under estimated, thus, we should consider our mind. If we take the topic "MIND" we can simply write more than 300 pages. It is having freedom, and beyond this it is to be very much honoured by us. Of all courses of the domestic happenings, domestic renunciation of life is the highest spectacle through which we can see and shut our mouth, we can have success in all our activities and we shall be conferred with a divine result, that is, Mukthi, As such, our needs are big, but our fate is not willing to give us, we should realise the fact and be silent for silence is the only way to dispose of our mental attitude from stormy to shanthi. As per human schedule, we have to begin our lively actions which should be neat and clear, otherwise, live a life of non-purity and as well the Devatha for poverty that is, Moodevi will permanently initiate and sign her residence with us. So we should avoid this tendency at all cost. We cannot do two or more jobs in various offices according to the government rules, but in the spiritual world, we can do various karmas at one time by the gracious look of God. That is why, we are repeatedly stressing that apart from spirituality we cannot get salvation of this human life and birth and death cycle. If we thoroughly analyse our visit to this world, it is nothing but to attain our own place that is Mukthi. But because of various reasons, we have this birth full of miseries, wherever we are, and whenever we call by any name God alone responds to us, because He is the Ammaiappar to all of us, so He has the responsibility to keep us safe and guide us as how to lead a domestic life. The saint said you are not having even 1% you are not at all fit to lead a domestic life, in domestic life, everybody will be in one roof, but cannot live solitarily and with all neighbours.

English knowledge is essential but we have to read and study our mother language Tamil, should be our own wealth and so we can easily understand our tongue power and thus, we can win all the cases. First of all, we have to increase our linguistics. Our effort is to be of the highest level and then, we can speak in other languages and thus, the pupil will grow up physically and mentally, then it will be easy to grow up normally, but, it will take sometime to be normal in all the subjects especially books, publications and market of shares, these are their cosmic duties towards the world for the betterment of this world, Therefore, we have to understand what is human life, for what reason we have come to the world as a human being; we should ask these questions in our mind, it is called athmavicharam.

The sparkle within ones heart and mind is ever fruitful, and one day, it will be exhibited through some channels, or somebody will pronounce about it and its efficiency. As a proof, a certain cricketer had the opportunity to represent INDIA in cricket one day match against West Indies; he had played several national games and his average is 99.9% and his record can't be touched by anybody else it is impossible. Such a great player, namely Mr. X (35) and we are going to see his playing authority and caliber all over the ground, because he has to play several matches in his home ground, and expect some good score from him, and the first ball, he is the opener, faces the first ball, duck out, everybody is vexed, the whole ground is absolutely silent and in the 2nd innings he had scored 444 n.o. who can believe, in that match India wins with 3 players to spare; this is the cruelty that makes him to be a roaring lion and he rotated his bat for 4 and 9 sixes. Like Neapolean he explained went, saw and won, this is the legendary sentence of the cricketer. Like him, he entered, saw and scored 444 n.o. what batsmanship the world has ever seen. Nothing, can be a dream, but he is -35 plus but has made all the audience happy who were expecting his legendary cricket match and this is God's boon. It has been dispensed by God to make such achievement. Likewise, in all games and sports, we can win the Gold medals, we are having these diamonds, but we cannot identify for our sight and for no responsibility on the part to be given by the government and private sponsors. That is why many are cheating others, and robbing, they need money, why should I work? It is waste. One of the quickest ways of income comes out of theft, he confesses his theft and tries to compromise us. If we go on talking about money and games finally we will be out of subject in this book, so we return to this book-related subject of realisation. Mind is the main embryo of the Prapancham and just as all stars and planets are revolving themselves along with the rotation of the sun too; such our world is on the possible way to enter into this earth. The Earth is the only place which is capable of man living Pradesh, but we are not having any kind of names of astronomy and its science, library, practical section, we have not seen at any cost, but if you analyse our sayings all will be true to the extent of exclamation. We are divine and our subjects are also divine. You must believe this concept; otherwise, nothing can be felt, sensed or understood through this book. For example, mankind is rigourously trying to step down in Mars, there is no possibility to step foot by any astronomer or astronaut. Some several years ago man went and returned safely from earth to moon; but up to this date they have exercised us to believe it. The reality is, it is a cinema set's wonderful creation and they, through radio had made a running commentary about this incident, but Neil Armstrong the man who was supposed to step into the Moon did not do so. And we, seeing this incident were all clapping our hands and cheering this achievement and showing our solidarity. After this, now, for the past several years why didn't/don't they try again to go to Moon? Mars…! try, try nothing can be done. As for Moon, it was all a setting of the moon and shooting was just going on and there was extraordinary talking about this incident, and still these foolish people are waiting to send man to the Moon; just....... just as they believe and praise the U.S.A. but nothing is true; everything is a set up, this truth will be revealed to the outer world so long this falsehood ought to bring their wealth and fame to the highest mark. If such unbearable falsehood is agreed by the scientists, because all are gifted in some way or other, something then, they will blindly sign and there will be no chance to go to Mars.

Without any special experiences, and a perfect Guru by Himself, on his own a disciple does not lift his longitude to the peak of spiritual discovery and inventing the supremacy of its own constitution. These are to be understood by the grace of Guru who is equal to God. The specimen of God or Guru also comes to us with our level of supremacy, he dispenses what the soul has to accelerate for a stipulated time and thus, the disciple is very much eagerly searching the super conscious stage of his Mighty Guru. The disciple believes that if Guru has spotted us, he can very easily atttain the perfection and mukthi with Guru's grace at all. As per the Guru's words, the disciple has to do his own findings and the needed patience is to be blessed by his own Guru, his other disciples chorously take in the intuitions in the presence of the Guru. Through phone, the Guru can tell it, but it is not honourable; and when He meets directly when time comes the disciple prays for an apology for the mistakes he has done in the past with date. Thus, the Guru pardons him and he will be free, from all sins and his soul will be so pure to take on the experiences within the stipulated time. Now the disciple is so much dejected through these activities, so the Guru pleasingly forgives all the sins and they will be having the chanting of the holiest Names of God and this. He showers His mightiest blessings on all and thus, they will have a well being life. The disciples are very much confident that their interior and exterior hearts should be with clear and clean thoughts to absorb His vibrations and verbatim. As the Guru can do whatever is positioned in the Vedas, if it is done, the disciples themselves to even millimeters, without the introduction, they can have the prasadham of the mighty Guruthi pooja and thus, they can lift themselves up to the plane of elevation; thus, Guru also penetrates Himself to take the purest prasadham and this will be the highest ritual in this case. And thus, he (disciple) will be the proceeding officer of this spectrum and he will attain sidhis and he should not try to show it off outwardly through any way and this will recharge his greatness of proceedings without failures in any way. Therefore, the disciple should not show anger and hunger for the third mind optional. He is not a man of nothing, we find and realise about Him, He is having the supremacy of God and up to Gurus period we can run our life without any troubles. He is also knowledgeable and a very respectable man, soul to us. If he even blames us, hereafter, we should not be angry towards Him because He is expecting us to be filled with His grace. Sometimes, we simply, idiotically blame Him and We should be blessed by His presence.

We should be with plain heart, and try to do prayer and we ask Him to guide us all through. Whatever we wish, simply, pray him with confidence, we will be blessed by His abnormal dedicated sakthi throughout. He has to bless our requisition which is to be fulfilled with dedication and satisfaction. Then everything will be achieved by our spiritual learning. There is only one universe, but we consider that there are 110000 globes rotating in the milky way as such; if He makes us to see and understand its science, then we will be contained a certain extent, so WAIT. A day will come, the disciple and he will go to one spot, there He will enforce those universal jalangals which, then, can be understood by the human brain and knowledge and attained within 2 minutes, otherwise, he will become a psychiatric patient and there is no medicine to cure him. So divine perceptions, when they are coming down as rain, we have to wait and fill our utensils and they will not come as we need it, this is science. Do not worry about anything; the Guru will clarify all the diffusions as graphics of Geological study which will begin first, and our geographical knowledge with Astronomical science, these two mix and form the scientific development in a very fitting manner of the universe and its casualties. Till then, wait and see our pupils are normally abnormal and their IQ is very sharp which makes them with full of education to pick up any job and earn more than 300000/- per month, they will not be constrained by anything at all till their last breath. These kinds of felicitations, not only appraised by the Guru; He is having a fine journey in astronomy, so. he knows the inner sequence of science which should be obtained and thus, we can lift ourselves to the exterior plane of science. So, try to live by your own consciousness, thus, Guruji will sort out hearts and thoughts, He will joyfully try to teach those universal truths. This can be sent as a letter to the Prime Minister; this letter will exist as history and will come out in all the newspapers, it will be publication without omitting a single letter in that passage, and we all can come to understand the universal truth.

Nobody can make us slaves, if he is born of this Indian soil, this is our majestic prosperity, gained from our situational soil, and our slogan is the best one. We do not accept to take a handful of soil and thus, we are loving this Indian medicine, which is the foremost, ancient material which was set as a land in this universe, called India. Day by day, because of our non co-operation rulership, the British men easily got in the Indian soil; some saw it is properties and then they invaded for sometime, all subjected themselves to the British Government, and gave them permission to take whatever ornaments and bars of gold, silver and other metals. They quarreled with our small provinces and they looted all of our wealth; we who were the richest among nations were reduced to nothing. But they loaded the wealth in various ships and took to their country and saved as treasures. So this proves India is the richest country in the world before the invasion of Muslims and Christians. Now we are borrowing so much of loan from other countries, but if we analyse our activities, we seem to be in the deepest sleep in a drunkard position. This is the first reason, our beloved India lost its wealth day-by-day. Our excellent, archaeological victory is not at all present in these foolish idiots and they do not have the courage to face us in the war front. But they destroyed its fence with stones and they did not battle with us because there was no proper reason. They tried to destroy India. Then how can we go on to proceed on the quality and quantity of the public relations. Soon there will be no name as PAKISTAN in the world's map. Sorry, it is the appropriate word that is suitable to be utilised in that place then, Pakistan must realise its strength and repeat them to their country's defence. It is a very good aspect, otherwise, it will not have place to be pronounced as PAKISTAN. The worldly helping nations, should bear this in their mind, not to lose their troops and weapons without any proper reason and if is good to return our country, will give you first peace and wealth and many soldiers' death. As a mother, I give you advice not to reside here, thereafter our nation will not be silent, Pakistan is nothing and so, all the people who live in the border they lose several things. So try to stop this war, it is not at all necessary. We want to live for many more years with a life of understanding as kith and kin. Thus, we believe that we are having so many friends and only friends.

Our nation is really a people without all the needs to run a peaceful life. Many of the people are not having Aadhar number, ration card and they are not having the chance to avail the policies which are developed for progression. These bloody municipal authorities do not consider all this. That is why we are searching for food and occupation. We are all ready to work hard sincerely but who is the gentleman who is going to give us a good job. In such circumstances only India is going on, and how can we fulfil our daily needs and where will there be peace in the homes? They, the Nilaswanthars are looking like beggars and then, what will we do for our hunger and thirst. That is why, the sale of plots is now considered to be a business and all the farmers sell their lands; they may have crores of rupees and they can live an easy life; thus, each and every peasant thinks and believes, because in this situation, they are horribly affected by severe illness; it is not bodily, it is mentally; so, we have to analyse their needs; if government helps them they will not sell their land and agricultural land and also live comfortably and bring the nation to the prosperous level. In the Central and State governments there is a minister for agriculture and what does he do there? Is there any minister who comes to a field and interrogates the farmers about their needs; and then they must discuss their work and actions elaborately. Why does not this happen in day-to-day activities in our nation? Then their world will fully compromisingly come to unite and will be prosperous and they can earn good price for their products. They can laugh and smile, thus, they can see God also. But what are you doing? instead of it. It is your first duty, sir. Not only India, all the nations of the World should cultivate and with the profit amount, can be used for several industries and commercial acknowledgement. So agriculture is the bottom hold of this universe, we have to have it in our mind.

Wait for 2 more days. Then normally rain will fall in all normal situations. When Dharma is not significantly noted as its nature, then, the people of these worlds of all universe are not going the way as He principles as He allotted to us. If we are dharmavans and kind-hearted beings, all the natural calamities will put an end to their illegal life, and everybody will live a pure honourable life; Mankind's particular significant feature is not an acceptable one. If he is losing his one eye, he automatically thinks the next man's two eyes should be blind, such kind of thoughts make us not to fulfill our desire and nature does not do its duties. So, we have to feel that our organs, all have some impulses, when they are disturbed some vibrations throughout the universe, by this method, photosynthesis is going on and the fruit comes from the trees. When we come to be closed with union and co-operation, our sole life will be disciplined and we will have such a great mind by God's grace and elder peoples blessings. Thus, we do our rituals in our world, many of them go in vain. Some finish with success. Both are all planned, designed and dramatized throughout our lives, there is nothing in the world would be grasped and therefore all our auspicious happenings are under the registration of our mind and world wisely. We cannot say that all are brilliant; but many utter fools are present in villages, we have to adjust with them and theirs and live our life with fluency and happily. We have to reap from Dharma into happiness and happiness does not all have a majestic look of any kind. So that we are all trying through prana yoga and may be all classes of yogic constrains, if we understand it through a true teacher we can ourselves become a Guru and then through our, certain vairagya, every nerve will have to meet impulses from one another and in this way we have to understand thoroughly, yogic excercises may be to the soul, but the soul manages to be fit for the conscious mind, we have to uplift us to the highest pedestal, and this is otherwise called cosmo impulses through which we can taste the inner Ambrosia of all the flowers. We only have to serve ourselves. Likewise, we are all living in this world and we can cultivate the relation between all divisions for we are the sole owners of Happiness and Ecstasy. If we taste this moral nectar, we should be fortunate as there it is flowing in litres and we should take bath in this pious water and thereby have sincerity in the end, our life will be saturated with the Almighty itself. Nothing in this world has an END; everything can be changed to another, but the embryo of the article cannot go to ruin, we can change it into another form itself. I am not doing anything miraculous but nature itself can change the whole environment and we can praise its majestic heroic doings. Therefore, if we are pious and obedient to God and Guru, only then we are considered to be fit, we are miraculous through God's grace. Otherwise we cannot mesmerise and do unusual happenings as an ordinary man. We have to live in accordance with God's and a harmonious situation.

Our traditional predecessors preserved and pressurised their own experiences in various subjects for the sake of forthcoming generations. Like Mr Ramanujam, the mathematician who left so many sums but of all some locks are shut up till today by their numerical no 7000. He was a born genius, as he is identified from the social and intellectual birth, of course, his birth is not abnormal; just as all births too he was born, but he had some Supernatural power by which he could do something abnormal and nobody can even think about those things; likewise Indians in ancient times, (no time is mentioned) they had been inborn geniuses and they put forth various universal truths department wise for which we cannot understand even the questions and we are blinking and trying to solve them through this geniuses brain power, nothing can be done, it is ashamed of that particular period, I say. We are all doctorates from Various nations. They are given medals and doctorates. They pronounce Dr. Yes, they do not want to put their initial also, they are very much happy if Dr. is seen on their letter pads and public notices. Likewise, they do buy their medals earlier at an easy rate and such phenomenon is scooping us not to come to a solution of these doubtful sums' answers, But, one day, a man he has the sakthi to remodel Mr. Ramanujam himself, birth will happen and via through him, we can have some of the answers which cannot be had now due to our inefficiencies. Such glorious geniuses were present that time and today India is supposed to be an independent nation, but is not having pure independence, financially we are not independent as other nations. Our finance minister and foreign finance minister meet together and sign to transact money from nation to nation with some rate of interest and thus, we are slowly becoming beggars. This is the true factor, go and see the fact, you will realise it thoroughly by your own eyes and the exposure, how is that? You, the chief minister of Tamil Nadu, when you are in your majestic chair you do something to develop this cultural highness of your own. There is nothing but delay in our duties and we have to work double heartedly and win.

Accordingly, our name should be kept intact and should be a welcome to all, always. He also verifies the doubt, the same from one another. Thus, the puzzle is dispersed. As our good thoughts and deeds, the public like us and they call us with a Good Name. Maybe the title that God charted Him to be His own son, and at all times, He will guide and guard others by all means till life times span. This is a born dispensation by Him only. Others never can do it, so they suffer. I am very much not angry, it is inefficiency to keep them from poverty or they are very much eager to have a watch.

Several years ago, Agricultural science was selected by most of the pupils and they were willing to grow new species of plants. Likewise, we too are to invent a new species and, we will not suffer a lot without green grams, rice etc., Therefore, we should set aside some minutes and try to cultivate a new genesis of agricultural development. Then we are the super power, thus, they are keeping well and in due course of time, they earn name and fame from the One who implanted us in the earth. Such, truths are inhidden against them, and we are well and make others too well. Our profession may be or not be the study of agriculture, but I respect the concepts of agriculture.

All the experiences that we meet, will be a lesson to all of us and assure us to be free from births. We never hate anything particularly and never give up anything for our own sake. We will follow certain principles, which are a hidden treasure to all types of people, all over the Universe. These are Universal accessories for the betterment of the whole mandalas, where there are some people and animals in existence. Beyond these, there is the one and only abode for us, the Divine place, where all will get peace, calmness and unity which is rewarded to all, that is the supreme natural power, which is symbolically, we teach all younger generations. So, they have to follow our concepts without doubts, then this is the state from where, there will be no wavering mind of all beings, thus they entertain themselves and get the divine perceptions.

We are always having confidence, to look after national problems, and all others' problems; we are ready to honourably treat as Indian citizens and they will be given food, shelter and clothes, thus, we do in all ages. So, many nations' citizens are seen here, at the same time, we establish some Dharma of constitutional laws and orders. We obey them well and as a result, we can be all times good enough to the entire satisfaction of the Almighty God. Whatever, our deeds should satisfy God, then only, the concern, will be ever successful. Otherwise, it will not flourish or it may caution us over all ages, and that is why we cannot do anything because they themselves put and shut the doors not to do any unpleasant activities. So, if God curses, our Guru can save us, if Guru curses there is nobody in this Universe, who can save us. We have to run to ruin by our own self.

We must live along with our belongings and friends to lead your and our life, do things which are constructive by all means; so, we should be very much desirable to do penance. Such characterwise people can do them, to their goodness then, the auspicious happenings will be blistering white to be gained for us. So, we give our generations wealth, is not enough the rich may be poor if we think this, we are not at all giving importance for wealth, it will not be loaded to one's funeral. But, it is not stable and everyone responds to it, otherwise we will not be benefited to some levels. So, wealth, will not save us until the end. Therefore, we have to feed all as annadhanam, we will not become penniless. There, are so many fluctuations in the journey of life to save and hand over it very carefully. So, if we need dharmas' assistance, all of us, will be benefited by our waves of dharmas. So, Avvai insisted firstly, do be ready to do dharmic activities. This Holiest Dharma is adhered to by one self, He alone can attain mukthi and freedom from births and deaths, a moral life will be dispensed by Him. So, we should render our earnest service to the people and to all organisms at our all best, thus, we can bring brightness and dharmic perception can be known, to save us by all means.

Thus, we settle our trend of medical care and treatment, given to others will be differentiated, and if all are in the ways of dharmic happenings everything is alright, if anything is mischievous, we have to be punished.

Is there, we are in need of such activities certainly not; then, why do we waste our energy to be utilised forever! Therefore, our dharmic sasthra stresses us, should emphasise not to go in wrong paths and they teach us to follow good habits; and do not at all do evil things to you and others. Time is going on please do consider this aspect, to have help through us, and, we should do whatever we can it will empower our names in His asanas. Then, nothing will happen untowardly. So, be free from all bondage and not face any quantities of evils and gains at our earliest. The entry of happenings to us, should have the best qualities and customs and adhering to shastric engagements, will enrich our business wholeheartedly, those who are appointed will expect our assistance for cure of diseases, betterment of all Tamil Nadu's temples and so on.

So, there is nothing to be unveiled here, be happy enough and spend your time most probably, sleeping, sleeping, and then, you will come home/ house. Our life will be full of ups and downs, thus, we do the procedures to attain Mukthi; we can easily attain mukthi by our activities, services. And, we have to render all of our deeds to be pronounced very well and God had impressed His sign on us, will enhance us to do the best. Thus, our thoughts and deeds, we are honoured by all, all eminent scholars gain true bakthi and therefore, our sensation will be broadcast at will and pleasure. So, for our generations, if we leave good books, will give a holy place of MUKTHI, This is the easiest way to be calm and patient. If there is bearing tolerance it is enough to grow with peace and harmony for their sake and globalisation. All educationists should live in one surroundings, then how can we call them to rescue. So, there they are scattered and be placed others will do medical attention to all.

Whoever may be, all regulations are very much suitable, to enter inside the territory, they all are waiting for live and fond of watching the game, and if, India wins, all are in a pleasurable mood, if they fail, all of us curse. Is it acceptable, that is a game, if two clubs or nations play the game, one side will win, the other will not win, these things are known very well, but they do not remind us to be nervous and earn money in the name of medical attention. Likewise, we consider the game as we feed you, sir, so do not worry, Be happy, God creates and He will save us in any circumstance at all places.

We have to take rest, is called 'REST? How is that, we do not know the meaning, our rites are pre-determined, such rest, whenever we, the body needs, we go to bed early and in the evening and morning not to know the meaning of this word, whenever we work, the body pain is not known but after sometimes, two legs will twine each other and thus, we believe that medicine can removes and dispense rejuvenation to a certain extent and in this way, we win matches. It is a game, no bother at all to be experienced.

Some think of us as God's avathar, likewise, we do not cheat; we do not expose ourself as we know all, we too had these types of activitism, we clearly see the matters End. And so, we have to be frank by heart and through some earnings, another best chance will be waiting. Whenever, we are character wise earning money, name and fame, we should be calm and harmless to lead longer life by means of the impermanence of youth, patience and selflessness. Then only we can be believed by the Almighty, as a member of their society. When fame and good name comes to us, we should be simple and without a luxurious life, it will surely give salvation, while we are living in this impermanent life span.

First debts and diseases, in case, we should not put into practice these things though it will dispense us with all comfort and abilities. So, we should be much careful, it is also cursed, we have no ways for salvation one rebirth will be given as a boon in this juncture, we should come out of our troubles, agonies and hence be free from all kinds of sins and curses. So, we have to be ready to move along with these desires. We are given an opportunity to be aware about nagadhosam, and first, we do eradicate our sins and curses thus, poojas are done soon, so, we have to be pure by heart and our needs should be kept clean and clear, if we follow these customs, when the period of prayer, we also set up for our home's welfare. Whatever ritual may be done but the basic principles like non-violence, not killing animals for food, should minimise our greatness of this birth. We should pronounce the name without or with meaning of those words, it will multiply some inner hidden truths. Then we can live a good fortunate life throughout our life.

If we attain sivasameepyam stage, we will be free from all kinds of modulations. Those who are well versed in the values of all concepts, they impress one truth, which is non-violence. Pure love towards all is insisted by God, will praise the greatness of one, who departs from us. We should not give up ordinarily a valuable friendship, it will give us mental strength, to attain moksha without doubts at all. So, it is valuable to say, green vegetables have strength rather than non-vegetarian foods. So, we will be very careful in certain food materials, and we think that we will fill up our stomach with ease, and we will not be verily affected by illnesses, poverty and so on! If your needs are this, we should do some rituals and ceremonies to be passed over political heads and for their qualities and quantities and as a result we can be allowed into Heaven which is the holiest abode of God.

If we want this finishing touch of our drawing, it should be drawn, first, whoever may be, win the race and attain Holy Samadhi and through which, Gnanies are implanted like valuable seeds or by pure young ones, so this time, we can be silent.

In Temple cities, marriages take place according to Hindu culture and they will be quite calm, and silence will be conducted and all will be safe and normal, then the embryo will form the nucleus will be split into 2,4,6,8,10 in such order the cell's, division is in action and they will feel fresh and his help will be a remarkable union of both of them. So our ancestors lived together and 'To Get Her' thus, it gives two phrases, which the holy Epic, Ramayana implies. Those who speak or give lectures on Ramayana and Bharatam, their aim is only accumulating huge sums of money but the true saints who talk on Ramayana, it will be effective scenes together as if on a screen. What is life and for what reason are we giving births? Nothing, God's will, sinful and blissful characters are born and they regulate us to live in such a way and civilisation is to be held on by the entire society..., in this way, they are happy and those who do not comprehensively live, God will seek nothing else. Thus, mankind spoil their entire life as meaningless. Such a life is more cruel than a tiger so, many more husbands wives do not reveal the truth to others and that is why, they are seeming to be happy enough. All are having problems, but nobody is willing to tell God, who is the best rescuer of any diseases, and all matters. So, we should be a rescuer and heal all wounds and dress them properly; God will heal it properly. Thus, sidhars are rendering very leading services to God and maintain peace between them, and that is why, their lives are not weighed by money, but they totally count their public service mindedness. In this line of prophets, Shiridi Sai Baba is one of them, acts as a teacher, holy spirit, real mohamrnedian, sidhan and so on. Whatever was imagined we come and do as they compromise like Shiridi Sai Baba; he was not a smoker, but they say, how can we wake up before them?

He is educated through air, panchabootha hireship and was begging from others, but he gets their karma and proposes to give Dharma needs; the poor people are not in an awareness stage, and they do not have any substance for themselves and himself. This is the problematic philosophy, within all these activities. We do not need anything during this world's life, ours is nothing but it is not to be compared with one another. It is the mightiest and we, only mystic puppets are dancing, singing and acting. Festivals are quite naturally done by Sri Nataraja, but we do not think about their holiness, but simply say anything about arts and artists, that is why, our poverty continues, does not leave us. If we do not have mind to felicitate, we should not blame them, as if knowing all and all. We know something about some items and we proceed our activities and all organs are to be as Gandhi's life. Nothing in this materialistic world to be praised or blamed, all are false facts. So, we the true sanyasins are in search of forests and if we are in towns, our style is to be an aloof one, confining oneself to the house only and for a few days residence, we say that it is our house. We have not brought anything to the world when we came after finishing our period we do not catch nothing; in between, some days, we own this or that, everything and all things. We are all cheating ourselves by means of Homely respect and honour.

Whatever is our nationalism, occupation, sects and creeds, in front of Him, we are one and the same, and because of illusions, we feel ashamed of these convergences and divergences; we have been given a boon to lead a life with peace and oneness of words, actions, thoughts and deeds, if it is achieved by someone, he is the highly elevated soul and He is honoured as Brahma Gnani and He is dispensed with Atamasidhis, then they render services through several ways, to be tracked in proper ways of divine life. One thing is to be borne in mind that is, we are not taking birth, as now we are; we do not have freedom about our birth and death, everything is designed by Himself, so, we have to be careful and blissful whatever happens. Lord Krishna explains in Bhagavad Gita thus:- "Arjuna, you are still in maya's illusions, so that, you cannot differentiate them whether it is actual or that it is maya, illusions;" thus, we too practice the path to lead a new way; and the forthcoming generations will be able to profitably gain knowledge and practice a new lesson. So, we can be 100 per cent educated; if all are educated then there will be no quarrelling with each other without pure wisdom and self realisation. This mundane world will be running on the rules and regulations, so, we have to follow it sincerely and we can taste the divine ambrosia of sathyam. In such a way, we will be dispensed with not having births and deaths' deep hell, but attain Moksha.

Whenever we are getting confused and are troubled with some unsatisfactory distraction of mind, do not call friends, relatives and neighbours, do call Paramathma to eradicate this inability and you can periodically, call Him; if you ask your problems, He alone comes in solitude, and blesses and showers His mighty sakthi. So, let us lead our life with consultation of His deeds and civilisation.

Such divine atmosphere that is given as a boon must be very much comprehended throughout our life and we have the Roopam of God Himself; we can raise ourselves to eternal bliss. Whether they are true or false, truth is the final happening in all risks and tasks and it should be understood by all; thus, our ancient Rajaguru's shaped the rules and regulations and taxes not to load the people in any way. Such kingdom is called Rama Rajyam and all the men are wishing to establish, a new era in this universe, and they have to bonafide their processes of all calibers and appointments because they are with Eternal bliss only. Therefore, the ordinary people are always striking each other for food and shelter but the dispensed always set for themselves some limitations, and thereby utilise even a second to live is not for living, for living mood and culture should be in a spot and thus, others will be benefitted in so many ways. Therefore, having the capacity of activities we can do it regularly and they should come into action or actionless. The actionless, while action is a great being, He is the best yogi who can sow Asatamasidhis ever and thus, He uses the universe by all means, so we have to bow to these gentlemen maybe not in plural, it is rare a single too. So, this man is not like the normal people, he is differentiating himself in his own style but he will furnish nothing horrible to the society. In all religions, sects, races, these persons are present with accommodation of their living presence and this is happened to be realised by those who are oriented to spirituality. Such a man does not wish to mingle or collaborate with all the people, but only with a few men and women thus, they will be blessed by all means and through His spiritual power, he also, understands the echo of spiritual column of Indian thoughts and he without preaching, through kasta mouna, does service by means of spreading vibrations all over the Universe. Normally, such men come, are born into this world live and die:- these formulae are not suitable for them, but they themselves are the one and only part and parcel of one commitment. Such eminent scholars are not seen everywhere but they differentiate themselves on their own and they will do miracles and good tunes will blossom where they sit or whatever they are doing. This kind of life is such a boon to us and they are like a light house. It is also Light, but its picturaisation is certainly clearly seen though they are out of Shores they are blooming a vast circumference and as such the sailors are benefited so much.

According to Indian Economical principle based on domestic affairs and bondage of relatives simply saying from what source, money comes and how it is being spent in several ways, the amount will be decreased but we have to earn money and thereby our bank's capital is never equated as

Nil. So, we have to earn money deposit some amount in the bank and keep our economic ratio stable always, it is comparable to none and we care for our capital and hence the interest will be huge to meet our national needs, can be developed and the interest will be used to the progressive systems, thus, it becomes meaningful; this is a comparative study of our domestic government the stability is in accordance with monitory problems. So we have some money in our hands, to be ready to meet our sundry expenses. We are free from the demands of children and, we can be careful to meet out daily expenses and we can derive some money to have a special dinner or anything else; so we have to step up our Indian economy towards the fulfillment of such things and we are sure to have a conclusion to retain the property and throw out our unnecessary debts and so on. But in the meanwhile the politicians capture certain percentage of money is swallowed by these mighty specimens of India itself. We are all going and coming to and fro; thus, what is the primary benefit till the stage of attaining so much wealth then, how will the nation go forward, how is it possible. Our chief minister passed away so we have chosen a massive leader to take over the post, but nothing can be done, which is a democratic one in all ages, these conditional nations are successive of these records. Then, our M.L.A's are acting as though they are not interested in earning money on this occasion but they are growing very much interested alone with her minority plus members of the Makkal Mandram, but they stand in oneness of mankind and thus, we have to overrule the whole nation widely, and make the nation prosperous and a glorified one, what can we do? Among all type of births, there are very few beyond sects and creed and religions. The dispensation of anything will be boosted up towards the ritual and we will be blessed thoroughly and attain an unusual body and this inhidden treasure can easily experience and it is the total cause of all things.

It is not only a tip of wisdom and thus, by using the brain entirely, we have won all the encounters of all facilities so that our old proverb says, One who has presence and utility our VIth sense can attain all success without delay or failure. Today, the children are getting good education and in course of time, they can easily understand the concept of the subjects and they can form, furnish the matter as early as possible: in such a way we are successful to hear the divine approval of our words, and His desire is nothing but each and every unit of life should be beneficial to entertain the body and soul with purity and it signifies that our hearts are full of purity by nature and there is no untoward incident in our life time. If we follow our needs, through which we can buy the necessities by a good disciple and he is considered to be the mightiest man and he will spread out the sequences like never stopping of any group of destination. Whatever we think to do, first of all, we have to concentrate our life with full of piety and faith in God.

Therefore, we should be economically sound, there is no problem to proceed with our earning task, ever and if there is ho house or holdings, or money, we have to face so many problems from all and automatically we fall into debt to somebody. Thus, we are materialistically weak, then all diseases towards mental associates and depression whereas, they attack us and we cannot survive in this world, is so difficult to run through the domestic life, very problematically, so our whole process of finding money will not ease and hardships in all will be in our daily needs, so we can create a position for not falling into debts and easily escape no effects of disabilities in domestic and external affairs. We are likely to be a Gnani ever; hence this synthetical world's maya can be thrown put, without its shadow and we can be easily living in this domestic world and so, we must earn something to lead this life in this mundane world, and we should not be disturbed by particulars and even others, thus, we can lead our life towards Eternal Bliss and our spiritual status will not be disturbed by any means; thus, we will proceed with our wants nearby and there is no business with you, but you are the master of your home, and everything is happening, whether you know or not, all things will come to action. And there will be no blindness in Economical field, there is no frustration and we will satisfy all departments. So, you alone can live as you decide; and there will be no delay in your works. And your family will be self satisfied as they will be happy and joyful ever. Thus, you also satisfy your ownself too.

Our works about spiritual world will be shown as an open book, there will be no joy or sorrow to us particularly and we will not be needed by the sources of this modern life. They are seen according to 'our organic system, all will exhibit its maya appearance and nothing is positive and stable, why is man running behind money, fame, demonstration of himself in the official life but we will never be a slave for these proposals and will be calm, and specially calm the steep deep silence, this is not because of others but our self-oriented silence, when we smile, then, we will be a proposed Gnani, this state is described and nobody can understand to follow or to have principles of their own field, thus, the whole Universe will be benefited because of our presence and thus, we can understand all, ourself but all will see us as their own thus, they make us to participate in this world's day-to-day life. There will be no damage of our overall life and nothing is there to succeed our life in this materialistic world; then now, we can know why these circumstances are like this, nobody can answer it, because a true Gnani alone knows the reason and He will be verily contented through the vibrations of all, thus, his seedlings will disturb ever, and he comes to clear others doubts but he simply adds some sayings, the true nature of others life, present and future, and how to live, with this science, he adds some Universal Truths, thus, he will be very happy and homely as he asks some concepts thus, man will be satisfied and will be the mike's loud speaker for his greatness; so people will come to meet us and have some moral tips, so if we wish, we can easily earn a lot of money, but being a true gnani will not become a slave to money, that is why, we will bow to Him only, not to others in this world, thus, we and you will be accompanions in life but between you and us, there will be a big difference available ever and ever in God's classifications and rules. There rules are ever Universal and we will be held to task, others will use our innocence and they will try to buy us for money; be careful. Gnanies are not money minded and they are very well educated, not academic in their approach of the world which is entirely different from us and our master; do feel this situation and we can easily come outwards to settle our own problems, and others too, thus, we should be guarded and be guided by God is the proper path to attain eternal liberation.

There are men of speech, but none, there are no men of action; but, we are a master in this universe, master in domestic life and others are not equal to us. Because others are holding something as though having relation to Him which is the only qualification, and that is why we are more respected, unless they are nothing. Because of these happenings, we are alone and we never mix with others in any situations. Why I and others too emphasise this universal nature of the Gnanis.

"Sorry", these gnanis simply say that for courtesy, and they simply leave the home, so, others should be cautious as they can be because of their fruitful life; they live, without illness, poverty, not failures, others are all slaves in their possession, will and pleasure, these types of 'EGOISM' is their real nature, what is the way, you are going to transform into something, they say something is better than nothing. These gnanis are created why, their lives are only because of Maya's illusionary illustrations, they will be covered and they never spell any word, to others feelings, This is not at all done by them, because they will say, we are out of senses and we are doing heavy work. Our lively activities will be perfect and not normal and that is Why, all will follow us our spiritual way only, we can realise it and thus, capturing capacity will be increased to the modest height and this world's honours, money should be with us. If fame is to be attainable, we should live with name and fame, and that is why, we are in this materialistic world and you are a statesman.

Therefore, our Guru is the certain treasure of the ever living concepts who can dispense what the Mummoorthis dispense to all. Definitely, from this type of Guru, one can attain the sharpness of mind can be felt, not realisation, it is in action and in all of your vibrations, there will be peace and natural child's harmony can be exhibited by all means. Thus, a sadhu is ready to heal all and dispense good education and thus, he is enough humourous, he will reshape this Universal University (earth) and live and his affection will be on each and every creature in this whole world. Then, he is honoured as a sidhar and he is personified as God, Himself, shows his figure to some only. The golden opportunity is one, only to look after his problems and fulfill his needs. So, if you speak or think itself it is enough, if you are against Him, ultimately diseases and poverty will arise due to factor of discipline and civilisation. Thus, normal people in this world all will come to this type and realise this spirituality and the application of this mighty soul. Yes, you can. Try your level best.

The supremacy of this human birth is only for attaining your own self by your own self and thus, you will come to and realise the fact "I" is the supreme power which can be felt like thirst, whatever drinks you do have them, but the thirsty will not be sorry, it will not do to be free from thirst because of these drinks', but if you drink water, within sometime your whole situations of discomfort will vanish and you will be normal. Thus, if you need good disciplined disciples, the master should be as she or he expects. So, Good people will come to us, the master, the mighty Guru and the disciple will be an abled hand whatever may be the problem and he will surely become a Rishi. Whatever manthra is given as Manthra and that which is pronounced with dedication of mind, it will automatically make your physical and intellectual deeds to come to an end at that moment the dawn of philosophical truths will be clarified because of our past births and deaths' grievances are fully erased from our mind, the empty and pure mind will be the simhasanam and you are considered to be the Almighty itself.

Therefore, our whole legends actually start on bhavadhaeVasudevaya- if you chant this holiest manthra of Lord Vishnu, will be dispensed with all of its effects and realise the ever living life which is nothing but, fitness as a member of the company of sidhars. By the by your saturation point with the mightiest Being will give life to yourself, and be embraced, thus, you attain a birth-deathless region of ever living concepts. The goal of human life is thus, attained by you, and it is the best dispensation. This is the highest elevation from abnormal to normal and it is a stage under below it, it will be a bonded life, must be gotten from evils and so, you will lose all your physical strength in your old age. So, do mind this Truthful Truth and situate your life with care and pass all, it is not the clowny situation. He/She, whoever may be, you should bless them not deeply. Then, you will lose your mighty power, will be a waste and do mind this concept. And, a lady asked whether her son will pass the Indian service test, there is nothing be worried about him, he has birth to rule over this earth for certain provinces of India. So, be confident, his is the suthra or formula to be satisfied. ok.

From all dimensions, if we analyse this materialistic life, nothing will be found in the last, death is one of restful time and leisurely, sit down in any asana as convenient to you, try to analyse your past, present and future nothing in the end, and something is better nothing an English phrase, but, in this circulation of activity, there is no use of the body without its soul. Try, do it and you will not be disturbed, and you cannot conclude anything which is a pleasant and cheerful one, for you, thus, she settled the fact between us. Therefore, according to the part and parcel of life will be their own ways, and they live with all comforts. Thus, they decide, by Almighty's grace they are having natural dealings to lead a peaceful life and so, others are calling them fully concentrated souls and Aacharya too. As such these accords, they are all having all types of rewards for themself, such noble qualities, will disturb one and all in the future and they will be normal in all circumstances and their classification in the society is so hard to follow and have opinion of him as the best descendent of God Almighty. Their one and only weakness is always speaking anything to anybody else. So, we have to train Him/her not speak and how to speak and where to speak, if this is known, and adhering to this philosophy, he has none equal to Him such a dispensed soul He is!

According to India, agriculture yields money makers, more than any other country in the world. In India all types of crops are giving so much of income than other countries. So India is the sole country with prosperous lands and they are producing much rice, fruits, nuts etc., for our welfare. Other nations buy some of their crops from other countries. But India is producing self- sufficiently and it exports such crops to all the necessary countries and so foreign money is transacted for various businesses. Therefore, we should concentrate on crop growing department and its development, our business in this agricultural field will be satisfactory; and they are somewhat costlier than the producing cost of those crops. In such fields, we are casually dividing lands into plots and selling them for an accomadative price and thus, we can settle our future. But none of them is willing. to work in our fertile lands. That is why, we are suffering though we know how to do agriculture and how to send to other places and make money, if we encourage them, they will be geniuses in agricultural sales and distribution too. Now, we may be living comfortably, but after several years, we may have lost all our lands and in its place there are, new, only buildings present and we have some tablets for breakfast and the same is for dinner also. We have to take some tablets, and in future, for supper, we have to take several tablets; thus, we have to be free from hunger and thirst feelings. This is going to happen steadily without any doubt. That is why our scientists insist us to do agriculture in our fields not to be lazy but create a new era of India. Otherwise our respiratory system is mostly in poverty, in the sense from selling our fertile lands. So, we have to carefully deal with this matter and take considerable action too. Otherwise, we have to be present in the Q series for getting some rice and other things from the government or end up with starvation. Thus, our natural calls will not be fulfilled with food and others. So, we must be aware of honestly constructing water tanks and the source of money is to be found and make it to be used by all means. Otherwise, everything in future is worthless. Our efficiency is to accelerate and satisfy our needs, so, we have to work hard, unless, nothing more in this world other than this way. So, we should not delay or discard our responsibilities, if it is continued, our poverty will grow upwards. This should be borne in mind. First of all, we should be ready to focus on agriculture in all ways, we must be, and the final result will be as tall as the Himalayas. We know this by knowledge, but we are not ready to realise it through experience. If one is willing to be a good agriculturist, we should be having all divisions, dimensions of agriculture in this way, we should try to the best of our efforts with our sole efficiency.

Therefore, first we should be always, throughout 24 hours, we must believe ourself as a farmer and then our cultivation will serve us as earnings and experiences. So, we should be ready to be follow culture, then agriculture is permanently giving us wealth. And then, every thing is possible, and we must be careful in planning and forwarding our thoughts into deeds, this is the choice of success.

Those who are teaching, speaking, fluently doing these two modes of life, but when it comes in our life, we are not able to catch anybody to get rid of these crucial circumstances, we can go to special divine temples, and seek His holiness towards us and thus, we can deliver to others the divine boons like health, wealth and all success. So, the men and women who uphold His holiness take all our divine principles and such things will keep them strong with these articles throughout their life span and their surroundings will be golden customs of our sathsangam. This will make them to penetrate the flesh and bony structure and leave them all to part from these evil deeds, then we will be really clicking the symptoms of godly amenities and thoroughly amend our petitions to whom, can dispense us on the pedestal of God, then is there any trouble and troublesome manuals? Nothing will be our enemy and if everything is in practical, they will come and have friendship with total surrender and thus, we mortally dispense the clipping of our life fruitfully.

As a human being, implicit faith, respect and honour should be given by those who are young. When you see elders and the aged you should bow your head in front of them.

Some lacs are secured by the eminent artists and they pay its tax to the government, thus, they are out of the income tax probes. If this is done by them to any other department, it is a waste and no necessity to do so. If tax is paid what kind of use is got. If it is not taken into consideration both of them will be fine friends, even as brothers can with a lot of money and thus, they can spend for natural calamities, atrocities and they are bothered about nature, they will donate some lacs of money for rescue operations and they will have consideration for the health of the society of their own privilege. Like this, we can expect their support morally and they can be utilised forever. Those who are earning lacs of money, they will provide for a large family of members and if they are ok, they will not be disturbed by means of the outer world, their field entirely depends upon their efforts, they can exhibit their all forms and frames will be shown to the outer world, thus, the producer and technicians will earn a lot of money and hence in the society, they will be considered and they will be useful for the society and can even go to the borders and entertain with some extra-curricular activities and thus, our soldiers will get rejuvenated mood and there will be no fear for anything that happens and their efforts are dedicated for the national integration and harmony. Therefore, they are given some privilege in tax departments and they are incharge of some intensive disturbances, and they will not be taken in consideration, their patriotism is over all kept silent will be eluded outside and they act as several politicians and our incoming generations will come to know their sacrifice apart from religions, creeds, sects etc., we are one and the same, in this all of us will struggle for freedom and unity among diversities and hence our exhibition will be taken into consideration.

Those who are living in this world without Education are said to be of eye sightless births, according to many statesmen. Thus, Thiruvalluvar insists on education's praise and pleasure. A car which is running through speedily, then they feel a mood of pleasure and that is why the car was called pleasure the never ending process and it is called pleasure. These pleasurable situations should be settled by us, and should we rejoice with love and pure affection. Passion and affection naturally arise from bedroom itself, if one who, he or she, is contended with pleasure of bedroom, is nothing but to have sound sleep, thus, one is saying at all times, one day he filed a case and through camera via cell phone is the sole witness, and they speak like a 60 year old woman. Suddenly stop the cell, I will give divorce at this moment; they are getting separation because of this female, the husband should give Rs. 2000/- per month for the maintanence but the judgement has gone through and he alone is still in love with her.

We have plenty of confidence, that our son and daughter-in-law are rejoicing their life with calm and sexual calamities, they, themselves put an end for those inconveniences and they are contended with self realisation through life style and our sketch of life is entirely modified into all of others and inners are sub-consciously nothing but wind. I have a trip only for two days, and the earnings about Rs. 80000/-has been paid on that day, still up to this moment I have not gone on any journey, so, bear with us and within 20 days, all the balance will be settled as cheques or currencies directly. So, kindly bear this uncomfortable situation, I have given to him, I am feeling ashamed and that is why, I ask for time, within that auspicious day, with the grace of Lord Murugan. I'll come directly and settle all the money, I thank you very much for your important forbearance, this is the good relationship says Thiruvalluvar.

Our life span is determined by the auspicious day. If I come it should be by auto and I have to search for it, if I decide to come by car, there is no driver, what will I do? Yes but I am waiting for you, some fear is in the heart and so I call you, everything will be in your hands. Ok, ok. I will start to come and throughout tomorrow will be here and finish the book at an earliest state of human life. Suffering is nothing at all but money is the President of all, this is the lesson we had at this time. Hence, you should be with Nagaganapathy idol, and worship Him with full of coincidence, your forthcoming generations are over all well equipped by nature and mercy of His greatness.

That is everyone must try to attain perfection in life, they need not go into the womb of a lady and through mitasis divisions, the senum is transferred to a fourth in size and the multiplicity of numbers every second they multiply themselves and the first organ which is formed is the HEART, which is capable of ticking throughout 120 years, the span of life. But it is reduced, on time we will argue about it. And the muscles, tissues are formed and they are collapsibly the supernatural creation is ready to push from inside to outside at the prompt time the baby is coming out. As per the instructions of the Almighty it comes to this world as he/she and the mother especially and all are very happy and the new born baby is crying and the sensual organs begin to work as such human birth is given to us as our own property, and everyone is rejoicing with the mother and breastmilk is the first food material, it empowers all organic systems and stimulates them towards construction. The construction of a house is easier than this manual or physical construction. Yes, there some permanent processes are going on and then, in the educational field, your approach should have a chance to realise the divine secrets and in this way you will have the insistence of God, you come to understand the instability of all beings and hence you start to look inside your organic systems and as a result your education will be marvelous and as such, your glory will spread over our artificial happenings thus, you have the manual set up of the construction of this human body and its miraculous growth and every season the body's structure seems to be some and exchange all of their culture and permanent feature of human life.

Human birth is so rare among all the varieties of production of mass is so difficult with all inner and external aspects, there should not be deaf, dumb, loss of organic system, kilpauck cases, these are given divine punishment to the organs that is why, Avvaiyar, Tamil poet, classifies the differences between us and other creations. So we must realise a human birth which was dispensed and their capacity should be ruled by righteousness and characterwise we should be with full of love, desire upon the Almighty, should be permanent, but all we see, scale and appointed syllabus's rules cannot be changed and we alone undergo with their foot paths, then only it is the Right human birth, as we praise is suitable. So, we must have everything who wishes to avail this. I am very glad to save money, otherwise, I am penniless and a tea is expected, such experiences I had, have you had such experience? what is your age and mine you know if I am in the bazzar, I have not enough time to resist and to use the latrine, 10 rupees is needed, what is the use of knowledge, so we must learn to earn, otherwise, we will not have any kind of respect, I know it, well, nothing doing. If you say anything, there will be no response to that occasion, so learn and accumulate money. This is our first teaching to the world.

We give the most convincing out sketches of the film industry for consideration. Thus, they can be scholars in a particular field, they can help the society's inner and outer world's and they exhibit all of their activeness towards their concentration, they can give some outstanding cinemas and thus, patriotism was expelled through our past exhibitors to the outer world and they will come when she leaves and where is she? He is afraid of these concepts and they will not be taken into consideration. They can easily help the nation in both materialistic and spiritual worlds. One's output moods are satisfactorily expelled, all will exhibit their values into outstanding phenomena of their consideration about the fields they choose. So our forthcoming generations can know about our past actors solidarity and compound status also, therefore we should take them into consideration as the formation and information about the society and world at large through the heroes. At their level best is an idealogical one, if they donate, it will be a boost to us, through their heroes and nothing should be expected or otherwise our needs can be satisfied by the influence of those who make themselves to liberally give to the nation, the amount may change but all will donate something to the nation wide consideration, they give and others will be induced to give some amount considerably thus, they serve the nation by their own influences. They donate beyond consideration to the welfare of the society which means all sects, creeds are beyond religions benefit. The giving hands are only allocated to some of the people and their donations will be under the circumstances, there should be no quarrel about the differences and systems.

Thus, the efforts are taken into consideration, one dramatic situation can be found at each and every movement of the people and hence our freedom struggle is so effective with the co-operation of religions and by this union all are diminished to Indians as a whole are all one and the same, and all the people come together and are struggling for freedom from slavery; we are not at all slaves but our original assets are borrowed or buried and taken to their consideration and all of this world's consumption of needs will be stealing the articles and their attitudes are based only under INDIA as consideration. So, we are requested to donate handsomely and liberally to the freedom struggles. Finance is an important figure by which we can solve so many problems, because we have no government, it is in honour and its position is enough, there is nothing to be worried; so we have to keep ourselves by the income and sundry expenses through which we can analyse the income and outgoing of the money's values. So, it is essential to keep an account note in which we must note the incoming sources and the expenditures we meet out, then, if they ask like this, the note will speak for itself.

According to thanthric and manthric methods which are taught, it will not be applied for illegal processes, variety of sensual desires and so on. The disciples should take an oath in the Guru's presence and in front of yagnas done to Goddess kali, and they come out of the Gurukulam and hence do penance and work for the welfare and betterment of this Universe. But the disciples have to live in this materialiastic world, they need a lot of money, hence they can apply his yogic current to the various processes and he leaves from this mundane status in due time. Many well wishers are asked not to do anything for the wrong sided people, but they earn money and cannot guide and guard even themselves. They are in the drunken state and are subjected to pisasus activities and they are failing to do good for the people. Then the next yogic master is selected thereafter and he also goes in these ways, and both of them do unglorified activities and as a result, they, after some time suffer the bad effects; two will suffer from various diseases and unsteady method of livelihood, and at the best, ruin their ownselves. Thus, two frauds diminish from the world. Such people they are, though due to their good fortune, every thing was going profitably and nothing further to glorify their abilities, and lost mental peace, they became psychiatric patients and they were never useful for themselves and for the nation and in due course of this field, they two are abandoned by Time factor, they never unite with another to do such works, but they were fully finalised as failures. And such these are released through the public and in the end, they finish their life's span and hence have no gain by or in the spiritual world. By their cheating mentality they could not keep our confidence for the welfare of the people, nobody is coming to speak leisurely, and as a result they lose everything and pose as if they have the divinity in personification but are useless and nothing can save them.

The primary duty of human life is nothing but, to attain the lotus feet of Lord, Himself, since the birth of this Universe the total population of it, Man finds to fit one another and they shake the earth, and count one, by one. They have statistical tolerance and they have the ready made statistic sheet. So it is very useful to be published by the government and it will be a boon to us. This is very much utilised at the time of general Elections. It is working enormously and they sum up according to the calculative side, they are very much classified so as not to take false total digits, if you take it as they write, then, nothing useful in our findings. Such as analytical science, they won't do anything apart from speaking and talking, and they are not respected by anybody, and everyone's blameful look makes them useless.

All our thoughts and deeds are taken off and modernised machines and fertilisers and mode of agriculture should not come to their own kith and kin. So we have to have co-operation among ourselves first then, we invite them to assist us. But this Mental darkness must be thrown out and scientific procedures will not be suited. Is it a question; try to have opinion from the public; though He is moneyless, He is not to be considered to be doing nothing. His thoughts will be of enormous help to the environment also...

We got freedom from the British Government. Up to this date, India is a vast, big nation, but the British Government wished to break India, and thus, due to their compulsion we had to form a new Muslim country in the name of Pakistan. They gave voice and they succeeded. Pakistan has grown day by day. Our wealthy temples there have been broken and they have taken away so many loads of valuable articles from all over India and deposited them as their wealth and established Pakistan, thus, periodically touching our micro heart beats they created a new formed Pakistan where only pakistanies will be allotted to higher positions, and posts; not even a single Englishman (Christian), can have the privilege even to vote in any election. Now there are Hindus, but there is no value of their immense valued human life. Thus, they are controlling the whole wide country and they always follow a touch and go policy against India. As per schedule, Pakistan itself thinks that India should not be in the world map. This is their ambition, and they are not keen to develop their oun country either qualitatively or quantitatively. They do not wish to be united, this word unity is not at all pronounced during their normal life and speech.

The nation which is independent, we can speak, ask, guide, participate in elections, vote with confidence and enjoy the rights we have got in these nation-wide sessions and self is having to win the votes. There is the President of Indian Republic and he is considered to be the 1st citizen of our country and thus, democracy is established, of, by and for the country. We are ruling our own nation, this is described as democracy and therefore we rule over the nation widely and we respect, honour our India as an ever independent country. Among all democratic nations, India is the first to have calculations and all. So, independence should be cautiously and seriously safeguarded ever. The nation wide thoughts and deeds are the profits of the country by the country's wise men and they lead their life with speed but without the slippery mode of operation. We are a socialistic republic and democracy is maintained in a normal way and thus, we should pray for its welfare and betterment. Therefore, we have to uplift the nation by our own efforts in all fields and this way we can win in all competitions, and others will give respect to us. So, that is why, we celebrate our Independence day; speeches by VIP's and distribution of sweets are not at all urgent, beyond this, we should be ready to sacrifice our life to the innovation of the Almighty. Thus, the nation will have hope of integrity and unity. Where have we come from? Nobody can say with identification. So, we have to keep this auspicious day to celebrate that we are indeed, Indians and it is to be maintained throughout nation's life. If we strive the nation itself will thrive in good condition so, we must be work hard with good will and pleasure.

There are many sects, creeds, religions and customs available with Indian Philosophy and there is diversity throughout. We resemble all in one sector of enemity and all kinds of people donate freely and thus, we easily can collect money from the public. Some people have given rupees one lacs during the kargil war, such mentality is in service to keep our mother nation with our production of weapons. Thus, the soldiers, why? all the people wished to give something upto the mark of their prosperity and property which must be valid during the kargil war and tried to give something and denote it as an honour and we will be majestic. We salute the public's presentation and thus, we will be considered as one of the participants who love others and our esteemed service to the society will be truthfully sizable in writing our nation's heritage and its class among all nations. This alone is one point which touches each and every kingdom. Many have plundered wealth from India and we have come out into the world and as such, we are serving the nation at our level best. Thus, we need all of their needs and then India will be a supreme power which has got wealth and health to face these kinds of troubles. If anybody is ready first you use your conch and let the battle start, and within some months time, all nations will come under the one nation INDIA. Then only, they will cultivate our remarks and total marks should be collected and the percentage of money will be distributed towards India's war field till the end of destruction. They are all concentrating on the weapons, but not the virtue of those who supply and produce the weapons, will yield as weapons and thereby we all will be ready to be in the battle field of the army and airforce and navy service with ships and submarines. May be, God created us to be in the place from 6'O clock, but then nothing is normally ending, so I do not prepare myself as a human being. Thus, up to the level of situations, all situations are made individually and all things are out of her service money and they do not consider her strength and valour.

The supreme One controls all kinds of jobs and occupations very well, but due to ignorance, we declare that we are responsible for all these victories and then we launch a party and do name it, and try to go all the way and become a member of the municipal council then, they contest the elections, they are trying to be an M.L.A., and after this they are doing some tasks elaborately in order to become M.L.A., later their sight is towards New Delhi, to seek a seat to promote as an M.P in the parliament and the general elections come we select the M.P and then, they try to get ministry post; thus, their political life is running and they really forward a few settlements, constructing electrification everywhere and some welfare schemes they go and make us to study to become M.P by their leadership's recommendation, he becomes a minister for power but no jeep at all. We have inner intellectual sector and is considered as the best man, who rules the world with scientific outlook. I am taking revenge on this INDIA to improve ourselves and suitably treat Indians and my first circular should be not to wear nighties and walk on the roads whenever they are coming out. All the colleges should educate their students thus. The name itself denotes that it should be worn only in the night time and not during the day and walk about everywhere. If nighties are worn during the day time, then why not go to your work place in nighties. If we copy, let us copy the foreigners correctly. Nighties are not their day time dress code. They restrict it only for the night. But we who are just copiers have made the nighties our national dress by wearing it during the day replacing the saree and half saree, walking on the streets without any qualms or inhibitions. Is this our culture? We are going away from the path of our culture and civilisation because of modernisation which is not a good sign. Another matter of concern is the chudithar, the dress code of Northern India, suitable, due to cool climatic conditions. Here, in South India, it is hot, hotter, and hottest. The uterus needs more air circulation. Thus, the saree is best suitable. Otherwise, the women have to face many health problems.

We also preach not to give importance to money, it is nothing but mere paper, may give you pretty handsome look, if the government announces that these currencies are not in action, then it loses all kinds of value, this is the philosophy of money, so, give respect to the man the One man and you can be taught Gnanam; thus, daily after taking bath, pray Him for 5 minutes and it is enough to saturate with the mightiest among the mighty, therefore, He makes clear His caliber and He has gnanam and leads life towards success.

Wherever you go, inspect up to the royal look, you will come to a conclusion that money and wealth are the sole authority which maintains one's name whatever you wish so, everything is weighed by one's ability and good habits they are linguistically significant, but there is no value for these words, if they come in a practical way, then, we will be treated as a Prince. So, every man is only weighed by his earnings and his balance in banks, thus, we make humanity to understand this world, by doing something, we will be arrested, whether this is a convictable mistake or not, we have some idea about this death and thus, we can go to bed and sleep peacefully. We will be happy enough to exercise to do good acivities, so our ancestral blessings and kulthevatha and Almigthy must bless us, if otherwise, we will be without any such thoughts of them. Because we are an astathathiran ...! Chanting your deities name gives you enormous power to your five karmendhriyas. If it is in primary state, everything will be blossomed by saints and yogis, when you come in person they can heal you with a touch as they are our Gurus.

Now, without caring about food materials, we are pushing and pressurising our children to study; they also act as studying. So, the parents should have an awareness of what is education. All offices, all staff are given the best salary for the their works. Then, why do they ask bribe to make the matter in favour of us. In the season of Deepawali and Pongal, we have to give some amount to all staff of all departments. They mischievously blame us and their department's works are stopped.

These Maharishis do not also stay in one place, they are wandering here and there and uplift the whole society by their presence by the process of application of love, service and so on. They are doing these activities which are admired by many of the people, and thus, they are honoured by all and they will be surrounded by people to gain something from them, like freedom from illnesses from poverty to higher level, job orientation, marriage. These activities are recited by their whole and sole presence and therefore, they serve the society and so they will be remembered by all. These Maharishis are sleepless, foodless not bathing at all; but near them no bad adour will arise from them. People worship them in due course of time, and such continued services cannot be done by normal people and such happenings will blossom by their Athmic strength and those who are interested in them, their advice, they make themselves as their pupils, disciples and some will reside along with them and do their level best; thus, their family will flourish to the extent. Such people are ever working for the welfare of Sanyasins and the public people. Through this serving authority, meaning their troubles and inabilities and He knows it and He blesses them and they will be cured well both materialistically and intellectually. The peoples grade of living will be raised to some extent and they become rich in money and they need something to give them self confidence. They will be blessed by Swamiji but he is in normal position and lives without poverty and so on. So the people are fully up graded by the blessings of Guru and God, and they will be impressed by the Almighty; dispensed with good health and wealth they begin to serve his Samadhi. Their last breath, will serve and celebrate all sequences and all other surroundings; a very compact Samadhi will be raised by which, he comes out and responds to their consequences and blesses them very impressively and the whole world will be happy enough ever. All people will ever live honestly with honour, discipline and through the penance of the yogi or Maharishi in the samadhi, the outer world will be safe and guarded by him in good fields. Such a recognised life is entirely wished by all for this reason, the whole area will thrive in agriculture, and many other crops, fruits and so on will flourish till the time is going on. This is ever living and pervading Samadhi like Shridi Baba's Samadhi, will transform itself, respond to all disciples wants and needs and give strength to them, and they will lead a life with no problems. All types of arts will flourish to the ecstasy and there will be no severe diseases and all will understand one another and thus, they will go, but discipline and character cannot be destroyed by God's and Guru's grace and mercy.

If we call on a medical practioner, a doctor, he interrogates the people. Asks them the time, and sends them away to go else where for the treatment, he does not have the humanitarian spirit to attend to emergency calls during night times also. The patient meets with death. These are not imaginary scripts. When you experience, such a situation you will know the pain.

It is natural that is why we can insist on their deeds. There is no strike, dharna or lack of efficiency and yet we find fault with other's work and dealings. This practice will not help to do rigourous agriculture, it will be responsible for the lack of growth. So, trust in our servants, will be a boon to us and others. Therefore, we do not miss out these workmen and along with them, we have to do our earnest work which should be to assist them in all the ways. This will help a lot or a bit to the strength of the buildings. This is the easiest way to go with co-ordination with the workmen and the proprietor. If this ego is not among the men everything will be happy and they will yield so much of cultivation and crops.

In the Indian geographical map, if you understand it, there is so much of fertile land, but they are all well educated, the best games and sportsmen are coming from Russia. We should not be greedy, instead of this, we can beg elsewhere and we must keep them safe, do not worry. We are ready to serve our land with water and fertilizers regularly, the crop will give us a lot of its yield. At that time, we feel the ecstasy of natural feelings which implicitly upgrade towards the highest peak of divinity. This is considered to be karma yogic mark.

Our ancestors did yogic exercises, are nothing but our ancestral yogic exercises are done by the body for a healthy long living life. This is therefore, to continue our duties fully merged with the profit of the cultivation. Gradually, day by day, we have to keep them safe in all ways, then see, what is the huge mark of profits attained by agriculture. Our inventions and discoveries are easily done due to spiritual manifestations. Thus, we should guard and guide the crops to grow with full-fledged yield and then, we should be ready to analyse its highness and supremacy.

If a man with all comforts and liabilities, will be dispensed through their ambassadors, everything will be finalised and Almighty, Himself, do whatever our epics and puranas and shathras mentioned if they are followed regularly, we shall get all boons without any doubt at all. Because of its useful methods if you realise it, you will be contented. All our necessities are fulfilled by nature. So God alone is the Head of all departments, if you think so, it is blunder mistake, but, if I curse you, your entire life will be a ruined one. So, please be calm and try to educate yourself and then, a place and time comes, there you can produce your excellent happenings should be in way of promotional situation and live a full-fledged life; if we shower our bhakthi and faithfulness is shown there will be no base for doubts and whatever, we do, success will be ours and thus, we shall be full of gratitude for ever. All of us need something in the circumstances and change of rulership, they differ from one another and we have not enough laws to prevent such five fold sins, so we, should not be involved in these five fold sins. Whichever and whatever greatness we should not do any harm to those people, who elect us of this mighty power.

Our pros and cons should be utilised for the welfare of others whoever they may be; we should pay them as it is. Then, God will alone come and place a good site, and He wants to be a restful nature. Thus, God is ever here, because we are all not known to all peoples. But Gnanis know ever expect God only. Therefore, God is the seer and sole controller of all metabolisms knows everything about all, without any doubt, we have to pressurise him to dispense such mind and abilities to achieve then everything can be done. We are always ready to convince us, than their theft mind's reception we cannot do anything elaborately dispose of everything in our mighty shoulders whichever, the task is, tell me I will concentratedly mind it always I can get a pure, irreparable solution can be realised by this Almighty. So, our efforts are accepted appropriately by others, if we do not try to solve it, how can I succeed in this risk? It shows your ego and innocence. Do not think so, body will lose all calories and give new blood throughout the body, we cannot do anything, why? Such an invaluable birth it is, and others can request us to do possible things and impossible things certainly leave the matter at its best cause.

The whole system and metabolisms are to be firstly finished we are taking time to spend it in producing this project as a first one. We can have 5 marks intensively, without physical assistance, we have done all the necessities to be fulfilled with ease and care. This is not the first time, man accepts our concepts but if there is something from us, it will be a miracle deed alone. Each and every action first comes out in our or others presence, common man can read and have result at once, our study never has an End, because, Goddess Saraswathi alone is studying ever and She is fond of learning all happenings. A fully educated man, by a mere look, it is understood, because of His calmness, His eves will stand still in nature. Always He is active and involved in action oriented happenings. He is never disturbed by anything and has sharp wisdom oriented exercises. He made something, not at all at the end of His time His soul is to be released soon. Thus, every second of time, He wishes to spend it for the sake of the society, whether it is for destructive or constructive purpose even after the expiry of that work He does not bother about the results or its publicity by any means of medias.

He is ever dynamic and does things for the welfare of humanity's health and wealth; He never spends even a half second unwisely, He wishes to render His service to the fullest mark, He is always a moody type, His consequences of silent mood, gives rest for the inside organic systems and He is very helpful for the society's betterment. Even, if death occurs to wife, He will not have disturbance of His own, He will remain to enclose all the proceedings towards achievement by all means. He is much active to do service. Each and every second He does something whatever is in the prints of a geographical note, He exhibits to outer world, the highness of kingdoms and their ruins is to be called off. Thus, they are living and were living, must be the chief co-ordinators of the universal love and peace. If we follow, then Rama Rajyam is quite possible. It can achieve everything. Everything is noticed by everlasting period, it may be a little, but their schedules will not vary and their suitable divine power, they are all still as the lessons of the 1st standard in schools, thus, they wish to make achievements and ever living even in their death, through which, we must and can expect good result. Necessity is the mother of inventions wherever, we are dynamic enthusiasts our output will be big in size and they are got rid of for those who have their negative approach. Such a while, if we discover the inner meaning is that whether it is needful or not, we have to launch their arrival, they convey this message, is very essential; and hence, several homes face destruction by nature. Naturally, we are having settings, to work and hence enjoy all, as they can…! the best thing we did, that is why, we went with umbrellas, why? because another man is walking along in the rain, we can share this umbrella for him too. Such type of our ancestors lived in the space of this Earth and they now belong to national wealth, and we must reveal their glorious deeds, telling in our volumes and often we have to speak about them about their surroundings and life styles, by this our children are to be very much educated and thus, we are well equipped ever in all the fields.

Our activity is only to put on Him, all our burdens and gains daily, and our habits and leisure activities are so much keenly watched like a supernatural camera, and all the registrations can be seen, and as result He comes to an opinion, and good and bad are in action; when we are in illness, we used to say that "I am not doing any untoward actions, to those who are poor, I have given so many packets of curd rice and water too". But, the voice convicts will not be heard by God. If He hears, God descends to us and makes us hale and healthy. Likewise, all things will be happening. So, we should be with consciousness of fear of our actions, then it is very easy to get rid of all ill effects. This is the Universal Truth of all and they should follow the rules and regulations for humanity, will minimise our deeds. He will dispense through His mere eye sight, we will be out of all kinds of illnesses and ever be a rejuvenated one. Now, we are knowing the way to come out of ruins, then, do it at once, God alone will rescue us from all of our evil thoughts and deeds. Due to our past karmas, we, naturally are affected by some innocent persons, we will not be rescued by all, but if sathya is present in favour of us, everything can be done through our efficiencies. Thus, mankind, particularly has rescue from all burdens. He will shorten these weights altogether, because, he measures our bhakthi towards Him. So, let us be devoted and pious men and thank Him for discharging out duties, then we can feel the presence of Himself. Whenever or wherever, we think or call Him, He starts to rescue us due to His mercy and grace. That is, He is named as kirupanidhi and thus, His activities will be bound with full of miraculous and divineful forms. We can taste them through panchaenthriyas and Gnanaedhriyas too.

Therefore, we should be very careful in all aspects of this mundane characteristic moments, trying to go elsewhere, all of our dreams may come to be true, thus, THE HIGHEST LEARNING IS THAT BY WHICH WE KNOW GOD, ALL ELSE, GRAMMAR ETC, ONLY LOAD AND PUZZLE THE MIND;!!! We are good educationalists but, our day-to-day life, is entirely different from what we are saying. We should be a proof to our words. Then only, we are considered that we are also educationalists. When we talk to others, our words should be heard. So, we have to see that our words our fulfilled to the satisfaction at the most. Therefore, our ancestors emphasised to make our path, as what we pronounce. Our words first should be kept by us and then we should analyse about others' recognition.

"There is a special old word" if we tell something important, they should keep our words, when multi-millions of money is paid not to do, the same. But, if we ignore others' deal, we should keep our words properly. Our thoughts, deeds, and actions are in a straight way, then, GOD, Himself descends to us and fulfills the matter with ease and comfort. So, first, we have to give importance to our words. Then, He will undertake our needs and deeds very quickly and neatly. So, we have to be keen to keep our words, our tongue has pronounced, such a person will be equal to Him and persons, give also respect and honour beyond doubts. Whatever, happens, we should be a witness, and we should not leave the proper special words, whether they come to actions, we should not give assurances. We should be keenly watching our words, till, they come into action and others will be profited. Thus, mankind should live an honourable life, as a result, God alone comes and gives dharsan of His own, thus, our human birth, will attain an approval among all.

All organs are systematically established and their metabolism is controlled so much by virtue of Godly fear and then only, we can have their relationship since the time permits. If we want to have good name in the society, we should speak very, very important words. Mere blabbering will cause troubles and agonies to all including us. We should live for our intention, there is nothing impressive to buy and sell whatever the things, that our neighbours have. The copying mentality, will lead us towards destruction, so, we have to fulfill only our needs within our source of income then, we can be beneficial to us first, and then second, we are also very much helpful for national integration and fame. Without any particular objectional selection, we are honoured by our deed and thus, we can lead our manual life upto the mark of respect. Whether we study or not, we have to be lawful according to our words, the whole world will be free from ignorance and patience, thereby adhering to these noble qualities, we can make ourselves, a true citizen of the Indian Republic. On the whole, we will be considered to be the best people all over the world. This respect and honour originally come from the lotus feet of the Lord. So, when we are ardently having such beliefs, then we will have no chance to have debts and if payable, its interest also. This is a blind procedure, as somebody sells their house and they are now living as orphans. So, we have to be very much careful to settle our debts as early as possible. Then only, we can participate and concentrate on the welfare of the public. Therefore, after getting our salary, from that day some money say Rs. 10/- is collected by all workers, totally it may come to more than one lac rupees, and we give to those who want a lump sum of money, and every month, they have to give rupees 10 with interest. Within several years, this company has so many lacs of Rupees. Thus, we can be helpful and collect money from us and giving it as interest too, then we finish our account, we can get some thousands of Rupees and thereby we can buy some gold materials and dresses and getting ready to face marriage, at that time, we will not be agonised. So, we should deposit some money in the piggy bank, and if after one year, we come to open that piggy bank, there will be thousands of rupees. Thus, we can make the poor into rich, and thus, we can spend and purchase all that is necessary.

Goddess Mahalaxmi is in the modulation size as money, so, we should do poojas for it, because all can earn money to their satisfaction. Most probably, some families are always running with uncontrollable budgets. This type of life makes them cowardish, and one day, they, all lose their souls because of these debts. So, we should be frank to others and our needs will be a boon with the holy order of Parasakthi.

If our intention and attention is equally maintained, it is possible to have success without doubt. But, most us, without knowledge or due to our illiteracy, we sign and get some money. He /she is poor and that's why, they are unable to pay the capital and its interest, they lose wealth for the cheapest rate. In this way, many of us lose our property and without money, are struggling so much, but nothing is easy to do and earn for our home needs, then, they take a conclusion mistakenly, because of their innocence, and lose their life once and for all. So, we have to settle our life within our budget, as nations, we too frame a budget, every month, and some part of money should come under insurance purposes. Thus, we will have money, and try to save the life from poverty and unavailability of health and money. Then, our innocence can be clearly known to us. Due to our uneducated life, we are breeding agonies and troubles, since four date of birth till the moment of our last breath success.... Success, what does it mean? when we enter into the competition, with mankind and others, we should win the race, whether we have prizes or not, it is not at all the matter, we have to fulfill our stipulated games till last whistle blows as mark of respect. So, we must have presence of mind and at the same time we should be generous, and give to the poor to look after their needs and they too will be with joy and shanthi when they are fulfilled. Thus, if one can live, it is effective to God, to dispense all their needs without a single doubt. We have to put our faith on the lotus feet of Him, we will be dispensed all whatever we wished, for our expenses. And, when we are hungry He will come in the form of rice and curry, if we are hungry, he will come and dispense money by any cause of His gloriousness. Whatever we need, we should submit an application to God without doubts and doubtful mind, have belief in Him, in due course of time, they will come as a boon to us under the Governing maintenance by the gracious heart of God. Whatever we speak, whether God is here, or not, nothing is profitable for both the sides. If you adhere to one principle, we should live up to the mark as a job and thus, we will be dispensed with both money and healthy life, till our last breath. So, our primary duty is to keep us from doubtless mind, and enough money to push the periods. Such a confidence, if we have, then, everything is achievable, and they are nothing but one bounce of air from His smooth, Rose coloured lips. Therefore, we here by insist all to be confident with gratitude each and every activity ends with victory and for this reason there will be no possibility to have life from other's assistance. So, we wish to lead a neat life with full of sophistication, all will come as a boon from Him and He keeps us throughout our life span. So, we have to put faith upon His Mighty Hands and lotus feet of the Lord. These will dispense us with whatever we wish and our essentials needs would be given without doubts and make us to have saturation after our last breath Sri Krishnarppanam.

Particularly, in the spiritual field, we should keep our tongue both Gnandheriya and karmaendriya; otherwise we cannot go upward to Eternity. Whenever, speech is necessary, just in short verses, we should pronounce our plans to others and according to hunger, we have to take pure food in very minimum quantity and the taste about the sustenances, we should be most careful for elevation in food control; we should be starving; but at the same time, limited food is enough, otherwise there are ample of chances, to be attacked by diseases. So, we have to oblige but not to oblige our tongue, then only Utter silence can be maintained, if it is possible, we shall have elevation in spiritual world. Whether we take food, or not, we should be ready to work hard for tomorrow's sake. So, we have to take our good food materials with gaps of time. It will yield a good result to our body and mind. When we are penetratively, hanging on as a spiritualist, we have to shutdown the mouth, ears and eyes, we have to pin always our ears, because the pure Otic system, what we speak, so think about the value of the words. Thus, we can have enormous strength to continue our duties without starving position and there is no necessity for a small rest. Therefore, we should consume a small quantity of food and if we try our level best, it will be easy to be free from untoward TENSION.

Now, Each and every one boastfully declares that he/she is a Bp patient or Diabetic patient, thus, we introduce ourselves before others. They do not know its consideration among their circle, what kind or type of conclusion will arise? But, these innocent people declare their disease by loudly thinking that they are sympathetically seen by others. What a foolish man, he is? Our salary, diseases, correspondence with ladies, medicine and Vedic upadesa Mahamanthram—these should kept as our sole capital money. Then sometime, we will be honoured in the society. Therefore, be careful about these lessons, and keep your prestige among all. Later many more secrets will grow up when you are aged, you can live peacefully, if your tongue is not kept so..!

Chapter - 3

Go Home to Live

Parents receive a secret order to keep us from the time of birth until their last breath; but we? so, we should be ready to keep them calmly in their old age, besides our wives and children. We may be the masters in any department, but, we should be the remarkable son or daughter to our parents. It is very easy to make them satisfied by feeding them and asking them their needs and our deeds should be converted to furnish happiness to their mentality; thus, their blessings fall on us and they shower the holiest blessings automatically. No entrance to any temple, chanting of holy mantras are not necessary to us if we bow our heads before them. We must discharge our duties; among all taking care of our parents is the primary one, and such women are being showered by the Holiest and mightiest blessings of them throughout our proceedings. As per their divine will and pleasure, our lives will blossom with beauty of wealth and health. So, we should be ready from this moment, to render our earnest service to them physically and mentally. Whether they expect or not, we have to discharge our duties to the entire satisfaction of our VIPs never giving up this service, do it at all times and in all circumstances. There is nothing more to be compared with their blessings; so, we have to be ready to do service to them physically and mentally. The service to our nation, Universe, gives us peace and harmony throughout our life. So, like patriotism, we should have enough directorship, to render service to the aged; especially, if one renders service to parents it is beauty of their life, if he/she protects all of the beings he is considered to be the Gnani and Karma yoga will be implemented throughout his span of life. And these effects whether it is right or wrong, it yields in due time. Otherwise we shall be punished and so, before speaking we should be in a normal equilibrium of mind and deeds. Our Budhi will work to a certain limit; but our sidham works and pulls all the bogies which are connected to it.

Though we are Ireland citizens, in due course of time, we were transformed as fish people who are now pure Indian fellow citizens. We both are rendering our earnest service to keep the nation. Now the U.N.O called upon those interested in war fields, can come and get their military weapons and be ready to counter attack, this is the main military multi-national concept. The patriotism which pulls out with such an energy, and free to fight with shooting guns, it is a thrilling experience and we cannot show our patriotism, and handful gratitude of flowers are for your feet. Because we are not ready here to start a fight with the enemies, we cannot do this better, thus, a jawan cried, but we do not worry about our warriors who are keeping India, a democratic country, the best and the biggest in size, but we too do not show our patriotism towards the national grade. We are really ashamed about the delay to start to send. Now, we honourably submit our crores of salutations. If you simply call, we will come with fresh machine guns and be ready to throw them away to die. We are very much afraid of a snake in the bed, but when all lights are on we see a coir branded like a cobra, just as we had done yesterday night. There are mostly 42 branches which make one jawan, and his cost may be 70 crores. If one jawan perishes, 70 crores of money collapses. Do you think that it is a police service and this is not the way to submit to the military masters. Who? The Major General is the only man, who believes in their efficiency, he retains them here and we thank him very much, because of the valour and service oriented lively activities, Long live India.

All are subjected to discharge their duties to the entire satisfaction of our own mind, that is God. But we are thinking that we are able to cheat others, it is quite true that we are destroying our inner divine power that is Bhagavan, he is still blabbering because, we are still not ready to apply the divine power in our life. So, if we go through our ancestral epics and puranas, they are surely emphasising us to be truthful to unite with all and then only we can understand our reality, and thus, man becomes God. They wish to be good citizens in the world; female gender is on the whole of turbulent character they wish to over rule male gender. That is why this kind of transferable to untransferable; we can earn and how to earn and learn to be ready to do whatever kind of work there is; their fundamental loop holes are found in our general political life. We, all are to be leaders; but very few are trying willingly to be head of the family, and this is the reason, they sincerely work so many hours and earn money to the betterment of their own family; whoever may be, everybody is struggling to preserve their ancestral fame and name, this is because they wish to establish good fame for our ancestors. Thus, the females are existing satisfactorily and sophisticatedly leading their lives.

For example, do see this scene, you witness daily on the road sides, many are uneducated, not civilised, without proper experience, and that is why they are still searching for a bun and tea. The husband works sometimes overtime, and they are willing to spend for their own welfare and their nation too. Wherever you go, you can easily see beggars stealing money from others. Most probably, we are totally ignoring our kith and kins' progression; they sit all round the bench and analyse the profit which they need. Our selfishness is uprooting the family; simply they get a divorce certificate from the court. The foremost, father, only has the responsibilities to be aware of keeping his/her family's betterment. Swami Vivekananda declared if he is given 100 youngsters and 100 crore rupees, he would transform all the citizens and they will lead a good and wealthy life. According to this period of life, I also have sufficient knowledge of seeing her each inch by inch, will not be among you. So, I conclude, females and mayasakthi, they are not well being, 0.001 may be chaste, others.....?

Parents carefully maintain their whole family with care and they protect their son's wives and children but at the same time, when parents are old enough, their children are grown up, but nobody is willing to look after their parents safely. They are not secure in their old age. Children think that they are a burden to them in their old age session, in which they will search for humility support and at least they need the security of the children. But in most of the homes they are only houses but not homes. There nobody truly shows mercy and respect to them. One son says that father will come and reside with his family; mother can go to another son's house thus, they simply look at the parents as a personal female and male gender; they never wish to keep them the father and mother unitedly together. These children have had good education, and have got a good job, that is why they are thinking that they should only look after themselves; but they simply omit the aged. Likewise, this human circle is going on, what is the solution; from their childhood, they should be brought up with grandfather and grandmother, and family background will be having such enough goodness to all. Apart from parents what are they going to succeed in their lives. Even brothers and sisters are quarrelling most probably, they are having meetings in courts in order to safeguard themselves only on the materialistic line. This is to be condemnably denied by them because they think that their ideas are natural and totally they, most of them "by omitting parents" everything will be theirs and they can easily live a life without the support of the parents. This is why, do we call it knowledge or is it considered to be wisdom; not at all, we should take care of our parents and others and nation will look after them. Everybody is excepting the government to be responsible for these things. Is it a correct expectation? not at all. So poetess Avvaiyar told some 3000 years ago man should die in his 60th or 64th age, death will be meaningful. So aged persons are to meet death in their 64th age. In this manner, our human life is considered to be meaningful. If it goes beyond limitations, rules and regulations whatever happens, God is the chief who controls and governs all metabolisms of life and every action. So, let Him give final solution.

This book concludes the weakness of man and his greatness as well. The Almighty controls this whole universe with His own rules and regulations; so nothing will happen; this is to be realised by each and everyone of us. We can trumpet merely that if man triumphs, everything is possible; may be; such conclusion is God's then it is possible, otherwise, we should accept the result of natural happenings. If there is death, we should bow in front of God, Almighty. If a building is constructed by an engineering graduate, he has many more servants to fulfill the job. Likewise, the metabolism and directions issued by ONE is omnipresent, omniscient, which controls and regulates the lively syllabi. We are all eagerly eating food materials, whether hungry or not, but without thirst, we take water regularly and we just believe that our metabolism should be ever in a state of satisfaction. Now a new trend has arisen. Each 2 year old child is pushed into school. Whether she/he gets education or not, she /he should not bother parents. This kind of mentality if rampant, in course of time, how can we expect a loyal, real helpful, son/daughter to be thriving. Like the parents they too simply act as if they are looking after their parents, we can say, within a hut, a man and female as wife-husband make themselves as Father/ mother, and look after their parents. We should expect this kind of respect and parents' care. We simply have the Brahma's shrusti in order to look after them kindly and smoothly, we just put children in school and we leave as parents. Parental care, without this, our sons and daughters and so on go in mischievous way of life.

Now-a-days we are very much proudly trumpeting that we have achieved so many inventions and discoveries in science, economics etc; by that we earn name and fame, all these, where did they come from? only from parents; we have to learn and then, automatically earnings will be very easy; without the holiest blessings of our parents, these illusions come to be real and natural so, our learning and earnings are because of our parents; these are possible because of our human birth. This is only because of our father and mother respectively. That is why, we have to worship them whole heartedly and thus, we can attain so many Himalayas and more in real life. Those who deny the existence of God, they without doubt, accept that our parents gave birth to us and our academic progressions, proceedings are only because of them. That is why, the most valuable man or woman is our parents, when mother dies, we lose our good diet and mode of giving them to us in order to build our intellect and mentality and outer world's existence; all of our sensory organs are controlled by the Almighty and thus, we exhibit our lives to the world only through them. So we have to pay our capital with interest to them. If it is possible they will be contented by all means. So, if anyone who is willing to reach the highest pedestal of ecstasy, we should bow our heads down in front of parents. The only pair of persons who do not and cannot do damage to their offsprings. It is a universal truth; do mind it, the younger generations, if we respect and honour their sacrifice and selfless habits, we will be dispensed by God without any doubt. Thus, our ancestors lived so many years and gave birth to so many ancestors. Our best History is to analyse our parents' Honourable hearts. Thus, we can attain the Holiest feet of the Almighty; the Holy Quran says, the good swarga is at the feet of the mother which reveals the greatness of parents. Let us pray and be obedient to them and elevate ourselves.

Likewise we have belief that our father is our father because our mother introduces him that he is our father; that maha manthra word, only one word gives us enormous passion and faith upon one man as our father. Likewise, if we have faith and trust Him by all means in all circumstances, He will never be apart from us. As is His will, so inwardly He can be heartily realised by us till our last breath. We must have so much faith upon Him as our father; likewise we have to believe Him in all circumstances and in the midst of acquiring worldly experiences and most probably earning money; and if our faith and trust is the most truthful we cannot be apart from Him, and also He will never separate us from Him; He gives a separate place for us, instead of His spouse. He is searching for such bhakthas and is ready to make us attain moksha that is the sole liberation from this mundane, sinful world. If He bestows only a glance with grace upon us, we can win any race throughout our entire life. Let us be ready to attain such an attainable and necessary goal of our whole life and therefore from this moment, verily, we have to form a relationship with Himself whole heartedly and verily we become the next messenger of god. He is always ready to give us the Holiest post; but we are simply satisfying ourselves with our simplest needs, fulfilled, we are contented. Hunger and starvation are different meanings. We must be with such hunger to become His sincere disciple as He is ever ready to acknowledge our prayer from the base of our heart and thus, we also become the godly saint and we can never give up our faith upon our ownselves. He is our universal master; He has the right to test us and give testimony that we are suitable for spiritual life; but on our part we cannot have such strength and power to test Him; if we test him everything will be around the table; such a situation does not happen throughout our life. If our confidence is an iron corridor, then nothing can shake us to remove us from Him.

The economics can be by a Gnani because of his vision towards I and God, his vicharam is always on athma and its significance is analysed and he will conclude and it will be, by his name, a new philosophy will be introduced to this world, some years, after they will be honoured as universal truths and he becomes an ever-living soul throughout this universe and he dispenses the best blessings to this materialistic world, and whenever evils are high enough, God descends and looks on this line of destroying this concept of universal truths, but inner hidden meaning of this life will not be suitable, and it will be the concept of transparency of everything towards gnana. This is the exact possession of human life and hence, they may revise the syllabus of forthcoming births and we have to listen to our surroundings towards success. The familiar and easiest concept is our needs are fulfilled by the ecstatic mood and we should be aware of this life's impermanent nature as it is unstable, therefore we have to find out the inner hidden treasure of this mighty universe. So all dimensions of this life should be furnished and their sequences along with the prolonged practice of the human tendency (ies) as such. The inner conscious is always with us, there is nothing to be feared and disturbed by anything and those concepts will be gone through wherever it is...!

Human life is eccentric and it is only as a mobile system, whoever can speak through it and whomsoever can buy it or steal it, let us know the value of money, thus, we all produce some transformation towards Mukthi. Because of this mighty concept, all human beings are with sense or without sense, they are proceeding towards mukthi, where there is no chance of births/ deaths at all. Everything is easy and comfortable and they will be thoughtless then and they will keep coolness of mind, the sole inner system will be towards its way to Golden Ecstasy only. Therefore, there are more fine fruits in your hands, but there is no conjugal life, he/she keeps them and there is no necessity to proceed with domestic life. So the easiest way for liberation is nothing but the pure socialisation of humanity and democracy towards the universe, will give peace and shanthi. But in this world he who has abundancy of money then there will be a circle of human beings and if he is wealthless, penniless, nothing will remain along with him, if it is maintained in application of our day-to-day life, peace and shanthi will be ever ours. The true gnanis will live ever whatever the circumstances are...! They are habiting other circumstances and their consequences are very tiny and their lively process is very little but never ending.

Wherever we go, return home to life, an affectionate sentence this is. Likewise, this earth always comes round the Sun and thus, day and night are in situation and these are not any tantric and manthric deeds. Only out of divine will, all these systems are globalised and according to these scientific universal restrictions, this earth is in a stable position, so that we can build bungalows and industries in biggest size. The speed is over and over, it seems to be non-rounding up, we believe, but science probes that it is rounding the sun too and thus, all the natural deeds are going on. Likewise, if we analyse the performance of science in the spiritual world, then, we can understand all the formulae, will be clarified and classified in detail. If we have geography of this universe, we can clearly know and realise the fact that nothing is artificial but it is quite natural, we have to go around the steps or footprints of this geographical universal truths. Each and every field has universal truths, nobody can exchange them into two or nothing, we cannot do this task because it is risky or will demoralize the situation of this universe. Wherever we are, we are the citizens of this earth whether we are divided into several nations. According to the situations, human tendencies, the nation wide circumstances are accommodated and, our ancestors have lived up to the mark that they could. Therefore, the philosophy of this Geographical analysis, we can come to understand some marvelous truths, explained part by part, and thus, we can know the total philosophy of Geography. In this way man gets the knowledge, in all these some are the inborn savants who have had training in this field, and they explain the universal truths, the whole earth is created and the components may not change, but its magnitude and philosophy is as follows;- if we study and experience the depth of geography we can be contented by several aspects of this universe and components. Two gases, oxygen and hydrogen unite, in proportion of the scale of one molecule of oxygen and 2 molecules of hydrogen makes itself as water which is in the form of a liquid. Thus, how is it possible? If this question is raised in the fellowship of scholars, they will analyse physically and chemically, finally they will submit one universal truth. Thus, we can easily understand the science of all elements.

The betterment of this universe is in none other than the mighty hands of our ladies. They have the power to construct and destroy anything and everything, that is why, God gives her to be loaded with a baby which she cherishes, second by second and the pain is not easy minded and that weight! She dedicates her part time of life, and gives birth to that child, what a sacrifice it is? Just think, if we eat the food materials, with full stomach, can we go around with the body, make another round and then another round, but we are ignoring such food materials and they who supplied them. He wishes to eat that amount of food materials, but he is blaming all else nothing but himself. With this type of stomach we cannot bear the inconvenience, but the would be mother, how she is carrying such a weight which is growing tissues second by second, she without or with fear makes the whole baby, then discharges her/him to this world, then, she upto some period, with full of rest builds up and restores her body with fine vegetables for strength. Such a motherhood should be saluted, otherwise, this universe, itself goes to its destruction. Do mind it. Whatever the males are having, and achieving, the females have the embroyo and after ten months, she gives her/him to the earth, in this one and only point, she has been upgraded, than all the male generations. So, as per Indian tradition, Mother is to be saluted for she is the pure temple and father's words are nothing but, all of them are the holiest mantras, we have to bear in mind and adhere to it day-to-day so that we can thrive in our materialistic and spiritual worlds. Both of them bless us, nothing is failure in our efforts at all. Therefore, God's favour is always with us and we must think well, doing mutual good deeds, deliberating on our words which determine us. So we should be keen to noticeably publish or release our words from our mouths.

One by one, the civilisation is programming in a systematic orthodox level, life is assured by a wife and she has the natural mind and is considered to be the chief minister of a region. According to cosmic power, everybody is scintillating their way to rectify all sins and give us a truthful life, So it is almost in need of medicine and construction fields etc., and this physical body has its own physiology and like every system it has one symbolic division and we introduce ourselves as the best of a home. Whenever bricks, cement come together and construct a building it is a house; but if all our relatives neighbours are dwelling there it is a home. Such examples in our entire life is sharpened through our wisdom and buddhi, a great, joyful life, it is dispensed by God only. Only those who are identified by Him, then it is considered to be the inner ambrosia's secretion and this is nothing but the Ambrosia of our human life. And all creations in the universe are suffering and also experience some happiness. These are just the experiences and we should take lesson to our heart for this is the simplest way to realise the truthful fact which can be identified by them; each and everybody will live their ways to the perpetual comportment. As such this schedule, each and every living organism metamorphosically regains our send power and we should import and export some of our natural gifts to those who are quarreling and victory will be ours.

According to the customs of our ancestors, what is the symbol of a true son/daughter as Indian Dharma which is insisted by Vedas, Epics and Puranas regarding the care and concern for the parents without any difficulty both mentally and physically of the parents. One who serves them as his own son and daughter is considered to be the most truthful heir. Therefore, all should govern their parents to their fullest satisfaction of them and their offsprings. Therefore, money is hereby wanted by the son/daughter. For this they should not demand from their parents in any way, if their son is running the family, then he is considered to be the true son of the parents. If mind of the parents is twinkling with sorrow and demands they are not compromised; so we can understand that they are not in the normal path. They should be encountered by the sons co-operatively, the parents will be satisfied and ever willing to live or lead a compromised life. If money is in the son's pocket fully, he, himself should think of the parents, they will give a single paise as their own willingly. There is no law and order to obey this custom. If, parents do not take care about us, by this time, what will be our position and we should think, through their satisfaction and tolerance only, we are still standing as idols in the temples. Therefore, in the name of son, he is not at all a son himself, if he is doing the appropriate service, while the parents are alive or not we should render our duty to them. We should fulfill their hunger and thirst. Can these things not be given at the necessary time? yes, it is certainly possible. But their hearts are not willing to do service to them, their parental care has been possible but son's care and duty is not up to date.

Whether we do or not, what is our Kulatheivam? this is the question, many of us ask several Poojaries with alms, and they blabber something and go and kill some creatures and with pongal they do Aardhana to God, they also say that this is the custom of worshipping their kulatheivam and if they miss, many of their neighbours also miss a good non-vegetarian meal at least for one day. This is why, they may conclude some mistakes on the parents. The good family is split and they also wish to divide their family into two or four as they like, and the property is sold and the money is divided into appropriate ratio and thus, they quarrel with each other and they depart causing separation from one another and among themselves. And after some years, there is no representation at their father's demise. Is it the prosperity of family co-operation, or not. All are educated fools, idiots and they not willing to proceed with their duties in time with confidence, if we clearly, dynamically try to achieve the goal, it will be so easy to attain the purest result which is confirmed throughout our mind and its branches. As such we can succeed with all our effort in our one and only path of sathyagraha, if you, all penetrate the steel heart of those we know very well they can be ruled over by our significance of heart and our education, it is not obtainable from colleges, but they are from the one and only universal university. Thus, we can succeed our ego and fire it well, natural and thus, we can have a pleasant way to attain self renunciation. So do try to imposture all our imprints of life, and thus, we can win and represent by which we can give trials to the pupil. And thus, they will be told of the versatile genius among them in their own life time and this is to be sustained quickly and more actions will be unloaded by us thereof. Whatever way we are discussing, we are one and the same and they consider the result is good not satisfactory.

Thus, we are in the belief that all the readers of this topic will have no doubts to reach divine life, and its pathways, and how it is to be attained; these excellent sketches are like a map, we rejoice in this work very much and execute it for all. Apart from our classifications about mankind, should thoroughly be erased from the encyclopedia; we have to form another, a fresh encyclopedia. Thus, our integration and mutual understanding should practically show its speculations at all times. Mercy, Grace, Forgiveness, forgetting, nearest relation to all is the Almighty one, and we should follow all the rules and laws of mankind; we can have a prosperous life and thus, we can easily attain the convergence with God, Himself. He shines like any form, and processes His presentation in front of a man. He cannot swallow the trace and shining is not focused because it may be some crores of Sun's brightness and heat. So, He Himself descends as glory, comes to us, with our knowledge of that God is represented before us. If you have full of sakthi from your penance, you can have the shining and focusing of His brightening light of the globe, will be presented before him and He has had the grace of Himself and thus, our prophets and Annonists saw Him with their naked eyes and rejoiced with supreme ecstasy; and they very much graciously pray the Almighty to give His presence to all Bhakthas and make them eligible to have His Dharshan too. This is the Mahans' or saints' inborn characteristic feature and they are living for a long time in this earth for the betterment of this universe. A father and a mother do not even think of divorce, but a husband and wife may conclude to divorce, because the appa and amma are characteristic features of the forthcoming generations. But a male and another female cannot attain this position and possession; and that is why husband / wife can divorce but appa/amma cannot be divorced, it is one's designation in this divine world. This is the basic karmic principle of this worldly phenomenon of all characters of all creatures. And, this is considered and honoured as a characteristic principle of human society. All tie-ups in this world are divine and they are characteristic among all relations, but apart from all relations, but apart from all relationships, this is the one and only which is dispensed as the beginning of the procedure to creation of another generation; and that is why we designate it as Divine one, by our instructions. Whichever and whatever the relationship is, of all these, the one and only relationship is worshipped and witnessed by God Himself in this abode, and so, whatever and whichever the creation is, human life is considered as a divine one. Of these, all creations are from their mother; this holy motherhood is considered as a temple, where the deity's words are the father's words. What he says, it should be Vedic truths and if one follows and constructs his life, there is no failure in his domestic life forever. It should be realised in everyone's mind. So, we first got our education from mother and father, AMMAIAPPAR; this is the universal feature and thus, we have to thrive on this, one of the oldest verses, we never fail in our efforts and if there is no suitable thing which is almost adhering, God will cut off, and naturally our pathway will be set up by God's representation, so, we have to satisfy our father and mother without any differences of opinion.

We are always speaking about national integration, but, we should be integrated in our day-to-day life. A man cannot know who he is, what his name is. He knows nothing about himself. If we know these particulars, we can be useful for others, if it is needed we can help others at a time of troubles. So, mutual understanding among our co-residents, we and you will be benefited in several ways. So, we should demonstrate ourselves for helping them if needed. But, in this juncture, who knows who? nobody knows. Understanding between one another will give peace and good fortune, because friends are by God's understanding. Thus, if you have a good friend, he will be with you in all circumstances because he, himself does not consider such words as his or mine to be of importance in their friendship throughout life. Thus, their friendship may end in marriage, bride from one family looks for a bridegroom from another family thus, they and their aged also want this combination and marriage is the sole motto which settles things finally. As such, they are living made for each other philosophy and they make their lives very pleasantly and they gain peace and their national language is pure love. Thus, they are living with love; and life is running with the speed of love, and a monarch should be in their heart with love for Jesus or karthar or velankanni. Thus, all religions focus their up to mark is mere Love. If we adhere to this, love will be had with good percentage and humanity will grow with peace and shanthi and thus, the world will be under the control of love. If love is not there, there will be no creatures, God will not make His shirushti. LOVE is the basic nadi cell to provide love, it is from God Himself. So, we have to show our love through our service and helping tendencies. If, thus, our heart is fruit ripe, its flavour will be wonderful and marvelous, admired by all. Thus, the personalities of good fortune how do they meet their End; there is no value to shed down tears, all should not lose the equilibrium of mind but get together to find a natural, permanent conclusion for the problems, which is necessary to make the world with one heart. They must think all in all in one purpose, and work hard with full of energy, then the canal should be opened within the stipulated time, and we must live very confidently with co-operation and co-ordinatedly. These are possible tasks to humanity but nobody is willing to do it for they are not with peaceful hearts, that is why they are speeding up making late, as late Mrs. and Mr., whichever our relationship is, we have to flourish our relationship, with forbearance to tolerate some do's, don'ts and wants and refusals. As per the relationships is not under the basis of purity of love, we suffer a lot, friendship is a must to everybody, and according to Thirukkural, we can see that Thiruvalluvar denotes its value in 10 directions through 10 kurals. Therefore, if we choose friendship, we should analyse its pros and cons relevantly and then proceed with both members. Firstly, we should be with full of confidence upon our friend, then there should be no suspicion in any situation, friendship will grow as flavoured herb, so we have to grow day by day, fluently and we should always be with the tendency of making each other grow then only, our friendship will be of the soul. We can tell our secrets to the other one, and nothing will sprout up in consequence of our subject ever. Even as a fun you should not suspect one another, it is all navarasabhava, that is why, our life will blossom with excellent growth. Friendship has no sign of religions, sects and creeds, it is apart from all, so it should be grown by our own intellectual oneness of hearts. Mind should be thinking the same subject that the friend thinks, this is the grammar for physical and intellectual friendship ever.

Therefore, we should be very cautious in keeping the friend in confidence with each other. When one member tries to do some mischievous action, soon the other should stop that event and thus, our friend should have a change and return to his normal mind. No such evil thought or deed will come into action. Both friends will behave well at all times, in all circumstances and then there will be no need for worry about having friendship with one another. Between them, no such evil related event should arise at any time. Thus, if you are ready to keep your friendship, it will be an excellent one and may all have best friends to all of us. Pure friendship has no religious regulations, they are free from friendship, but it should be chaste in all situations. In this way, our ancestors lived along with their friendship up-to-date; Avvaiyar-Athiyaman's friendship is the best example in this issue. So, we must have friendship with whoever it may be, it should be truthful and chaste and a full fledged one, if it is flourished with flowery flavour, God Himself is presenting Himself at all times. Rich and poor, sects and creeds, poor-rich should not come in the way of friendship. It exists over all our worldly regulations, it has some rules, that are demonstrated between the friends, and they do not overrule it in any circumstances. Thus, our friendship is with the other, patience which means one with another, and capital of this friendship is only apart from Love affairs; our friendship always shows the way to all how to live, why this birth is given, such questions are asked. It has answers, so, if our friendship is always pure, truthful based relationship which can flower ever. Moreover, innumerous births, our friendship has been growing with honour and majestically, this is pure friendship and this is always truthful between them. If the two friends (persons) recognize the glory of their business, occupation and their designation, are all nothing in front of friendship. So, Love and friendship are two rails on which many chakras go fastly, thus, it is a journey and it is illustrated through friendship. Our secrets are to be told to one another, and they never expose them in the public and it is kept, or one member is not revealing the mistakes with full of confidence and he tries to save the other not to do such disqualified actions throughout his life. Our truthfulness is the original convocation to our connection. At first all will not respond to this segment, but in time they will praise them because of their character and good conduct. Character is always more powerful than all others. This is the good life through which we be ever living in and beyond this world. There are 110000 Andams and in each Pramandam an earth which is having in which these kind of people and objects are all in action. So, The prapancham has all characteristics which are out of reach. May be, if astamasidhis come in perfection, we should not start with these to have supplementary and easy ways, we should not exercise before others to have a majestic honour and name. So God is the sole Master, the whole prapancham and He is ever pervading and that is why, which means we are near Him. Then the natural contentment itself comes without any cycle of (births and deaths) henceforth. So, we should not weep like all, we should be firm and stand simply and cause goodness and, the betterment whichever we process in the world of spiritualism. We, never hand over money is the only one motto that we have money and money cannot give all to anybody and thus, first, we realise it (supreme truth) and our brains is some what not functioning sharply all along. Thus, the world exists, ourselves too enter the ether, invited by Devendhran Himself (chief of all Devas), and honour us and do pleasingly give us pass to go elsewhere, everywhere.

INDEPENDENCE is the aim and goal of this nation. Now how much sakthi is essential, this is our motto, and thus, that Nation is to be got rid of from the map. This opinion is one, and Muslims they are standing verily not arrested, decision of my ownself and it can be made a law, Pakistan is not in the map, if you need, call in his name and which nation's laws and regulations are anxiously respected our laws and therefore sweets for our victory. Maybe within one or two military systems, then the war is stopped and the jawans are playing football. You, the chief of the authorities get rid of all thinking and give special honour and Hospitality, should be given and we should be a good friendly nation ..! And we are a powerful sakthi which we kiss accordingly. After the King and the Queen come and sit, the music ceremony will commence ... try to remember, and do the needful. The King's politics and administration coincide with each other and they unite together, with the wisdom of worthy persons, ministers, they ruled over the country naturally with loyalty and royalty and they stood still as a scale in a grocery shop, give new, lawful government to the people, and all are living comfortably; the give and take policy is admired by all and they obeyed rules and regulations with piousness, the country is well conducted and each one's presence is important in the Dharbar Hall and they treat all as the same. In their, they cultivate drawing, sewing, cooking, agriculture and so on, going on developing peace and shanthi throughout the kingdoms and live freely with truthfulness. Thus, their nature and naturalness is maintained without any fault and nothing is wanted by them as allowances. They do not know bribe and other unlawful authorities, they live with divine perception. Thus, the whole nation is living in a normal condition and they live understandingly without failures. Wherever they go on with their doubts, they win the race with distinction and they do not fall from any status, thus, their rulership is peculiar and they are satisfactorily felicitate each other. The genealogical ideas are very much honoured and they grow well day by day, and thus, nothing is incorrect and they lead their way very smoothly and they treat each one as themselves and plan to develop in all ways and the growth of all cultural arts and agriculture is marvelous and there is no simple mistake in their workmanship. Thus, we can utilise our time can be enriched with lots of activities; and if we exercise our duties regularly, we can achieve all things; and such exercises are ever good for health and our excretory system will be scrutinised at all times; So, these exercises are necessary for all of us. Our studies should be coming into action, then only, we will be benefitted in all departments of home accessories. And thus, it can be very much beneficial to our daily important things; as such, all vegetables can be bought in freshness, and they are very much useful to our daily necessities. So, if there is place, which we live, all facilities can be got in an easy way and we can live genuinely till the last breath. If we wish to go to Sri Mariamman koil, Sri Abhiramiamman koil, we can take a rickshaw and we will be very much lucky enough as there is no inconvenience. God is Great; if we study to a limitless level, if we do not worship God, there is no use of this education; thus, Thiruvalluar states. It is an universal gem of good verse. And if we are learned, it is not enough, we should be living with comforts and this is beyond our selection the model of the house, as such all are houses; but, if it is full of members and happily sitting taking food, then only, it is called 'HOME'. Thus, therefore, we should adjust and understand their normal qualities and so, we should grow with friendship, then as a relation, it is considered to be consciousness's section of human relationship. Thus, we should have good relation with all and that is called HOME, and we must call others as our relations, then, there is no chance to meet with war; battle and competition at all. So, if we try to form a HOME, we should cultivate our works and understanding must be cool and happy allied commitments by others; they are admiring such kind of relationship between a man and a woman who unitedly live a long life about 70 years. These make us and others ,what a tie up between this couple is it possible or are they acting? So we are honoured by them and nature gives us all our needs as boons are admired by the Almighty too. They are living most probably an animal's life but our mode of life is ever based upon god's dispensational surroundings. Do bear this fact in mind this is the greatness of India.

The major and much differentiation of thinking about mankind, is completely different they think, that animals ,with the foot steps of animals, are struggling for life, this kind of truth makes their life animal like. But here, we are in the depth of animalhood structural scripts, and in between the long period, they modified into mankind and they cannot live like us, according to our, rules and regulations. If we analyse the modes of life, our approach about anything, some culmination of divinity will shine as a remarkable truth. But, if you analyse those lives, there is no footmark about manly doings and happenings, take an example of their cinemas and dramas, there is no livelihood, art of culture which cannot be seen ever at any cost of life. Therefore, they are living animals, take an example, whether he is a muslim or not, do not collapse your mind about religions, that is the Taj Mahal is considered to be one of the excellences in the world. It is a memorial of both husband and wife which took 14 years of penance to finish this task which was built by so many thousands of workers, in memory of his beloved wife. In other nations the walls are some muddy walls, flowery gardens, erection of iron bars and so on, but our India expresses Love (truth) between them which is a true marvelous beauty of manlihood. Such a life, India teaches us, the value of life beyond sex. So, according to us, still souls are bound there, and thus, we honour and respect the Taj Mahal the most beautiful among all greats in the universe, not at all in this tiny world; so, we bow our head towards their true nature of LOVE, and now-a-days we are often saying I LOVE YOU which is collapsed with sexual desires. On the marriage day, the couple, how do they behave between themselves, will be the same as our life should be an establishment at all. So, this is considered to be a Truthful life.

Apart from sexual conjugation, one and one rejoices in their presence is enough, if they live comprehensively, it is the Golden opportunity, that dispenses. If this is renounced, the couples live together, but, their motto of each one, for the goodness of the two organisms. These metabolisms are the same, when we follow intimately seeming due to Budhi, this secret will be elaborately explained by God. Just born child is growing with mother's milk (sheeram) and the baby grows big and bigger, it needs so much of nutrients to lead his/her life, beyond breast milk, it is considered to be proper parental care. In Zoology, parental care is a topic which explains the mode which animals keep their offspring and its recognition is quite abnormal. Such as, all animals bring their young ones to a valuable period, and then left alone, but mankind, age to age, we need parental care for sons or daughters care is needed, due to age by age, they surely lose their courage, valour and their mind becomes hollow, hence they think about their future. That is why, earlier, we wrote that the parents can bring up 12 children but those daughters and sons cannot even support the parents who have lived altogether. So, this state should be reformed from this age. Parental care of Father and Mother depends only on the development of their off springs. But his son's and daughter-in-law's care only stand upon their children. This is the gap between generations. This is to be ousted at our time of leading, they must give preference to their parents but now those fathers and mothers give preference to their generation, then they prefer the old beings to be considerate. If we know the difference between generations, we can live a peaceful life without any kind of doubt at all.

In old age, they are not able to remember their tasteful canteen or kitchen cooking, and they automatically lose their confidence, that is why, they need all support and they believe that son or daughter's affection will give them peace and shanthi. They think about death, and that is why, they are afraid to die, he whoever, may be a champion batsman in his young age. Confidence is lost, and hence they are very much useless, they think about themselves. This is the underground reason they feel ashamed not to live a life of solitude. From beginning of their marital life, they need none of the others in all angles, But, in old age, they are in need of safety and security which they look forward to only through men and women, simply, saying they become childish. Therefore, we have to get rid of our own feelings and must live for their sake and then Almighty will bless us, but not giving such type of care to the aged oh, young period, try to embrace your parents with love and care. Thank you. God bless you.

In old age their confidence is some what weakened, and hence they are afraid of whatever they see, hear and even to eat, they neglect these items, and they simply say that they are not at all hungry, thirsty because of fairy mentality. All their age, brings solitude and they, who are available in the home do not look after them at all, the male or father in this age, his younger age, a champion of billiards or any other sports and games, now if he thinks about it, automatically, he lacks the confidence and has fear for everything. So, we have to treat them as our children and thus, they flourish, they can live some more years. Let us do this duty to all parents and treat them as Almighty! His mother maybe all India champion in foot ball tournaments and even, we can see many silver cups and gold medals, they do not care about them, but losing self-confidence, they look at one another. If I die soon, who will look after my wife, thus, he murmurs. In turn, she says who will take care of him? she is always with tears. This is the quarrel between their mind and intellectuality. They should be ever blissful, we can make it so at once. This is the golden opportunity to do so; your wives will ever be blissful. I am not at all cheating you; if you both are blessed, you will not meet such a kind of situation, never you have to suffer, this is dharma also, chance and hence they are praying intensively and now I am standing before you. Varam, means in Tamil Give me a boon, thus, they save us, so, their prayer is called upon and so we are living, and trees also do penance in order to get boons from God. Thus, each and every temple has its own proper tree and hence they are worshipped as God, we worship God and they are everliving and scientific miracles can be done in due course of time, so they are jeevanadi of all creatures with the blessings of God and they are to be governed and grown and name and fame will automatically come to us. Whether they wish, or not, we should look after them in every aspect. Then, by seeing these concepts, our daughters and sons will grow with the affection of their grandmother/father; and in later years they will in turn grow with affection to their grand daughter/son; they will reopen their eyes, by it, they will be contented; if we do our earnest service like giving coffee to grandpa, and grandma they reserve punya karma and they will be blissful and ever growing up with success. Such, a great thing, that their blessings can do. Whether you believer or not, I wish to share this point with you all; likewise, a couple derailed their parents, then after one year, they both become blind and their status has no form at all. But the father and mother live under the control of their daughters. So, if we need to taste ecstasy, we should do our duties to our parents and God. Giving food materials is one of the best Dharams insisted by our saints. So, we implant such confidence, our young generations will hopefully discharge it as a duty and in this way they are fully bestowed with a holy seat in the Darbar of God.

According to all the vedic principles, we have to grant their needs, because, in our young age, they brought us to the rejoicing mood, and they gave sustenances and satisfactorily, lived along with us. So, it is necessary to discharge our duties first, and then everything should be second. They had sacrificed all to the betterment of our career. Therefore, we must make this service as our debts that we have bargained from our own young age. If you lose confidence and metabolism there is nobody in this world to clear the illnesses. So, do consider the future and discharge your services to the entire satisfaction of your parents. You are well educated but, why do you not serve the aged?. This is their karmic results, by telling this type of cruel lie here itself, your entire life will be changed as a super most hell. If you do not at all get their blessings, nothing is lost, if they curse whole heartedly, you will be no more in this universe. Do bear this concept within your heart and mind.

If we render our service wholeheartedly, then, it will be given late, but, if they are late, who is there to get it. So existence of our parents, we will never bother about anything, they tried their level best, and they satisfied our innerself, their love would penetrate our heart and thus, we are still able to stand on our own legs. Even this age too, we should render our service, God, Himself comes and renders His mightiest service and makes you to live with wealth and health upto your last breath. Therefore, My inner self awakens; and you should look after your parents and your father/ mother wholeheartedly. Thus, we receive their blessings and live with a divine attitude.

A bunch of feelings can be read through the neopalium of head it is interested in sexual allegations. Try to understand the process of human life. Human life is commonly created with playing, running, walking, sexual allegations. After our life death, and rebirths are human qualities but if they are not such human beings, nothing useful because of their life, and they struggle with each other at every opportunity like this, they are creating different opinions, then they are to be shot at sight. If we do, most probably some crores of people will have to be shot down, there is no sin at all. Whether they are men /women, must be useful on the earth, they must do marvelous job and should live a normal life. Through this our offspring will be produced and we create this kind of population. One couple has to take medicines and finally an operation has also succeeded, but the rest; what can we do? Nothing, we have to adopt otherwise, it will be I live for you and myself, thus, we must have a peaceful manner, if you are capable of calling father/mother what is the use of it, nothing. I usually tell in lectures, if there are no children, do not be cheated. We are all expecting that our children's life should be noticed and we are saving amount for their educational upgrade, but he secures marks in IInd term examination. Suddenly he has had a fall, the father's mind is upset and then returns to normal, 72 hours of rest is needed. He is given glucose titration, and now he is very well but he does not think about those children.

This is their remarkable destiny which He has written at the time of birth but, technically he is a versatile agriculturist, like this, all parents must watch their sons/daughters will and ambition; if we direct them in their ways, they will earn more money than their fathers, now he is happy enough and he also works, earns. He earns and all family members earn and run the family very well. We tried through education; but God determines this only through some nature of education and their industrial works, never compare one with another by which they come to a conclusion, do not blame yourselves, you have been brought up with good culture, character, and they are two sided coins which are transferable in His MUKTHI, so our ancestral poets and gnanis, where did they educate themselves, please do note the Universities. Avvaiyar did not go to any university. She was not awarded Bharat Rathna, but still they were telling universal truths.

Why should we study and what is the reason for reading and capitalizing on such scientists, savants and so on, because of their scholarship and their physical and intellectual service to the world? If they read they themselves are witnessing their life, through their life may give us a good or bad timely effect how to lead life with simplicity and confidence. Guru is one who eradicates our options of stealing, false hood and sows instead truths; those who are prostitutes, and marital sequences in the name of triumph of the union of couples are said to be separated, divorced. It is a huge punishable fact in any circumstances, Husband-wife relationship does not need separation, if it is imaginary, is false and conduct Bramahathi Dhosham. Hence, from this bondage, we have to live separately for 18 years that is what the Manu shasthiram has said, "If a couple's separation is not on their own accord the people who are giving verdict as sathya words, live like sentenced prisoners". So, in any circumstances, we should not do this kind of sinful, most effective ritual is not recommendable. At all times, they should live in union and the wife is responding to cooking and serving her husband, then in due course of time, he will realise the fact and reunion between them is a choice for them so, we do not say this for everybody as a couple, to withdraw the relationship between them. That is why, Saint Viswamithrar took Ramachandramoorthy to Janakai and marriage arrangements were made ready by Dhasararaja and kaikeyee's marriage which is done by her in due course of time and they lived together very well, and that is why, Paranapavithran Sri Barathan gave birth was steadfastly done so, saying or pronunciation of the words is not acceptable in Tamil literal World.

Therefore, we have to live united with parents, grandfather and sons, daughters- in-law and so on, it will be seen their ever green lively options in spirit of living. That is not constructed by spending many crores of rupees, having a car, a two wheeler, home is full of servants but there is nobody who is in good relation to her/him, is it a life? Not at all. Thus, some years are gone together, they meet their inefficiency and surrender the old aged persons. This convenient life is sponsored by all. We went to a Home to get their blessings. Nothing is seen in the hall but one 56 inch Sony television attached with several speakers and it is equipped to give bliss to all, but from the next room, a voice calls somebody to give water, nobody is there to respond to the call. After some time, we went into the room, a very old lady is laid on the bed, and nearby, there are a few mineral syrups and syringes seen, she cannot even speak fluently we asked nothing and gave the water but she is not in a position to hold it and so, we drop by drop gave the water by our own culture and risk, what can we do? Nothing more, we did not wish to be there and left them with the Iron bench, there she is lying down as a so-called equipment and they think that their mother is in rescue. But, really, is that her condition? nothing; but the soul is pending at all so, we have to follow their golden words and living like them through which we can establish such a blissful life.

Like our old aged persons in the homes and streets, we without notable reasons, are scolding them because of their inabilities, they cannot ride a bicycle or walk quickly and the 18 year old is scolding very much and by capturing those concepts, the aged persons do not do anything, and apologise to him because of the loss of time. This will not be noticed and, he rides his bicycle very quickly and goes on! But, we wish to advice them. When they are more than 80 but up to the 80th year, what is guaranteed to the young man, is there confidence to live more than 80 years, and you should walk quickly and it is better to run in an Olympic competition, why so you scold the old man without respect and honour. I ask you one question. Do you have a span of life up to 80 years? certainly not, this kind of tension brings you sugar complaints and blood pressure and so on. Try to understand the old man's mind and treat your grandfather or the oldest man of their generations with honour and respect. Speaking is very easy, but, when we maintain these words in control is very much difficult and you have to be scolded by whom, who is just 8 years old. Where are we going? Try to walk in a straight path otherwise go home and tell, "I was going to be killed by a child on a bicycle who scolded me in such words". We are living in the shadows of our parental care. He has a degree but last 4 years, his potentials are due to his father's income as pension and grandfather's tax fees. He is, nothing, but, his grandfather from his mother's side; What affectionate parents and grandfather too. If you lose them, time will teach a long lesson to you by experiencing their habits. After returning from town or city, the slang that these youngsters use now-a-days is offensive and uncultured. What kind of subject and languages, they had got from their earnest professors and vice chancellors. They simply call another just as a cow calls, it is big noise adamant behaviour and after this activity, we see only educated idiots and non sensual geniuses. What am I to do? They have studied and then, they got their degree as per allotted, and the university gives them convocation in the name of half of the signature of department heads and one witnessing this together with our fathers and mothers and collectively clap a long time. Thus, they are graduates only according to this degree, they can boldly say they have finished with a 1st class, then they are searching a good job, because their parents spent much time from the age of 27, now they are restless. So, we are going to work, and will they spend more time on pilgrimages to various places and only learn to accumulate spiritual elevation. Thus, our efforts are going on. We now think about the word marriage we have to choose one among many.

Therefore, we should live our life with full contentment and satisfaction, otherwise there is no crooked way to enter into God's highly ideal palace, then we will be pushed down and it is not certain, we may have another human birth. Thus, we have to undergo till our judgement time finishes. Let us keep our mouth and ears, not to speak openly and it will give us detachment at our own risk. Try to assimilate all happenings for we can stand still when we perish, we have to have dharsan of God. Such a goal, go to their native places, God is so merciful and His mercy is Sathiyamaev Jeyathae above all, only sathyam will exist, because it has two powers, one is controller of Athma and the other is punishment in order to realise the habits of our past thoughts and deeds. So, from our childhood period itself, we have to give training as we give food. At that time we should tell them some morals thus, we grasp all realities and its universal truths. Purity of mind, activity, conception and grasping Education, Holiness, Chastity, being natural............these are the noble activities, basically all should follow till their last breath.

Our nation India is among all countries the one which is a karmic bhoomi and those who have done penance, can be having birth in India. If the world is a home, the pooja room is considered to be a boon for us, where we will not do any untoward actions; whereas, America is considered to be our industrial area Japan is the kitchen, Britain is the war forcing field, Switzerland is for extra curricular activities and as such all the nations are activated in the same manner but, India is pure, clean forever and this is the Moksha Bhoomi where we are having human birth, is a dispensation to us, and thus, we should pray and thank in a private room. May be all the parts of our home are dusty, India is free from dust, and silence is the most powerful weapon to the whole Universe. If one's silence is real, it will control, console all the problems and as such humanity is ever growing and thus, we can live with peace and harmony. We may have 36500000 crores of money or American dollars but hunger, thirst and appetite and whenever we are sleeping, He should make us awake, otherwise, we are not men and women, and others simply neglect our names and simply call us corpse. Such an impermanent life, that we own. Within 365 days plus worldly days make us to live in this world; we can earn more than 3650000 dollars, but it is not easy to live such and such days, when we count it, our nature of life is based upon our inhalation and exhalation of air. Such a jeevan point is fixed in our body and that is why, we are speaking and talking; what a word, we pronounce, everything is weighed what we accumulate in the name of wealth, but not health. In this same sort of lively period, we are quarrelling with each other for wealth and some wants. Our needs are endless; and we have to content to be free from our sorrows and failures, then only peace can be achieved by one another. Love is the word which is not mentioned in its real meaning, only male and female unitedly live for some years and if they unite with each other, there will be no doubt for a child. But, apart from religions, sects and creeds, we have established wife husband system and religions have arisen to keep chastity as well as understanding. So, if there are various rules and regulations, we have been maintaining divorce in so many marriages. So, many pundits, according to their astrological knowledge and analysis, they said, that the horoscopes of many are having unity with each other, then how does divorce happen? We cannot go and question the gentlemen if we do they will convince their own neighbours and relatives by their false and meaningless words.

So, God alone gives and forgives; Man gets and forgets; that is why, their fate is in action and as a result they are very much afraid of married life and so, we should be careful in choosing a bride or a bridegroom. Our knowledge and wisdom is having certain limitations. Apart from these, we have to rejoice or trouble ourselves and so, we must have faith upon the Almighty, we can assimilate anything whether it is positive or negative and its repulsions too. Whoever may be, God gives this life and so we have to happily endorse it with the consequences and thus, we can be free from bondage and units. A unit is a home. We can build beautiful houses but not a. home. Home means, all the members living under one roof, such united family alone can win the race. But, today, after marriage, son/daughter with their relations set for them a magical family and thus, we are troubling ourselves so much. So, we should cultivate what is needed in order to live for all and for all creatures well being.

We are living but understandingly, there, is this most unanswerable doubt. So, we have to resign our husband/wife designation or distinction. Marriages are made done only to live unitedly. A father and his wife (mother) unitedly live and make their children grow up, give them education and then marry them off. But, all these sons and daughters have no sense of power to look after their parents. It is a pure philosophy and their wives intuition and sex allegation, they hate their parents, and today, we see that good friends are not present here and there. Not at all having a friend is a curse; friendship is a boon to one who is blessed by Him alone. Those who are brothers, neighbours, relatives, but Friendship with a noble man, is higher than ever. And if such a friend is had, then, it is considered to be the top most boon which is considered to be a boon to oneself.

True friendship does what is what and it identifies ourselves true love, so, friendship with male/female will convince and their main balance is only love and affection, and friendship cannot be explained by each other, now we are having so many friends, but Only for fulfilling some desires. If he is our friend, we can marry his sister who is so beautiful, such theme is basically taken and cinemas are coming. But, True friendship presents himself and herself to the entire satisfaction of anything and everything. Truthful Friendship always convinces and consoles our heart with full of contentment and it forgives all means of acts without punishment. There is no tension, untoward doings in connecting with pure friendship. Mainly, if we pray for a good friendship from God, He, Himself descends for us to be in friendship with Him. Example, Sri Sundarar and Sri Parameswaran, their unity is exemplified by one word, Friendship. Eswaran Himself walked to Paravai Nachiar's house to make them united in their domestic life. Such a way, He descended from His seat and hence, bhakthi and fear are the necessities to maintain our friendships. The Fear of God is the beginning of knowledge - proverb, it can be utilised and be made possible only through the Almighty; without Him, we cannot do anything; such an experience alone makes us pure and ever God-minded. Then only, we can really feel the presence of God and His omniscience. According to His will and pleasure, our life is going on. If we assimilate this concept, we can live quite satisfactorily. Without surrender to God, nothing is possible, we can say, that man, if he thinks, he can do; not at all; if we win, it is predetermined, and all beings are living in this world and all their metabolisms are entirely different from one another. So, the Chief Controller, God should not be blamed. He is always merciful and an eminent scholar, an all pervading, knowing preceptor. We have to surrender to Him, then He will take us on

His own as His son/daughter. Then, we should love Him. That kind of love alone, dispenses us ever ecstatic stillness and full hearted happiness/ Anandham.

Whoever you may be, first bow your head before Him, then His sight will be merciful and gracious; otherwise, He will not look on you, by any means at all. We live as husband and wife and unite with each other, but there is no surity that the embroyo will form; likewise, we can act, but, He alone can take decisions. This point should be borne in mind, always, then nobody will be in a dejected mood. Because everything is done by Him. Then there is none of our business against the mightiest Heart of God. Some people say, there is no God, I am very much deeply anguished; He is forever, this is the answer, I got, no doubt at all. How are they able to utter the word 'No', how is it possible, and we do not want an opinion. All are remarkably in our mind; but in our old age, we are just a little thing, once again a child which is not in our mind at all, then how can we be cured, we cannot succeed in our progress herewith. We are all having mother, but, for some reasons, mother - son sentiment fails between them. What is the reason, I am not knowing its answer at all. Likewise, one birth's others' love and care is herewith, cannot explain but, Sri Ammaiappar is the greatest Parent.

Let us have this kind of livelihood. From the beginning, parents had worked hard to earn money and particularly, they spent much money for children's education and naturally, they are well settled. Also they performed their marriages, up to that time, they had given food, shelter and knowledge of all worldy requirements and they are out of form because of age, retirement etc., they beg pure love from all and even live up to 100 plus years hale and healthy. But due to generation gap (we particularly use this word) they think themselves that they are being omitted from friends, relations and males, like all to do this or that, as they were dynamic, productive by nature, but females will settle their survivals will definitely bother ourselves and all the others too. So, we have to keep them very correctly and then, we are well-beings upto our generations. After one or two generations everything will perish so, we have to look after our aged men and women not casually but with special care and good condition too. They expect purity of heart and love from others, their offspring, children and grand children; they have to believe that they are loved by everybody, and so nothing to worry and they will be free from depressions and disabilities, commonly and they will signify or show signs of what they wish, it should be fulfilled and they will be quite normal and therefore, they will not side show, and swear at any one of the family, thus, they are confident and they live for a long time, because of our love and care. So, we have to spend time for our previous and next generations and in this manner they will be living along with gratitude and long life's ambition. They should live for a long period over 100 years, and they will listen to everything and their assistance will be a divine boon, which enables us to have the best thoughts, do good deeds and have fruitful results. Therefore, if they are in a contented mode of life, they will quite naturally bless us wherever they are, we will grow day by day, when our generation comes of age to note down about marriage, our aged people's survivals and their knowledge and experience will originally help us to take the best decisions and their opinions will sharply help us to our development by all means.

We will have not noble thoughts when we are in tension, anger, sorrow. These qualities will not arise from us and there will be no harmony everywhere and all will not be dipped into Divine Ecstasy. Therefore, we stress that time is very suitable for us to get independence from births and deaths, and therefore, we can saturate with Almighty itself. All people are thinking and provoking their habits without any misery and our income will be enormous, and if it is possible, we should perform rituals and penance. So, the divinely dispensated souls are enhancing their wealth and they live with ever shining Shanthi. Thus, births are given to us and we descend from Him as man. So, we have to return to our ancestral world, because, our natural nationality is Kailas where Shree Sivasakthi are ever deserving to be present. If, we attain this, then we come to a conclusion that there is nothing beyond them. So, wherever we come from, after our manual or worldly journey, we should return to our original home. In Tamil, a phrase is seen. "Go elsewhere, but, return home to live'—Thus, we are sent as the representatives of Almighty, and there should be combination of service oriented mind and enough rest. So, it is called 'REST ASSURED!' thus, we come to complete a rotation/circle about this life's general happenings. In God's perception, our mind finds the traces of the values of our livelihood, and hence, our profit and loss is settled. Like a one month old child behaves, like that, the Athamasadhakan treats himself and others. He has a conclusion, nothing is in this earth which is rather good, bad, dear, near, ugly, happy, sorrowful etc., These manuals are only present according to our natural perceptions.; Naturally, everything is on chirustic period, nothing is notable by anyone, and there is no impact of getting success, prizes or failures. Thus, we do not have to bother about our loss and profit. Such a man, never cries with sorrow and never does victory that makes him, a proud man of head weight. So, the ignorance should be got rid of, then, we will enter into this Holy world. And, we are satisfied by all means and this is the total gain of this manual life. From that Anandha state, if we come to see this world, everything is out of our repulses and we should not be responsible for what are said to be truths and lies; thus, man can win matches, and he takes this earth, like a playground, and we can be ever living full-fledged men and women.

If we wish to be a Super Power nation, we have put INDIA or Bharat, earlier we had mentioned the different names of our country. Higher officials are requested to do the same and save the nation. Indians are the most educated, but they are not enjoying like others. Because, our thoughts are if, verified, all INDIANS think and are confident that they are having so many responsibilities like Appa, Chithappa, son, brother, eldest, daughter, husband, servant, chakravarthy, M.L.A., member of council and so on. So, on account of this he cannot live happily and contentedly because, if he does any mischievous activity, it will affect our home's guardianship and sharply thinking that we are one and every one is considered as ourself. So, we cannot live, whatever our mind shows. In other nations, a single man is not at all ready to think about these kinds of relations, that is why, divorce is a common process, and they are simply living for some years, wander without proper reason, Husband-Wife tie is broken without any fear, that God unites us but we are given such power to be living saliently like Himself. This is the quarrel between mind and intellectuality. They should be ever blissful; we can make it so. Do make it at once. This is the opportunity to do so; your lives will be ever blissful. I am not cheating you, if you both are blessed, you will not meet such a kind of state, never you have to suffer, this is dharma also. Most probably, they use the word when they consider 'I' but an Indian pronounces as 'We' that means the plural forms which are behind us and thus, God's nature and form is seen with so many heads, eyes and hands, they reveal the many relationships that are ever living and we truly furnish ourselves as the chief of a home. What a nice embodiment it is....!

If one thinks that he is not - 'I'- but as 'We' there are more liabilities to oneself and he is confident first of himself and then, we consider as singular. So, INDIA is still adhering to the true rules and regulations which are registered by God; not by saints and prophets. So, our sole civilisation cannot be handled by others, they are admiring such a kind of relationship between a man and a woman who unitedly live a long life for abut 70 years..! These make us and others wonder, what a tie up between this couple, is it possible or are they acting..? So, we are honoured by them and nature gives us all of our needs as boons. They are living most probably, an animals life, but our mode of life, is ever based upon God's dispensational surrounding. Do bear this fact in mind this is the greatness of INDIA.

Chapter - 4

Intellectual Search for Divinity

Godliness, cannot be attained within one minute or one hour, whole life span is not enough to establish our mind with gurgitations. Exercises and their implementational foot steps over the plane of mind to establish this, we first, should have patience, thus, we can attain peace which is ever present in ourselves. It is possible to be free from all of our unnecessary problems; so we should prefer not to content ourselves with these mere materialistic sadhanas apart from this, there is an outer sheath over life; it may cause its reciprocal needs throughout our entire livelihood, by feeding the starving, giving water to those in need of water; thus, our hearts should be compressed through peace and chastity. We are all always opposing one another; and are cautions over our organs; this is how we find out starving thirstful, elements on the surface of this earth; we have to find out a universal solution and thus, we can attain eternal sweetness. Those who have won the outer world are respected very much, but at the same time, we have to win over our senses; they have to naturally stand still; so, we have to control it by our mind. If mental equilibrium is kept, then all will be easy to make things normal. This is the universal fact. We cannot win our senses but we are given as a boon by Him, to keep our senses in our control thus, our outstanding phenomena will blossom thoroughly and this is the easiest way to have control over senses, their reflections will be quite normal throughout our lives. Such mind alone can sustain peace and while living admist this mundane world, we can realise to taste the inner nectar of our whole life. Then, it is very easy to pertain our lives with ever lasting peace, non-violent characteristic one. So, we should be very much aware of our thoughts and we should be ever more careful over our senses, and it is the only path to be united with divinity. This universe is always fine if our efforts unite with unity, it is ever easy to keep it on the best level of its own natural position.

This confused life is full of ananda, as such several people are thinking and hoping to live without leaving it and they are very much fond of having all facilities. We can live a comfortable life without any doubt. But, with enough experience, they start to realise the worthlessness of the whole world. There is no change of permanent choice of happiness, and these sorrows seem to be our foresight and we falsely acknowledge this life is full of Ananda. In any corner of this earth, there is nothing, particularly Ananda is not in pursuit because of maya or illusionary sight, in different angles, some happiness is in all activities and this is false. When we come around the incidents and actions, there is nothing which is having permanent happiness or sorrow, which are identified falsely, when we look, these objects are the orientation of happiness. Naturally, we believe there is only happiness in each and every action in full, but there is only sorrow, when we search for it in the earth; for upto the mark of realisation, we can come to know and realise that happiness is itself maya and nothing in this universe is happiness and sorrows are ever a particular proposition of this mixture of all activities in this world. There is nothing, filtered as happiness and nothing can be segmented as sorrows. Everything is the illusionary appearance, because of our para chemical view and that is why, it seems to be sorrow or happiness. If one had passed his examination, he is happy, and if he passes with distinction in several subjects or is the first student who had scored more than 98% in all subjects, he is happy, another has passed, but has only scored within 40 marks in each of the subjects, then sorrow is the option, graceful acceptance from others and that is why, we formerly denote that everything is according to our right of knowledge. He has passed but marks, do not permit him to join higher classes without doubt. It will be a dream if it comes into experience, then it is miracle. Thus, sorrow and happiness are rolling over us. What we think as sorrow, there is something which repels as success. So, both feelings are actually available, but we weigh these facts because of the creation of those sensual assessments. Senses with mind have oneness period, its illusionary perception is exit and those who are involving in those exercises, have the exhibition of happiness and sorrowful activities. Though the activity is done by us we are not responsible for our activity and hence, Bhagavan in His Gita, particularly notes, be a witness, nothing in this world will include you as a member of the action or inaction. So, if one is capable of being a witness to those happenings in front of him, is nothing but the illusions of his own mind. This is the great, notorious view of this universe. So, no one is responsible for his activities or even the activity of others.

May be our thoughts and deeds differentiate one from another but desire is ever not changeable; such crimes can be pardoned in the name and recommended by those men and women because of their own circumstances. Like houses built by one and only engineer, he makes 100 types of houses with all conveniences in the houses and they if we tell them will build 100 types of houses and in all the houses the mode is changed but, commonly we call them houses. Thus, the whole creation is universal and this mode of classification is because of their own will and pleasure. Through God's vision everything is equal and haves and havenots are to be divided by us not by God. He does the whole creation with all facilities and many consider them to be permanent. Our crucial fate surrounds ever and we fail in all our attempts. Mens' desires are uncountable, so we have to suffer a lot, if we obey and fear God, then our life will be a satisfied one, and everything which is given to us is the mighty boon of His grace and mercy. Thus, we call Him merciful, and in Tamil, there is one word which denotes the kindness of God forever is karunyam, this is the best stage of the humanitarian race and thus, our life will be entirely blossomed with divine nectar and scents, because there He is in His mighty residence and where is His residence, it is as simple as the pure HEART. In Hiruthaya Sthanam, He is a dwelling factor by which everything is controlled and conducted regularly for the welfare of the society. All possibilities are due to His mighty and mightiest happenings and they, all are embracing with goodness and forgiving mood, should be adopted by heart are called saints.

If we keep silence and patience, we will one day achieve our aim and goal, which is derived by God and He expects at all times, our characteristic phenomena of peace and brotherhood harmony. We speak and lecture in a hall of fame, trying to earn and learn how to make money; but by mere accumulation of money, we cannot buy our inner conscious' contentment and satisfaction. If we really attain this, we should always be keen over our senses and their reflections; now, we are in the sense, all fools, idiots and what we see, that is only true but maya is on the way of our migration from our materialistic omnivorous mentality and we should be turned around into manlihood and divine beings. Then only, we can proudly say that we are living a full fledged life; we are instructing others, but we do not emphasise it in our mind. Our education and tongue power are utililised only for earning money and thereby we can buy weapons like anger, anxiety desire and that is why, we are not able to keep us on the pedestal of godliness. So, if we wish to have divine life there are such rules and regulations, which are given as a syllabus by our ancestors, and they had practiced them throughout their lives and affirmed shanthi and peace. Let us have the divine peace by all means.

According to our circumstances and time factor, we believe everything is done by us; this is the failure fact, because our do's and don'ts trail, will give us no confirmed solution, everything is altered as an altar, He remains controlling everything in our favour or otherwise. If we realise it, then we will be saints on one side of the coin. Then, by having experiences and facts we meet together daily and secondly we can be taught lesson by lesson which is His mighty education. There are no books, no rhymes and rhythms and we praise the Lord because of His glory and consciousness of Him. Thus, He adds all of our civilian civilisations, and thereby we are all considering and concluding that "'I' am doing this or that, "I am educated yes, 'I' am going, walking, talking etc". This 'I' the letter, the word, the happening and it can be held up in any circumstances in all universal truths. Therefore, it is considered as a main fact for us, in mathematics, 'o' is an important factor according to -'o', whereas if we take into consideration is the main factor which makes all numbers as valuables and non-valuables. So, mathematically, a master and ask him about the Mighty power of 'o's greatness. This 'o' was found in action by an Indian, we proudly trumpet this valuable fact to all. Thus, our maths subject is over ruled by Him as an existence of time factor. Time is a characteristic factor as 'o' and it is considered in maths field as a catalyst. It does not undergo any chemical equations. But it is the master which resists the strength through out the universe.

If we are ready to cause in the midst of all, first we have to stop our talking and should give preference to our best thoughts, deeds by realising the uncertainty of all. Nothing in this universe is stable it is the natural fact and thus, we should adhere to the rules without mistakes, we shall attain our originality within a second or fraction of second. First we should be ready to be a good pupil; then it is quite easy to be established with oneness of godliness.

Such men or women seem to be rare in this materialistic and computerised life, if we search them with full of patience and penance, we can find those rare ones in our own life time. All Gnanies and prophets have not directly jumped from the Ether; they also have been given to us through their parents. So they are to be honoured as they possess the signs of godliness and divine elevation. If one wants wealth and health, they will be dispensed only through selfless service to parents with sincerity, at the time when they are in need; so should be classical and lead an epic oriented life which will give us mental and physical peace and good character. Then our creator will be contented and dispense a lot of wealth, health and so on. Therefore, we should be ready to give up to show our gratitude to the nation and parents with will and with Ecstasy. It is sure our daily service to parents and nation and our conscious deeds, we shall establish a new world and there God himself will come and sit permanently; these kind of experiences were described in our normal life. Whatever happens we should not lose our consciousness but be patient to cultivate our thoughts and deeds to the level of peace and shanthi. All our sages and saints were trying to imprint the values of penance and kasta mouna (deep silence) it will dispense us with full of our needs; if we are satisfied with our deeds there will be no one who can cheat others and all will be considered to be Pandavas, in the sense, they are equal to God. We are struggling to preserve our buildings, our cash, bank balance, buying new cars and living a sophisticated life; it is possible only through giving respect and honour to our wealth. Some people may not have money; but they are satisfied heartfully with whatever God gives. We should cultivate and plough sowing good thoughts as seeds, we can establish a Rama Rajyam certainly in our life time. So patience is emphasised herewith.

Within a second, attempt, we cannot attain this symbolic result or over all in one night. We can attain the unexplainable, but implicit state of honour which is respected by all deities; thus, we can be free from sorrows-worries - miseries and attain supernatural perfection. Each and every individual's natural habit should be too much of patience and silence, we are not with these noble qualities ever, if we are still standing on the path, we should be handed over to Him automatically. In other words, it is called non-violence, patience, self-dedication and penance. Penance is the only way to attain bliss; then nothing can disturb us by all means of materialistic collapses. So we should be always aware of these evil acts. There should be evils, surrounding us, but, we have to win the race, for this, some natural qualities are essential, our ancient scripts denote to the point of tips for our lives. This human birth is not at all an easy one to get from God, He, alone makes a syllabus for this certainty of His own, and we should be climbing on the ladder, without a mistake, then we are one and the same with Eternity; thus, our ancestors teach their invented truths to all for our own welfare. But we don't notice anything, even not be opened with our sensual organs; we are all cheating one another, and thus, believe that we can live a full-fledged life, but these should only come into action, only through proper exercises and then our lives will be a meaningful one. Thus, Nature created us, and we must obey to the entire satisfaction of God through our thoughts, deeds and results.

'I', which is full of this fleshy body says this is my hand this is my leg this is my eyes, this is my ears. So, what does 'I' mean? We know without knowledge, we believe that this fleshy-bony structure is ourselves. It is a universal false concept; when we enter spiritual analysis we can know and realise the fact of 'I'; it is nothing but PRANAN, which controls 10 Air systems, through which we are actively doing our deeds daily. So 'I' is nothing but a part and parcel of Paramathma. If we understand this fact, we can easily attain spiritual perfection. Thus, our thirst and hunger start towards the path of self-realisation. If one realises this universal concept, then he is an Anandamayee, while living with this body. Such phenomena is subjected to be the aim and goal of human life. We should be aware of our senses, sense organs and our mind should control our whole metabolism, thus, we can liberate our soul whenever we wish. These are jeevanmukthas.

Mind is to be on the plane of peace and harmony not by doing yogic exercises, but whatever we do, if we do them with true pious dedicated significances, we can attain even jeevasamadhi. For example, saint Thiagarajaswamy did not at all do any Thanthric modes or even Ramakrishna Paramahamsar or even Sri Ramalingar did not do any specific yogic exercises, but by their piety and dedication they attained their deities very simply. They did not only do namasmara of God, they saturated their soul to the mighty feet and they are now, beyond time, they stand through their mode of simple ideas and procedures; they are still living ever in the hearts of devotees. These customs are characteristically imposed on our life, then the benefits are to yield for that we have to sow good thoughts and deeds for our young generations. Then the forthcoming generations, they can easily handle this life, without nothing in this universe; without money, we cannot live peacefully, this is a false concept, and therefore, we have to do good activities and good will rise from good hearts only. Bad will rise from bad only; So, we have to retain on the basement plane of peace and uncountable thoughts may rise from the hearts, bad hearts show ill treatment of our senses, so we have to omit such thoughts and their trace of destruction, we have to elevate ourselves to even equal godliness, such foolish men we are! so, from the childhood, we should nourish them with good citizenship and Bharat will rise to the pedestal of peace and harmony, thus, we can elevate us in the best ways. Our thoughts only transfer into deeds. Such a society should be eagerly transformed. There is always some misunderstanding between two groups, ours is dharma another is adharma; finally "sathyam" whatever may be the problem, we can come to a non violent solution, by which we can understand the sakthi of Dharma. God is operating our Universe only on this basis of Dharma. Whenever some test is put between these two, sathyam only wins. Because of its existence violent, valourless beings will also be punished and furnished; so, we must be careful in adoring divine principles and try to lead a peaceful, calm life. There is a fact, nature will exhibit in due course of time, and we have to wait, wait for that moment, nothing in this universe as conduct or misconduct; we just divide our activities into two and we enjoy about our thoughts and deeds. If we think hopefully, then everything will end with success. So these concepts are ruled over all beings. God is great, He is the mightiest among the minutest. He is omnipresent all are pervaded by Him, without His grace, we cannot do anything, if He insists we respire and it is only by His instance that we reproduce, inhale and exhale to the responses, and He is the whole witness for all thoughts and deeds, without His guidance we cannot survive at all. In this universe, full of oxygen is present, when the jeevan is living long with the organ systems a whole metabolism is running off; if he discharges, from this fleshy body, he cannot do anything and He is the processor, One who pervades all our metabolisms; there are innumerous metabolisms in our body, but we cannot do anything without His order, will and pleasure; we cannot do anything why? He is all knowing. Though adhering to the simplest way to attain Almighty's grace, we can easily without any kind of efforts reach the highest plane of liberation. Liberation is nothing but total surrenderness, all these are possible for those who attain mental peace, thus, livelihood is going on, and we, honestly should be with full of surrenderness and bhakthi. We are not at all surrendering to God, Almighty. So we spoil ourselves and others too. We lose our wealth, peace and harmony, all because we do not entertain our inner consciousness; we are all time passing doing yoga exercises only for good health and mental peace; we do not have inner eye sight and proof but we wish to live happily; it is in our hands, simply to chant, if we do chant the holy mantra of God intensively and sincerely rejoice with oneness of unity, saturation will be ours on the search.

DIVINITY what does it mean? Everybody has his own conclusion about this term Divinity. It is nothing but purity of mind and action and goodness of our deeds and thoughts, also to be with full of purity and shanthiful confidence upon the Almighty; then only, we can realise the full meaning of the divinity of everything. Everything has its own nucleolus as it is, everything has its own divine power which is within the embryo of the nucleus and it is to be realised, not explainable, in words, it is simple to say anything about the abundant subject of the whole universe's rotation and stimulations; so we have to be responsible to know about ourselves, first; it is the best knowledge of spirituality. Now, there are many rishis and munis and peedams all over the world; just this one question is put to these people that is, what was their last birth? where did they live? and who were their parents and how many brothers and sisters they had? what was his/ her educational and monitary qualifications in that birth? and how many years he / she lived in that birth? Is there any sage or swamiji in India or all round the world to answer these questions? They know something about epics and truths from the books. They learn some basic tricks and simply cheat humanity, earning more and more recognition, medals and money and lastly they live their life in jail and die as orphans. So, the forthcoming young generations beware before entering into this spiritual world. If your are dispensed by God, you will be blessed by Him and His grace makes you a great gnani, and one day this world will salute us and many disciples will follow our preachings, no more secret steps are needed. So, do not be in a hurry to achieve this by your own efforts. If God had proposed earlier in our births, we will surely get His Ultimate Dispensation through His own protection and guidance. So, have belief in my words. This is not at all a book which is written for name and fame and money. It is God's words, every single letter is His letter; it is not mine nor is it my own wisdom. It is all the intuition and insistence of Himself and that is why, I have taken such a very large tolerance and patience to type every letter to present it as a book and give it you and it will preach to you not by mere words; before your naked eyes God Himself alone gives His Dharsan and makes you to understand this manuscript and you may have a little practical knowledge of spirituality and about my trials. Therefore, be confident at all times, to have such huge patience and tolerance to have a seat in the universal university where He is the Principal and the admission purely by Himself and not by any recommendation or so. He Himself selects and elects each and every candidate with whom He is contented Himself and makes him pure first, and then He will teach the suthras of spiritualism which is the Brahma Nadi of India. This Nadi is the principle for all the holy scripts of Hinduism, for mankind's final liberation and by which one can attain self realisation and through which all the Vedas and epics originate their own concepts which are taught to mankind for their welfare.

If someone asks us suddenly, we have to tell them frankly with fluency, that amount of frankness and truth, in our statement, as our answer should be clear and clean, thus, we do not think badly, it will be the throne of God, our mind is plain and crystal clear and we should think about the good and only the salient features should fill our thoughts. If our thoughts are clear and clean, our deeds will be bright and with Godly exhibition and we can go with the train and our journey will be nice and pleasurable. Therefore, our character and conduct must be praised by the teller, and the third party. Our life should be planned and our needs are to be very meagre and if we live thus, God will justify it and His blessings will always be with us and we also, by His might blessings He will place us on the Holy pedestal of ecstasy. So, we must keep our heart and mind with full of good thoughts, that is, divine thinking and we should be neat with a crystal clear mind. Of course, God will come and sit in our mind. For this, no money is needed; we should surrender totally and of course, our deeds must be blessed by God, if our mind is not trubulent, that is fine and divine. So, such heart filled thoughts should be the HEART of us. If we are having His blessings, that will be the noble heart and His presence alone cleans the Ether and fills it with divine power always. Therefore, we should be united by doing prayer and doing noble jobs. All the festivals are to be celebrated with piety and peaceful character. If we do our deeds in this way the Noble soul, the Almighty will bless us always and our prayer will be noble. We hope all the needs, will be blessed at the proper enhancement of God's sthuthis. In this Kaliyuga if we chant God's name with bhakti, we will be surely blessed by Him and we will be near Him and our deeds become divine and attain His satisfaction. So, we must keep our mind very solid not to be shaken by this wordly notes and then the angles and sidhars will very easily come and go from our heart. This is not an easy deed. It will only happen because of our mental oneness and divine co-ordination. So, first we must try to get His blessings thoroughly and then, we can have His mighty blessings and we will get the help of the sidhars to assist us in our mighty deeds (Astamasidhis). If it is achieved our pure thoughts will be transformed as deeds and the course of our life will be divine and therefore, the divine aid is to be swallowed by the Almighty. Mankind has a propensity for acceleration and achievements, but God alone notes and watches our thoughts through our angles, that is why we cannot cheat our mind, because our experience of mind will be the witness number one as the witness of the Almighty's court. Thus, the conviction or prize is allotted by God. So, we never think and do anything which is not rightful to do in action; if it is done always, the punishment will be serious and we cannot escape from His mighty government and we are not having any such ability to get rid of it too.

A suitable environmental complex is present, the agricultural pursuit will be very much favourable for the cultivation of crops. Just we have to work hard, to give us a perpetual configuration of the agricultural field and farmers are intensively praying to get rain they should cultivate the grains from this earth to fulfill our needs and save for sale. If this kind of life is led by the farmers they will be the richest people in the world. We are all having strength to cultivate but at the same time they are too proud and have much head weight and because of this, they lose all their profits and benefits. So, to eradicate this good bad habit, we have to work and entertain life, to the entire satisfaction of the Agricultural System. And such all the farmers now-a-days are not seeking to yield the result of agricultural ways confidently; if we fail and do not respond we lose our income and the situation of a farmer and sit in the home and feel very much for their distress. Then how can we achieve good yield in this field? Nothing can be expected from our high class fields there is nothing seen and how our hearts are trembling. So we should pray our Surya Bhagavan and do special pooja to have its best sway. We have to succeed in our progression and thus, we are all ready to work hard, but no pleasurable result can happen and such, the owner how can he smile as per his cultivation; what will be the situation of our statesmen. We had much education because of the approval and confidence in our beloved agriculture, now, we are starving with hunger and thirst without water, both are not gotten in an easy way and we how can we get profit and, proceed with our job and trade. Thus, we expect a good result, how can we reap a good yield in the way of mere studies and getting marks may be up to 89%. What is the use of this rank card? By birth, our commodities had been earned only through agricultural fields, thus, an agricultural college is running for the past 41 years. There are innumerous peasants who do work. In the fine tender morning, they wake up from sleep and start to begin their daily work. They plan as what to do in agricultural period, who sprinkles the medicine and fertilizers to the young ones or saplings. This is the superior priority to do what is fine. We are studying and playing and spending our time in postponing our studies just for fun we cut one period of class and spend that valuable time in juggling and after the bells rings, we go, to our next period of class trying to understand the particular subject from the magnanimous professors. We are going to grasp the lesson with a big sort of understanding and finishing the test, papers are given to the examiners and they leave the class, the students start to get out of the classes, and some students go to the mess, some sit under the shade of the neem trees and are speaking on several topics and they normally look to be very gentle and they are very pleasing to refer to their conduct and character which is very good. There students should proceed to do higher studies. There should be a renaissance in the education field, we should produce masters like Mr. Krishna Menon, Dr. Radhakrishnan and so on, Our beloved INDIA should be ever filled with savants and valorous people and that is why we start the basement of the college studies so as to mould each and every student, that is why, all the students, when asked about their S.S.L.C. studies where did they finish and how much marks they got ? they blink without answering well. Now the bell rings, and all the students begin to go the classes and the all professors are ready to teach them, but the students are not ready, even though they pardon their mistake, what is the matter, and how to pronounce, these are taught by our teachers, but they themselves teach these styles, how we can project our life with education only. In any way, we can earn money, but we are studying to earn money because of the qualification of our education, we wish to have 3 times food for all the days. That is why we get short tempered, sorry for that, and whatever, you are studying, go through thoroughly and proceed your studies with meaningful education, this will feed you by any means in the world. So, try to accumulate your wealth is education and pray God to give proper and special education, through which we must be embodied with Education itself. So, try to achieve your insistence through the students and the teachers, the correspondent should be on a common level and thus, we can have practical study through this type of education. We are all having good knowledge, it should be with wisdom, then you will be appointed as the dean of this university and thus, the government will be pleased. In a college, the correspondent, the Principal, the Founder and various scholars and students are sitting in the huge hall and first class mic set is arranged, First, the Principal delivers a short speech about my particulars and my service, thus, he has given some introduction of myself. He repeated the matter and he called me to speak for 45 minutes; after 45 minutes they all asked for specimen signature and to bless them. They celebrated this small incident as a celebrities programme and gave some momento and money. Thus, all are given chance to go out and listen to my lecture. Lastly, the principal came and she narrated the delivery of lectures, is to be analyzed for about half an hour and she gave me a pilot pen as a presentation and requested me to permit her as my disciple and that she would learn from many more gurus and thus, attain mukthi. This academic and periodical system in materialism and spiritualism is not suited in any form towards Self-realisation. They never continue to be in correspondence with these aspects totally and thus, our steps should be with the uplift of our cultural and situational status. Therefore, we should credit our life with the establishment of a spiritual founder and thus, we had several leaders, and if the time arises that they are conclusive not practisable, this forum will stand still to form of a peaceful forum the controversy will not be disturbed to the fullest amount of rituals and ceremonials.

According to rules and regulations of Nature, all Dharmas are one and the same, if we analyse these truths, all are giving tips to live a full fledged life. They are also giving their opinions as their own experience, through their attainment of gnana sidhi, they are flowing like water in a falls, they are never without water in any season. Thus, the Gnanavans also give us a pathway to go through in our life and attain how it is? But we just listen to them and do not adhere to them with a mind full of confidence and sacrifice. Without preparing ourselves to do penance to the highest stage and accept His presence, never, wish to have anything, because the one and only fixing article which is subjected to be with us i.e., GNANAM, and thus, they become Guru-disciple holiest relationship without passion. If there is any passionate action between mother and daughter, then the relationship is not at all a penance filled life. Nothing can be expressed due to capability towards this world by mutual understanding. So I quote:- "If you give, I will give you this;" this is materialistic compassion, but no bargaining between two; cannot consider to be ours and they will not yield anything without approval of science or spiritualism.

So when our pure organs are in good condition, we can remember the names and we can attain perfection. So, from the age when we are interested to know the value of His name, we must start to do smaranai always and then our life will be fruitful. Everybody is having several types of ambitions but nothing will be fulfilled, what is the reason? They do not know anything about their analysis. The reason is nothing but their background life has some fraudulence. Then how can presentations be given to the accused? Therefore, we must be noble in living, and in all aspects of human life, if it is possible, God alone, comes and gives us all. Thus, please understand His gracious heart to give us anything; be ready, but we are not having such good personalities. For studying, job seeking and then to maintain and continue in the job with our working ability we have to have his Grace. Some are giving us promotion by promotion and thus, we can be a managing director for the whole factory. If we are so we do not have any searching possibility of a job, it will search you and make you to sit in that job in that factory. So, you should be like this, you will be the job holder and prosperity will come of itself. Likewise, due to your true bondage with the factory and its development, your help and hard work, you will be the icon of the factory. So if your bhakthi is truthful and if you have belief, if you come to us, everything will be coming to you at the perfect time. Likewise, if you search Him with love and bhakthi, He will come and give dharsan to you automatically. For many bhakthimans had God's dharsan directly, thus, many examples, are seen in the epics, puranas, even in this kaliyuga some bhakthimans have had dharsan of God. We are coming to know through archeological witnesses and they are everliving and they represent without body but natural voice. Those are specially called and worshipped as sidhars. For example, Sri Ramakrishna Paramahamsa, Sri Ramalinga Adigal are some figures who had seen Him and had heard His voice, that is, God spoke with them. Likewise, if we live a spiritual with ahimsa filled life, we can have His presence. Hearing, speaking and grasping through mind, His kalyana guna vaibavas, in due course of time, we become a Bhagavatha Bakthiman and thus, it is the easiest way to have His Dharasn. Then our eyes will be glittering by His divine dispensation. Then we will be a sidhan and hence we can speak and do divine dispensation. Then, we will be a sidhan and hence we can speak and do divine moral activities and wherever we go, there will be the divine surface which will be started by Himself. This stage is Self........ is SELF! Therefore, we have to have confidence first on our self and, we must turn it towards Bhagavan. Lastly, his soul will merge with Bhagavan's Holy feet. This is why, our interest is also facing towards His Dharsan with mild, milky words. This is why, we should live a divine life. Thus, all the religion's Vedas express their ideas with multi proofs.

Wherever we are, whatever we do, He is looking at us and though, we should also think about our mistakes, then we can have salvation from maya, and get pure wisdom. Therefore, we have to chant His Holy Name several, innumerous times seeking philosophy from epics and doing our daily poojas. These are the ways to attain His Love towards us and if it is done, God will be ours and He is ready to watch our thoughts also and thus, we can attain natural perfection and surly we will guarded, governed and organised by Him ever. Time is going on so, we must be very careful of time and so we should spend time in chanting His Holy Manthra, in due course of time, we ourselves become Gnanis and the world will have knowledge through our preachings and the society will be benefited in all sections. That is why, we are beyond sects, creeds and religions, do not consider them at all, praising Him without any colour and gender. There is a bond between us, we are all mankind, and we have the right to seek His presentation, through dedicated life. Thus, we should dedicate all, and everything will come through by His Divine Grace, if this dispensation happens, there is nothing more to be obtained in this world, and our mind will not accelerate throughout time to time. Take for example, RAMAYANA. The essence is GO TOGETHER...........GO TO GET HER. If we analyse its true meaning, we can easily get help and unity will be possible in all aspects and we can get everything because, He is the owner.

All of us daily discharge our duties throughout day and night, we must have dynamic power to do it, that is why, our overall sakthi is promptly saved in the liver, the power house of human acceleration and thus, we can be so full of strength and no more tiredness in between their exercise. All spiritual exercises need strength in the physical body and then we can be strengthened throughout with sakthi by taking good meals. So in kaliyuga, according to our food and its consummation, our soul will settle with prolonged life, and this should be borne in mind. Therefore, we must see to the quantity and quality; we must take food materials according to our own age and situation. Thus, we can maintain our duties with fullest satisfaction of our soul and mind. If we have the privilege to do cooking and distribute them to the bhakthimans, it will be marvelous among all thanams (donation). For this, we should elaborately speak about this; as such it is the thing considered to be the peculiar experience to avoid the coming vibrations and in future we will be without spinal pain, many pains and of the joints of bones. Such diseaseless service can be realised when we struggle with diseases, so we have to take fresh green vegetables. Good exercises and daily walking, jogging are considered to be the exercises, should be done morning or evening. We will be hale and healthy, thus, we should proceed with profits and benefits only. Therefore, as per time if we consider this body's strength, the life time will be noted.

An ideal life should be led by us throughout our span of life, it must be only through discipline, we can earn crores and crores of money and be very much learned and have many degrees and doctorates, but with ideological survey in our life, everything is a waste. Therefore, we must set up our mode of life at all times, by sustaining it with Sathyam and Ahimsa, then only we can live a meaningful life. It is possible, we have to control our senses with our mental power and thus, we can win over our lively activities and win the race. There is no necessity of wealth, education and so on. The one and only needed thing is enough if we are chaste throughout life and thus, we will be equaled with God; and all creatures will salute and they will follow our life's style throughout their life. Such a phenomena of life can be possible if we are disciplined and do the needful and keep away from evil thoughts, unnecessary rituals and ceremonies; this is the first wanted necessity to have a divine bonded life. So, we have not to sacrifice anything, if we neglect bad thoughts and deeds, everything will be divine and there will be no ego in our mind and by our activities, automatically, we become sadhus, and live liberally at all times among all the peoples. Without ego, the life will be brightened with divine glory and it is the ecstatic life which is repelled by our thoughts and deeds. As much as we are integrated with mind and deeds, our life will be acknowledged by His Almighty with truthfulness and glamourous, charming, ever-green proposals of God Himself. This is the aim of ourself and thus, we can attain the top of life's Holiness and Highness. Thus, we are at the bottom or on top, there will be no balance between these two and we do not bother about our life's consequences. Ordinarily, we are thinking so much about our survival with full of equipments for our comfort with full of electric instruments and home with full of servants and thus, we calmly sit in one place, press a calling bell, calling one to do this or that, and fulfill our needs as much as we do not move anywhere, and as such we suffer all kinds of diseases and illnesses and taking so much injections daily for 4 times and swallowing a variety colour of tablets and capsules, countless number of tablets for our rescue from diseases.

Among all diseases of our organs is our mental depression. We are also spending thousands of rupees per month and for its rescue, tablets and injections too are added. Is such a life a good successful life? Not at all, we have to do our needful activities by our own efforts and we can say boldly "I am the chief of this family, but we are a servant". Most of the ladies are sleeping even in morning hours between 10 to 2 pm. Are they meant for domestic life? We are punished by Him, because of our foolish activities and for our known and unknown sins done in the past, present and future. He knows all, and everything, without His wisdom, we cannot even do anything, this may be a sentimental concept, it is the universal Truth and we must have belief in this concept and lead our live with simplicity and nobility, otherwise, if he takes His mighty Whip in his Hand, the Whip will seriously trouble us and will not be excusable and non-stoppable; no recommendations will be considered; so from that situation, we have to escape from the hell in this world itself. God is Mercy; but if He punishes us, it will be for our upliftment and at that time, He seems to be very cruel to our sight. So, from this moment, we have to escape and we must deposit our dharma and sathya, mercy and grace alone prevents us from His punishment. May be it is punishment, in the sense, it is not at all our punishment so, it is entirely different, if we turn our table, as He wishes,

He, then, will kiss and encourage us to the extent of showering His mighty blessings on us to do the duties properly and executively and also He will bless us to have success in our all actions. But human kind does not do like this, from this small incident very long and large commitment will be prolonged throughout our 2 or 3 or more generations, they are extending their non-touchability with each other. God may be cruel to us, but the posture is like that, at the same time, within seconds, He cools down and blesses us to the very far extent and like a passionate father, He will exchange his passion and love on us. So, He is nothing but our father Himself, He strikes; after sometime, He will give us sweets and ice creams to soften our heart and at the same time make us realise what were our mistakes and how do they all not be repeated in our whole life; thus, we are noble and very ecstatic in doing our doings perfectly and neatly for our own satisfaction and others too. This is the difference between God's and our's. So we have to extend God's grace like Him. We should do our daily activities and then, we also will be God's shadow and have the trace of God on our body itself. If His sketch is graciously stressed on us, everything can be achieved by us because of His Divine Power. Such gracious power, He has. He is ready to share with us but we are not having such efficient qualifications and authorisation to attain those divine qualities. If we try and try to attain it, it will come one day and it will do whatever we order, for the welfare of this whole universe.

Entire silence both internally and externally will expel the outer world and in this way we must be ready to cultivate our mind with passion and pure love, otherwise, we cannot do not anything to attain Godliness. If we straighten ourselves with these classifications, all clarifications will be shut up and there will be silence which is compared with ecstatic supreme silence. This is oneness of mind and deeds. We should cultivate ourselves in this manner in all our services. Therefore, sanyasins, live without any materialistic moments in their lives and they can move towards liberation. The eternal liberation is the sole motto of this human birth. Whoever it may be, their goal is this and this is called Moksham or Mukthi. In other words, we can name it Ambrosia of concentric circle's unparalleled plant kingdom.

All the creatures are the reflections of the Almighty, itself, but, we do not have that kind of IQ, because all our needs are satisfied only on the plane of mud, earth, that is why "I know everything and anything and I believe that I am all pervading and all knowing ..." is it noticeable? We are all puppets of God, the Almighty, who creates and guards and finally He,

Himself pulls us to His abode, according to our situation while there are so many contributions to the divine path, they are shining very much into this materialistic group who are always immersed into money and wealth alone. There may be somebody who is crying and weeping for His real dispensation. May be one, one among one crore may be the Gnani who seeks Him and attains Mukthi when others are immersed in this materialistic life without failure. We are all entertaining ourselves throughout life only money is the main factor of our cultural aspects. So, are we expecting any special searching mode to climb upto the spiritual world. The only way we have is to thoroughly surrender to Himself, then we can attain all things and we are the best human being in all subjects. Our worldly handsome, priceless, costly articles cannot search Him. All are going to temples with some thoughts of Him but not with bhakthi. What is the difference between bhakthi and attending temples daily. Try to differentiate these two facts, if you cannot, call me I will clarify your doubts. According to me, today we need only Sri Narashimmamoorthy, not just Vamana Devar. Nashimmamoorthy with that type of uktram, then this world will be reformed and Ramarajyam can be established without doubts. So I pray the Almighty, "please do come as an avathar and you alone can make this whole universe to establish sathya and sathsanghs". Mankind's real and natural temperament is sathwic and vegetarian; but they are all ready to be in a queue to in take food without cost in the name of Dharma. If this world runs through, how can we attain our particular junctions or stations.

He may be in any kind of human circle, some of them may speak, some will listen, some will eat food 3 times a day, some do not take even water; some do some miraculous sivaleelas and these are the samples of His doings through which He protects the people and gives them liberation. Their motto is to transfer humanity from the passion with materialistic mind into Athmic perseverance and precedence. If we are involved in His circle, we will also be gnanies while living in this mundane life with kith and kin. He has good practice, when He wishes He transfers His mind into materialism and when He wishes to show anything abnormal, He can do so, thus, He recovers the public and preaches to them to do good deeds for the welfare of all creatures and all Jeevans when you are present here and abroad. This is the universal thought, which makes us to promote the beings betterment of their qualification, without any yogas, but they will be uplifted to Moksha or Mukthi by grace of Ganapathy. Whatever we think, do, complete fail, pass all are the mightiest sakthi of God; even a single finger cannot be used without His assistance. So, we should learn how to earn God's mightiest blessings and our Bhakthi makes Him to run to us to fulfill our activities into deeds and thus, our human birth is meaningful. There are a lot of creatures according to His will, are in this world, but God only can and has the power to pronounce everything, we are learned and that is why. we know something but God is all pervading because He is in all forms and formless also.

When God's immense qualities are known and realised we acknowledge, that this mixture must be distilled, which is Ambrosia, and this is what each and every creation is searching for. For this attitude, we must educate ourselves in a variety of subjects, then, after education, each and everyone from one department gather and they should be inevitably concentrated towards their life's motivation, they are doing their journey with Athmic conclusion. Thus, they bring everything into action and surrender themselves to Him, because they have to exercise and our illness should be cured, and this procedure will be for a long or short period. May be 90 days or 12 days. This is the scale of input of the medicine, it will cure you by all means with medicines, thus, God Himself comes in different forms and we have to be awake in a mood of expecting Him. If this is real and truthful, then what I say, will be in a plain road, and you beat whatever is happening in this world. Everything is illusionary, nothing is real; everything is mortal, this extreme supremacy of mind should be practiced throughout life and this is the way to attain perfection; so it has been concluded by a blessed soul (ALLAH) otherwise, NABI, who is an annonist who gave the Q-ran for the welfare of the whole human society and by which, we must follow its regulations and regulate us towards divine saturation. May be this is the path of Islam, these golden theses are nothing but our wealth which is to be understood by everybody and the whole mankind should salute him. Give respect to him in this way is not at all enough. We must inspire the words and follow strictly these concepts. Then it is quite sure to attain him with flowers/ offerings. Therefore, we should practice all principles, of the Vedas, so to say, all the truths should be first known from a Guru, and live with these truths ourselves should be changed to Godliness - oriented men and women, then whatever the force is nothing will affect us in positive and negative ways. So, guru's Gatdatcha is inspiring it should be saluted as God's representative's words. That is why, we are insisting these truths to all to express our betterment of the world. Thus, you and others along with the prophets go to his home bless them, give valour to expect whatever may be the problem, we should face boldly without any kind of doubts and God is our's, thus, our situation must standstill and fight with the foe and then final result, Success is sakthi's. Thus, this worldly story lives cork and guardianship along their manifestation of your eye vision. Though we are having eyes, they have some power through which we can see objects from just 20 metres, but the wisdom is Eyes; the eyes of wisdom can see all along the prapancham without any profitable dinners and so on. So we should be always keen in discharging our duties correctly and thus, we really hear some unknown subjects, this is not true, but they are giving you some false certificate and we with our authority must develop him first and then he must find the spiritual man who can do whatever we cannot, by God's grace and mercy. Therefore, we must be very cautious about whatever is in action and as many happenings, you should know the original, and the false goods should be discarded one by one. You alone examine it and you can set up an electric clipping and save all for the betterment of mankind. This is natural spiritualism. First try to understand what spiritualism is and then you can be living throughout your life with gun mood. It is dispensed only by God Himself. We cannot make it or shape it, that is why this gentleman is beyond your knowledge and wisdom. He is nothing but one of the molecules of His greatness of God Himself. If He exhibits Himself his personification, and privacy may be disturbed, that is the reason He is not seen at all on roads and canteens, you and your followers must pray God every time with your mind, whatever you are doing, you must have mind, thus, whenever you involve in these rules, you should follow them and go on through with piety and with one mindedness, should be on the path of growth and thus, we must elevate ourselves first, then you can easily elevate others too in the easiest way. This is possible only through Gnana yoga, and that is why, we are all working, working and working our systematic Thathwam (philosophy) by following these principles.

Of all creatures, the Almighty is the creator, preserver and destroyer, in this way He represented His Roopams as Brahma, Vishnu, Iswaran and they have spouse and their domestic life is as ours; thus, we can know the value of this integrated life's salient feature and this is the Dharma, is the first of three divisions; thus, Grahasthasram is the best by which we can give a part of the meal to the hungry and water to the thirsty, and thus, you can retrieve the society from downfall. You are the representative to give all Annapraatham daily, so it considered and described by the Epics and the Vedas, dhanam only will reinforce us to Mukthi without any special penance and athyathmic principles to be done by us. This is the most ironic and majestic dhanam which pushes into Eternal saturation by the grace of God; we can have Mukthi only through Annandhanam, thus, we can know and realise the salient feature of this dhanam and we should promote it in huge size of numbers and spread it throughout to our youngsters to do this dhanam so that they can be dispensed by God Himself. Through this dhanam, we can shine in all types of our efforts and our privileges. Like this, we can easily know the best reference of Annadhanam (giving food to all citizens). In kali yuga, only food only cuts off or extends our life span. So, food is essential to live with sakthi to do Dharmic rituals and ceremonies and personal life's activities. So, we should give food to those who are suffering from hunger and thirst. By this we can satisfy the Almighty, and thus, we can be contented with peace and harmony. These two aspects make this universe to direct it to do all the passionate works through us for the welfare of the society. Therefore, we, however must do the needful to give the least to atleast one man or woman food and water, so all will get food and water and God will be pleased, thereby His creation is out of thirst and hunger. This is considered to be the best instrument to enter into the Ecstasy in God's abode. Therefore, we come to know the ecstasy of Annadhanam and its remuneration which is dispensed; what are they? We should keenly note the point and you will find annadhanam at least one daily by this holy ritual, your whole generations will have sathsandhanam etc, will be blessed by Dharmadevathai without doubt, it is sathyam. Many of our ancestors followed this method, they had very imposing positions in this holy residence of Himalayas where Sri Umamaheswara is residing. What a boon to those who are doing Annadhanam! see what it does! Here by, we come to realise the benefit and its glory which have been described apart from regions and religions, all are mankind and we will continuously do Annandhanam upto the mark with our earnings. This Annadhanam has so many holy dispensations; one is, you can become Eswara Himself, if your penance is faithful to all devathas, they will honour you as Eswaramoorthy, so try to follow this principle and be happy till last breath of your generations.

According to our birth, our fortunes and misfortunes are determined and we must respect this ritual, and keep ourselves to the entire satisfaction of Lord Umaparameswaramoorthy. If they are satisfied the whole universe will be contented because they are this universe, and the major contented figure among all principles is Umaparameswaramoorthy. If they feel free, every being will be happily adjoined with satisfaction and they are very near and dear to us and keep us as eyes are kept by the lids. Each and every creature is born in the earth and so-called the other worlds are living on their own and they are very well being concentrated with food, shelter and dresses, these three are the most important necessities to all of us. If we wish to have it, we must do dhana and dharma, as per divine rules. Annadhanam is especially noted as a divine one for we can rule the part of this world. Through God's order, they are all presenting others the presentation to them by their Guru Pathini Herself. It is enough to attain Mukthi. So, you must realise the sakthi of our ancestors. Some are not having even the naked organs and others will not be in working their daily schedules. If we follow our schedule of humans' circular, given by Almighty, at once we shall be the properties of His abode, there will be no doubt at all. It is our experience and thus, we narrate and explain to uplift and better this ether. If oneself is trying to attain one particular place, if he runs, some distance he may not run after this, he must have rest, but man who is simply walking to the place, he may attain the point just late but he arrives the spot. So we should mark our aim or motto, and store it into our whole nervous system, and in this way we should perform our domestic life, our activities are nothing but Divine as we are all having good education and discipline and really we will be saturated with Divine Ambrosia. Then there will be no births and deaths, thus, we are all back from those domestic compulsions and need not worry about whatever job we got, for the welfare of our nation and our home itself. That is ecstatic posture, there, what will be there? Go and you yourself realise the feature of this realisation. This type of spiritualism of all sections, are nothing but one, they are having one man principles and they are explained in their languages and the circumstances and rejuvenation, they are spread among the people, that is all. It is nothing but, any division among all by mankind. It is very close to God only. He, himself operates this cycle very intellectually and calculatively, no error is possible. He feeds and keeps all created materials in a righteous velocity. Thus, we generally will come to know His physical and chemical and mathematical sums, when they are operating in day-to-day life. We can meet them happily with the proper answer, then only they clap and astonishingly realise the marvelous Sakthi of the Almighty. Therefore, we should obediently, truly sincerely joyfully obey God Himself, first He will be voice without form, makes us to realise our presence in various hectic circumstances and thereby we can realise the pervading process of his total Sakthi through His mark of inspiration. Then, from the next day, you will right away have all appropriate things, praising the Lord, and preparing others to praise the Lord with full of confidence and honour.

If He comes into your heart, He will encourage and enforce you at times, it is only because of God's will alone He can dispense it, if you attain it, first you need to surrender thoroughly, and do your duties very well with your heartiest fullness and not lying in any circumstances and not spreading about anyone. Try to keep full of silence in your inner mind also; keep your body and mind clean and clear; if you are living thus, for 30 days continuously, first He will make you feel His presence by spreading good flowers fragrance everywhere and your mind will be with full of peace and shanthi. As a result, your inner and external organs will work without any repair and you can discharge your duties to the entire satisfaction of your superiors (consciousness). Always, be with this mode of life, we or they, no necessity to keep you, you alone be silent and oneness of concentration on an object and thus, your soul will be in the abode of God. There your experience it is to be described by you. The narration with your own commentaries will be sweeter than anything in this world. All will be thought of by your heart as your own brothers and sisters and they too have the same feeling whenever they see you. This is identical theory of spiritualism. Our mind does not impose us to do and be a characteristic slave like worker in our occupation and we will be the rank holder in our materialistic and spiritual life. All are one and the same, you do not want to quarrel with others and there is no necessity to know others' comments about your experiences. Then you will have the scenes of divinity and miraculous happenings will be bestowed by Himself, for the upliftment of others lives, and your own life is totally encouraged by yourself with the saturation of spirituality ever. Thus, you will be very truly forwarding life by your helping others, not at all in the sense of a slave. Maybe you will be riddled by your neighbours, but your range in front of Him is entirely different and your manhood actions are transformed into spiritual embodiments of reflections. Therefore, you will openly try to spread His glorious acts and deeds and spread out God's principles and thus, your time will be spent on. Your life span is prolonging for several years. These, like our ancestral saints and sages, you prolong your Ayul, life span period will be long enough and your duty is emphasised by the representative. He, Himself will come in front of you with fleshy and bony body expressing the needs to be done. It will be pronounced to Him and thus, He will be doing sacred things for his disciples and make the villages as towns, towns into cities, cities will be metro-cosmopolitan cities and as such little by little you change those villages, towns, cities and all types of cities with spiritual enlightenment and divine peace and all follow their own principles as they pray. The significance of the penance and upto the mark of this existence's morality can be remarkably and thoroughly understood by ourselves. Of course, these dedicated soulful men and women are the most blessed people, and they are uplifted by Irai Nesargal (the Thiruthondars) are very much fond of God's abode, as like that, God alone in His time has interest to see His Bhakthimans very well and their minds will be read by God in His time.

In this time if she is silent and passionate of Him, at the very second of time, she will be blessed to be a saint and thus, she will be helping the people of the world by saving them from illnesses and mental depressions and wealth problems. Brother's brutal actions all will perish and he will set a flower herb there and make it steady as pure brotherhood. You will have thousand acres of land as your own income. As he said, within one year, they bought 100 acres of this earth with fruit park and they came in a chariot and took our Guru to that spot and He also stepped down from the chariot and walked for some time, and blessed all of them, very consciously. They are very much pleased and they say, first what ever the income will be every single nayapaise will be donated to your God's service centre, that is, 12 crores of rupees had been submitted in front of our Guru and they kept their words and as per our teachers words, he accepted that money and gave to a confident disciple to build a solid building with width and breadth for residence of all disciples and with three times of full meals. All are very much pleased and they work hard to develop that park as Devi Sri Sathya Loka and Vaikunda. Therefore, our own creator, preceptor, who is the Almighty God will do what is written as our fate, apart from this, He will look after us and do the needful as mighty of the mightiest and doing always the best in our life. So, be with confidence and He, himself does not know His effort's significance. So, be confident with full of goodness and, surrender your life in his lap, then, watch, everything will be yours and you will handle this town through your unexceptional service by which another true disciple is gotten for our co-operation. Be happy. Do not worry.

A machine is designed by an Engineer and he has the copyright after finishing the work, likewise, God also created us and He certifies that we are having the qualifications to reside in this world, and not the death date, because, if a man knows his death date, he will be controlled by anybody. His atrocities will make all the people worrying about their own self and like this he will be a rowdy element, he creates wrong paths to certain people and our shanthi and peace will be not in action, and we prefer to die, for it is better than his misbehaviour. Many, apart from our normal life, everybody will suffer due to his activities and there will no peace of mind in this world. So, if we want to live joyfully we should not enter into others independence and let them live their own life with consciousness and truthfulness, the fundamental root of philosophy must be chastity. If, we sustain our chastity with us only, all will be dispensed by the Almighty.

It not only depends upon our physical activities but it purely resides with our spiritual strength. This alone will give all possessions of His will and pleasure. So, we have to satisfy God alone, and this is the only one penance enough to enrich us with divinity, you need not search God elsewhere; He will be merged with us as astral body. Thus, man can have the chance and rare chance to keep himself with divine power that is, God. To keep our chastity, we can give anything to equal that only, so it should be kept alone, without losing it in any circumstances, it can be achieved only by God's dispensation. Of all ideas regarding Vedas, Chastity is encouraged for our betterment to live with identification without any practical side balance; we have to be God's essential Gunas and as such, we must keep these qualities only, all will surely come to me; nothing can be done; everything depends on the strength of chastity. So, our ancestors particularly emphasised chastity's Highness into words for some reasons. It is notably excellent which is kept as a Gem, our entire life will blossom with fragrance of the lotus flower and it gives peace and pleasure without separation. All are living with contentment and joy upto the last breath, we do not know the proper way, we are doing some activities, is there eternal peace? there is nothing; likewise, she/he may be disappointed most probably. If you wish to attain this highest position, be quiet, and observe silence; Athma Vicharam is the fundamental way to serve us to realise ourselves by His mercy and grace, because He always is with full of mercy and grace upon us, if we utilize it, we can climb to the highest pedestal of God very easily.

So, those who are very much interested in Sathsagam, alone can perform like Him, then, His privacy is occupied by the Eternal Ecstasy. This is why, this human birth is introduced, when we compare with other beings, the per cent age will be very much breathful in counting; so this human birth contains all types of animals' livelihood and thus, He differentiates a true man, can be selected. In this natural enrollment, only one person can be called a MAN.

He, Himself, due to this selfless thoughts and deeds, He is considered to be half part of the Almighty. Then, we are calling Him as incarnation and garland Him, grasping His experiences, but they do not undergo the path, to attain Eternal saturation. In this chance, our creator proposes a noble heart like Him, if we find that holy soul, we must recognize Him as God's Avathar.

He always notes each and every action and its underground situations, which are done by mankind, thus, He proposes us or disposes off with us. In whatever name, you call, there will be no impulses from Him. Even if we mystically pronounce His Holy name, He sanctions all our needs, with a merciful heart. May be parents are very much fond of us. But, in some circumstances, they beat in some brutal ways. Likewise, He has all responsibilities over us, The Creator, He never shows anger, because, He does not know what is anger, such a heart filled with peace, He has at all times. He is ready to forgive all our evils; and boost up our good deeds, so, let us know that God is always, by all means, a good preceptor over us. His mercy alone keeps us, free from illness, poverty and so on.

The instant requirement is one and only bhakthi, to gain His grace and Dharshan. If it is with us ever, He will be with us by all means-This fact should be and must be believed from the bottom of the heart, and Buthi and Sidham. If it is true, the Ever truthful God will be with us at all times and circumstances, not only with us, His personification will be upheld wherever it is necessary to the outer world and thus, we will be the incarnation of Himself, we should have this belief upto 100% percent. Therefore, He is always ready to come to us nearby at the speed of more than light and sound, but we are not having such belief on and of His arrival. That is why, we are worshipping with fear and our worship is not upto the mark. If, it is upto the mark, everything will be His assistance and guidance, all our things will be finished successfully with current speed. If we switch on the next second the light will blossom, likewise if we call Him with full of confidence and surrender, He will give His Holiest dharshan at that very second and fulfill all of our needs. Thus, our deeds will be successful by all means; nothing can done without His ordinance and redemption, all the laws and regulations can be changed by His Excellency, because everything is His own civilisation and creation, and is having the right to exchange all of those laws and regulations to the extent of His will and pleasure. So, we have to settle that all our things are not our own but His own things and they can be remodeled and exchanged accordingly. So, we must be ready to face what His change of order is and what is the realistic thing, we can know only out of his grace and mercy, if we have pure Bhakthi.

He is in search of our one and only bhakthi and purity of heart; have's and have nots He does not weigh us. He proposes to give order what is not to be given; everything is in His Mighty Hands and all the Universal activities are all in His own desire and thus, the whole universe is rotating and metabolism of all creations are going sensibly; So we should realise that all are coming into action only through His rotation so that we may live sinless and comfortably and without disease. This is because of His mercy upon us without partiality according to their karmas done in this birth and also past karmas. And the future karma upto date is waiting for count down and so we must be very much careful to face the consequences. So, we should do and think good thoughts and do the best deeds, thus, our life should be. Everything is coming from Him, will be wonderful and marvelous, so we should do penance or Tapas over the glory of Him. By this we can assimilate the glory of His presence and we must murmur His name not murmuring, but chanting fully the holiest names of His excellence. It will give us perfect Shanthi ever thereby we can do everything successfully. Thus, He, Himself exhibits and Mr. 'x' does it and profits from that, so His Honourable heart will bless us with such a good self and He, Himself gives His excellent position and makes us Himself and He is proud of seeing this scene, such a merciful heart He has. So, we have no fear of anything to go with Him. Apart from Him, we cannot understand by our Budhi and feel His excellence by our sensual organs and heart. We can understand His gracious heart and how much ready He is to come near to us to make our life blossom, we shall feel the vibrations of His excellence, we must be ready to invite the presence of his Greatness and it is not explainable, because such an incident is unexplainable, and it is the greatest incident. Above all, there is no other greater incident in this world for anyone to feel or attain in his life. So Tapasvis and Mumoorthies are doing great tapas to have His dharshan and it is considered to be the minutest among all the happenings in the spiritual world. It is certain for us at this moment.

Our human birth is overall a divine creation, through which alone, we can attain God, all else are to be doubtful. So, all should realise themselves; thus, our annonists, gnanis and prophets emphasised us to realise the fact soon. Then when we come to a conclusion, we can rejoice ever in the Mighty kingdom of the Almighty. Apart from these births, Manhood is the Mightiest birth which is a dispensation, by which we can enrich with all abilities. Thus, our human birth is honoured by God Himself. Our final state of this birth is nothing but to attain our natural abode, where God is dwelling; God is everywhere, but particularly in the mind, seated on a throne, without haves and have nots, His attributes are quite abnormal and His mode of looking at this world is entirely different and His approach is normal. They are totally dramatic; perhaps, all are very good actors and actresses and this world is the dias.

Our traditional concepts reveal Character, Wealth, Education and rules and regulations. Dharsan of God is possible for the character -wise man. We will be considered as the priceless man. We should stand on our own legs—this phrase comes from Sivavagya Sidhar-thus we should be in all times and circumstances.

The value of human life is immeasurable: and this is a golden opportunity by which we have to analyse ourselves, inner and outer structural contents and where the soul is. We have to realise this life's ambition, that is why, we are dispensed with this human physiology and cytology, through which this ideal truth should be realised through our countless births and deaths. When we come out of this miraculous circle, we have to reportedly conclude our soul through senses, this Supreme Truth by which we have to understand the contents of human life. What to do? And what are we to do, thus, we must give a clear lesson to our sensual Indryas and this is the aim of the human life, and such, we can teach a lesson about life and death; then everything will be easy to assimilate our life span, how long have we to strongly run through the path of life. First we start the history of this life's modulation, we have to understand the human's life contents and thereby we can sketch our life into parts, become parents, bringing up the children with enthusiasm, introducing our human life's situation and surroundings, life's ambition has to be taught, identification of our relations and neighbours, introducing the uncertainty of this human life; thus, we should be ready to make ourselves to attain the goal and, we bring our child into this world by which the child will rule out its strength and valour to bow to the commands of the Almighty and through which thoroughly the whole physiological science inside the body, regulatory life, their autonomous service throughout our life is to be checked. This is man's boost and this should be presented towards the human life's perception and perfection and by these, we can attain endless ecstasy. We can rejoice by each and every activity and thus, we can become Mumutzoe, the first stage before a yogi or gnani. Our entire subject of this organic system is the one and only one to achieve the goal of this immense life. We are quite interested though we are taught this science from childhood it will help us in the middle age classes. We can educate the present life's needs, and they will understand which is profit or win and which is failure, we are thinking, a fail in one class is a failure and we try not to live and misunderstandingly commit suicide. Is this the result and profit of education, certainly not. Failures may be not failures, they are binding ourselves in the same class, and give more training and exercises and make us pass with good marks and pass is the designation, this is to be understood with education; but instead of doing this, children simply put an end to their life; if this is buddhi, what will be the benefit of doing the rituals and regulations.

Our education is not at all giving us any fruitful result. Then, our educational systems, lessons and presence of classes are utterly a waste to all those pupils and teachers. Though they are educated up to M.A. (Master of arts) there is no use of their studies and experiences. But if you honour their educational qualification, their age, you should give honour and respect, we have to introduce ourselves through our answer papers, each will be marked more than 70% of marks in each subject, then they will be proud of the pupils and their self confidence and ability to secure wisdom and they themselves proudly recognize them as a big shot of those people; thus, both are very well versed with their progress report, the whole family appreciates them; this is the honour for your education and this will be used for your cultural and civil progress. Many praise the progress of teaching technology and note the model of how to grasp knowledge through education. Thus, they are profited; likewise, our presence will dispense education, wisdom and health and wealth. If you wish to hold these facts simply Bhakthi is to be forwarded towards Almighty without any kind of. particular expectation, you will be governed and dispensed everything and you will be a changed stranger, and this activity will give your relations and neighbours too much of value towards you and they praise with presentations and money. This is what you are interestingly expecting from them. Now everything is in your hands. Enjoy. Service, makes us supreme among all.

For this, we are here as human beings, otherwise we will in the form of other creatures, will not fulfill our desires. First, we should cultivate ourselves and then we can influence others to the fullest customs of spirituality. Otherwise our bhakthi and our spiritual exercises will be the one and only way of exhibiting the breaking of coconuts with bananas and worshipping thus; this may be the L.K.G pipil's standard and in this way we cannot penetrate our life throughout the span with pure gnana yoga. In this modern world, the whole world is copying the word 'Gnana Yoga' is taught through our institutions, the cost for 3days is this, for 5 days it is this and so on... such advertisements are seen, but what do they teach? in what way do they educate, what have they received from their masters, nobody knows and it is not expelled, through the outer world. Something is going on and they are saying something and that is taught by them and they say some experiences have been attained by them and so forth; thus, they convey but the fianal result is NOTHING is accomplished according to us. The spiritual awakening is not at all as easy as we speak or tell through words; we have to pull out all of our organs first and then we can have an experience, the starvation of these sensual organs, and to tolerate them, then tolerance is nothing but it is considered to be the PENANCE. Without our knowledge our inner organs to do spiritual excercises are switched on to do their beginnings and thus, temples are necessary by which we can be started as the solar dance of Lord Natarajar is the symbolic representation and hence we can attain all the responsibilities and their results to the entire satisfaction of our soul and mind. Mind is without body; body is without mind; both can now be operated by soul, this is the Hindu concept, but the other religions do not accept this supreme concept because they cannot and do not climb up to the mark even a millimeter behind our strength and length and that is why, they cannot digest this supreme truth. When they come to the highest level to the entire satisfaction of those concepts, they will be integrated to discover the truth of the concepts of these philosophies and this is the over all supreme truth among all concepts. Therefore, we should cultivate our linguistic (English) power to a certain extent. Thus, we can be a genius in English, whichever, word is suitable, we thoroughly know English grammar and we cannot commit mistakes when we are writing or speaking, are very easy to do well and eloquently. So do not waste time, try not to prolong your power in linguistics first in Tamil and then English. When we pronounce Rasham, our linguistic pronounciation Rasham, this could be a great mistake in linguistics. So, we should clear our mistakes and prove that others are picking up this advice as per schedule. Whoever may be, if one clarifies our doubts he will be honoured as Guru and our mistakes will be erased and new royal English should come out of our mouth. Therefore, we have to speak often to attain a linguistic style, will be corrected by them and they teach new lessons to us and they will clarify our doubts at all times. Therefore, our grammar is unmistakenly maintained only we can boldly use English words. If we have enough will, we shall enforce our title to the extent of the royal English words' origin and thus, we can be well versed in English language from A to Z.

Our Gurukulam's education is the finest way of outcoming disciples who are well versed about their subjects, and penance, and they never deny to do service to all creatures. Lord Krishna did His service to His Gurumars respectively. This shows that we too must have the tendency of service oriented life to elevate very quickly. Modernisation with SENSUAL ALLEGATIONS should be ERADICATED. The highest learning is that by why which we know God all else load and puzzle the mind. So, character is hereby equally said to be the soul, without education we cannot elevate to the Supreme pedestal of Eternity. Our aim, today, is accumulating money, wealth in various places, should be one's requirement is VERY MUCH ESSENTIAL, TO KEEP OUR ACCUMULATED WEALTH; SO WE SHOULD BE CHARACTERWISE STRONG WITHOUT MISTAKE. IF WE FOLLOW THIS FROM OUR YOUNG AGE IT IS SUPERFINE and for this qualification, God will shower all of His blessings on us.

To these kind of mahathmas is presented heaven so marvelous and most beautiful among the beautiful. God is the whole witness of all beings' attitudes and service oriented mentality through which they are having fame and name. If He accepts us, high, then we are all having the ticket of Dharma and Sathyam which are two sides of a single coin. The toss should be up to the mark, thus, He weighs people always and their nature of thoughts and the circumstances of their deeds. So, whenever we are living here, we too should have a mind of dharma and be fond of truth. Otherwise, next birth will be a waiting to these culprits, therefore, we have to live a life which is acceptable by God, Himself. We are struggling very much to lead our human birth fully and contentedly. Otherwise, re-birth will be given with some bonus and we will not at all get salvation at all times. If we wish to saturate with the union of His kingdom, we should think well and do good to others by our mind, thoughts and deeds.

So our bhakthi may be having some unimportant things, but God knows all and ever witnesses all our thoughts and that is why, we will be given boons from Swamy. We are not afraid of God, if our sincerity is capable of truthfulness, we will be certainly blessed by Him undoubtedly. If God does not hear our wants, the whole mistake is due to our own ignorance, ego, anger, thirst and hunger. We are going to temples, churches and mosques, but we never pray to be made free from bondage. In order to ask, we pray Him to dispense a rich and wealthy man with a long period of life span, then, automatically, be crowned by these bad qualities and our whole penance will be wasteful. Our ancestors were ruined in this way, and finally, they undergo births and deaths; such greedy minds never have the dharshan of God at all. Simplicity, in all aspects exhibits our true bhakthi, and therefore, God alone comes before us and does whatever we need and dispenses us the medicines for all our diseases. The truthful bhakthiman will be always speaking, doing penance and thinking of God only. Thus, we can identify such holy men. They never give place to anger, hunger, thirst but they will be ready to bear these inconveniences and through their pure bhakthi, they attain God's holy feet. Such truthful men and women are today's need. There are lacs of men and women, for speaking but very few are having the dispensation of God. Only through non-violence and sacrifice their whole life span is spent in order to get relief from unconditional births-deaths cycle. So, if we wish to be blessed by God, we should be ever pious and such a typical mind is to be consciously ours ever. Then, our efforts are divinely twittering like thunder and lightening. When we go to sabarimalai Lord Ayyapa Himself, stands in order to receive this truthful, original bhakthiman. We have to attain this holy state.

We, all are very much keen in attaining Eternity, according to my Goodself, only one second time is enough to have that opportunity, what is needed; one thing Patience and hardwork to reach the goal and broadmindedness. The ever blissful will attain this superlative activity without unavailabilities of good things. Now, we do not wish to assimilate this concept ,and there is only one way to do it, selecting the task is correct or not, and past, future karmas' recognition and disciple's growth in the department and so on. One servant is gone, the master weeps; the leader leaves, then the servants do not respond, between these two, who is the master? Try to understand the meaning of the phrase. Likewise, we completely consider marks, that the boy has secured then who is the master. So, do think. Likewise we are weeping and crying before a doctor's presence. He says, he has done the best, and then everything is in God's hands; so is there any more of doctor's diagnosis. Likewise, we are not at all crying and weeping before God. If it is done, no herm will occur. So do pray well and believe that God has mighty power, through which He dispenses good health, this kind of confidence, if it is done, all are well. But we do reversely, what fools men are..!

We should pray God, for everything and it will be given by Him, when time comes. Likewise, if we are submitting our grievences, He solves the problems, but we are few in number, who worship and pray the Almighty to grant such and such things. He is the mightiest among all. If our prayer is correct, He will save us 100% so, with full of belief our demands will be surely rescued. Otherwise He will not do anything for us. So, God sees the heart of oneself; thus, we do, what is to happen? Nothing more to convey. If He thinks to give anything, nobody can stop it; at the same time, if God does not think to give, whoever may recommend, he will not at all get from Him, therefore, we must understand God's heart like it, He minds the heart, if it is full of love towards Him, He is the one who possesses all by His Mightiest Sakthi. So, there should be no shyness when we go in front of Him. Those culprits cannot go first and do not worship him at their level best. So, they are dejectedly blabbering like some animals. This attitude should be eradicated, can be, we should save our life.

Then, a matter is to be remembered our inner ears and physical body do not do anything, which is not at all life. We have to feel the uncertainty of our body; its shape varies as we are getting older, our panchboothas do not work according to the intellect, will be sure, that we are all in queue, to attain them. Without entertaining these obstacles, no sort of civil beings, betterment in all situations and we have to obtain patience and do penance, we must use our time and date, thus, if we do in regular basis, our mind will be everlasting, our memories will be in the righteous ways, absolutely not for materialistic needs, if this kind of liberation is given, we can have some food which gives us strength to physical and intellectual fields. We had a fine certificate about our tamil poetry, it says, we have reached the pedestal and so, others need our help, we do not do such business, we, but are nicely getting disappointments, who is to be believed, I hope personally that tamil will, is going to guard us; but we are dejected for a while, now we are alright, and will receive all through our goodself at an earliest date. Do avoid cowardish exercises, do pray Almighty, ever never stop, with full of confidence in our hearts we have to think about His deeds and chant the holy manthra and this will lead us away from such inabilities. We can win over these happenings? No, it gives us a goodness and importance to have a heavy heart with full of confidence and through which we have power to be thought of. Never discourage yourself by your own thoughts because God is dwelling there and is the unseeable ability, but He sees ever and everything so, we are to be thankful for all that we had, have and good earnings and listening is going on; this means that the world is full of divine perception and alright to be giving devaprachnam throughout our day, we can easily declare to have earnings of some thousands per day. But it is not acceptable to us we have to earn more than the amount, as we can live a luxurious life till the end. Then we can easily enter into the palace of Godliness and thus, we can transfer us into savam, that is without buthi and siddham, so we should not blame for this loss even more sanyasins or ourselves because the cause is in the forms of conditions.

If you wish to have ambrosia you should be in this procedure for about 5 years. After that time passes, you will be dispensed with such secrets of truthfulness of the Athman and how it survives. One may be a multi millionaire, but in our world, he is nothing just one of the creatures. What is creation? The first question's answer. I do not apparently convey if it is implicit, express our vibrations, it will be like oxygen molecules and thus, will breathe. So through your breath you will have divine sort of happenings there and as well as will be knowing what is death? These questions' answers will be erased from your mind and analysis of both of them you had lost time of growth, such manners of Maya dwell in it, you should get out of it, do chant Rama manthra intensively, you will be free from this cruel situation, after thorough medication of your own reference, you can get it very easily. While this message is given to you particularly the disciple and the Guru will be down under for some time and at all times you are in the Blissful ecstasy, it cannot be spelled out, and cannot know the inner hidden treasure of your own self, thus, a day or more, one moment will be enough to make a sidhar, therefore you should be ready through doing athmavisara, you will be awakened and finally, you will have the booster without fail. After these consequences your survival is too short and your natural saturation will be held as stars or planets through the milky way of astrological positions. You will serve all and you will be worshipped. An inner most feeling round you, you will implicitly insist to hold on, by all means at all times. So, go through according to your Guru's definitions and demonstrations then it will be easy to save the sum of your breaths, that is the one and only way to be with the Athman, the physical body is given to all of us. Try to chant manthra with pure confidence.

God is everywhere, but we are not having such gifts given by penance to see, chant the leelas and His glorious deeds. We must be free from these worldly happenings for some minutes, in those times we have the deepest thoughts of God, and His earnest dispensations, given to us. Thus, if we have significant thoughts, it will give both materialistic and spiritual strength both in this birth and henceforth of times. Therefore, without the pronunciations of His presence we have to try to some extent to have time to pray and thank Him for His unexpected gifts that are given to us. If somebody has been endowed enormously with health and wealth, that kind of people, one day, they must realise the true factor of the impermanent nature of this life, as a result, they will detach themselves from this deepest materialistic life and will try to hold God's hands for their convenience and since these efforts are done, they will surely be blessed by Himself, and attain the highest pedestal of Godliness. So, sathsangam is more necessary than solitary prayer, because it is a group which many members get together and discuss many divine factors and through this mode, we can attain rich knowledge about God's efficiency and Man's inefficiency. Such thoughts give him/her, to enrich with the bliss of the certainty of mental steadfastness. This kind of eternal life is to be dispensated; that should be the prayer offered by us and through this continous prayer, at one time or other, some metamorphosis will happen both of mind and body in today's life, we will be able to attain the feet of His Holiness. Saint Manickavasaghar said, if you look after God, with tears, certainly you will be blessed and He will grant you His beautiful, ever shanthiful characteristic sketch which can be seen by us. This boon is only out of His mercy. In such a way, our prayers should be at the most empowered to control our senses and through our command they will react and there will be no responses for the activities, but the waves should be from Himself and they will give peace by means of shanthi and contentment. Our entire life should be dedicated to the Mighty hands, such belief will give us more strength to meet out any kind of challenges in our life's survival. If we need one thing, we should apply to Him, with sincerity and faithfulness. This is realised when we get the merciful activity for our sake only. Until then, we do not have such confidence to have belief on His unparalleled grace and mercy. It cannot be compared with anything else in this world. Our help is done only expecting something from the affected one of their family members. But He never expects anything from us as His remuneration, come and go, it will be significant approach of his Eternity. Such action is on the full flow, we can easily attain confidence and faith will grow steadily upon Him. But He does not show Himself within the empowered prayer and confidence. He gives tests, after innumerous experiences only, He will certainly give us His superior seat, equal to Him, will be bestowed by His truthful mercy and grace. His heart is most widened, and each and every human being is expected to pray and thank Him with full of realisation of His presence. To some He will be just voice without form, for some people, He will appear a structure but no voice, very few people can attain His presence with form and voice, such people are very much countable among all the population of the world. His mercy may differ from one to another, and this is empowered not only by God, but by the ones whom He has appointed as messengers and duty fulfilling authorities. By this we will get such periodical posts, and thus, we will discharge our duties to the entire satisfaction of Himself. If He is pleased with our doings, He gives Himself as the most empowered gift. It is achievable only through this birth(human beings), so that this birth is noted as rare, unexpected, God's will. Whenever we or our parents wish, this kind of body and daily discharging our duties will differ from one another, from school to school the syllabus is different, but the lessons are one and the same, if one realises, it is sufficient to get liberation.

This life's primary goal is to attain our beginning original state, which is the abode of God, up to this time, we are also an embodiment of God only and due to curse or His will, we have descended to this earth or some other places in order to return after this our earthly survival. So, our ancestors insisted us with a sathvic mode of life, for which state, we have to discover the point and the mode of attainment of the soul. Thus, we should be able to realise the natural truth from our own experiences, and this life will be fruitful for us and the creator too. Otherwise, we have to return to this Universe, to experience all sorrows and agonies of the ether, and in this manner, we will be certainly rotating with the speed of the planets and stars. We can get rid of all of our sins and dispensations. In this juncture, we can attain Divineness to the entire satisfaction of the Almighty, because He is always within our heart and controls all and regulates our organ systems without any consequences(bad). He is towards us to attain our natural phenomena of life's goal, Liberation, that is, getting relief from births and deaths, what cruel experiences are births and deaths? If we realise the metabolism of those experiences, we will never try to prolong time in this earth; such a horrible experience it is? How many months, 10 months what a long period, we have to bear all sorts of illnesses and inconveniences, day after day, in the womb the baby is growing within the embryo sac, well and at the time of delivery, we see the lady, she will be suffering with full of horrible secretions, one after another, the pain increases and then, she gives birth to a male or female baby, those who have undergone through, these types of experiences can realise the responsibilities, nothing is in our hands. It is in His Mightiest hands, He Himself without form and voice ejects the baby from its residence to the world. Just like that, at the time of death, what type of agonies we have to experience. If it is remembered, we will not at all want to offend. Because of our affection on this fleshy body, we are having so much of jealousy and ego, but we have no notion of the soul. It is insisted, one day the baby will perish, but the soul is ever living, it cannot be buried or thrown into the fire or pyre. It is Siranjeevi. Therefore, the everliving concepts of soul must be illustratively realised, and it is the way, through which we can attain the Holy place of Divinity. Through our materialistic life only, we can realise the innermost nucleolus of the atom by atom, thought which we can easily realise the value of the body and soul. The everliving soul should get new and new fleshy bodies each time throughout time, it is the will of our creator, because of this, we are undergoing very new experiences, through which we can get rid of all desires and affections, so, we have to put a full stop mark, by which we can realise the truth, that is, no one in this wide, spread world, has ever at all experienced and fulfilled all his desires and needs thus, if we realise this truth, we can get rid of all sins and actions. No more desires will arise from our heart and mind also. For this reason, we have to be free from desires. Desireless mankind is today's necessity, and to be fond of nature to avoid sins; and Dharma can be established with pure Divine basis.

Therefore, we come to a conclusion about the clarification, that this life is a boon by which we have to spend each and every second, and try to realise the value of life and then, we should think of the Creator, the Preserver and the Destructor, by which we can get Gnana and through Gnana, we are free from all types of bondage of the earth; then we come to a conclusion that there is no sin and no remuneration for our pure acts too. If we in this way, try to live without any obstacles, He will finally show His face to us and thus, we can have the Vishvaroopa Dharsan of Himself and attain Mukthi. There is nothing more for attaining because our soul, like an atom which has served so many crores and crores of years of livelihood that has gone through, the Eternal Rest is required. That is why, God gives and dispenses the soul gets freedom from each and every oscilation of the glimpses of worldly aspects whether they are active or inactive. And that is why, our ancestors are insisting on us to get rid of, from the worldly anxieties and get free and not be bounded by any kind of boundaries or limitations to lead a full-fledged life by each and everyone in all the situations. Therefore, some restrictions and boundaries are clarified by the Vedas, Epics, Puranas and Stories. They come forward to have a good remark by all creatures of the society and therefore, we have to proceed with good thoughts, deeds etc.

Human tendency is with the restrictions of this fact, but, Maya, itself has the ability to provide a wrong pathway to the soul by its natural grasping of bad thoughts and deeds, original is rare, but the duplicates are several and it is the sharp example to this version. So, we have to have truth in mind thus, we should not go by the intuition of bad habits and therefore, we should be always awake to get through to the truth of supremacy; hence, we can come out of the world of maya and anything illusionary will not be picked up in any way, So, such purity of mind, is now needed by Humanity, if they are transformed in this way, natural calamities will be reduced and pure peace can be inhaled by the creatures of the world.

Of all births, the human birth is considered as a boon dispensed by God to the soul, the soul never changes into any other form, it has no destruction, it is ever living from age to age, in all ages, according its karmas. The soul takes birth with a fleshy body, which is a composition of five elements and so this human birth has the top most rank among all creations of this Universe. It is only because of attaining the goal that is, saturation with the Almighty, that we have come from that original abode; this life is a mere temporary one, and so it has no value, after death, the soul remains deathless, it has no birth and death. It is everliving, that is why, it is called Siranjeevi (Ever living). If this Universal truth is realised by us, there will be no taste in the worldly objects and we can make ourselves clean both materialistically and intellectually. Therefore, we should know this birth's sanctity or creation by God, Himself. If throughout this whole span of life, we have to struggle hard all for nothing but wealth, we believe that if we have more wealth with ourselves, we can be contented and right royal life will be ours. It is a false concept. Money is necessary for leading the life to some extent only. But, there are some things here which cannot be bought by spending lots and lots of money; for example we can buy very sophisticated bed, but not sleep, we may buy so many books but, there can be no easy route to get a good educational standard, by our money, we cannot extend our life span for a single second. In Hospitals, we see this sentence 'Doctors dress the wound, but only God heals it' by this we can come to know the value of our medical science. Whatever thing we find in this world, everything is only through God only, victory or defeat, failure or success they are determined by Himself, we may try several times in order to get Victory by all efforts, but it is in His hands. If this one and only concept is realised, man will not go after wealth accumulation. We are earning more than 36500 lacs of money, nobody says that he will survive 36500 days; if this is mathematically analysed, it is one year (365 days) if we live 100 years, it is just some hours in God's measurement. Therefore, in the Bhagavat Gita Lord Krishna Paramathma revealed that "I am the Time and the factor of times, present, past and future, if you realise it thoroughly beyond doubt, then you can feel the presence of Myself." That is why He is worshipped in the Universe, so many people have seen Him and have talked to Him with friendship as the basic factor. We are hearing, seeing our epical dramas, cinemas, etc., and we sense the vairagya in them, but when we return home, we just ignore the essence of the epics. So, we can say these soulful epics are just in the form of discourses and sometimes, they are seen through dramas. But there is no gain by this kind of vairagya. If we wish to attain God, we should be ever ready to do anything and with full of confidence. This sincere confidence and simplified patience make us sadhus and the experiences in life make us the sincere, purified soul which is saturated with Almighty. Therefore, we must have full of Bhakthi for all of our deeds are only through and by His will and pleasure and every thought is noted by Him, by this belief, that we have, we would not involve in unnecessary thoughts and deeds. Each and every action which is performed in any way, it is known by the Almighty, because the cause of them is nothing but God only.

We are struggling so much because of the curses of chaste women, natural destructions, violence and also no dedication on the peoples' part. We commit many more sins and that is why, we ourselves are reasons for our own obstacles. So, we should change our mode of life from this minute and chant Holy Manthras of God and decide to dedicate to live with Nature; if we do this there will be no time being obstacles and troubles, at any cost. Therefore, we have to change selfishness into unselfishness. If all are well settled automatically, we among all the people will be having a satisfied life, otherwise, our life is no good for us first, and others too. Like all the creatures, man is living and is perishing one day. If we think very much about death our desires will vanish and Gnanam will dawn. Therefore, death is only for the body, not for the soul. It is SIRANJEEVI; it is ever living, with the order of the Almighty. There will be necessity for us to think about our REST ASSURED....our creator is ever the controller of all happenings and He identifies each and every creature; He knows everything apart from HIM, there is nothing in the universe. Whether we believe or not, He is not affected by anything. But if we are in search of God and our search of God is attained, our life will be led by peace and Eternal bliss; otherwise it will be filled by all means with all kinds of miserable happenings and for sure lose our mental equilibrium, thus, our entire life will be a waste and it is equal to creatures life styles.

THE HIGHEST LEARNING IS THAT BY WHICH WE KNOW GOD, ALL ELSE ONLY LOAD AND PUZZLE THE MIND, according to this verse, we should be awake and alert at all times, to seek God, we must do sadhanas and exercises throughout our life, and thus, we get liberation. It is an Universal truth. Truth alone blossoms from the very near truth only. Therefore, we should truthfully lead a truthful life, as such, we can be a truthful human being, and thus, we can attain the Eternal Truth. Like a Railway locomotive engine, it will be running in the same speed and reversely as well it can run in the same speed. Both ways, pulling and pushing, it has the same speed, likewise the locomotive engines are constructed. So, also truth alone can survive with its same way of possession of Dharma and itself can make us and others to adhere to the same dharmic ways as it is having the same speed while pulling and as well pushing. Therefore, we may have to live a long period of life or a short period of life, we should earn justly as a truthful man. In this manner if we get fame from others, then our life should be the same even when congratulated by all and so we will be worshipped as a Devatha. In this process our ancestors are worshipped in the name of 'Kulathievam' by their following generations. This is the way that man becomes God. If one has attained this stage, he will take incharge of controlling this Brahmanda's regulations and all the creatures will be fed at the proper time, and births and deaths are to occur at their appropriate time, whatever God wishes and does He should discharge all His duties to the entire satisfaction of His own self, then only He is considered to be the right person to hold the Godliness, He must discharge all His duties without failure. All will worship Him. He has to fulfill their needs and at the same time, He is gracious with merciful character. But at the same time, when the fixed time comes there will be no reconsideration or delay in sanctioning death and giving diseases through which gain or failure must be dispensed without any grace to that particular soul. According to Him, everything is equal but according to their karmas, they should be punished or forgiven by the person who is immersed in Godliness. His trials are done without any fluctuations or there no forgiveness will be sanctioned by Him. According to their karmas, they should be punished as the rules of Garuda Purana, and this divine person is to be honoured with respect and bestowed with God's presentations. People who come to Him should be well wished by Him. Thus, his rulership should be done without any partiality.

WHAT ARE our thoughts, they become deeds, whether they are good or bad, when they come into action, they will view their origin and their service to do take away our Jeevan or fly out our jeevan. So, we have to normally be with good thoughts, of course, encircling us, a Cresent based Thejas will be formed. Beyond this round (holy) there is nothing or nobody who can penetrate and we will be safe in this materialistic livelihood. So, it is stressed, that we should be full of noble thoughts and have good thoughts, and thereby we can easily serve all. So, we should impress this nature of thoughts and deeds, therefore, we have to take birth in good family. So, it is possible to have good thoughts and they are moralised into the best happenings. Such life is designed and dispensed by God to man. So, we are to be ready to do and get good result from our over all life. This human birth is gifted by God Himself to make man realise about his body and soul's energy and thereby, we will get His mercy on us fully, thoroughly, what we introduce to our soul and body, will be empowered with full of divine sakthi, as a result, the whole Universe will be enlightened with Harmonious Ecstasy. Thus, Mankind becomes divine if it is divine, there is no chance to do evil to anybody else.

All are wise to be liberated from passion and co-operation, this is the only path where if it is obtained, we have to spend our time in preserving His name with chanting and this will enhance and guard us at all times. Those who are surrendering mentally, towards God, they will be guarded and guided at all times, circumstances by all means. Almighty takes incharge to keep them hale and healthy, and gives money as a boon for their sufficient survival, thus, they are controlled by Him too. So, they are not to worry at all times, because they are the sons and daughters of Almighty. Bhakthi, devotion and complementary mentality are the needs to become a fellow in His diary, -Sir, our name is entered in His diary, there will be no harm or shame without doubt. So, first of all, we have to capture His mighty source of all, we have to rejoice soulfully. We are going to temples in order to pray but we stand before God as beggars, we wish to have a house, car, money, education for passing, and nothing more than these articles. He has abundance of articles. There He expects LOVE and sincerity to hold a boon from Him. But, nobody, bargains this sort of a process of business, so, He dejectedly shuts down His shop and starts to His Abode; where everyone likes the Almighty. He resides for ever, (Yoganithra, sleeping while in waking state) it is a boon of God and thus, He preserves all worlds in His control. Such a Sakthiman He is! So, we must bend our head and salute Him for His greatness and eradication of evils. So, fearless life will be owned by us and therefore, we should not involve in things that are hated by Him.

Whenever, we are free and leisurely sitting, do pronounce Sri Gayathri Manthra this manthra chanting gives us everything without any doubt at all. If this Holiest Manthra is recited with Kastamouna stage, its power is very much effective, Gaya—means body; kalp—means without destruction; in all times, ages, it is ever living, that is why, it is called Sri Gayathri's manthra. Whatever ritual is, first we call Shree Gayathri devi to give us Her fullest blessings, and thus, we should finish the penances and manthra-chanting, thus, our prayers will not be in vain. So, we have to have as Upadesha from an eminent scholar/pandit of Gayathri manthra, and after initiation, we can proceed our activities, whatever the activity is, everything will be fruitful and a success. So, Gayathri manthra chanting's uses are abundant and it will keep our astral and fleshy, skeletal body in a fresh situation, and it may dispense all those who wish to have it as their own. Thus, after knowing the value of Gayathri manthra, we should spend our time in chanting it, we should be ready to have immense value of human civilisation and cultural customs.

In Bhagavad Gita, Bhagavan Sri Krishnan emphasises, "Among all the manthras, I am GAYATHRI manthra", thus, you can realise its immense value and do not waste time and if you chant with full of silence, you can be boosted by wealth, health and nothing untoward incidents will happen. So, we have to pick up this holy Gayathri manthra's chanting will give us good character, good name and fame, abundant wealth in our day-to-day life. Most probably, if we chant the Holy manthra, we should practically realise these mundane experiences and so, we have to be patient and peaceful. Throughout our life, we should not have a nick name, i.e., Innocent man, likewise, we are called by all, automatically, one day, God exhibits us as a patient man, free from all types of bondage and they will feel guilty minded and thus, Sri Gayathri devi, where in these situations, will not be present. So, Be careful and beware of chanting manthra with full of faith and confidence. These qualities bring us peace and contented life. The word 'Satisfaction' cannot be rewarded by Lord Uma-Mahaswaramurthy, because, our mind is always rotating around materialistic particles and articles.

Those, who are very much interested in having connection with the Almighty, first get relief from evil thoughts, in consequence of their consequences they should abstain from several activities like drug consumption, ladies incidents, not cheating others by any means, surely adhering to and cultivating response to yogic principles, orthodox views, pure vegetarianism, fearlessness in all aspects and activities:- these are the fundamental needs, WILL BE SANCTIONED TO HIS ARDENT DISCIPLES, day-to-day necessities, all will be gotten by His mightiest will. Thus, the entry into the spiritual entrance and one day they are given convocation with Vedas principles.

Why should we adhere to vedic principles in our daily life? Because, their contents are ever Universal, their and they are ever-living concepts, in both ways as per theoretical and take them in trials, they are ever suitable and their profits are innumerous, their concepts are ever-living and according to our mode of life, which is insisting us to follow them, because, they are ever Universal. If one takes into consideration and follow the principles, he will get salvation surely. So, they are immortal and they are by all means, crossing our day-to-day lively activities; such divine power they have. So, they are in action, even after 10,000 years, whenever, we go through them thoroughly, they are evergreen and our concepts of human life are mentioned up to the marks of life. Therefore, they are everliving concepts, and have the power to enroll in our lively assets. So, if we go through these universal values, they give different meanings and thereby we can set a new life in order to grow with chastity, most powerful media, and this is the secret, by which we can attain Eteranl salvation. Then, if they are enforced in our daily life, we can realise the principles, which are contending, give us peace which is eternal; also, those who are not interested in God's presence, without their senses, if some crisis arise, they too hear to do sathyam as Vedas, in such a way, they are including the everlasting concepts. If we follow them, we are profitable enough, and these concepts will be concentrated, one, who has life sentence, can write up his life without a single mistake.

Therefore, all the Vedas grasped by saints and rishis, through their spiritual power, tried their level best and gave them for our own betterment to us. In our daily, today and yester, and tomorrow, these concepts are ever unchanging and they come along with us by all means of usages and through which we will be benefitted both in materialistic and spiritual, they are walking with the guidance of them. That is why, they are honoured as Vedas' and it is adorned in churches, mosques and temples irrespectively and all the benefits are for us entirely. He, Himself will be a companion, to lead a liberated Eternal life. Those who are not interested in these concepts, they can just leave from the church, after finishing the ceremony is over. They come to the churches, because they are searching Jesus in churches, outwardly, but He is in the midst of all happenings of our day-to-day life. Time will come, we can remember our concepts, one by one, and then, we will be liberated from sects and creeds. So, we should be beneficial, whether we utilize our Vedas or not. The one and only reason, may be, we should live with peace and without hurdles, if a vedic man is able to conduct dharmas, which are including them. So, God has given these concepts to only one and through him, all are bound to be respected, honourable to all of us. Then, we will be satisfied with our own life and these are ever unchanging and ever-living specimens of our life. Naturally, we have two minds, so, should concentrate with only one. You can be well and good throughout your age ever.

Among all Almighty's creations, mankind's metabolic system of all fields is extra-ordinary and even doctorates exclaim about it, and its operation throughout our human body, its shape is not properly known, by anybody else thereby science is not a proper channel which can prove its- METABOLISM AND ORGANIC SYSTEM'S AUTO WORKINGS: we have education, thus, we are medical practioners, and we check up the patients and dress wounds; but, our Almighty heals the wound; finally, the doctors tell the patient, which is a mighty creation in the Universe. So, if

God's mercy is with us, we can win any kind of race, and we can be satisfied with our activities. We are living morally throughout life time, but, it is not at all sufficient, we must acquire wealth and health. Such boons can be dispensed only through His Mighty power. Thus, human races are running, and if we trust ourselves dedicated throughout our whole life, we can win the race by all means and get contentment. Also, we all wish to perform a good life and we should not be affected by diseases and illnesses. But if He sets right our breathing we can live easily. Our metabolism cannot be realised by even all eminent doctorates. Here our scientific field bows its head, without knowing what to do! So, we have to be cautious and it is not enough in the case of God, so, penance and acceleration of mind in order to search the Good Being to realise the facts. But, our working and should be sincere, and nothing horrible can happen happening in favour of us. If we shut our ego of education, wealth, and approach like a child, the final stage, we can win the race; thus, Almighty has a powerful heart. He, dispenses all our efforts to have success with ease to be served by the people and for the people. In this way, we can win over the scientific world.

Chapter - 5

It is Now or Never

'Time and Tide wait for no man" :— This is one of the finest proverbs and an Intellectual, Universal Truth, when we finally do try to analyse this we can come to so many conclusions, thus, just if we miss a thing within 20 seconds, what is the collapse between failure and success and thus, we are always in action through our mentality, we will give its honour and utilise it very properly; so, then we compromise that everything is in action. According to our karmas, we meet victory or failure we are listening to many more scholars elaborately explaining the acute meaning of time, we, then utilise it properly and we are happily spending our time, in order to achieve something in our life time. So, our ancestors gave IInd place for worldly happenings but the 1st place is rewarded only to discharge our duties without a waste of even 10 seconds, then, all will be safe and secure. We are simply speaking and earning some rupees from the organizing committee, blabbering something with relation to Ramayanam and Mahabharatham, or Periapuranam and Thiruvasagham-fully pronouncing, will be believed to have lightening dawn of Sun, we also make us divine, and thus, we can attain salvation. So, our motto will be ready to do customs wide relationships and must do whatever procedure to give and take these policies. Therefore, we should do our rituals and ceremonies at a proper time to do the same.

If we are lazy, and sleeping without stop, we have to earn, money is the common trade. But, we definitely know the value of TIME, we do not waste even a single second. OK. If time's worthiness and value is not known, what will happen? A patient in a serious condition who is admitted and eagarly waiting to know the result of CT and MRI scans and waiting till it comes and reveals, that something's serious but, not at all serious, instead of playing indoor games, please do chant the Holy manthra of your God's name and praise His noble qualities, such type of prayer will us give a boon as miracles and cannot be exchanged as 'CAN', such belief will give us both intellectual and materialistic strength to face any kind of final result. So, we trust ourselves in God, and expect miracles to happen, when we are in an unconcentric period, dispenses good health and wealth. According to the Almighty, if our prayer is as good as even in nature, the result by which the doctor can save capably the patient. Such kind of Bhakthi, hereby is needed to achieve all things, when we witness god's mercy. Such mercy and grace can be given to all souls at the same time, nothing will be miserable and we can achieve all doubts into fulfillment. It is only God's sake. His immeasurable sakthi, can do anything and we can elevate us to the abode of Heaven. This is also one of His mighty gracious looks that we have.

We are believing that money can provide us all our needs; but it is a false concept; if it is true, many cinema Artists will not hang themselves and finish their lives. According to our ancestral scriptures stressfully note down that our efforts fail but final result which will be allotted by god will be a truthful one. So, due to our actions, they should not prick our mind at all times, in all circumstances. So we should be very careful in choosing our thoughts to be transferred into deeds; if everyone is having sense of humour and simplicity, they can be free from bondage, and automatically we become sadhus. Then, God from the sanctum sanctorium will ever be in search to find and trace such type of truthful devotees. So, if there is devotion universal love can flourish without any doubt, we are in need of so much money, wealth and health; but our efforts do not coincide with our deeds; we are all having different kinds of mind. It must work hard, may give up all our needs due to the situations, we are punished or regarded by Him. If His support is with us always, we can have darshan of Him undoubtedly. So, we should be normally ready to live and leave; this is the simplest formula to get rid of our karmas, deeds and thoughts. Such a man is called and honoured as a prophet or Annonist.

All nations in the name of self protection, are all concentrating on manufacturing bombs, which are very dynamic and are not utilised to produce electricity or fertilizers; on the whole their concentration is to be ready to use these weapons for war; violence is everywhere, we can see, in cinemas it is a powerful media through which we can spread out the importance of peace, or domestic relationship, the value of human birth and its integration, but we sow much violence in order to make a good collection of money, and in the name of cinemas, we are spending crores and crores of money and we earn multi-crores, but to the society, they are not propagating any salient features such as non-violence, sacrifice and dedication. In our old films they emphasise husband-wife relation and the value of patriotism and so on. Today, we are readily preparing cinemas, not only do we bother about anything but they are only money machines, for that, we can go extensively in the civilised mood and we are ready to destroy our cultivation and civilisation, thus, we spend our time and money, but there will be no signs for the development of the forthcoming generations. They only escape from these materialistic views, dynamic creating of our sense of confidence to certain extent to be calm and patience. We have to cultivate natural qualities, when a child is born, we have to turn the table from "A" to "z". Then we have to find out some so-called graceful true friendship of nations, between our kith and kin; otherwise we have to destroy our mankind without any collapse from outer strength. Our governments should pass resolutions to make these people march towards nation's pride.

When at the time of our birth so-called relatives and friends, all with smiling faces are gathered together and sing lullaby in words and they christen a new name and those have participated share sweets and sandal paste to exhibit their happiness and the new one too; and the name of course, is old and we should be getting all others by means of Good character and best conduct or marvelous education etc; for such special casualties, we should be named by the society as Socrates, Neoplean, Vivekanandar, Bharatiar, as they may have other names, but the society titles a new wonderful name as these. As per principle, all children will have good nick name and thereby we should elevate ourselves through every second of time. We should dedicate our work to the nation. Such kind of people are known as the padmashree award winners, according to myself. We must arrange to live our life by dedicating it to the nation by our selfless rendering of service to the betterment of mankind. Therefore, if our conduct is without any repair, all the other aspects will be going the best way and earn good name and fabulous, extraordinary fame; thus, we are pronounced because of titles, our neighbours and especially parents will be honoured by even churches too. What a brilliant situation it is! As such, we must cultivate our civilisation throughout our life with education. We should go through any hardship to show our responsibility to work for the development of the nation and ourselves. As per all the laws of various religions, the basic principles what they stress is one and the same, but when we go through with patience, we can easily understand mind of the nation. Then how do we keep its independence without any sacrifice. Those who sacrifice their lives now, our nation is being elevated through all the policies and thus, we should try, to elevate in all directions. India is probably the most efficient country and it never has been fond of waging war with other nations. Its motto is to live co-operatively and rule with obedience with our own possession. The government is to work hard for the welfare of the people and we should do what they stress. India is an unequalised country among all nations.

To get rid of the situation of the Mars, we cannot even think about this trial and those who travelled in rockets (3) fired up and there was no gain or loss. All this is poetical, just imagination. A lot of money was spent in this regard, and we should not continue this non-sense oriented activities and make others fools too; it is to be surely condemned, not to believe this falsehood. But there is no belief in Indian rituals and ceremonies which are the total elaborations of science, they are insisted upon as pure truth, which can be agreed by the people. We say this in the belief of their spiritual oaths. This is idiotic to us, but the performance process is true. We are fluently throwing our wealth and manufacture many varieties of destructive weapons and sell them in the world market, as such they earn a lot of money, and thus, they are pure reasons to encroach upon vital activities throughout the world. If U.S.A. is controlled with by natural calamities, everything will be normal and naturally human beings will be with satisfaction. Now, that nation is cheating in the name of science, we are all buying and preserving the weapons or sell them as all old iron particles; thus, we are losing all a lot of wealth and our nation does not realise the fact. A day will come, all the citizens of the world will realise this is true; What has been said in the beginning by the Indians is 100% true; we are all being cheated by those bloody idiots in this way. That nation will be begging before all the nations. After this state, the whole mankind will be the Guru to all the nations and thus, we can be living smoothly and honestly. Our sole prayer to God is to please give us proper knowledge and power to keep our ancestral customs and to have to tell the truths in our ethics, they are nothing false, they are the fact that we have to understand. If you are to come to me, I will clarify the truths and the whole human society will live with peace.

This is considered to be the Ananda life, but, crores and crores of people feel miseries and difficulties, for example, I want to say one thing, that prostitution is now-a-days, confirmed as not at all a fault to the society, and they are living, and thereby they are earning and they, same time, themselves cook and arrange for tea etc, living with and like all other family women. They are not doing well and according to God's government, it is the most sinful incidence, we understand this truth fully and realise through soul, but, they do not neglect this majestic job and they live more than other women's life style; but they say that they are working for some time, and then they earn money and do not expect anything from others, they do not care about ration card and voter ID, but they are living they say without any damage to the society, and thus, we request you to condemn them.

We have to stand before the court of God, when there is a notice to us and, then the punishments will be severe and we should neatly and clearly conduct such things. If we are interrogated the punishment will be extraordinary and arrogant, and you cannot even imagine, how it is? Likewise, we should be ready to gain the support from God, and all the surroundings will be with full of the brightest light, which means, truthfulness and patience, and thus, the spiritual education is seeming to be very easy, but it is so difficult to lead it and for gains of this divineful activities. Thus, we should get salvation through Godliness through our emergency, and must do our duties. This type of manlihood is with us, you cannot enrich mind of each other. We must not have our name involved in about any mischievous things. We should adhere to humanities goodness and politeness, with these, if we handle ourselves we will purely go on in this way, and thus, we can popularize ourselves in these duties. If an idol of Goddess or God is manufactured with full of resistance of rich divine power pranaprathista is essential to store it with godly honour in the idol and, if we keep it in our home, with Guru's upadesh, regularly, we will be alerted at all times, and our inner consciousness will be always to chant the Holy Manthras, regularly and we will properly go into the path of divine sovereignty. Very shortly, we are going to give some initiation of having divine presence and magnanimous situation that is to be a saint or sage, position and possession of Godliness and without your knowledge, you will be the blessed person to preach His Glory and mercy; thus, you too will be considered to be a Muni Rishi and then, you are very alert in maintaining this divine class without any trials and thus, kilowatts of yogic current will be produced from yourself, and it will enlighten the mind of the disciples. Now you are also a Guru and thus, some truthful Mutt or Peedam will be formed and you will be blessed by God and you will bless all of us and thus, we are getting the divine appearance in our heart and all will live their life with full of peace and divinity.

Though we are all residing in these materialistic situations, this maya world will vanish when Gnanam twinkles in one's spiritual approach and it is but the Truthful life alone can exist up to the cosmic reflection of fertile and good persons and those who live characteristically and adhere to the spiritual principles strictly, they alone live with our classic life generation to generation, some kind of progress which gives punctual victories in all our consignments. Now, we are thinking and doing that we know everything and all there is nothing in this universe we have to know, everything is ours by heart, and there is nothing to proceed, this knowledge world. Therefore, man fails, this is our invention; where education, wealth, health is there is agankara, everything will pass away and all will diminish; and there is nothing beneficial done to us by them, because our cause of life is nothing but they cheat all, but cannot cheat God; if He is alert, they will be punished with the divine whip and nobody can escape from this crucial renunciations. Most of us, think that this materialistic life is a full happy joyful life, but they when they step into the pool, then only they can know its bitter fragrance and its slippery mud, thus, it is full of miseries and there is nothing in this life; no happiness; but somebody has some peace and they are with wealth. Even for one minute we have no happiness thus, all are knowledge collapsing without mixture of these two things. So if we are without no support from others we will be nothing and, if we have a choice of situations, We can say that everything is characteristic and if we search misery, there is nothing that seems to be.

Wherever and whenever we have time, we should utilize it and express our ideas with proper understanding of the audience. If we set a bulletin, it is to screwing their mind and we are perfectly doing the proper handling of the public audience's expression and their impulses. Therefore, when we have a chance to give an idea elaborately explain our ideas and conclusions, by which we will be an eminent lecturer and demonstrator about any event. Thus, if we are not able to express, our ideas and regulations, for the next time, we have to wait or at that time which will be the modern trend and the ideas will change altogether. Thus, our idea will not be considered, that is why, our chance of expressing should be delivered without any hesitation and objections. Such a way we can have a place in the midst of the audience, we can boldly express the impressions of the ideas, the public should be noted to the generals of the departments concerned and they will have a chance to re-examine the deepest thought of this and their final endings. So, you should use the idea expression, and our ideas, are expressed without any misunderstanding in classical language and those ideas should be up to date; it is a conclusive one, and why do not we take it as the conclusion? Let us think and surely implement it in our schedule without failure. Thus, if our idea is coming out of our forum, what is the joy of our heart and our friends and neighbours. Do try to achieve it without delay; thus, we can understand our hunger of the play and within it, how much deeply we penetrate towards the earth to have a drop of water, such an opinion is this, so do not drop out the most valuable chance anywhere. Friendship and enmity will be taken into one plane and give us permanent peace and true understanding can also happen. If the play is being played following its rules, such power is inside the play. Play is nothing but the understanding and taking everything into consideration and our relationship with other players will be as classical as much as we had, this is understandable throughout our life and such model will be classified with one another, then the understanding will vanish and we can understand all in a nice way. Therefore, the mighty sakthi, which is having, the true play is. It is deeply having such strength and it makes them shake hands without any discrimination; construction will be in all fields and thus, in the world, we will be the super most sakthi, thus, the other nations will realise into their heart. So, do try to flourish friendship and it is possible through play, we should encourage all games and sports to the extensive account. This is the easiest way to share peace with one another and make them understand each other to have good relationship with kith and kin, and so to play a constructive force of all signs. Now-a-days, especially in cricket so many stars are sprouting and they play and their remuneration is quite according to their level and they never think about the scale, thus, they are encouraged, why they play so classically and secure good runs and wickets and fame too.

So, we should play any game and in one chance we gain victory in two ways, one is playing the game and another is trying to promote the game's introduction too. As such so many fantastic players life is wasted because they are not given opportunity to exhibit their skills. Politics and money are playing a hand in the selection and the play is hand to hand transferring, so if we choose basket ball icons, are here, football experts and geniuses are more in number but we are not at all selecting the dispensed players; if we identify them, all the cups in sports and games will be for us Indians. Such trained experts are here, but we are not having the sense to identify and make a good team. I challenge the government also. Therefore, steadily and without desire for money and recommendation, if we select some eleven boys they can win even the world cup in all games and sports, I can challenge in this regard, such winners are in India, but here nothing is suitable to anything. People are concentrating on hero worship and do claim some of the do's and don'ts; then how can they show their pure skill in all the sports and games. If we appoint a new man without prosperity and wealth, do call him and give him the chance, see how much skill they are having, you can finally see their huge potentiality. Thus, our ancestors gave and dedicated their whole life for the spirit of games and sports. So, we initially and truly give priority towards the big selection of the players on the grounds of their skills, throughout their career, then if you send them into international grounds, see, what will be their wonderful achievements. You cannot narrate them in words; only implicitly feel the caliber of the games and sports. As such a lot of icons in all games and sports are passing through roads and grounds; if they are identified and given connection with the national squad, then we can see their whole strength in batting, fielding and bowling, they keep wickets too, such players were in our squad, and this is the easiest way to make money, that is why, our nation does not have eminent players and trainees to our contentment. If we sincerely and truly try to select out good players, they can be gotten within a short period and given good practice and training, and teach morals and rules of the play. First he must know how to play, how many rules are there, he should note and then come to the ground, within 6 months, they will be geniuses if they play the game and sports, they exhibit their skills to the entire satisfaction of our officials.

We are having a golden, excellent chance to live as a human being in this birth, we must utilize this chance to do good deeds and attain personal salvation, otherwise if it is wrongfully lived for the name sake of life there is nothing to be blessed by Him and we cannot get rid of births and deaths. So, doing our prompt deeds salvation will be a sure one. Whatever we do, we should start as a dedication to Himself and begin our deed, nothing will be a failure and everything will be without delay and final result will be the 1st class end. So, we should be living with thoughts of Himself alone and this will give us all benefits and gains. Wherever we are, but, we should be with His thoughts and chanting the holy name of God. Chanting will give us permanent Shanthi to make our mind go in the path of His way and thereby we will get our deeds successfully done. Most probably, all are to attain success in all of their deeds, nobody likes failure, if we need success in our deeds, we should fix an attachment with Him always then our deeds will be Himself, and so victory will be the end of the courses. So, chanting His name with divine mood we can have success in all our deeds and His presence will do quite good to all the creatures. That is why, God Himself is born in this earth for doing good to all, but we never understand His deeds and we blame His deeds, after knowing that He is Universal, we fall in love with Him, at that time, He will be seated in our heart and the one searching His place attains nothing.

Our human life is nothing but the certain creation of God and it is given to all, nothing but the one who has the ability to withstand with the boon his life will be fruitful towards Enlightenment. Whether we have sense or not, our life will be modified into a knowledgeable one and play a big role in this materialistic life and therefore, we should be ready to live and ready to leave; thus, we should set up our lives as the setup of our conclusive perception. The divine perfection is up to the mark of perfection up to the Highest steadfastness and we have to spend no money at all. In materialistic life, whatever we wish we have to spend money, but in spiritual life, no money is needed, it is related with the oneness of mind only. So, if we have mentality to realise the Passion of God, we have to know nothing, as else, this is a way of realising through pure thoughts and mind's oneness. We can even celebrate kumbabhisekam without a single paise, we can fulfill it without a single paise, for that, the only need is to think thickly in our thoughts to do kumbhabishekam in our heart and this is the easiest path to do any celebration. So, if we wish to attain Him truly, He will be ready to give us His holiest Dharsan before us, and all. Confidence and surrenderness is the much wanted need, if we are having these elements, in our heart and deeds, if they are blessed by the Almighty, He Himself gives Dharsan before us and dispenses His glory and grace.

There is nothing as maya. Only truthful life is exhibited. Such life is to be opted by us at the same time, we should give the statement to achieve that this is our goal and aim, then our triumph will be up to the mark of perfection, thus, this human life will be beneficial to all. Then, nothing will not be possible to attain in his mundane life, we have all divine qualities and we can be with shanthi and peace in our mind. This type of peace is emphasised by saints and all spiritualists, then the earth will be full of confidence and divine. This is in other words, Rama Rajyam. There we should live a divine oriented life. This is possible, we can be blessed by God, instantly and thus, our life will be utterly meaningful. Whether we have confidence or not, the whole universe is unitedly operated by Himself this must be realised without any doubts, thus, if we construct our humanity into socially oriented mundane life, it will by itself transfer into a place ever oriented with God.

As according to human life's rules and regulations, their insistence may differ, but the main embryo sac is only one which is meant to be realised by all. If it is in day-to-day life, there will be quarrels with each other, and all are having right to walk in the streets with hands swinging front and backwards, but it would disturb others. Likewise, we should maintain even other religion's regulations, and they can pray whoever they may be, our Bhakthi is universal, God alone will come to invite us to His divine hall. He will serve food and finally give water to quench our thirst. Such a merciful person He is, you all must know the illustrations by seeing with your own eyes; otherwise, you never know anything about spiritualism and we are striking with harsh words and sometimes, it may prolong as a big quarrel. These types of people are nothing but foolish persons and they still have 100 crore years; they do not know God's supremacy and His broadmindedness. Therefore, these kinds of persons, what can we do? Go abroad and they should be given special rooms and they can live with peace and honour. Whether they know or not, everybody wishes to attain God, because He is the only refuge who has Ambrosia and it is the only one medicine which can cut off our long procedure of births and deaths. Then only we can live with peace and shanthi and thus, all the worlds will be majestic in nature and we can give solutions for all kinds of agonies and disturbances. The divine solution for all disputes, universal peace, only one rescue is this, this is always divine. If we have this mentality always, nothing will be happening untowardly. If quarrels and problems arise we have to speak wholeheartedly with peace of mind, then there will be divine peace and this peace is standardized throughout the world. We are all speaking, but we do not have the tendency to bring this peace about in all places, in all times, so to say always, if this is adhered to by everyone of us, there will be no time to quarrel without human nature. If we live peacefully throughout our life, the one and only way is to hold peace, if one is angry, the other party should be calm, if that party is also angry we cannot do anything fruitfully, we should calm down our mentality to normal plane of peace, thus, peace enrolls its divine quality into an everliving concept which is PEACE only. This is emphasised by all our religious monks and Gnanis. With anger, nobody can do nothing; this is an universal concept. If we want success, we should be like the sweet sugarcane and likewise, we have to taste it, then its real nature can be realised, likewise, if we are trying to live with peace and harmony, we must be with peace and always we must be in control of all senses, and then peace will be the same as peace itself. It is residing in our mind, we should search it, because peace searches peace, then where is the second peace? So, whichever it may be, we have to maintain peace within our heart and think for atleast ten minutes, then our mind gets soft and shanthi, thus, peace can be regained. Peace is a marvelous weapon, which can change even an atrocious man into Paramasanthavathy.

We should rejoice about His toughest and rarest happening which is a boon to us, because of our saintliness of all births and this is the boon for us to have the Dharsan (Holiest) of God in front of us; we should not waste His presence by mere logical sentences, as we require, we must not have these, as a bond, instead of these, we should have a boon that His thoughts should be always with us and ever we should be with His thoughts and we should have the work of spreading His kalyana guna vaibavas all over the world. Never ask for this mundane requirements because He is the Almighty. He is now in front of us, apart from Him, nothing more positive a thing in this world to have as a boon from God. So we should have the boon of His presence in our mind at all times and circumstances. Then, He will be pleased and give us that boon of penance and He is always with us and we are all with the thoughts of Himself always. Then what is the greatness of our life? Everything can be achieved, but would not experience it with Astamasidhis and never use this greatness to spend for the worldly things, instead of this, we should assimilate His holiest names by chanting His Namasangerthana at all times, everything will be had by His grace at all times, by any circumstances and we shall happily and contendedly live our life. Every second is to be spent in the ecstasy of His holiest Leelas and Gunabhavas, and we should be the image of His presence. Once again we request the same opinion, not to spend the time in accumulation of wealth and our needs of worldly things, instead of that, we must spend our costly time in swallowing goodness and betterment of God's Leelas and Gunabhavas at all times. We should rejoice and taste the nectar of divineness. Apart from this Golden experience nothing in this world to rejoice in thoughts and deeds, so try to understand the greatness of this ever living, deathless experience of this kind. As such if we have it our life is a boon which is presented by His mercy and grace and as a result, we are born to have the greatest experience of this kind and nothing more to do in this world as our duty, for attaining this glorious experience, we are repeatedly born in this earth, so many times we die and perish in this earth and turn the table for several crore times. Everything for attaining this miraculous excellence. His presence is suddenly happening in front of us and our eyes have the penance to see His Sthula sareera with His heartful desire and then, we have all sakthis. But only if we are living with politeness, with full of sincerity, obedience and truthfulness, these are boons dispensed by Him as we lead this spiritual life beyond the level and keep the level of confidence upon God for He also should not be far away from us.

Whenever we close our eyes, He should appear before our inner eyes and if we open our eyes, He should be before our naked eyes, in this way so-called spiritual life should be operated by Himself too. Hence, all people should attain this glorious, unequalled, unparalled life, and rejoice in the presence of His majesty. To have this experience we have births and deaths cycle and whether we wish or not the cycle will so round us to make us have the modifications. As a result one day all of our cycles will end and this divine experience will be on us and it will stand still; if it happens, it never goes apart from us, with this joy we have to dip our soul fully and as far as we rejoice, and apart from this mundane experiences, this is the only happening which is called the TRUTH and it is the super most happening in our whole life. Because it is the result for all tests we have faced, put by God Himself; those who are having interest upon Him, He upon us, would be able to Interpol these experiences and tests and thus, the pure One is gotten from among all dust. We fired with hot fire, and in the last experience we got it, as such we passed tests, in some tests, we failed, but at the last time, He make us to pass the final test, and gives convocation of His glorious blessing. Now our entire life is a meaningful ideal philosophy of our own life. There is nothing equal to refer to this amazing happening; and so we have to be ready in the midst of all happenings in this spiritual line; we should be picked by Him with full of delight and divinity. Therefore, we become divine and our whole life becomes divine and our entire life's biography becomes divine. We should saturate with the divine nectar, of spirituality, not taking birth in this universe again and again. In this universe, lots of entertainments and enjoyments are available, but nothing can give us the highest pedestal of divinity, so we must be very careful to retain our spiritual experiences and our attained boons, without using them for silly things. Thus, if we do, our power of penance will be reduced and one day it will end with nil balance then we have to do penance vigorously and then wait in which birth, we are going to attain that greatness. Nobody knows, so, we must be very careful to use our spiritual power very limitedly and without wasting it, we have to retain the sakthi with full of concentration and it must be worth wisely growing day by day and such a day we will be having the whole worth of divine sakthi to retain us in the holy abode of the Almighty.

Our voice to God can be heard and He will suddenly come and give His responsibility to heal our illness both in mind and body. So that, swamy is named as Abathbandhavan. He has several duties, to deliver on such date, we will be His children, firm disciples and thus, we can attain the hope of His firmness and therefore the Head office ordered us to follow the rules and restrictions. Otherwise, we will not be suitable with nothing, thus, mark us. So that, at an earliest date, we should get a caravan through this philosophy, nothing will happen untowardly, which exploits us in any means, we close these philosophies to our own house and rejoin with all. Everything is the truth and we are having sufficient knowledge to have the sight of the divine philosopher, God. If we wish to consider that this nation is full-fledged, what does it not have as its own? First this nation must stand on Her own feet, fine agricultural upgrade, considerable amount taxes. Beyond religions, all should be under one roof, maintaining peace, non-corruption - these qualities are essential to consider our nation as a Rama Rajyam. If all the nations in this world are keen to maintain peace, without fear of war with industrial development at the same time, one Rajaguru is importantly needed to the nation's development. The Guru must be characterwise first class, always thinking about national integration, dedication of his life to the betterment of the nation, these qualities make oneself as Rajaguru. This kind of humble but courageous man alone can be a guru and he alone can show the path in which the nation must go every step to step, it is possible, our life and all of the peoples', well being will be sure and daily we will with smiling faces with boldness and valour surrounding our hearts which is given by God. No person of theft is essential to develop each department, and thus, the whole nation would be ever peaceful and it will be considered the well settled nation is wanted by all types of population. The whole human beings are to work hard to develop all the nations for having one solution. That is each and every nation should slowly but steadily clean their nation so as to do away with atomic weapons; in all the people's mind there should be peace, not violence, it is supposed to be gained through tolerance, we have to get rid of from these natural and artificial riddles. Everybody in the nation should have good education and there must be trials of body building, and our potentiality must be served for the integration of all nations. We can automatically develop in all fields of education. Though we are speaking one language in that particular state, all the statesmen should know as many languages so as to make our literal department grow like a tree. There is no deficit of educating ourselves in several languages, there is no harm to us. We should study many languages and we should have enough pandithyam (mastery) in that language so as to translate into our mother tongue, literatures of other languages. We can in this way uplift our wisdom to perfection. Who is the author of this book? very fine, we just say about the book and thus, we can win it. The author is the master of that language and through his educational standard, he has translated that language's treasures of literature. As a result we can have more books on various topics from various languages; so if better to educate our pupils first in the national language that is Sanskrit. If we have knowledge of Hindi alone, we can go anywhere in India and there is a sense that we are utterly Indians. Whoever they may be, if they too have knowledge of Hindi they can easily go and return to any place very easily. The language problem makes us not to go anywhere as our mind thinks. This is to be erased.

Whenever, one thinks of controlling his sensual organs of the body (throughout) and whenever, they are needful, we can make to do as we wish. How various physicians examine, give several injections, lots of tablets have been taken; but there is no benefit at all. We generally hope to live with physical and intellectual strength as are enough and above all, we are eagerly tied up with various departments and trying to establish our own business and our life. Always look out at others and particulars of them are easily covered by us, but we have to know self realisation, how is it possible? If we decently behave like a gentleman, give and take respect, thus, the two parties may live without controversies. Those who are living with their problems alone can deliberately arrange good result in life, others, simply spoil their and others life without any solution of their mistakes. We should educate ourselves and then others. Likewise, the first bell should be for the consent of the Headmaster. Ok, sir, what can we do? tell us an easy way to solve the problem, all are asking this teacher, he does not speak anything. Thus, some minutes go by. They conclude that the adamant teacher herself hoist the flag and then, 2nd time the flag has been hoisted by the Headmaster and he is very happy but nobody congratulates him. Then, they disperse; all of them dispersed within five minutes; likewise, politically, all are with the dream of chief ministership, how then will this Tamilnadu thrive? Not at all. We are all ashamed because of this action, the matter is simple, but the consequences of the action are severe. So we should prefer everything; but, the nation is considered to be the 1st in the world. Economically, one may be weak, but humanity's sight, he is a gem among all and has character and Thayai and grace. Such persons are in need in today's political and social life, if we practice our children everywhere, all sects and creeds, beyond sex and religions, we can establish a new era in our lively situation of the universe. Today, we are in need of forgiveness, tolerance, anti-corruption. We are all paid monthly once as remuneration for our duties discharged to the nation, but why do the people, who are working, need bribes, this thought, if they can think wisely, the nation will be superlatively number one among all nations. Apart from meals the man does not note the word, 'enough', which means, whatever, whoever gives, there is no measurement to loot the articles with or without permission. What we do to the newly constructive Indian policy, we have to work without bribe and no gossips forever to which the nation, itself develops in all sections marvelously. Thus, we must work hard for the payment by the Government, it is a boon and we are all not at all sincerely getting rid of these evil spirits. If we live in a right way, all the creatures will automatically help to develop our curriculum to victory.

All are willing and wishing to have divine life, but we are knowing the path how to make up our life's pattern, and first of all what is life? If we find out the answer to this question, then we will be the genius among all fools. We mention all as fools, because, everything in this world is not permanent, everything is unstable, then we believe that all are existing beyond eras and that is why, I see this world as a foolish one. Our remarkable task is not to get recognition and not at all to be praised in any public forums, but our foolish activities are considered to be the champions, and they are given medals with cash prizes to encourage them. Try to analyse our Olympic and other events, they are the job of the activities of five sensual creatures, if we do it with some organisational acceptance, they will be honoured and their prize money may be 50 lacs. What do they do? Nothing, but lift up some iron bars. An elephant will do this very easily; some are running and they are given prizes and cash prizes; what non-sense is this? a deer can run faster than man, then prize is not given to right person. A kangaroo, can jump a greatest distance, nothing, then they, the organizers try to exhibit the creatures' out put and their nature is out sketched in the name of competition and we are all crying and enjoying these foolish activities. Then even if 1000000000 Jesus' are born in this land, they will also fail in their attempts. They have given us a sketch to live a wealthy and healthy life, first class ideas are given by them, but we do not accept and adhere to those principles and we make a fool of ourselves and others also fools too. This kind of monopoly is to be erased from our competitions, and we should cultivate our civilisation, cultural programmes, our ancient arts, dances like those games that gave us both mental and physical strength to overcome Maya from our ego and give righteousness. Then, such a man is so-called and honoured as man; otherwise, nothing and nobody is honoured as man. This pitiable grade of manhood should be accompanied with our own society and do not and need not go outwards, there we can do what we think, that are unknown assignments. And in the end, our karmas are united with bavas, so have we to resolve us from what we are doing. Then, the answer is no. Is it considered to be a normal human life? No, certainly not. In this place exactly all dharmas, are revealed in special recognition, but the land is nothing for we did not come along with it and all things we earn, they are not our own savings. Maybe somebody is having Levadevi business, that is, some amount of money is given every month, the buyer has to deposit its interest as they pledge it, and in the final instalments we have to give the capital plus interest, this is more or less done with some small amount; but some do it very elaborately with ease, and within the place, they earn lots of money and lead a comfortable life. Thus, we are doing many businesses and when we are treated by illness we cry "Oh! God according to my knowledge I had not done any sinful activity, but this disease is troubling me very much, please save me". Is it a lawful business or not? When we are deeply thinking, our mistakes are elaborately known to us. Several sins, we are doing as we know or not, we are always having the tendency to do sins without fear of God, that is why, the world is fully seen as sinful. That is why, many are naturally troubling themselves because of their sinful thoughts and deeds. Likewise, our chain of sins are going on. So we must pray Him, to forgive all our sins and dispense a natural life and thus, we should live comfortably without any sins; if our prayer is thus quoted, we will be surely embraced by Him and He Himself shows the natural path to go through with faith, goodness and sathya, then, Heaven there the abode heaven, with its saturation is the major aim of our human birth.

"I can do anything ....!" this is a version, we certainly hear from out of our mouth once in a while, thus, we are telling others? Is it true? Can we produce anything in this world? certainly not. We know and experience always, but are trumpeting that we are having sakthi that even a hill can be lifted by us. But, when it comes in the practical side, can we do anything? certainly not ? Every thing is the wish and pleasure of God only. If, there is fate we can do it, then only we can do it, this is God's prediction. May be, all are graduates and post-graduates and doctorates; can we extend our life span? Is it in our control? No. Everything is possible only through His order and grace, we can succeed in our position and possession. Nothing is in our hands, and if we wish to live 100 years life span, if we wish to extend it, can we do it? Nothing, we are earning even 100 crores of money, but we cannot live beyond 200 years. It is the universal truth. Likewise, we are earning one lac rupees, can we live one lac days. Nothing is possible. 100 years is equal to 36500 days only. Within this illusionary life, we are dreaming about such and such dreams and live selfishly but not for others. Nothing can be proposed by us; God alone can do anything even if is to dispose. If God thinks, He can do whatever is necessary. If we have His guidance and assistance, we can weigh this world, only through money as a scale. Other than money, nothing is in our hands, we cannot write up our whole life. Within 36500 days what are the things that can be done by us? and just think about its consequences of the things that we do. Lastly, the answer will be nothing. Therefore, we have to seek refuge in Himself and live what He had written as our fate. This is the easiest way to get rid of these mundane feelings. If we really trust into the majestic philosophy of God, everything which is done by us will be all fruitful and nothing will present itself as painful. Always, mind is controlled by His power, and He, Himself submerges with our heart thoroughly and all functions and activities delivered from us will shine with divine dignity and those activities are helpful to us and always for others too. There will be nothing, whereas we note, everything will be beautiful and excellent, there are no evil effects from Evils. There will be all faithfulness, sincerity, truth surrounding us and our deeds are only the ejection of the Divine power. Wherever we see, only shanthi and tolerance will emerge with controlled sensual power and behaviour of human beings will be higher than all others. Without permission of Him nothing will happen, so everywhere we look, all are divinely dipped things and there is nothing against divine laws. Wherever we go, everything will be smooth and all the people will behave with one will. Another method of living will remain and there will be no failures or mental depression. All will think that we are the sons and daughters of God only, so, let us live with passion and love. No more cheating process and thieves are nil in number and this world is praised by God, Himself. He will praise about the world's daily duties, discharging with satisfaction and dedication. Therefore, we have to dream that this type of world should be established by His esteemed grace and mercy, Oh God ...! Thus, we pray Him. Prayer has its own power and vibrations. It slowly and certainly brings us near to God Himself. Suddenly, where there is no matter at all, God Himself comes as an Avathar and He makes the world just healthier and stronger and having Astasakthi's control, and there will be no beggars anywhere, all will work hard and earn money and live most comfortably with their own earnings. No servants and no masters; this kind of Equilibrium of life is present every where, and we closely live with full of love and dedication. The whole universe will be full of shanthi and peacefully covered and God's presence will be swallowed by each and every man and woman. All this distinction of male/female will be adhered to henceforth as per law, we are all living with equal bhavana and Maha Gnanies and Paramahamsars will be high in number and they are teaching the society the philosophical truths, about God's presence.

Now-a-days, we are materialistically living like machines; that is why, we do not have a chance to know about the value of human birth. It is not at all easy, God proposes oneself, as a human being. In this birth only, we can think of God's glory and have holy darshan of Him and even we can talk to Him. Such a merciful attitude God has. He knows everything, because He is the sole creator of these beings and controller too. Everything is nothing but He/His modifications, differentiating one from another, He performs all leelas to the welfare of all beings.

Thus, this human birth is worthy, but we are all wasting the glory of it. If we continue to follow the spiritual processes, one day, we come to realise the true value of this birth; so, do respect and honour our soul and body; because it is the abode of soul, try all exercises, in due course of time, our goal can be achieved.

We are wishing to live several years with full of health and wealth; then, all will come in action, likewise, somebody's life is blessed. But, Human life is always worrying, So nobody, is going to taste the nectar of this life; and then, they perish. Satisfaction of mind with budhi, sidham, knowledge and wisdom are essential to be a Gnani. One who hates rituals, ceremonies and are blabbering some statements, are called and respected by the innocent people as God's representatives, but that alone is not enough to think like that. .! we have to undergo spiritual aspirations and then, we have to weigh Etheism and Theism. Whatever Dharma and karmas are stipulated by the positive side, are also emphasised by the negative side. They, both sects make us to realise the universal nature of happiness and sorrows. Those, who love them first, can win the human race. Such a victory magnifies them to attain complete and thorough happiness i.e., Ecstatic Liberation from all types of bondage and we should bear in mind this universal principle that Nothing in this world is profitable and loss. Mere explanation of our findings will make us to practice all natures of common lives. Those, who are well versed about this transformation, then, no doubt, we are entering into the diary of God. Such a mode of life is essential to us in this situation; and hence we have to earn and keep them as our capital, and it will be, become a huge amount. Then, from that interest we are showered by our Mahasakthi, for the welfare of the human race.

You can first give food and water to the hungry and starving people, then you give them good clothes next, you can make arrangement and for them to have good education, if you do these three things, then you will be equal to God Himself. So try to have these divine qualities without failure and mind it this is our goal and we should achieve these divine powers and three dharmas for the benefit of mankind. Thus, you will be leading to get rid of bad habits and try to acquire heavenly thoughts and noble deeds, within the short time, you will attain God's principles as it is. Then you can serve these three noblest activities to all the people beyond sects, creeds, religion and all; your eyes see a man only as a man, not his creeds, religion and all; your eyes see man only as a man, not his creed or religion, you will seem to him as a godly trace before him and in yourself, He sees God and he waits for your external service because you give him the most three needs of mankind food, shelter, education and everything, then you will broaden your service to the horizon of this earth. Of all these services, the whole world's noble people and crorepathies will start to do this kind of service. Everybody will have education and by their education they will earn money and lead their life without others help or assistance and thus, the whole universe itself will get the glory of God, and this is called RAMARAJYAM. By this way only, we can establish a truthful universe and hence all will be noble and there is no fraud, bribe and extra curricular activities among the whole society. Everywhere we can see the glory and mercy which is flowing through the heart of all people. What is the defect in this world? Nothing. This world is to be established, our scholars and savants are trying to install it. If we begin this is in this second itself, within a short period we can see Rama Rajyam. The highest fame for this world is nothing but to be full with peace and shanthi, grace and mercy, life will have pure Bhakthi.

Those persons who are ever starving and hungry must get food and water, all are to have clothes, and shelter, these basic necessities are fulfilled, then, there is a chance all will learn to earn money and have knowledge of this universe and they, themselves will live by their own effort and can easily, solve their and other's problems too. Thus, our leaders are formed with good name and fame and all the people acknowledge Him, as their leader and he also dedicates His whole life for welfare of humanity, So, The society grows in the fields of health, education and industrial development and they make innumerous good things for weather forecast and for the welfare of this humanity. They are so to say Annonists or prophets, and their actions are all for the nation's development, but they live a very normal life and they do develop, always think and think about each factor and bring it in deeds, and as such the nation develops from the basement level. On this basement only, we are all constructing other sectors such as agriculture, philosophy, politics and chaste performance in the regime of all Governments. Their actions are for our forthcoming generations not for themselves. They never think about themselves, they have only 4 dhothies 4 shirts, 4 banians, 4 underwears, and one spectacle and they live and take food only by their own remuneration which is given by the government as M.L.A salary. In that stipulated amount, they send some money to their mothers and keep themselves also and help the students, especially children to pay school fees and giving pencils, rubbers, pens, and they too are living, such people and they are ever living and thus, our nation is slowly but steadily progressing in all the fields. If we are loyal and royal to our rules and regulations, we too can make INDIA, as a Rama Rajyam within one year. This is the challenge that I took ...! All are trying to get the fulfillment of this aim, but we sometimes, not at all remembering our goal and aim, that is why, some kind of downtrodden happenings are on the way to this procession. If we work hard and without rest and respire this aim as our sole life, we can definitely get to the target very soon. So, we should take an oath, we must work hard and patiently make our INDIA develop in all departments and with others' blessings and co-operation, we should maintain our Highest position in all departments as soon as possible. There is no more time, we have to spend time for that, we have to attain it within hours, so, oh God! please do sanction our prayers, this should be our prayer and belief and work hard for the development. We, and the nation should contemporarily step forward and upward to attain, we can give all help to the other nations too. This type of spirituality must be pronounced by India without failure. Failures may happen but we have not to get rid of our hope and stiff belief upon ourselves and God, we can achieve the goal one day. That will be the day of Independence and Republic day for us. They are the only true holy days for us. Until then, we have to work hard to the development of the nation in all angles and thus, we should be not only in mind, time, but we have to mind "TIME". Apart from time, we are all working hard in each and every field of departments and get fruitful results, automatically we are counted as the 1st among all the nations' development, and thus, we can regain our majesty throughout the world. If we try hard and faithfully, God alone will help and assist us to attain the goal with pride and graciously. With this boastful assistance, we can be ever Independent in all subjects, there is no chance of us being slaves, any more and we can erase this word slave from the dictionary itself. So, by the grace and blessings of God, we must go forward timingly and work whatever we know and as much as we can. We can try to develop in our respective fields, inch by inch and attain the super most elevation point of the Highest Mount and thus, we uplift India to the superfast and super most elevation in all fields and development all through. Hence, our nation will be pronounced by other all nations, when they quote the name of development. It is, indeed, achievable, practical, but with full of confidence, if we work hard with systematic mind, with all united, our nation will attain the foremost point and thus, nothing to worry or have any sorrow about anything. All things and instruments are made by us and if it is needed, we can sell those instruments, if other nations know this fact, automatically our neighbouring nations all will shut up their mouth and anus if they try do something wrong, their tails will be cut off. They should know this truth very well they know our power and utilisation of the instrumentations and their usage. Thus, we should come up forward and live with peace and shanthi. No sir, there will be ever peace, India declares, this will be our top most slogan pronounced by us and all of us.

When, we analyse the Education field, it is a very pitiable one, here all give preference to English, but government does not encourage the people to know, Indian's mother languages is not English not at all our language, the politicians spoiled 3 of our generations preventing to educate in Hindi but, we are very keen to educate ourselves in English, now all are speaking, mixing Tamil with English and thus, it has saturated and has become Taenglish; we are writing, speaking and are ready to know English but none is ready to know Hindi. But, in Tamil Nadu, hindi films run like an Olympian athlete. If this is in action how can we make all to know Tamil's ancestral quality. In Tamil, some specific literary products are present. Other languages do not have these kinds of literary treasures. So, we have to make our offsprings to know TAMIL'S caliber and its archeological study of its immortal value, if they, concern with the language's authority may be, good to make its immense values of Tamil to be known. All are willing to know it with grammar. We can go to any part of India, first and know its time of preparation, and its divine power can be realised,, and then we will be sound enough in Tamil, Hindi and English. Thus, we can know at least three languages, by which all can make trades with all and in all directions. So, this is to be done and practically brought among all in our day-to-day life. Politicians must stress this concept and it is necessary that while we are not knowing Hindi, but that we are Indians and we have to say that Hindi is our national language. So, it should be done without delay. All three languages, Mother tongue, Hindi and English.

Even though we are savants if we do not know Hindi, we cannot go on a tour to our capital city, New Delhi; without Hindi we cannot see and have dharsan of Lord Viswanathar.

In India, the only problem that we are actually struggling with one another is about which is the national language, we have to know it very well and they question, why Hindi language is to be known? Now you have not insisted on this matter, why so you concentrate on Hindi, should be learned or studied thoroughly. We learn to write and concentrate to have wisdom of that language, because, it is declared that Hindi is our national language, as such, we have to be ready within a short period, we trained them at the most, and that is why, all students from various cities earn a lot of money and they own a house, and buy a car. So others are willing to study steadily, you all should have knowledge of Hindi and its grammar very well and you, all should be good as you can. Ok, students are ready to learn oh, parents, please permit your children to have knowledge of Hindi within a year, they can go elsewhere, anywhere growing to the best positions and an ornamental person to our own nation, INDIA. Do come on. Let us have knowledge of Hindi and thus, we can do trades all over India, and will happily celebrate all the occasions. Then, we will be bold enough to see sights of various parts of the country when on tours and pilgrimages. This will boost international money, and our mode of living will be elaborate. Our 3 generations have come down in the field of education but, if our children know Hindi, they can go elsewhere, they can do any business or occupation anywhere in India alone, will be significantly having the finest stage of economical departments, and through all the trains, we can continuously make journeys without any delay and expenses. We can go and speak Hindi, wherever the place is, we can have all of our needs and thus, we can build houses in our places, hotels and temples of our traditional deities. Hence, we will be one of the biggest democratic nations and this can be proved in this generation itself and without leisure time, if we work hard and with ease, we can expand our business all over India then India's position, just do imagine, everything can be done only for the sake of all peoples and others who are coming to see the beautiful sights, temples and our libraries etc, will be astonished. Within a stipulated period, India becomes a superpower nation, hence, they will not threaten us and we can independently respire our own prana without sects, creeds and religions, we are working and constructing new industries, companies and we are all going towards pure salvation.

Just if time permits alone we can bear any more violent people in the battle fields, and one concept is there, if India fights with another country, they should be afraid of death; we can make this false concept, into winning style of war fields. Jai Ram. Our INDIA itself is the one and only dependent country over God and all things which we are doing is a boon got right from the beginning and if He Himself fights we will win over any nation in all fields. Thus, He is the master of all matters in only one stroke, it is His boon and we cannot do anything about it on our own. Just obedience will make us to win over, whatever the problem it is ! So, we are living without fear and passion only because of His will and pleasure. That is why, we name children with God's names and at all times we must pronounce His names and thus, we can win over any kind of problems from outside and inside too. Our mentality is running through goodness truth, sathyagraha and non-violence are the basis principles which are established and so we definitely go to war irrespective of their kingdoms, we do not give troubles, agonies to the nearby countries.

We are very much struggling to live a fulfledged human life, till our last breath and it should be exemplified by us. Our life may be ordinary, our death should make others to cry. Our departure should make them feel how, noble a man he is? Such name and fame oriented symbolic life which he lived, gives others a lesson to the word life; we may struggle for shelter, food and education but we should be counted by the Almighty. To certain extent, our noble thoughts and deeds should be a lesson for forthcoming generations, our life should be noted down as a lesson to those who wish, can select and get doctorates even. Such a marvelous life is ours. God should be astonished and so without any enquiry, his entry ticket should be issued to us. Do think in this angle, what a symbolic life, God has forwarded to us, in order to earn and learn and learn to earn; but we can earn; we cannot learn to earn; vice versa; this is not at all an easy one to come by nature. Those who are doing the best, to all, surely, they will be remembered by all means. Our materialistic life should be blessed by our ancestors and God Himself should have satisfaction through our mode of life. Life should be a fine file, likewise, life should be quoted to live like them, this kind of life, God expects from us.

We, all religions, sects and creeds united together and fought Englishmen, as shouting 'Quit India' and it is called most probably, a massive peoples' movement, without their Religion, they came to fight with the British Government, The propellers of 'Freedom' plane took off, to get rid of the British. Most of the people, beyond religions etc, fought in the path of ahimsa against the British Empire or Government. They were a treasured uneducated people, but they were ready to make their hilly places into fertile land. Thus, they prepared everything which was at the level best for use. Every zamindhar acquired a lot of fertile fields, and was it just, but they scolded them not to give up their fields. They periodically told them, your signatures are in my pocket, and there all people's documentation of all the fields and they own the richest money holder, and stopped, their notice within 5 minutes of time, there is no necessity to provide our lands but we gave up our nationality and ownership's fact; what kind of allegations are there, then, they got ready to go out of this ground, such the whole of Tamil Nadu's 1/3 part of Tamil Nadu is owned by documents, because they do not fill it by themselves, and they are interrogated about how this shop is running? Just a glimpse of lawyers all over Tamil Nadu gather together and were fond of filing cases in the subordinate judge's court, let us know the final result of our lands. The whole British Empire suddenly stopped all their allegations and rightly, they pulled off the cases against Tamilians. Just jambavans in mental and physical strength, if you study lessons daily, then after six months you are a genius in taking a decision, how to react to get freedom. Thus, our leaders posted each and every one should hand over this or that job, by which we can automatically get freedom. His opinion is common, and they are murmuring, taking the sticks, to strike their organs with full of the fire of anger. You do not have such forces to win over India very easily, certainly not, the bloody Pakistanis must enter into the border, but there will be no leg to step up another foot on this soil of India. But, they have a clear cut idea that India is having big army forces; Aviation system is so fine; but the naval border cannot be considered as a safety side. They wish to fulfill our dealings with them; like a wish our drama comes to an End.

Due to their inefficiency to win a war against India, is quite natural, they do not have mental strength, to win over the Indian Republic, though there are different men and women, their own languages is that as the same. Thus, if war is declared, within 20 minutes period our tri-colour flag will be hoisted in Islamadbad's assembly. Such scene can be brought about by us, but there is no value for peace and integration in our day-to-day life. So, we are going about, respect is given though there are relationships and own custom of friendship. But they say that they are willing to even unite with India, but they do not show their weapons out of fear complex within their surroundings. Thus, they are doing their jobs and when war is declared, we are ready to face it, and final success will be capturing Pakistan, and that is why, each one of us may belong to different sects, creeds and religions. Therefore, it is insisted that we are Indians and are willing to fight against them any time. We are ready to face any kind of war. The result will be a cherished one, therefore be quiet and be patient our dreams should have sketches to build an orphanage, that is our own desire.

Apart from religions, we are running our life peacefully, but the Politicians kindle the people brain wash them and try to increase the strength of a particular sect or religion or so, all of them go in search of someone to get this help. Whenever you can, you can give money. As such, we should live an amicable life together, but the politicians conclude and come to a point to make the land a war field. If it is so, Indians will unite together and fight very well and make India as our own asset. Therefore, we will not give up the Indian Republic to our enemy. Certainly not. It is an assured promise or even God's order. We think and believe that a mere 70 years of earth's residence with, diseases, I am not at all a hunter; likewise, my valour and courage will; periodically and systematically form this secret of winning life is only our dream, but we never do keep others as enemies, but we always treat you (Pakistanis) as our own brothers and daughters. So, we declare our suit between India and Pakistan, should follow Panchaseekla agreement between them.

Up to this, one language's personalities are introduced, is enough to emphasise us to know the value of one languages ancient temperament and its literature and grammar. Whether you are interested in literary English or not, we should be fluent in its grammar, otherwise, we cannot speak a single line in English correctly. So, try to realise the grammar of English, wherever, whoever it may be try to understand its fluency and hence you can educate yourself with good English language. In English, there many literary works by many scholars who have given us many novels, stories, poems etc., these are very beautiful to read and understand its embryo of those literatures. Our sleep will be far away and up to time ends we sit near him to attend his imaginary literature of all languages. OK we are ordinary people, but He is a divine birth who has victory over thirst, hunger and sleep and these aspects are capable only by divine ones and these gurus are masters. If there is a general acceptance we will be very much happy to bring out literary production in our own style for 20 years time. I am here to produce English literary concepts like the work of Nosterdam. We can produce a new one about future incidents with date and time. It will help those who rule and they can escape from the destruction of these concepts. As such our duty is to discharge our duty and not expect anything as its remuneration, they need money, for me there is no connection to money at all. If I need a cigarette packet, I simply ask you humbly, you can bring it and hand it over and fulfill my desire as a brother or sister. Then particularly why do we wish to have money? Nothing but it's a waste to save it. Those who are interested in English language to know and realise its greatness, I am ready to do it as a service, a duty to this nation.

There is no war between ourself and those who do japa with authorisation of Christ, is nothing but the dispensation of Himself. He is the king and Undoubtedly hearing this lecture if you are having confidence,,

I will guard and guide you by all means. America does manufacture machines and total income of America depends upon manufacturing weapons, selling them to other nations, who wish to have it, they sell with some percentage of profit and in this way they maintain their monitary status and call themselves a super power. So the undoubtful enemy should be got rid of to keep our mother nation from destruction. If they make, made such weapons, all secrets of the instruments and machines should be kept. So, it is suitable not to buy several number of weapons and dresses. If they think about us, are we your brothers? O.K. Through this way we can be satisfied to manufacture SLV rockets and they have been exemplified several times as success. So, we can save and gain more dollars, it may be some crores of rupees in Indian counting. So I insist our scientists should concentrate to manufacture the best weapons and sell them. We can be the biggest royal military land. We salute India's tolerance, satisfaction and dedication.

A student goes to school to educate himself daily, but when examination comes, he also participates, but the marks are single digit. The same teacher who educates all of the 40 pupils, one has scored 100 per cent marks, but our student has Zero mark. Here, who is to be blamed. The second person goes to school as a duty but the former goes to school as doing penance and that is why, he grasps all from the teacher, then he can secure good marks, good habits and so on. But our student is not at all interested in going to school but for time sake, he goes to school, and this mind is oriented with extra curricular activities as street- walkers. They lose their excellent life and spoil their lives without any development. So, we should blame teachers; we have to tell our students, what is education and they will smoothly try to have a degree, then by earning money, they live contentedly. Then, they realise the importance of Education. Education has no limitations; their education will feed them, yielding good conduct and character, they will serve domestically and also our nation; they do not waste a single second in their life. They plant some saplings here and there, and they grow like the old trees and give enormous results for betterment of the universe. Those who are not interested in education, we have to find out what is the field, he is willing to concentrate, their worthful field then he will be a genius in that field and learn to earn money and lead his life calmly and peacefully. So, this world is read vastly so, everyone should be prepared to spend time to make others genius in one work or other; and thus, he can save his own family with full of luxurious equipments. So, if one is not interested in studying, do not bother about his studies. Many more are more than post-graduates without education in the school, college and universities; these persons settle their super tax to the government. So, everybody has his own talent; if we find it and give training in that field, they will earn and learn the sequences of life; so, with sincerity, pious heart, our loads are to be placed on Him. He will prepare us in the best way and thus, God reacts to our callings without failure, and our lives will be twinkling more than the educated ones, this is not that we are not supporting education in anyway Do not mistake us. Those who are not studying! well and then, should we conclude that they are useless; such concepts should be eradicated and find out their phenomena of life in their particular field; if he is trained he will shine like a pole star. Doing Dharma, speaking kind hearted words, giving and forgiving qualities do not at all come regularly through education. They are our inborn qualities and if we adhere to these things we will be honoured by Himself in person. There are many examples in our epics, puranas and scriptures. So, do not be weak; try to achieve something while living in this world. There are many more dimensions in our life, but we have to choose our level best and keep trying on to be a real human being.

Our ancestors gave up their invaluable life and they got independence for our nation. The English men have gone but now our INDIA is in the mighty hands of all citizens. Our creations, wealth, health, nobility, chastity all exercises, our achievements, education, neighbours, friends, well known personalities bank balances, are our own will and pleasure, these all round men and women, including doctors cannot save us or even prolong our life, even for one second. They are saying we have given full medical exercises, herewith you, pray the Almighty. So, doctors are going to die one day, but nobody can live forever. This is the presence of His Almighty power; then death occurs, some are weeping, then they do up the customs, and all conclude, at what time, the body is going to be taken to the graveyard. This is the normal custom for all of us. Therefore, God proposes, man disposes, No man proposes, God alone disposes, this is the fact which is suitable at this juncture. Upto some time man will succeed in his duties, but apart from these factors some things are out of man's reach. So, the sole preceptor is God only. Let us pray God, for having liberation from all illness and inabilities. If He remarks, anything will happen without any failures. The fear of God is the beginning of knowledge. So, we should always carefully deal with anything, that is done only by God's sake and this confidence makes us prosperous and also hopeful. If we surrender only, He will dispense all our needs as they are in His mighty hands. So, we do pray intensively and carefully with bhakthi, otherwise, many accessories are only granted by Him, in order to succeed in our concepts. Over all we have to worship

Him with full of bhakthi and renunciation. He expects only these qualities from us.

We, from all the nations, emphasise peace and tolerance, is instructed all over the world but some are not ready to give up their scientific weapons which are trumpted by them, this power should only be used for production of electricity and scientific progressive matter. But these nations are ready to sell them for manufacturing atom bomb, hydrogen and nitrogen bombs. Is this the development to establish weapons or to develop our integrity over peace and not for sale to make bombs? Their main commodities are made with the aim of selling weapons which are ready to be launched towards a target, thus, they destroy the unfailing point and they are telling stories like some peace oriented topics, but their organisation is making goods throughout day and night to earn money very tactically. So, I curse this nation which will soon be destroyed by natural calamities, to international sentiment they are but truths and nothing else; they acquire and earn several crores of dollars through selling their commodities and they are luxuriously living without any danger; hence, they also act by speaking about devotion, religion, faith, extra-curricular activities and so on. All are false so to say as they are doing in their normal days. They are for selling those weapons and teaching them how to utilize them on other countries and simply proving India is also strong as even the U.S.A. cannot win the race. Just like words make the U.S.A angry and they said, if we have confidence about the several happenings, within 24 hours, we can hoist the American flag in the parliament (Indian), so we should not entertain false opinion about our strength which is as powerful as the U.S.A. This is nothing but India's power will be deduced into a sakthi producing nation and we cannot fall down. We should not make any wonderful invention or discovery, we are mingling their mind and intellect, is going to fire down and these will be normal and India is the superpower and hence, many eminent leaders spend their time by boosting us towards destruction. So, we must be very careful to avoid such ill links which would pull them out and sentenced without any grace and mercy.

The results of agriculture, as well as we analyse this kind of botanical gardens. Why should these be without consultation from US, these wise people all are running towards all failures. Our Human words have immense meaning. The dormancy in metabolism clearly shows symptoms of what the disease or illness is going to be maintained by parasites; thus, science shows signs but, in agricultural field, if you analyse cleanly you can get some symptoms of those activities, likewise, we are there and here because our heart always thinks of fertility of the lands and questions why, this year we cannot have some huge profit? Suppose, this is the doubt in the heart of the agriculturists whatever you show we will not be contented by them. Therefore, we have to make it so fertile, and this will never go out because of our mind is made up of mundane assignment. Thus, all minds of the farmers are interactly weighing because of this loss and they have to be normal, they with all members go elsewhere, they get shanthi. But our concentration and mental rulership cannot be kept among some crores of people only one Man knows and realises this fact, that what should be done to equalize the loss of the tiring body is also a confidential person, such, cases are to be attended by the village agricultural officer who comes; we have to put questions about the betterment of agriculture, what is the reason, we have lost all and how can we get money. Please do say any way to compensate this ungrateful land. Thus, we have a chance, but who is going to fields to plough and crop. Our father, why? I am ready to take plough and see to all my agricultural activities and think why these kinds of losses come in action. If time is not favourable to us now and those ways, if we think progressively we are cheated. So, we cannot blame Rain or Man.

If they are diabetic and with blood pressure, they are all ready to help the jawans and our nation will thrive in several ways. Thus, India is always an independent country, she never thinks of slavery. In the past time, unfortunately being slaves and now all are having free air and free thoughts, these kinds of thoughts make us to be a weapon to win over the world, if others come to war Do or Die the phrase which is given by Gandhi, thus, people without strain faced the consequences of the country, such favourite Indian human warriors the night they come to the spot and come to know about our boldness and secret of victory, because the Rajaguru, Sri Sanakian born in India and he knows about the pulse of India. This is the moral opportunity to lead and we are knowing some tricks to attain victory thus, we can win nations and their friendship. The Universal unity makes many of us the supermost brilliant people will have an illusion, we can make others fools and how they can be cheated? There we know very well according to our wisdom and you, yourself knows the steps of the meaning 'wisdom' and thus, one could survive at his best and they drop Ambrosia nectar drop by drop nectar like this, we can provide our gap in the mind which means that all of the educational benefits are made to vanish, the extreme ever living Truth alone here overrules.

Because we have all things, we are getting settled which is a boon dispensed by the Almighty, which means all our comforts done by us or

Him, there is one reason behind it, that is to step up and proceed in the right pathway; He knows everything and all thing's cause of sudden expenses and worthwhile benefits, which are dispensed by the Almighty. But, actually the pathways of the Almighty to reach salvation is very difficult, but these types of courses will not fail, and it is for us, may be, in one or two places the encroachments will be there. It is very hard to assimilate by all means this is so-called maya, which is always weighed and kept clean, then, we have a happy mood and assimilate that our land is surely ours, no trespassers will not even do entry, thus, our mind comes to a conclusion and the owner will sleep, eat, wail and he can do all. Thus, mind and spirituality both cross one another without fail; so, we are all convinced by all kinds of people, and therefore with Gandhi's leadership innumerous people do service as their duty and always there will be freedom struggle, lastly, they are convinced, thus, people feel it to be the freedom inhalation of oxygen, What a moment it was! A fine and one; people are in this thought and they are melting like a metal. Such a fine situation, we were not at all present, what mahapavis we are? No, one thing is encouraging that we have no more chance to have the inner feelings of a slave, O.K. It is in our memory by all means always.

Thus, our forefathers struggled for about 200 years of slavish life and now, we are all independent people, we rule for, of the people and by the people democracy, which means what was mentioned in the law books, but we have so much of slavery items and we were slavish people till this moment; such slave in various fields should come out of those clutches and we are here, now only, we independently inhale such oxygen of freedom which is taken to live comfortably and this is freedom's victory. So, we have to analyse the doing's and undoings, thus, we should inspire ever this is the mighty prayer towards God and He will honour our feelings and in every way, He will dispense us independence and democracy, and all the best felicitations, come through their experiences, our lives will be meaningful. We should not be hungry or thirsty and suffering very much and remain unsatisfied. So, we should be out of these agonies and then that day when it comes it will be the pure independence day. Then, only we can celebrate as pure, utter Independence day in all our proceedings. Once, just such a remarkable day will dawn when, we can unitedly celebrate as one India and its remarkable day that is INDEPENDENCE day which is an achievement and then, we can undergo whatever rules and regulations like rules of the road as well and we are remarkably honoured by all, such invitation and felicitations, we never exercise it thoroughly and we, ourselves only prepare to take special refreshments, thus, that important day will be spent by us utterly. Like this day, once in a year, we should abnormally develop to higher ranges as others whoever they may be and taste our independence thoroughly.

Thus, our leaders had always been in the independence crisis, all had worked well with the fiery spell bound humanitarianism, they saved this land from slavery but they who passed away, may be, now they are in independent nation, INDIA, but yet no one can come to the home, calling bell should be used, and after getting permission only, they must enter the home. Is it independence? Please try to understand this question, we are trumpeting that we are independent but, we are all purely in that stage, we are still in the dependent mood, and we are working but few know the value of Independence. A female cannot speak to her parents and brothers and sisters, this type of homely situation, why does it not enter into the homes. If then we can say our nation is an independent one boldly. Independence means without others support we have to live solitary, by our own incomes, leading our daily life. That is not much explanation, of course, we live independently but with others guarding and guiding, if we live alone, that is not independence. It responds to all calls and living by our own income, thus, entirely, in solitude, this life is called independence. Such persons live calmly, and if they are stimulated by any means, certainly, they will respond violently and their woes are towards catastrophe. So, we have to arrange some amount or we must provide them food, shelter and dresses, if this cannot be given, they will act in such a way and throw away all by means of their independence. Such familiar personalities, I have met more than 100 persons, so, we have to know their capacity of mentality and strength. When they need, they will not call you, but in his/her surroundings they call one or more persons and they will be permitting this noble heart, to do something for them, they never call their sons and daughters and even their husband/wife. Such infinite independence, if they are disturbed, their responsibility will be quite sensual, extraordinary and they will do whatever they can, anger will be like Sri Bhagavan Narashimmamurthy. So, it is very clear and so, we do not disturb them in any way, then they will be calm, realistic and responding to all discomforts and disturbances.

It is God's pleasure and He appoints others in His mighty diary and He focuses His concentration towards everyone's home and some news will be got. He sends to your home or hospital and he understandingly requested some doctors to please attend this case, how can they the doctors say it is a fiery occasion and fail to do the necessary treatment as they may be tired as to work without minute's rest. If God takes rest for a second, in what way, this earth or universe will be normal. So, those who are having noble mind, help the patients, we first of all give first aid treatment, then we can send to the Government Hospital, there are a lot of good medicines, and by producing the medicines and bio-chemical productions, so do not be late, be quick, you will have a point of heaven and your forthcoming generations, will be in the hands of mighty Sivaji Ganesan. In the court they asked to remove the statue and court is pending though the public are very much appreciating by seeing his films. Remove the Actor's statue as it will be a disturbance to traffic, and this is not even prepared for any cost, more or less one crore of shivaji's personnels have been signed and they will give one of the best judgements, not removing the statue, he is not only actor, he was a member the Lok Sabha and he donated lacs of rupees for the freedom fight and he, whoever they may be, asks anyone to come and have dinner first at his house and this is the man, who does not act as a philanthrophist. To many he has said, 'I am ever in the hearts of crores and crores'. This alone goes to felicitate his capabilities. Let us see, what Government should do? Please wait and see.

If oneself is a scheduled tribe, he will be honoured by a rare destination; thus, our government is trying to attain the plane of Eternity. If we achieve this co-operation successfully, then our nation will be honourably the best among all the nations; so, we should eradicate all our mistakes and thus, we can establish a peaceful, worthful unity; so, all citizens should be educated invariably. And all over the world, there is no one who is an illiterate. Education gives us not only job and money, it gives us patience, chastity and good life. Livelihood of our ancient Divine poets come into line of contribution to yield them and we should sow them thereby we can attain the goal and aim of human beings. All beings are living but man has several rules and regulations of his own; if we adhere to them with consciousness the whole universe will be heavenly, style of literal, lively position, so many more annonists came to this earth and preached their principles to attain Eternal peace and divine existence. If we have to take into our mind we have to live the simplest life; only searching for food and water will be worthless. Our education then, is nothing but waste of time; so, we should from this second, we have to understand civilisation and progression, and we have to establish our life well and give pleasure to all.

Moreover, our needs are innumerous and we are all working hard, but earning a small amount as remuneration, that is why, God's offering by each and everyone by us, is very small and it is not at all sufficient to do the tasks. So, our prophets emphasised to put an end to our needs and our deeds should be to level of the best. Otherwise, we will suffer a lot and cannot live very comfortably, but up to our last breath, we demand each and every deed they expect a huge amount or whatever they demand, it will be given from God, otherwise he or she does not prepare himself or herself to a satisfactory mood. Man is always in between needs and deeds; the two turbulances make mankind as slaves and man is not wishing to get rid of this kind of desirelessness. Desirelessness is a balanced mind which is actually very contented in all circumstances, this is the one and only way to escape from bondage, thus, we shall do good deeds and our needs will come under His mightiness and He will sanction these things. But man is never satisfied or contented by those deeds, then other deeds and needs await him and pull him in front of them and he will not be happy enough. They too introduce multi wishes and they are a never ending process. Thus, if you live a simple life which is ever a "sample", if we understand this, as we think, the mode of thinking if it is wrong enough, our entire life will be a failure. So, we must situate our life within a campus of originality, and piously, if we have fear upon Him, it will be the beginning of knowledge. Thus, we attain wisdom in our life to the entire circle of existence, and therefore, we should swallow facts, the unpleasant happenings into us. Truth will speak for itself, it will give us strength both physically and intellectually. But, our needs and deeds associate with one another; they are travelling on two rails as the train runs, so, we have to bear the steps up to the mark of wisdom. The fear of God is the beginning of knowledge, if we adhere to this principle, then it will be a law to humanity's welfare and betterment, it will thrive as we demand. The main need to a young sapling is only one bucket of water, it will give enough strength and its livelihood will be designed by the Almighty and in this way it will give rejuvenation and the service holders attain some shanthi towards God. Until then there will be no permanent peace in our life. If we are well enough, we can serve the country so much. Like this teaching, our ancestors revealed each and everything which was taught by them through their poems, prose, classics and through some proverbs and phrases. If we get in touch with this literature, we will maintain ourselves to success and succeed in whatever we decide. This mode of organisation over the features we go through with all success, and there will be no failures and success will be determined. Victory and failure may be mentioned literally and these inconveniences enable us to live with contentment and satisfaction. We should be satisfied, what is dispensed by the Almighty, then only, we can proceed our process into true minded beings, whatever words come from the mouth must have some significance of the word's execution and this is the reward to that word and the satisfied mind is the award to ourselves. If we think like this, everyone will flourish with peace ever since.

Therefore, we have to develop the nation towards professional careers. We have to keep our independence ever and we should not do harm to our national integration and so on, thus, India will survive in all ages, So we have to be pandits in the Tamil language and the national language and wishing to grow according to our customs which must be necessary. If there is a leak in our velocity, nothing happens, we will be again and again slaves to someone and thus, our integrity and unity will be not available in our modes of livelihood. So, the loser will suffer a lot in the name of partition. All humanitarian's of these relatives will survive on the basis of confidence and thus, we punish them. Partition of the land is one fact, and another is they have to be separated forever. Some one lives in India, and their relatives will be in Pakistan and there is no possibility to meet them again and again which in not at all active in life. Thus, we are all losing our own brothers or sisters without seeing them, as punishment forever. What a cruel happening it is!.!

Partition means about wealth, if there are four or five members as representatives, they divide into two groups and they equally share and whoever wishes whatsoever region, then they can own the settings of wealth. And if we go to courts, two choices are there. One is INDIA, and another is Pakistan such a crucial situation will be going on without an end. So, this partition, should not at all divide us men and women; they made partition with the cost of bloodly relations and they have to obey their rules and regulations. Like these deeds so many discomforts, we have to face without failure; and it is a very big sin. God alone gives us sisters and brothers. We have no right to do as we wish; everything is previewed and they, alone should accept their wants according to the natural effects and there is no choice of choosing as per our desire.

Due to partition into two countries, there are more inconveniences up to this minute, but we have to take this division as a good thing. As such, our every action and deeds and needs are according to God's will and pleasure. There are no preferences and recommendations to be sanctioned as our own. This is due to fate, almost. And we have to accept the livelihood positive to us and as for our regulations and rules, there all kinds of facilities can be taken due to our politically oriented sects and creeds and also through religions. Such sectors can overrule the country, by the by they can fulfill the commandments of God. In the name of God or divinity, lots of atrocities are going on, and these elements are swallowing as per their own pleasure, they bend the political circle into a complete round and making this, they hope that all are permanent and every regulation should be common to all of us and they provide the natives or its citizens to go through and fulfill their desires but will not be successful in their main body of meeting; such, cruel activity is to be avoided, and all will be punished and remain without getting degrees. So, this is democracy; if it is not in action, it will be dictatorship between them and their desires depend on them alone... they have to suffer a lot and nothing can be achieved so soon. Our precautionary deeds may help or we cannot do whatever we desire and we will be cheated by ourselves and we are the losers of our desires and fortunes and misfortunes. Therefore, we have to maintain an equilibrium between the people concerned and us, will be a fruitful result, it will give laughter in our whole life; such reasons, we have to think overall, and recognize them into our desires and take a conclusion within a second and thus, if it happens, nothing will be in action so, we should properly overrule the regulations and make them as Rules and governmental decisions. If this is possible our recruitments will be beneficial to all of the citizens.

The elimination of strength is only for the accumulation of God's priceless grace and merciful look upon us. This should be the highest learning and earning to us while living in this world. Like a conventional father in churches, God acts through us, ready to forgive all of our sins and dispense us with the best. He gracefully forgives all of our ill habits and orally He serves us to make us as the most noble beings. He takes us in His abode and we have to thank God, for getting this marvelous body infrastructure and its metabolism and the excellent configuration by which we do our karmas without any kind of expectation. It is our duty, which God expresses and insists by all means. This is the natural science of God, by which we should become a part and parcel of His embodimental organisation. Our entire span of life is not at all for dancing with drinking liquors and playing for some amount, sporting for medals and so on, nothing. These activities are done very easily by animals, a leopard can run 136 km speed per minute, can we?this is the game in our Olympic competition and swimming, running, hurdles jumping, Iron ball throwing these are done very easily by animals. We also very idiotically give medals and money for these actions if they do it like animals. In these ways, we boast we are going towards the developmental side. But eventually we are going backwards towards animalhood. So, ponder seriously on about this concept. In the name of illusion we are unknowingly not prepared to attain the unparalleled

Aanandha (sat/ chit/ anandha). This strictly is very much the human's fond goal and we too can live a life of goodwill in our life. So, do not waste even a second of time, every second is countable, and thus, we must make ourselves pure and divine to attain God's possession can be realised without and beyond doubts. Therefore, we have to spend our life time, in searching Himself and so we should be ever in an awakened state always we should be alert to attain Mukthi. We can attain Mukthi, the supernatural power. All men/women are divinely blessed. They can show the right path to all and teach how to lead the human life without any hurdles and puzzles and attain the final point by our own efforts which is to attain Himself. This is the aim of human birth. After the death of such disciples, their body may decay, but the soul will be omnipresent and will always have connection with the Paramathma, so therefore we are nothing but part and parcel of divineness. In such a way, our human life should have an End. Then, such a life is said to be prosperous and purified with shanthi and peace, these two aspects are one, and the only way to attain it is to be filled with patience can be attained. 75% of spiritual awareness is within ourselves and remaining 25% of spiritual elevation will be held through the rest of our life. We can extend or shorten our life span's period and hence, serve the society for its betterment. This world is ever in a good condition, if we wish, we can make it ever blissful, by the way of divine will, which are traits of mankind. The invaluable unparallel and ever blissful life and therefore, we should thank God and pray for the same in our forthcoming birth also.

All creatures are living in this whole universe, they are taking food, copulating and producing their offspring; all metabolisms are likened to mankind; but man alone can realise the creator, if it is achieved by us, that is the total goal of our life and henceforth our activities will be glittering with divine prosperity and, there will be surely no obstacles that can disturb us. Our duties can be discharged to the entire satisfaction and contentment of God, therefore we, will be Brahma Gnanies. This stage is emphasised throughout our human life and as such, if we lose this and are deeply involving in this materialistic and maya world, our life will not be in any way special after birth, we are crawling, then try to sit, then try to stand, and we try to walk and run and then everything is usual as an ordinary being; so apart from this most tight schedule of our senseless human life, we should consider life as a ladder, by which, we have to attain the Eternal plane surface, that is Bliss dispensed by God, Himself. So this Universal supreme truth is emphasised by all the vedic principles in various styles and languages therefore, we should start to do penance with the thirst of God discovering process. He is in us quietly but surely, and without realising this truth, we are searching for Him in the outer world. How is it possible to have a dharsan of Himself? So, our entire life should be entrusted and surrendered always to Himself only. This is the only way to have a pleasant life and leave the world, without passions and admirations also, and final target is Eternal saturation. Though we are post-graduates, gold medalists, we are well versed in the subject of our study, when we ask them some questions domestically or privately, they cannot resolve them, and getting confused, some suddenly are making an end to their life. Therefore, with patiently waiting for His mighty Grace over us, our entire actions will be glittering with divine fragrance and flavour, therefore, our ancestors have given us rules and principles to adhere to. If we follow this right path we can attain mukthi, there is no doubt at all, as a result our entire human life will be meaningful.

When we are meeting so many failures and disappointments, then we should confidentially come to a conclusion, our past karmas' reflections are burdening us and when the time of justice comes there will be no more troubles and agonies. Our parents, brothers, sisters and so on, are dispensed to us by the Almighty, but our friends, we have to choose them. They are also the reflections of past karmas. -When time and presence of mind arise, you can accept our concepts, you should rely on them. There should be no qualifications to question, whatever it is. But, to tell answers properly, we must have experience and self realisation and so, our ancestors and forefathers replied to all the questions. All things will be furnished with good and satisfactory answers which are dwelling inside of all proofs. We are not willing to know them but, just, our presence of mind may answer some phrases and questions. They do not know either English or Tamil grammar, then only you can be a master of two languages. The Quest of knowing the languages, thirst and hunger should trouble oneself, then some food materials and water happens to him by God's grace, He automatically accepts the presence of God and His unexpected standing. So, it is correct that God is very much ready to come to us for rescue; but, we pray Him not to come; such silly things are to be eradicated, then, their lives will be blossomed to the highest level. All the deities in the temples symbolically stress to surrender, then we will be rescued by all means. But, we are not ready to realise the facts.

In Today's very urgent, speedy journey to go elsewhere, we do not have time to concentrate on the facts of our religion. If there is a will; automatically, there will be time; whenever we sleep whenever we eat, whenever time is allotted, we go to films for time passing. Our ancestors had so much time, they built temples and sabha mandapams, how did they have the time? In those days, there was no newly constructed conveyances and conveniences, but the people used their athmic power, chastitic wordings. They flew over fire and stepped down on water and crossed the sea or rivers. They too, were human beings like us. But, their confidence makes God's heart to melt, comes there and helps them in constructing new universities and temples. Please do see our sculptures on the walls of the temples and museums and we become astonished about their capability and their confidence over God. Thus, their bhakthi and confidence brought God, Himself for helping to construct such holy palaces, temples and so on. In Trichy, KALLANAI trumpets the will power of karikala Rajan's eminence in constructing that bridge, it is irrepairable, and it trumpets our engineering supremacy and its magnanimous engineering. What a wonderful service to the nation! long live karikalacholan's supremacy...! And go see the Taj Mahal on the river bed of Yamuna, its miraculous engineering and that is ever appreciated by so many generations. LOVE is LOVE..! This is can be realised, when we are there.

In all departments, we stand still, and we are not equipped with new mechanical engines. But they constructed palaces of the kings and houses for guests and Dharbar mandapams, are realistically immortal ones. So, we should first salute the holy hands and the lotus feet of those noble souls. Their devotion to God, loyalty to kings, when we think about them, our hair stands still throughout, the thoughts mingle with air. Such divine kings ruled over India. So, in the first chapter, I mentioned our emergence of power, eminent scholarships in various fields, their memory power and worthful job oriented science for all, we must bow our heads to their holiness, because, their faith, has the super power, through which they have had the holy dharsan of God and they spoke to Him /Her in the form of mankind and they blissfully constructed temples palaces and strong walled forts. They lived united and they sacrificed everything to the development of the nation and if war was declared, they all went to win over the enemies. Such kings and the common people were very much quarreled by Englishmen, and got independence after their 200 yeas of rulership. They, the foreigners stole so much of gold, silver, platinum, and precious stones. Thus, their nations become rich, but india, still concentrating to learn and earn money, in such a way, we are brought up. Whatever happens, it is divine will, and we have to postpone the pain and when time comes and insists, we should show our valour, just like this manner, we are still struggling with nearby countries, but loss or gain, the two are troubling us because our culture is constructed on peace and shanthi.

According to the past karmas, we finalise a list of diseases, illnesses. Thus, we are troubling ourselves a lot. Now, the situation is to gain spiritual peace; otherwise, we will be inspired by evils and there will be no peace of mind, harmony to the body; our ancestors, sitting under a tree, told several Universal truths, and these are now-a-days, become practical and we should be worthwhile till our last breath. So, if we try to realise God's wish, then, we can have all the possibilities and they, whether educated or not, we can serve the universe in every department. To attain this status, we have to have good education and it should be analysed by our senses, especially God. Then, we will be the top most doctor in the medical department. So, inner confidence is the utmost need. Sri IRAIJI, He possesses several crores of Rama manthra chanting and it is enough for all by means of uncharacteristic quarrels with each other.

Now, we come to have power and are going to do penance for all achievements, and thereby, we can attain all in all. Now-a-days, we need good character wise men to handle our problems and if it is possible, one man who is strictly imposed by good character and peaceful mentality, alone can raise us to the pedestal of Ecstasy. This is our aim and goal of our given human birth. So, we should keep others and other things outside, and we have to accelerate our brain, and the solution will succeed through 360 degrees angle, and we should be living with peace, non-violence and charitable heart. Thus, what shall you do to achieve this, he replied the senior policeman, we should find out the breath of life. My ambition is to have permanent meditation, natural medicines and save our lives permanently and be enriched with wealth and health and name and fame, it is this only our master wants to achieve. So, total surrender is not to be avoided and this goes on, and we shall have victory in all aspects.

If our aim is great, God will sanction good health, abundant wealth and always surrounding us, good news, everywhere, we can taste the Ambrosia of life. So, have confidence upon God and surrender totally body mind and soul and you will succeed. Then you become part and parcel of the Almighty.

Human birth is a holy one, which is not dispensed by God, as easily as possible, we have to jump and jump from all births, and lastly we have this invaluable Mankind birth, such as, we have to return to our own residence, where God dwells there forever. We are whoever may be, all our habits may be different and one's left hand's thumb impression is never compromised with one another, such grand Engineering master, He is! considered and worshipped as the all pervading master, and that is why, we are offering flowers, doing poojas and colourful temples are erected. Whichever creed, sect, we belong, when it is GOD, it is one and the same which comes to the Supremacy of the soul and for this reason, we have to be ready to worship Him and Himself, there is no doubt at all, that is why,, we worship and make Him to grant all our needs, offering poojas on several occasions and this will dispense our heart into unity and integration. If we wish to be a man, (good), we have to chant His Holiest name and fame, we will be automatically, granted wealth and health. Those who are showing their bhakthi, by chanting manthras, some may sing songs about their deities, and all rivers submerge with the sea, likewise, we are the rivers and they finally get into the sea and lose identity. Thus, we have to concentrate on the Holy names of the Lord without expecting anything.

Whenever you have time as leisure, do chant your Ista God's name, should within the mind and in due course of time everything will vanish from this materialistic world. So, we have do to one thing, i.e., thinking always of the glory of the Lord that He can do all things and that we are well and worthy of life can be perceived by the Almighty only, not at all by our careers or professions. Therefore, we should be always patient, chanting the Holy manthra by getting it from a true Guru, and we discharge our duties, all will end in peace and kalyanam. So, there is no piece of time, allotted to ask and tell Him, to save him, it is certainly not in action; God is ready to be present there, where ever the place is, He can come through yogic exercises and thus, we have sidhars to help the Universe in a good condition; and thus, they all will enrich their burdens into the lotus feet of Himself; in due course of time, we can discover the reason, then we will be contented by means of Godly existences. So, we should pray God without fear and shyness. We should call upon Him, when we appreciate the glory of God, everything will be quite natural and nothing miserable will happen, so, our heart returns from tension to normal.

Now-a-days, we have no patience but standing in the queue, expecting to meet the doctor and return home as early as possible. Patience is must needed, that is why we call him patient (patience) Time alone heals our problems, if we wait for a little bit of time. Whatever the diseases the problems are, we have to be patient and earn name and health. Likewise, God checks us to have the strength to bear all inconveniences and finally which is the winner! At that moment, He dispenses His excellence of Viswaroopa and the disciple becomes a half part of God; if it is thus, given as a boon, we should not stand overall on egotism and arrogance and our behaviour, if it is steady, in due couse of time, everything will vanish from the brain. So many diseases trouble us and our primary caution is to get rid of all. Therefore, we should unitedly be adoring all karmic principles and we and our home will be made divine to some extent. This gives us a peaceful situation. So, we must have practice to chant manthra of our God or Goddess, instead of troubles or hectic financial problems arise. Only for our sake we call upon Him, asking so many questions, but He should be rewarded for, He comes to rescue us and return home satisfactorily.

The salient feature of this human birth, so many tongues are necessary to describe its value. In our body, all organs are necessary, but the most activated and with full sensual tips are here, by which we know the taste of materials. So, it is doing two important works, one is to speak, or sing, or be mouna, at the same time, it is the cause of knowing smells and taste the matter which is taken as appetite. To pronounce words, the tongue the most important organ has the most sensual part of this human body. Whatever, we put into the mouth, first grasped by tongue, at the same time, the taste is acknowledged and thus, we are able to take it or not. We conclude and come to a conclusion. The body's clear nature is to intake the right food, it tries to assimilate and make energy, otherwise, within some seconds, it expels those sustenances outside as vomiting; so in our body, tongue's role is very necessary and it has an important role over the whole body, so many organic systems are going on, but tongue is the basic of all organs, by which we taste the food and half of the assimilation is getting over inside the mouth and the porridge goes through the food passage, such trial is necessary to succeed our digestive system. So, this tongue should be kept very alert among all and get use of it, must be exercised throughout our life. With thoughts or without talks, tongue is the main controller of this human body. There are more activities which are done through tongue. If tongue is not working, we cannot taste, not speak, and not think, this is also a salient feature of the tongue. It is created for tasting our food materials. Apart from these, a very important task is performed by the tongue. If the tongue speaks wrongly, then it is the teeth which buys punches and we are loosing our equilibrium of mind; so tongue is to be worshipped with piousful heart and should thank the Tongue for its marvelous part of discharging its duties.

Finally, one day the man is found as a corpse and then his parents become mad due to mental depression, they will be in psychiatric hospitals and we have to pay a lot of money.. because they are parents, is it not? As a result one pure and whole family goes to ruin in our sight. Thus, their family members, neighbours, friends leave them aloof and they are severely affected by serious happenings and in-due course of time, all of them look to have lost mental equilibrium and they finish their life as they need not live in this corrupt world. How? they do not wish to live because, they realise that they are moneyless, respectless living is not at all tolerated and thus, the whole family is suffering very much and they are afraid to enter into the town, they finish their life briefly. These are in practical way of life. We should eradicate these non-sensual activities, whatever happens, these are according to Divine will, and work hard and earn, free from all their debts. But, they are not willing to live a life, that is why, they leave this world brutally. All the younger generations should try not to follow this; please, then you will be dispensed with holy blessings of Lord, by receiving this kind of morals, we need not go elsewhere in search of peace and shanthi. What they invent from substances, then, they realise these are from our inner self and thus, come to realise this concept before God and like this you will be free from all agonies and troubles.

One thing is to be realised by all, if one is not having debts, then he will be considered as a multi-millionaire in the world. Some quantity is realised in our life, we can feel the ecstatic moralisation. God created all of us. Then He has the commitment to look after His generation. Thus, our saints tried to establish their love in the relationship of bondage. They were not nervous, and whatever happens they would be quietly sitting and reading some moral books. Such balanced mind is needed to all of us. Do try to have this as boon of our life. God creates all the organisms, and He is responsible for their foolishness and doctorates, all are controlled, if this fact is realised by us, we will be an independent being in front of God's sanctum santorium. So, we do not believe Education is only for the sake of earning money and getting luxurious things; such unwishable thoughts and reactions are to be deleted by all means. In this way we have to come out of this PRIDE, the divineful life can be imposed on the sculptured mind. He, Himself chooses His residence, and in Saivites 63 siva bhavana holders are equally worshipped because of their still heart and the depth of their bhakthi with confidence, they gave up ego and others, they lived freely and finally attained siva sarupya. So, we too have sense of humour and we have to prepare to surrender in God's Dharbar, every being will be taken under the risk of His own. Therefore, they should have faith and trust in God Himself. We should safeguard ourselves from 3 things. One is fire, other is debts and third is diseases, if these are mistakenly grown, we will be the losers of our self. Try to understand the inner meaning of this sentence through which you all will certainly realise the value of this body and soul. All are the primary wealth of Himself, so, we have to be ready to live and ready to leave also, in this way we teach him to grow with self confidence; but he is not aware of realising these mighty words. What shall we do? God only knows everything and if we surrender to Himself, He will dispense with health and wealth, offering all of our necessities at all times.

According to scientific formula, each and every action, has its own, reaction. It is from the theory of spiritual field; it is quite truthful and a universal happening. If someone does mischievous things to others, automatically it will be like a boomerang and it will return to us with interest therefore, we should be very cautions, when we do activities; by which nobody will be harmed by all means; Thus, man elevates to divine aspects. When, we think to do harmful happenings to others, without any doubt at all, we should face the controversial side reflections, then we have to face their pros and cons. So, we should think good to us and for others; this habit will post us up to the grade of divine level; such noble persons are ever purified to an extent and in this way they, without any particular prayer and penance, attain Samadhi status and hence we can serve all in any structural positions. So, we have to speak or tell anything, which is very easy. According to Thirumoolar, he stresses us to avoid harsh words towards others.. If one who blames us in unparliamentary words or language, we have to react with peace and tolerance which is considered to be the highest range in spiritual world, and it is possible, we can attain Ecstatic liberation through the mighty, merciful eyes or God directly. Thereby it is so easy to tell others, whatever truths and false concepts, we have to be with full of patience and Shantha bavana, we utilize common words and thus, we will attain calmness and pure heart. From the pure heart only, we can educate ourselves first, and then others. This activity can be very easily done for, the betterment of ourselves and others. So, we have to practice this phenomenon, then lots of penances, and multi Vedic principled yagnas are done, that kind of truthful results, automatically is deposited in our account which is transferable into God's bank. So, we should be ready and educate ourselves to use not harsh words, instead of these happenings, we have to deliver the best thoughts and deeds for the welfare of us and others, thus, we will be satisfied and others will approach us irrespective of religion and respect and honour us by all means.

When we are in angry mood, do not speak or write anything for the people; it will make up a status of false conceptional respect, and lose the true friendship and neighbourhood of all will be lost. When, one man stands with anger and is in thirst of doing ugly deeds, they will return and penetrate us in any way. So, sweet words will give others and ourselves, some kind of divinity oriented deeds, as a result, we will be fond of several people; so, our friendship and relational aspect will grow perpetually and with concentration in all activities, that we had not used harsh words. That is why, we usually say, that THE RESPECT IS IN THE TIP OF OUR TONGUE.....! If we try this alone from today itself, we can harvest good and fruitful results in due course of time, all will assemble in front of us, and they also appreciate us because of our sweetest words; There is no monitary loss materialistically, we haven't lost anything, by speaking smoothly and calmly. So, let us try to hold on to this concept and we can attain the glorious status among ourselves. If we pronounce good words, our mind is full of contentment and peace thus, it is easy to proceed with our procedures on a winning note and we will be boosted, dispensed with good health and lots of wealth; So, let us use very easily understandable, considerable words through our tongue and earn a lot of friends and neighbours. Thus, our worldly activities will be so normal and no miserable happenings will happen throughout our life span, because, one who has the sweetest words, Swamy Himself considers them as a penance and He will be ready to put us on the lap of His Holy body. Then, what kind of hindrances are we specially to hear to attain it ? Nothing more than, God is standing before us, which is the most valuable thing in this world; so, we have to tell whatever the subject is, it can be revealed IN A SIMPLE, WITHOUT USING TIGHT SENSES, EASILY UNDERSTANDABLE AND SIMPLE LANGUAGE, ALL WILL BE PLEASED TO HEAR AND TO TELL ANYTHING IN THE SIMPLEST style without boosting our literacy, the dias is given us, to explain a subject with ease and without any kind of misunderstanding and thus, they will be rejuvenated to some extent. So, by our utility of language properly, all will be pleased to hear what we tell on the dias. Whenever we tell something, automatically we also hear them through our inner and outer ears, so, we have to use fruitful words and thus, ours and others would be getting pure and naturally our deeds will blossom with rest and peace.

When we are speaking something, that subject should not be long enough, thus, the audience should think and have confidence to listen to us without editing and so on. Such type of speaking will encourage others to do noble deeds, therefore, we have to utilise our mentality and good sense, towards the betterment of society. We are all always speaking or telling or asking about something, but, there is no necessity for a long conversation, the concept can be revealed briefly and hence, we can grow with patience and restful deeds. Here, we wish to stress something which is considered to be the noblest happening and self-oriented experiences are imposed by us in our daily activities. First do not use harsh words, do not hurt others. Do not think and feel that we are the geniuses and all others are idiots and fools, such kind of thoughts will make us fall from the top to bottom. So, we have to utilise good, easy words to reveal Good sensual explanations to others. It is a divine boon.

Chapter - 6

Wisdom for Elevation

India is a karmic bhoomi, where there is no time for mankind to spend even a second or its fraction without proper renunciation of life. Those who are willing to attain eternal liberation have to follow our rules and regulations and thereby they can be peaceful and lead a peaceful co-ordinated life. May be, we are educated and learning to earn a lot of paper currencies, gold, silver, and platinum ornaments, lots of designed clothes, but these never come with us to the court of God. So, we can be always aware of our thoughts and deeds, that is why, prayer and lovable heart towards others is needful; we can cheat our consciousness but not God, the Almighty.

Motivation of life should not be disturbed; but life's vibrations will certainly attack is the essence is quite essential, otherwise we will not be energetic. If we have belief and total surrender, are only for having a good result in our life, by showing Bhakthi and worshipping sharply without any bilateral assignment, we can have the best felicitation which is given to us. If we want to attain from all, we have to respect first and then show it to others, it will return in 50 per cent above the range of our respect which we show towards others. Therefore, if we get up with anger, we will sit down only out of synthetic commentaries. Nobody will be fond of our words and they never will be taken into consideration and nothing can be achieved with fulfillment.

Those who are willing to lead a noble life, they must be ready to get rid of evil thoughts and deeds, because our body and soul are dispensed by God, and they are to be utilised for the divine purpose only. If we do not use it to realise the creator, our destination of human life, we have to submit to penalties like diseases and illnesses. Due to this, a proverb is in our informal language, "The fear of God is the beginning of knowledge," there is nothing in this world is stable. All things and activities are unstable and nothing is permanent; everything we see, hear and sensual allegations are impermanent; if we realise this universal truth, then our life will blossom like kurinji flower, our heart will be in a normal status, and thus, we can lead a peaceful satisfied life. Our life's ambition, the basic principle of human life is to saturate with Eternal bliss. That is why God created the marvelous body and all the inner and outer organs through which we should predominantly thrive with civilisation and Self-Realisation and thus, we will be free from births and deaths. This body is composed with five major elements and they rejoin their components and the divine soul without doubt goes and joins its origin. We are not at all thinking about this truth, and we have accumulated we can taste the nectar of lively ambrosia. We are doing a major mistake, in order to live easily, we transform into hard hurdles because of our ego, without character and discipline then what is the way to attain perfection?

Most probably all of us can earn Rs 36500/- and more than this amount, our wish to live 36500 days is rare; so, within our life span we have to do deeds and obtain an honourable seat by God Himself; such person, is a bakthiman and man of karmic power, such warriors are very much in need to accumulate strength and produce some scientific miracles. All others, are wasting time in gossiping about others and spend their life in going through rudely, not trying to be participants in His diary. Whenever we come to act our action, our motivation is to accumulate wealth and money and are keen to watch our bank balance and so on. A fine bungalow, most uncountable well finished cars will not withdraw our sorrows, agonies and all evils. Within this life time, we should penetrate all the evils, we have to win life by all means just as a race. Winning point should be our concentration thus, we should make our life very useful for us and ourselves why, the whole universe, too, by, patience and calm, people can attain ecstasy.

Our ancestors too had led their life time as ours, but their service oriented, divine power was utilised only for the welfare and betterment of future generations; they may have belonged to various sects and creeds, but they taught us apart from bloody nonsenses. Due to our sexual collaborations, we wasted our innumerable priceless time factor which is entirely dedicated to the welfare of the society. Finally they attained Samadhi. It is not to be compared, and considered that we are going to be dead. They spread universal brotherhood among all sects and religions; thus, they are popularly known as sidhas. Something is better than nothing. Now-a-days the Art of yogic exercises are popularly adhered to by most of the people; thus, they believe that they can purify mind and intellect and it will be very easy to attain peace. What is Meditation? Even our masters, so-called for acquiring mental stamina to race through any problems in the midst of this materialistic burdens were very much confident that yoga will eradicate all our sins and give us ideology of subject and art of living. So they spent money for yoga, but this is not at all the way to keep body and mind, and then they simply have confidence with characteristic phenomena of the Art of living; in this present period nothing can be fruitful by doing some breathing exercises in the name of yogic exercises; and it is very different to keep clean both our mind and body. Apart from these simply to say that by these practical efforts we cannot attain anything by which we spend more money and thereby only ruin our body and meditation and there is nothing to do so; it is the simplest way to get rid of the burdens; we simply spoil others too, by spending time in the morning and evening hours. We cannot attain anything of ecstasy. So if we do namashmarana of Holy God alone we can make us pure and clean; thus, we can simply attain our inner conscious mental equilibrium.

If our thoughts and deeds are on the right procedure to attain salvation, Bhakthi yoga in this kaliyuga period is very easily fruitful to be saturated with Divine honey and our human birth will bloom to the Highest pedestal plane of ecstasy. Bliss, enjoyment, efforts are having their own limitations, apart from them, we cannot attain anything through bhakthi yoga. We should entrust ourselves in doing godly activities which are only evolving from our inner confidence and pure bhakthi. WE are not at all empowered by anything that moksha can be attained through yogic exercises, through which we can for some hours, retain ourselves to be with calm and peace; but if we believe to attain Ambrosia of Athman, we should be ready to accumulate Tapas with one-mindedness and then all sidhis will be possible through bhakthi yoga. May be we are learning to earn more than 36500 lac crores of currencies, but they have no value in God's government. There, if we want entry, our own consciousness should be full or Dharma and Sathya; otherwise, our recommendations, cannot be taken into consideration even, our shouting of materialistic agony, our crying will not reach even the nearby ears of God. There He will be silent and deaf; thus, we are doing our sins, that nobody is not witnessing our good and bad deeds. But one universal truth is He knows all, whatever is happening amongst us, that is why, our sages emphasised, "The Fear of God is the beginning of knowledge". If we adhere to this factor we will be very much out of the clutches of sins. The difference between good and bad is not all realised or digested by mankind; we are doing such mischievous actions, He is all pervading and that is why, our ancestors lived very calmly, simply and characteristically worthwhile upto the mark of the Almighty's our creator, preserver and demolisher. This is the fundamental factor of our physical knowledge, if this truth is realised throughout our lives, we will never entertain uncharacteristic thoughts and we will be free from ego, desires, have's and have not's. Thus, we will educate ourselves in all respects.

Without mercy and sense of the mentality of preservation, we have trees from our forests and we do not wish to cultivate our lands, thereby we lose our universal Right over this universe. We are very much proud of our multi-cuisine bungalows, types of cars, types of food-materials. But our motto and goal of life is to turn around our mind on one centre, that is, we can be without enough food materials, and now-a-days, we are destructing our fertile lands, transferring them as plots and thereby we hope, in one hour of time to be crorepathies and owners of very much sophisticated bungalows; but we should bear this in our mind, nothing is stable in this universe, everything, each will perish one day. If we have purity in our mind a little money in our pocket, our lives will blossom, and we are all searching for such noble souls.

Whatever we think and proceed with deeds makes us as such good beings in due course of time. So, we have good things to think with their meanings, to the highest level and thus, we can derive some good results. Also, we have to behave well with noble, good hearted neighbours and friends. All are given by the Almighty; friends also; in the sense we make good friends to perform intellectual and universal deeds and thereby live a full fledged life. If a good friend is not suitable, we should take books as our friends and derive good fortune; one day DEATH is certain. Within this period, we have to do good deeds; so good characteristic noble thoughts only end with good fortune. 'Go together' Go to get her this is the inhidden treasured meaning of human beings. As such, if we wish to yield the best results, we have to be ready all the time in all circumstances; we must have good education first. Education makes a man a noble man. These men and women are capable of constructing a new Era and dawn of wisdom, only by which we can attain peace and harmony among us and ourselves too. Whatever we do, it will be the noblest one. When we think of our past, in our old age, we should be proud of those thoughts we had; and deeds too; may be India is an ancient country. We should construct and shape an Era of our life, and the forthcoming generations should be ready to follow our prints automatically. So such a life should be dispensed only by God. For the fear of God is the beginning of wisdom. The highest learning is that by which we know God; all else only load and puzzle the mind.

There is no substitute for hard work; now we are ready to do any job; and it is only for money. But our thoughts are not sharp in their nature; each and every deed is not in the sense of national integration, linguistic proportion; accumulating money within one day. We should be crorepathis; but not in the sense, we are delivering our services to the fullest contentment of the Almighty; is it possible; yes ! it is and can be made possible, but we do not agree with these concepts and each and everyone is having some motto to achieve their goals; many, many innumerable schools are going on, but they are not capable of making man as learned and hard hitting personalities. We are cheating in every way and by that money we wish to live a highly sophisticated life, and the dispensation of our thoughts and deeds will be countable only because of our original thoughts and deeds. When God's court opens, we are not able to see His merciful face and demand our needs; such cruelty will be seen on the face of god; and thus, we are punished; today we can cheat all tax departments, courts with money and social representation, but in the court of God Almighty when we are standing there is nothing or no one who can recommend for our evils not to punish us. Everything is pre-determined and in such a way, we have the best thoughts and the best deeds will be automatically natural; this type of men and women is considered to be the good children of nature and thus, we can get rewards and regards.

If we have enough knowledge of the English language, we can easily understand the topics treasured meanings. Otherwise, we, first pronounce "Rest" meaning our tiredness should have some leisure time, and 'Assured' means totally our inner organs and our soul should be not engaged with anything, after rejuvenation, we can work harder than at the first attempt, and thereby we can finish our undertaking work undoubtedly. But not in this sense, this topic is used, then what is its true meaning. Yes, I have to clarify, the readers doubts and then it will be easy to digest the book, interestingly and by which we will be geniuses in English. I openly declare this phrase's inner meaning is nothing but Do live with full of confidence Now, you go through this book thoroughly you can learn to earn and earn to learn. This is the capital of our lively business. Whatever we do, with full of confidence, we can achieve this work. In this sense of wisdom, the services about sidhars are going to be explained in detail. Now, you, are all knowing the meaning of this title, and it will help you; you will be a genius and you can have abundance of knowledge, finally, be worthful geniuses. Now, a new trend is in custom; if I see a man, sitting on a hilly rock at about 1 p.m., I come to a conclusion that this man should be a sidhar, otherwise, nobody can stand or sit on this hilly region and that is why with my imagination, I make him as a saint.

We may be educated; without fear of God nothing will be successful to the betterment of human society. Really those who are crying for peace and demanding to establish over all shanthi, cannot achieve peace by pronunciation of mere words. Our leaders also emphasise this concept on stages but after getting down from the dias, they will be keen to create problems and puzzles and load the people with so many problems because, they kindle the lamp of peace with brutal minds; so our efforts end with failure. In this universe, any war in the name of land acquisition there is war taking place. Such fools and idiots make the universe unsettled.

Those who are mostly interested to uplift themselves by his/her own efforts by a spiritual life, they must be eminent with these concepts and thus, they can uplift their soul to the eminence of Godliness. So, we have to give first preference to this Brahma Nadi which is the sacred and most respectful one which is implicitly born on its own to us. Through this, we can understand what is life's ambition and aim to be attained, through which we can attain final eternity, ecstasy, which is the final goal of humanity and lastly by which we can attain the solution of our whole life's fulfillment. Therefore, we have to understand the holy secret episodes at various varanas on several topics. Many saints and sages illustrated its concepts very well with their own knowledge and wisdom in various languages and which is relevant up to the margin of time and attitude of humanitarian civilisation. But it cannot be understood easily, and if we are blessed by that Brahma Nadi itself, we can uplift our soul with proper understanding and its operation throughout our life span of time. So, we should know its value of truthfulness through our materialistic education, and vedic chanting. Thus, vedic chanting has no proper temple or holy situation to chant it, it can be chanted in any place and at all times. Thus, everything will be made holy and proper prosperity attained. Naturally it is having its own power. As such, its holiness can be understood, it cannot be illustrated by verses, but it can be implicitly understood by the soul only. Thus, we should rejoice with the soul by the soul of all. The Mightiest soul is Bhagavan Himself, we are soul (with) and without soul but, soul is ever being present in all times, according to god's will and pleasure, they act in their day-to-day action of births and deaths but everyone is subjected to rebirth and death as they are bounded by births and deaths, ever, without this cycle there can be no survival in anything, but body or bodyless there are Pisasams, Vedalams and Boothas etc.,

(Panchaboothas are entirely different from these evil spirits. Therefore, all the epics and purnas emphasise to do good deeds and ever be immersed with best thoughts of Bhagavan and chanting of His names and thereby we will get rid of all kinds of sins; and thus, we lead a divine life. This life becomes a meaningful one for us and others too. Our human life is so precious and nothing is parallel or equal to it dispensed to us by God's grace, and so, should value its invaluable wealth. Only Dharmic thoughts and deeds are to be performed by us to uplift us and make us so divine; otherwise, there is no meaning of the soul's divine creation. That is why, this point is insisted so many times in various places throughout this book, because we are all having plentiful work and deeds to acquire wealth, name and fame by Maya itself. But this is not at all the aim of this human life, this is only to preserve the value of human life and we have to grow day by day, minute by minute to enter the plane equal to God's place. Yes, it is quite possible; and we have to think and our deeds should be in the path way of processions which are maintained by God's sages. Avatars insist that we can be also a survival saint throughout our life span and this is to be achieved without any outward perception but we have to practice it through our inhalation and so our entire life will be divine.

We have to pray and chant His Holiest name throughout our life, we cannot go beyond the limits of modernised life. 'Modern' means, I don't mean this 2017 and on going periods. It is only the purity of mind, speech and our deeds. Others should give authorisation and certificate for our character and pure mindedness; our inner mind is the witness, it never lies; it is the supremacy's representative which is dwelling always within us and governing out thoughts and deeds and giving us all communications of the Almighty; He has appointed the Sun and the Moon and all the stars witnesses and His own possible witness which is governing us at all times in all circumstances, and that is why we cannot go beyond the limitations of His order. He is Sathyam; and Sathyam only always wins; there is no single incident in this universe, that can show us that non truthfulness wins in any one of our efforts; so, in this world, we have created so many posts such us police force, court, CBI and so on and appointed persons to govern the nation and regulate this nation towards normal life. In this manner only we have to maintain law and order. Therefore, we have to be most careful in our thoughts and deeds; but, some ask themselves, O.K., everything is right, but why and how are these atrocities going on beyond our limitations. It is only the illusions of Maya; we must win this maya, it is only possible when we have strong faith upon Him.

We have to perform Sathsangams with learned people and discuss the Lord's leelas; this is nothing but, truthfulness; if we discharge our duties, we can attain the holy Dharsan of Lord, and He, Himself comes in any form or voice without form to save us. Therefore, we have to pray God to dispense us with the everlasting truthfulness and sincerity to uphold good principles. Naturally, human mind is always worrying about wealth, and daily we have to earn wealth in any way, but nothing is passible and if this universal truth is realised by us, we can always be in an ecstatic mood and thus, we will be a part and parcel of Godly happenings. Wherever God is worshipped with good belief and confidence and total surrender bavana, He Himself comes to give us what we are asking Him. Everything will be dispensed by His mighty grace, we can have the positive approach of this universe, so, we have to pray to Him with tears, the whole human body and its metabolism, and we to thank Him always not expecting anything from Him. For we are created by Him, and He knows very well about our needs and deeds. He is responsible to adhere to all our efficiencies and inefficiencies. Thus, we can come to know our strength and if it is realised thoroughly, can be not at all disturbed by this world's happenings, and ever be with full of excellence. In any way, the Lord is not far away from us, He is in all nucleus of even a single atom and one only cell itself; so, we have to perform good deeds and thoughts always throughout our life, to make us majestic and have nothing to worry and be ever happy. When our parents are in a mood of conjual love we are sent by god, through our mother and our father to this universe in such an auspicious occasion, we came to this universe and insisted about our needs and deeds; everything is happening only though His own will and pleasure. So whatever our efforts are, if He proposes and sanctions only we can achieve our aim and goal with victory. Nothing can be possible by mankind to achieve or gain anything, everything, even one cell jeevan embryo may be is created by itself and through the process of God's will and pleasure, it starts its life span and one day, death occurs. So, everything is in His Mighty Hands. If we have strong faith in His efficiency, we can be always be full of satisfaction and contentment. This Maya universal life has limitations and regulations, so we, must have fear upon Him and all our needs fulfilled by His Mighty grace and mercy only. We boldly say that we have achieved all only because of our efforts, example a man and woman are united in conjugal love but the creation of the embryo is His Mighty will, and so we have received our off spring. Emphatically nothing is done, by our efforts, it may meet with failure. But God's mercy only gives us success in all of our deeds and thoughts, and thus, Rest is Assured.

We propose something about the thought which rises and comes but as words, we except their deeds instantly. Is there a justice in our thought, it is wrong, but a crop when the first sapling (new) forms 3 days will be taken, within the second itself, it is to be in action, how is it possible. Likewise, we determine our careers to be finished successfully and its profit should be seen in our eyes, utterly within a stipulated time. Instantly everything should be in action, and this is not at all close to the declaration. We may have brain, through which from the ether itself, the vibrations universally stable for a long time and the result of paddy crops should take at least 6 months and then it yields its generation as rice in a huge amount of formation or creation. We must cultivate ourselves to the entire righteousness in our analysis and then, patiently, time passes away, we can get baskets of rice, and it is to be collected and then, they are giving us the most valuable income due to this cultivation. Absolutely, this is the system which is taking place from age to age forever too. Patience is very essential and too to good follow in the all the departments. Therefore, if we keep our mouth and mind, very spotless we can attain the supreme seat of ecstasy. Various authors and Acharyas declare this moment is normal but extraordinary happenings boost up their needs and deeds. So we have to be silent and patient enough and possessive of the Almighty. Thus, we should cultivate all as Gurus and we can profit by their services as a philosophical study and thereafter they are considered to be the mightiest adherence of good character and conduct.

When the sects, creeds and time tables vanish from our society, all will be first class in this world; you are all having lazy mood and nothing attached sathu like mentality, you are all troubling Himself, that is why, I write this book, to know the classical period of studying and grasping from this education, and thus, we will be happy with our kids and children; we will be turned into some other way, we just start to throw this name and fame and, we can be job oriented of claimimg good wealth, health. I request you all to nominate otherwise, and go through every earlier moment. So, do not confuse yourself and all. If you are in a negative mood, what shall we do? In the home itself try to chant Ramanama with one pointedness, so do chant with confidence and dedication, then we will attain peace and hope to manage whatsoever we have to face is very simple. What is grief and happiness, try to understand, everything is illusionary and imaginary if you hold this concept, then, all will be in your focus and oneness among all. To attain eating, creating, reproducing and dying - these are not only our mannerisms as human beings. You can get rid of all analysis and artificiality.

Whatever the happening is, do not cripple your mind, all diseases have proper medicine, and there are many departments in medicine, but a doctor cannot discover where our mind is; if you identify this classification, nothing will happen to your physical body and spiritual mood; transfer you mind and transplant into various minds' action and try to discover your mind. If mind is discovered, identified, then nothing hence in other fields. Therefore, go around Sri Ganapathy and worship Him, you will be out of all kinds of sorrows and do not murmur try to speak colloquially.

According to our politicians, they are very much selfish while delivering their speech, combined with kumkum pottu, it is nothing but it signifies them as the motive, the first daughter of Moodevi (goddess of poverty) will give the note and I should do it, fool, nothing will happen to shake our hair, try to understand the Lord's exercises and final expectation now changes as godliness, our action will come to an end till the judgement comes when you are in the court.

The king's politics and administration coincide each other and they unite together, with the wisdom of worthily persons, ministers, they ruled over the country naturally with loyalty and royalty and they stand still as a scale in grocery shops gives new, lawful government to the people, and all are living comfortably and give and take policy is admired by all and they follow rules and regulations with piousness, the country is well conducted and each one's presence is important in the Dharbar Hall and they treat all as the same. In their rulership they cultivate drawing, painting, singing, cooking, agriculture, and so on, going on developing and shanthi sets in throughout the kingdom and all live freely with truthfulness. Thus, they rule the country with all priorities, they normally work hard and earn money and live with all worth growing subjects. So their naturalism is maintained without any fault and nothing is wanted by the name of allowances. They do not know bribe and other unlawful authorities, and activities; they live with divine perception thus, the whole nation is living in a normal condition and they live understandingly without failures, wherever they go on their doubts, they win the race with distinction and they do not fall in any status, thus, their governance is peculiar and they with satisfaction orally felicitate each other. Their genealogical ideas are very much honoured and they grow well day by day, and thus, nothing is incorrect and they lead their way. The very weak they treat each one as themselves and they plan to develop in all ways and the growth of all cultural arts and agriculture is marvelous and there is no simple mistake in their workmanship. Thus, we can utilize our time, can be enriched with lots of activities, and if we exercise our duties regularly, we can achieve all things; and as such exercises are very good for health and our excretory system will be scrutinised at all times, thus, exercises are necessary for all of us. Our studies should be coming in action, then only, we will be beneficial in all departments of home accessories. And thus, we can be very much beneficial to our daily important things as such, all vegetables can be bought in freshness, and they are very much useful to our daily necessities. So if there is a place in which we live, all facilities can be got in an easy way and live genuinely till the last breath. God is great if we study to a limitless level, if we do not worship god, there is no use of this education, thus, Thiruvalluar states, it is an universal Good verse. And if we are learned, it is not much enough, we hold our living with comfort and ability and this is beyond our selection the model of the house, as such all are houses, but if it is full of members and happily sitting taking food, then only, it is called a home. Therefore, we should adjust and understand their normal qualities; we should grow with friendship, then as a relation, it is considered to be the conscious section of human relationship. We should have relation with all and that is called home, and must call others as our relations, then there is no chance to be meet with war, battle and competition at all, So if we try to form a home we should cultivate our work, and understanding must be cool and happy allied commitments.

We have to repair all departments of our nation, for integration apart from creeds and languages. We have so many customs and civil rituals but no quarreling habit is installed, let us have good looking, charming goodness of face. This should be had by all of us. This is the 1st symbol, that our nation is stepping through real civilisation and national integration. We, should be ready to serve the country, not individuals. Thus, the nation also does its duties to the welfare of all people correctly, if these two co-incide once, then everything will be divinely oriented and God alone comes and goes everywhere on earth and to His natural abode too. But we should be ready to invite Himself along with all angels. If we have faith in God, if we do criminal things, He will punish us, then the whole nation will come to the original orbit of discipline, now, who is God? Is there God? what is He doing? these foolish questions are already encouraged by our youngsters and the society does not respond to it thoroughly, and it is one of the reasons, because of our earlier announcement of prostitution we see the chapter on advertisements. Now our aim is to become a Doctor with crores and crores of money- the honours are heavily wiped with money mindedness, that it is making us not a man, but a worried man too. There will be no separate suggestion to get peace of mind through ourselves. If we stop our whole non-sensual activities, then automatically peace and harmonious life will be established as its own caliber, which is annexed by God Himself.

The course of structural physical body's strength is upon our delicious and sakthi yielding ground nuts, dhal and all edible things. The strength for all is increasing day by day, and our body is physically giving enough sakthi for equilibrium of metabolism, which means the truth of happiness and enthusiastic life. If all are well, first we should keep our body, to be maintained as a circuit house, we have some separate place, where we are in our own positions and thus, we use our power to attract all for the welfare, of mind and body. Thus, we should take more medicines and keep us as a diseaseless person. Really, we should lead a life of no disease. It is quite possible to take over police custody and if they call us and some others, we are questioned boldly and normally they ask some questions and see if we have answered in our ways and they permit us to go home. Thus, they interview for electing persons of mental and physical welfare of that permission and then, they scrutinize our bio-datas and we are selected as a policeman, and undergo several physical and intellectual ways to keep us to win over our woes. Thus, we are selected, are tested in physical trails, and must pass in these programmes. Interviews are conducted in all subjects, our approach and body language, how we are working at that time, and they try to ridicule the fear over their knife, we have to move out of the reach of the knife, and we should write answers to the questions; thus, our optical, ethical, and cytological experiments are tested and we are selected for the further trials to make us true policemen and they file their life as a conditional mother who realises his son, by means of internal legal and ideally they encourage her to be fit for all kinds of experiments and we are put in Hindi classes; knowing Hindi both to write and speak thoroughly and even we write the synopsis in Hindi, it is a good fortune by which we can step in the ecstatic world and we can look at our allotment of service very well with super satisfaction of all our masters. Masters are always well versed with the martial arts and they are pronounced in Karathae and so on, trembling arts are very easily seen to be practical and they manage with these arts, they create a new culture and they live lonely with privacy, thus, they are not known by the earth people. Such a fine art which originated from Tamil Nadu, then it spread over India and thus, they capture the martial art as the pavithra bava ecstasy among the arts. Such art is now, come to the streets and they give us both money and claiming interest.

The interesting feature of living is LIVING --- Human birth is a boon to any particular Athma, through which all organic systems are in operation and it is the consciousness of all the systems which are in control and they are possessive to habitation of the particular aspect is nothing but Athma, which is unseen; but it is implicit to feel the presence and through which the metabolism is in operation. Thus, 'I' controls its movement and also the neighbouring aspects of sub classicals are also in control; we should pronounce, the Almighty of Athma's presence. It controls and at the same time, it also controls other 9 pranas to be in action that is successfully imperative to govern it and at the same time, the other 9 appanas. Main and subsequent metabolism may differ in the middle of life, but all are governed by the Mighty Athma which is ever living and indestructible and so He is considered to be oriented Athma, which is where this is at all times, it will be significantly serving all profits and blessing all at all ages.

Even today, itself, there is a friend and he has not realised that He is swami. Like kuselan met Sri Krishna as his Gurukula friend, because of His healthy wealthy status, kuselan's wife asked why he could not go to see Sri Krishna, He is not only a friend but you have both been educated in the same saint Santhibeebi Ashram. If He identifies you, everything can be boosted up can you go and see him? Thus, she explained, due to poverty, to eradicate this, his wife emphasised that it was wise he started with an handful of aval made from Rice. And he went, but at the gate, the keepers did not allow him into the palace. They said that Krishna did not have time to hear his words. Suddenly, swami, came from within the palace and embraced kuselan, and introduced him as his best friend in gurukulam, now he is not well, I think so and he asked kuselan what was his in hand and to give him something as a friend meets another, they share their friendship, because Krishna is wealthier than the new comer; thus, Krishna asked, suddenly, he took the aval in His hands. He unveiled the knot of the Aval vasthra and saw some Aval in it and he took at first a handful and all of them had taken aval and they were also satisfied at that time. He thinks about his situational life and gifted him with each and every article so that they transform themselves into good health and wealth. Thus, Krishna is ever ready to dispense them, and He associates with all deeds. Kuselan returned to his hut, but there was no hut. People standing nearby conveyed to him that she was his wife and 27 children they were his sons and daughters. Kuselan felt emotional and he exclaimed the wealth that was dispensed and he prayed Him for His good doings, but not to transform him. "I want to be a normal male child, with full of names, excellency and ecstasy, so do dispense nothing but the one-concentration on the glorious state of Krishna Nama" (name). Thus, kuselan became a wealthy man but he lived as a gnani always. It is the sample of krishna's dispensation. Thus, if we call on Krishna with full of confidence and surrenderness, He is in the vaikundam along with Sridevi. Such a proper penance is here and we must celebrate all days as ritual ceremonies, Thus, once asked Him, it is already dispensated. Go through. This is the aim the true bhaktha needs in directional without diversion. Thus, ever thinking about Krishna is so much of Anandha, other things are perishable and that they are unstable, not permanent ones, and ever thinking of God will proceed towards Mukthi, and that is why we wish to have God's dharsan and live a satisfied ratio of democratic sense and he can be also witnessing this growth with cultivation. So, each and every one is done, if he perishes all will blame us, and that is why, I am away from that crowd says Krishna. Thus, Bhakthi is to be nominated as a No. 1 in our life and that is why this birth is demonstrated to us. Therefore, we should be along with the Head of the family if we see Him, we will be profited, like this, if dharsan of swami alone can dispense anything, if you know the fact, then we will not offer anything as our needs. So, our needs and deeds should be full of consciousness, understanding these are nothing but God's modulations and thus, we reach Him.

One point should be remembered always that whatever we do as deeds, they are the thoughts-deeds-and satisfaction at all. If we surrender to Himself with His noble notification, there is nothing in this universe to be afraid of and hesitate in any situation at all. Whatever He fixes it will be fruitful when the time comes. So, we should be waiting for the hearty grace of His priceless mercy. If He is not willing, that deed will not be fulfilled even by our own efforts. According to this universal effect and decision we must set up our plans and will always win the policy. Mankind can propose, He disposes, that is why we should be charactewise the best, nothing horrid will happen in our life till the end. Of course we must do our duties according to our age, then the whole world will be ours and we can have normalisation of mind because our mental seat is given to Him. So we should give our seat to God, where he will be seated and give judgements for our deeds and thoughts, thus, He is in the Dharbar, then only, we will be benefited. So, the fear of God is the beginning of knowledge. Do have it in your blood and mind; never withdraw this universal concept; if you analyze, you can write a volume. Whatever we do, if it is a success we are very happy and give parties to celebrate it in a fine manner and if it is failure, we are filled with sorrow and become very much dejected. This kind of differentiation must be removed. The equilibrium of heart and intellect should be always on one plane of life, not by our own self. Self ... is not this body, it is the soul, it never ends by whatever force we try to do it. So we are able to have births and deaths.

Do take pure vegetable food for 48 days without even egg too, all your food consists of nothing but mutton, chicken, fish and whatever are considered as non-vegetarian. Only vegetarian food will guard and guide you full well. So, do not worry, be happy, within 48 days, your body's colour will change into pink, constipation will disappear. The fear of God is the beginning of knowledge, for this sentence, if you analyse calmly you can get even more health and wealth. If you are healthy enough, then, you earn wealth in a new way and rest will be yours. So, do not be afraid of anything on your side. Also we must enrich our war strategies and the yogic exercises, that push oneself, to upgrade the military services. So, please do develop in all fields of military services in order to overcome military pressure from any front; it should be upto the mark and beyond it. It is limitless, which is further expanded by the mindset of other nations which think about any signs of war. Though we are beyond sects, creeds, and different religions people are here our ambition is to unite with each other though opinions may differ, from one to another and we should be all along with one another; if this is done only, we can only truly know the unity in diversity and what it means herewith. So, we must respect and honour our whole family, that is, the society, thus, we should also realise the exact meaning of these customs, and we will be the predictors of the whole world.

We are characteristic in our principles and thus, we can make money in various businesses and dedicate our whole life in such a work, earn money and live comfortably but we are absolutely under the control of our mind; we make money and thus, save the same, if we come across expenses for a programme in the family the estimate may be Rs 12,000/- we can successfully conduct the programme with only Rs 7600/- and rest of the money is saved; we win the race and save money and buy a new house, or start a new business and learn to earn, and we will not spend money for medical expenses and so on. We control all sundry expenses and are residing in a comfortable house and make it all our own, we save money and the ration card can be utilised in all types of income and thus, they are becoming rich. But others like us, middle class people when they have, they are so much careful about even a single paise. They question which is ideal, what is the benefit of doing this, what will be the profit by this way, in this style they calculate all of their have's and haven'ts and do whatever is necessary or not. Even they can wear a shirt for more than one week, but we cannot do this kind of saving the money in order to face the future. The next one is thoroughly ready to spend money if they are asked by others, giving all notables, and their importance, even 100 times, we have to go to them, explain the marital and material life and its do's and don'ts. Thus, we have to know the importance and they are ready to spend their money without any kind of control and thus, we have something in this box. But, they are doing non-sensual activities to the extent and trumpet themselves as rich and the richest. They copy others in order to buy articles like them whether they are necessary and their words are put in hell. Thus, the IIIrd division of people are nothing to be noted, their income, wealth, is a welcome, and even they are ready to spend Rs. 20,000/- to pay for each and every ice cream, then you can imagine the spectrum of their life's style and they are countable in our syllabus. They do not worry of money because their ancestors have a lot of wealth, through this income they live a gigantic life and their mind is not at all having mercy, gratitude and even education. They live as their mind alone recognizes, and they do not respect anybody, they, just rule over their estates. And they do not know or recognize poverty, hunger, thirst and so on but they do not wish to know these condemnable life to follow our simple life. They accumulate a very popular name, always keep some elements with all rowdy qualities in order to recover money from the penniless people. Thus, they are living a life without any struggle. These people should realise this global part of the world. Then, they may become kind hearted and will spend their money for the welfare of the public and ultimately earn good name and fame among all. So, there are so many ways to endorse our points for the progress of all departments. Thus, we can make our INDIA as a super forceful nation and make INDIA as the first in all levels. But, these kinds of people are not willing to do, their co-incidents insist them not to do such kind of expenses, and whosoever, wishes to wind up our name and fame are countable in His world. And we have to provide some unsatisfactory mind, then we cannot spend even a single paise for the development of the whole humanity. So they do not at all thrive in their own and personal life.

This life is always an experimental one, where we are all tested, and through our marks and ranks, she/he is considered to be the 1st, IInd, IIIrd; thus, the ranks are modernised towards further studies. Such procedures are in day-to-day life, and most do not want to take full marks. The brain IQ power is wonderful; students discontinue higher studies, we cannot fetch bright students who are not able to continue higher studies. This is a pitiable one, too. So, we should not give rank according to marks only, but rank, value IQ and range of grasping other subjects, conduct and character these should be fundamentally taken, and given seats to further classes. Our poor

India cannot develop because of this recommendations and financial floating. This is to be done away with very well. If we follow this system our very own geniuses can be discovered and we can give subject wise marks and the IQ gives him/her the supersonic post in administrative care or materialistic position. In certain cities there are no eminent doctors to examine some of the serious disease; these doctors can give medicines only for dysentery, fever, headache etc. They also give us a reference letter, to see other doctors in different cities. Though they are very well educated in their subjects they know nothing but give us a bill for Rs. 12,000/- for the treatment; we are blinking our eyes and certainly pay the bill in the counter. Now if we take fast, whenever we can, it will give us a very fast relief from the discomfort. Whenever our well trained doctors examine us, they can diagnose what our illness is, and they will give sizable medicine, and we go with the medicine and with food control, will recover very well within some days. As days go by, everthing is alright; parents should give royal food like orange juice. If there is sleep without disturbance, slowly and steadily we return to normal and sufficient food can be taken. Orange juice is a very good pain reliever. Thus, our troubles are excused and we have to say thanks in a vegetarian style by preparing Nivetham and worshipping God with Bhakthi and penance. Then serve nivethyam to all. Thus, this Annandhanam is done, and all will be normal and divine they become sensual and proceed with normal health and wealth. As per our Vedas what is described as the punishment, not to do poojas without nivethyam; is it possible to carry on thus, by Goddess kali.

Try to have big breakfast in the morning, and we can live with full of strength up to 79 years and above, it is salvation force. Do mind it all, whoever comments anything about us and our actions, do have it in mind, we do not take it into consideration and then analyse that opinion whether it is correct or not, thus, if we go on thinking about the actions' dynamism, we cannot at all proceed with such comments. Whatever they are commenting about our activities, we should not consider them to be analyzed, and thus, we go on with our ideas and reciprocally of course reflecting on these comments, we have to finish our actions and our thoughts should become deeds; and should not hide from those perceptional perceptions. Therefore, we must have an iron heart, which cannot be melted in any situations; we have to go with full of confidence, and so we can succeed with our efforts. Such victory is the ONE we have to take into consideration. Thus, we have to proceed with a crystal and clear cut mind, we will be fit for consideration of hope and achieve our goal. It is not at all some comments. It is the resourceful system and we have to take consideration of our acceleration towards all our activities and we can attain all efforts with effectiveness and straight forwardness. If anything goes out of form, we have to think deeply and consult some eminent people and we can take ideas which are full of clarification and thus, sort out our thoughts; this gives good formation of a permanent temperament of character of mind and oneness of mind with intellect, which leads us to the perfection of certain oneness of our efforts. This aids us towards the perfection according to our present and future. So this will not only intergrate and answer our obstacles, they will solve the problem towards shanthi and peace. Therefore, we can attain oneness of mind in all activities and thus, we can attain the fulfillment of any situation in consideration of absorption of the best qualities of a normal divine life; this is the goal of life, it is in sidhi, our life will be meaningful and this meaning would clearly guide us towards such phenomenon of the ever glittering light of confidence which will be sanctioned by the almighty and we attain Gnanam as quoted by the Vedas.

If this stage is achieved we will be able to fulfill life's management very easily, because our duties will be done by the Almighty alone. So, there is no necessity to be worried of the future or the present. Every second of our life will be under the guidance of Him, so there is no necessity to be troubled by whatever happens. We can confidently lead our life with full of divine power. All the actions in our life that are going on are to be considered as predetermined by Him and as such there will be no bad remark to be pointed out, because its master is the Almighty. Therefore, we should not suffer because of the thought of deeds and consider our maintenance due to the unnecessary vibrations, it is common for mankind, will not be in our day-to-day life. So, be alert about what is happening, you do not think you are undignified; it is the duty which is operated by the Senior Operator and thus, you can be free from all unloyal concepts. So total surrender, confidence are the most essential to live with victory and succeed in life. You should not dream about your life with such illness of mentally collaborated fits.

We can face our life with full of satisfaction and with total surrender to the lotus feet of God Himself. Therefore, we should live with purity of heart, doing our actions with full confidence in God, and the main point is the continuous confidence upon our efforts and with the file of God's presence who will satisfy all our fulfillment. If we are living in His path, everything will be a success and everyone is considered as pure and confident, according to our perception, Thus, we can be chosen by the

Almighty Himself and we will have fulfilled all our aims and we can possibly live up to the mark. In life, the most needful is total surrender to the Almighty.

According to our cultural and spiritual and materialistic harmony how do we estimate our development? According to the nation's agricultural progress only we should understand its value. We should understand the value of the nation and its classical contribution to all the member citizens, this is main account of God and thus, we must love God and try to work hard on our own in the agricultural field. By His Grace we will supply to all the nations. Thus, we must earn and live purposefully. This is our prayer. It is His ambition, I am very much happy to give a sample of His ambition to this nation and I garland once and it will fill Him with garlands through all others. Truthfulness alone keeps a family with oneness and there is nothing to specify the most important situation. Likewise, where there is happiness, there is God, it should be understood by our own experience. Our nation is the primary agricultural nation, and if we have to thrive in earning, we should concentrate on the development of agriculture and thus, we can be the masters of agriculture in the world's records. Such a great event is proposed only by the people and the government, then India will be the super most powered country in this world. We have to buy so many weapons, they never keep us in right time, but if we do trade with all nations, there will be no chance for a war or even a battle between us and the other nations. All are attached to one another which is unseeable, but it happens to be felt, this is the cosmic correspondence with man to man and creatures with other creatures. For we can live comfortably with peace, if we throw all our weapons into the seas we should live a peaceful and admirable life, then God alone comes to our homes for having even water, such a nice Rajyam will be factually established all the people and God Himself, make their names very stylishly and they give us so many titles, and thereby we can be honoured by more statesmen and our nation's prosperity will be gloriously celebrated with pure happiness and enthusiasm. Violence is the second weapon, we have to drop off, even a single pistol and thus, we can surely exercise an effective and spiritualistic life, all along the nation's without any doubts. Compulsorily we are working for the development of all countries, but there is nothing remaining as per our dreams, we now come close to touch all hearts with love and enlightenment. Thus, we have to attain the target without any kind of mental requisition, and our children are in the way of thinking, this is yes and this is no, if they start to analyse, then their mind will be collapsed without, fear of God. Our ancestors may have done many sins without any fear of these controversial quotations, what will we do; if we come to understand by experiences, we will be particular to compromise the two sides and thus, we can create a new era of new evolution. This betterment of world is enough to get rid of unusual activities and thus, we are all happily talking about very healthy subjects.

All our efforts physically or mentally are only the basement of serving the society and earn money and thus, run our family without any failure; this is the media of consumption is to be our ownership of controlling our organs throughout the paths in our body, but they should to be controlled without any conditional play, as such we have to try and do whatever the concerned job is but we have to see here and there, if there are no vehicles coming on both sides, then We can proceed our passage without any damage. If we work hard as per our schedule, we will have money, as salary per month; as such our efforts and actions are only for earning money to lead a common life; if there is no money in our hands respect or honour will not be given by the society. So, if we want recognition and privilege we have to obtain crores of money, and from that minute begins the clarity of such highness which comes by itself. Therefore, we have to worship Bhagavan at all times anywhere and we must earn a lot of money. But we preserve the society in order to earn and learn those very important possibilities which are considerable to those who live in this hectic problem of life. So, money is must without money, we have nothing to be done to the entertainment of worldly happenings. Those who are parents, sons and neighbors, may be, the seats are given only if they pay money to proceed their negligible daughter's negotiations.

Though we are all sincere in each every action which we do, it should be nice and truthful for us and all, it should be our motto and thus, we can lead dharmic life through yoga, that is easily through bhakthi yoga which will shield us at all times. If a plan to construct a building and if we cannot construct it we plan to do a special pooja to all deities and thus, all our sins will diminish and we can do the work promptly. We must with pleasure do the pooja to all and we can have peace and shanthi. Therefore, we should be prepaed to accumulate our sakthi which is nothing before divine sakthi, we are throughout only acting through God's decision. So everything will be finished and furnished to the entire satisfaction of oneself. Of course, we can uplift ourselves to the best pedestal of peace, that is Bhagavan's almighty grace and through this way only, we can get rid of passion and materialism and obtain spiritual elevation of our Gurumahans. Therefore, we have to get trained. Gurumahans also should come with us to know what Aanandha is and how to conduct this. If these Gurumahans are known by us, we must bring them with us and see and hear the manthras chanting, they always think about us and we shall be promptly peaceful moving towards this spiritual elevation. All are worshipping according to these poojas and direct our thoughts and mind towards God's Roopam. Thus, the Guru sees, next day, he sees thus, he sees once, twice then it will be innumerous, and he can register the Roopa of the Almighty in our mind and imprint it in the hearts of his primary disciples who are selected as equalised students. They take them as lessons and do it vigorously but their aim is to construct a temple in their mind and call him towards their mind and thus, their mind will be ever clear and clean. Thus, our life will be the same as the Guru's. Just doing this, we will be free from bondage and we can stand still in our mentality through which nothing will happen as we plug out the reservoir; thus, we can be benefited through sathsangam without failure. Sathsangam, is the easiest way to attain Mukthi, because, where sathsangam is held there will be lots of money. We can stand still, our mind will become strong and courageous to tolerate all, this is nothing but tolerance. Tolerance is in other words, called Tapas, if our tapas is truthful, our clean and clear mind will be trained by nature to withstand these good and false records of our heart because of our activities, and then, we can do all rituals and ceremonies and the beneficiaries are satisfied and they bless us to give elevation to their worlds. So, the pithru duty should not be neglected in our life. Once in a year we must perform the rituals for they will bless us surely and through this way, we will be honoured and blessed by our ancestors and they will be our mind and we will have extraordinary peace to renounce our life. So we have to make some room for materialistic life and at that time we can make some money and get the necessary things to fulfill the family needs; then we have to climb up to the majestic place of Godliness. And if these thoughts do not occur in us, there is no value to our life at all and ever disclaiming sakthi from others. So, we must seek the residence of the Mighty Soul, and if it is properly experienced, this is the utter probability of clarity of mind and thus, God will be seated in our mental throne and we will have peace.

This peace will not be disturbed by anything and we should be ready to seek even Sanyasam. Till the heart disconnects all the sums of this materialistic world it will not at all be sanyasa; who detaches even mother's passion, he will be considered to be a true sanyasin. They just claim themselves as sanyasa bhava and there will be attachment or detachment from and for other objects, considered to be the systematic life of the world. In this situation. a golden verse said by Sri Vivekananda comes to mind,

"I do not stand on my mother's back in order to give and get some pleasures by my wife. According to my mother, my wife will be an ordinary woman. After my mother, she will be the queen to my daughter-in-law". So, we represent all by women- hood, thus, we salute all females. Because she is the practical roopa of dedication and satisfaction. For all our failures, we may educated ourselves with many reasons, the only reason is, not doing the Karma Pindam. If it is not given yearly once, and we are very much troubled by hunger and thirst. If we do the needful at least once, we will be dispensed with all materialistic benefits. So, we have to be mindful of the duties towards them with honesty and pure service, Then will be blessed with health and wealth and they will also bless our every action to gain victory. That is why the Tamil verse says that mother and father are the most important gods according to Tamil culture. If we salute our parents, then it will be the Mokasha to those who are truly, sincerely, obediently serving their parents, they are entitled to Mukthi with no tapas and pooja because without parents, we are not here. This is the most important verse also.

Those who are interested in spiritualism, first, they should hear His glorious deeds through Bhagavathar's lectures, and chanting Bhagavan's namasmaranai, always, continuously thinking of His names and thinking of His presence. If we cannot think of Him because of our full working time, should be worried because of not being able to chant His name. Because of Namasmaranai of His glorious deeds of His Bhakthas, it gives us enormous strength to do anything in this world. There is nothing better which always gives happiness; and nothing there is in this world here to give us sorrowful activities. Both tastes make this life meaningful in the midst of sorrows and happinesses, we are choosing both the categories according to the financial situations. Very few people are working and earning money for their daily needs, in the midst of this hectic proceedings we do not change our mind to chant Bhagavan's Namasmanarani. If he does not think of Narmasmaranai, he feels that he is nothing and thus, he must be with the capital, that is, God's grace, interest is the consequences of daily life and he unites with God always and has merged with God Himself. Without chanting the name of the Almighty, Namasmaranai or not to do namasmaranai he cannot live normally and cannot be with peace and shanthi. Therefore, whenever, whatever he is doing, he should steadily fix his life with the Almighty and he is very much troubled that he is not able to have dharsan of God. So he thinks and tries to chant without delay. He is always trying to have attachment with God Himself, and thus, he is living his life with full of satisfaction and contentment. If we are going in this way, always, there is no differentiation between good and bad always, by the grace of God. Everything will seem to be only happiness. Whenever we cannot do namasamaranai, some agonies appear before us and we cannot live a normal life. Without His presence nobody can live a full-fledged life, thus, he thinks and that is why, the impulses of concentration of mind will be stable and those thoughts of spiritualism is never apart from him. Therefore, we have to chant His name and holiness of charity should be pasted on our mind, and our mind is the seat of God. And thus, if we submit our heart as His residence, it is recovered by Him, then our mind never slips from the remembrance of His Almighty without any feelings and disturbances.

While we are living in this materialistic world, we should never get rid of our thoughts of Bhagavan. The depth of our Bhakthi itself alone measures our interior sakthi which we get from the Almighty and this is always with us and we have to find the significance of His presence in various roopas. Thus, the Almighty exhibits Himself in male or female or whatever He thinks about our presence in His heart and so He showed the interior presence of us in His heart. Bhakthi means not at all the density, potential in all forms of itself and we should ever be in His heart; this is natural; but it is essential that He, Himself should be present in our heart. As such, Bhakthi is the calculative method of His and Bhakthiman's goal of life, as we are having some ambitions, God has some, does anugraha to the bhakthimans and lift them to the ecstatic potential and density. Thus, both are realising each other and this is the highest level in spiritual life. Whenever we think of Him, our whole body is trembling, which is the first sign of spiritual enforcement which is in light and tears roll down from the eyes without any reason at all, and the sensual silence floods our mind and we think that our Ishta Theiva's mentality is accumulated by all the organs. Silence only is needed there and mind speaks in mind itself. This is the mental silence and we are getting into the heart of God and He also does have His sight on us, thus, we can feel the presence of Himself. Whenever, he or whoever it may be, they speak about spiritual substance, the bhakthiman himself also is accommodated by the same feelings and he comes out of this materialistic world and enters into oneness with God. He is having capability to force his variagya through penance into others. Thus, true disciples are transferred and oneness of Himself is formed and he is never with alms, without the thought of God. This is a divine boon to oneself by the grace of God Himself, This stage is not formed, it is the one and only fruitful result of spiritual harmony and thus, the pure bhakthimans are living a life not for themselves;

they are for the whole universe. He can spread the spiritual energy throughout the universe and such waves and vibrations, the people are having ultimate aim of attaining the spiritual sight ultimately the Mahans and sidhars must be in search of the bhakthiman's presence and they will be without form but with voice. Thus, the Almighty's harmonious sound can be heard by all bhakthimans and their mental equilibrium is not ever disturbed, because there is no other sakthi in this universe to destroy this Oneness of mind and spirit. The soul, even if it is travelling elsewhere, its concentration is always with the trail of Godly divine oneness towards us. Therefore, we should be ever watchful to have these vibrations and thus, we should be melted with bhakthi and karma yogas. In kaliyuga Bhakthi is the small, but very fruitful way to attain His grace and mercy slowly but steadily. Thus, it is in our hands we got the divine grace to obtain oneness with God always and this stage is to be determined by ourselves and that is why, we are very silent to taste the divine vibrations and its experiences too. If we are in a library, automatically we will be silent, but in the cinema theatre, we are speaking one to another without any break and in a cricket ground, there will be noise only because of the audiences' promotion of a player's play and they applaud and make, exhibit their inner joy towards that noise, that is all.

One who is merged with the ecstasy of godly presence, He/She really avoids naturally all of this worldly needs. They will be out of this mundane necessities and they live with little needs, and they are encouraged by their soul itself, as they are always concentrating their existence on Mother's grace, both will make them bold and encourage them to bring out of their knowledge and wisdom of Godly existence towards the presence of the Almighty. Thus, the bhakthimans are trying to acknowledge the Krupa of God in the simplest style. Therefore, we have to renounce life and have to lead a bhakthiful life through which we can entertain ourselves and others. This capacity is due to Bhakthi and total surrender towards purity of mind and we have to create the qualities of sympathy, grace, mercy and so on. Gods should be nearby our hands so that we can have the Anugraha of them, and have to be simple by all means. Our bhakthi should be solid and the social and spiritual life should be our neighborhood action and relationship with Himself. If this stage is our sidhi at any time, it is a boon to us and we can serve the people and make our life the sole perfection. So, if we have perfection in our deeds, then our life style will be keenly pure with ecstatic perseverance at all times. Though we are out of the sketch of manual life, God Himself stresses up to do the needful at the time of penance and thus, we can do the best of our deeds throughout life. This is possible and therefore we should stand up with purity and steadiness of knowledge, can set up our life with pure knowledge and wisdom. Our inner eyes will start to see the divinity in all creatures and in this way all will be with the parasonic ecstasy. This stage will not repeated to any side. The one universal truth is we have to realise, that is; once if God's entry into our paraorganic system, no chance at all to be free from these attachments, they only are the one and only intellectuals and spiritualism. This is the system of life which has the entertainment of Holiness and Higher Attainment. Therefore, if the chance of entry into spiritualism, there will be no manual exit without spiritual world. Without God's thoughts, then, we will never think of anything about Himself. Clearly, we will be the Almighty and we are considered one of the partners of spiritualistic partners among Bhakthimans. Thus, our situation is set up by the Almighty and we will be lifted towards the frame of Godliness. This is nothing but the entrance of godliness by all means of life. Then life will be clearly understood that all actions are nothing but the perfect one among all probables. So, we should try to construct our activities towards high knowledge and wealth, these are possible, but no use of these, though they are obtainable, one second is enough, but 0.5 seconds is essential to forget these articles. Thus, they have the value among saints. All are doing penance but the appearance of God, we simply ask Him to give wealth and life span and its length, and is there any VIth sense in work, no, Nil.., if we are dispensed, we may ask Him to dispense Himself to us and sanction Bliss and ecstasy and finally for us to be merged with the lotus feet of Himself; this must be the requisition of the Gnanis. But, certainly, we are all fools that is why we ask such normal questions and so, we have done nothing achievable.

Whether we are a crorepathi or even a beggar, the exercise oriented body, always showering good fortune and even after we can be laid down in Samadhi, because this kind of death, is somewhat called self realised Samadhi and many will live well and they will get benefits and profits through the vibrations of the Almighty. In this spiritual field, to attain God's influence, we have only one option that is truthful bhakthi, determination, penance and soft sustenances; these will elevate us towards the steps of spiritualism. So, we must try to increase our thoughts of God vastly and the materialistic class can be had and given to us as Acharya Sambavani (REMUNERATION)Such poojas give us contentment and focus our bhakthi towards the deity. We interestingly believe that hereafter, nothing mischievous will happen, all the Gods will stop those ills and we should be keen in magnitude and significance. These poojas give us more bhakthi and confidence over our self, and thus, we will have normal life beyond time. Therefore, we should be always still and alert to attain divinity and then, we will be one of the Astamasidhi's mankind and thus, we can do what is needed, it will come one after another, thus, our life should be profitable while living and even after death, because we have no chance to give alms.

The family circumstances should be fully understood by the public; but there is no banner or advertising board for me any where if you search for it. Thus, if you show such advertisements, I will give Rs. 1000/- each. This is not the proper channel to expose myself and others' recommendation is not at all enough to explain about myself and give instruction; if they know, it will be more than 20 minutes. First of all I am a spiritual lecturer, secondly a writer, thirdly a poet, fourthly a TV Devaprachnam programmer and, apart from these a good family head. Thus, I run the family with good administration and good character and conduct. If you explain to others, the time required will be 30 minutes. Thus, 1 have not done anything, and in words also I have made a statement of myself to all and please come to know Devaprachnam or Jadhaga results. There is nothing in my life, at all. So, I want to run my life smoothly. But according to my sleepless and restless life, from place to place without good food also, I am affected by diseases and I lost some money and time without knowing and doing deeds for others unnecessarily. I have understood hereby, every one should take rest as he works hard, otherwise we will be restless in our old age; thus, it was known practically, now I spend some hours as rest and then there is power to do my duties without delay and failure. This is an art; so we have to understand this occasion's projection through my presence and proceedings; it will give satisfaction for both of us thus, we had taken a photo along with all of them. So, honour must be given by others and it is not good to trumpet to others to give us honour. It is not at all our business and such honour which we give to our servants, they must be pleased by our hospitality and thus, they say one by one about good inference and representation. So we must be educated from the outside, and this will help us to earn good name and fame and our performance of one vaibhavam and its gloriousness. All are in the mighty Hands of Allah, so we should not exhibit the occasions, we have to thank Him to help us to do the programme neatly from beginning to end. This shows our obedience and patience. The procedure of the reception, hospitality and send off are praised by all, up to the mark of understanding.

This book is, because of exhibiting our today's society's unnecessary environments, they themselves create for them, by their own society which meant for education, is not given preference, but we are thinking about civilisation and modernisation of our own society and thus, we lose our mental equilibrium and are suffering from severe diseases, because for example, YOGA, this is today's world's trend in the name of long running adaptation ironically, they are said to be the destruction of the basement of humanity, that is consciousness, then everything will be automatically spoiled by ourselves and when time comes we are all weeping, at this time, we come to realise that we have lost our privacy and our own solitude and its co-ordination. Generally, we never wish to live a wrongful life throughout our life, but due to construction of our society's constrains, we are unable to follow the regulations of mankind and that is why, we are reducing our supernatural energy into untoward activities, and thus, we are not profiting anything in our day-to-day life. This is to be modernised and have to live long with the best qualities of mankind. So we innovate ourselves as ignorant as there is no way to escape. We just ignore the ongoing activities and this is the composition of not mere letters of the alphabet, who are entitled in utilizing our consequences of pros and cons and therefore we should have all these compound sentences.

Like this, in philosophy we have to proceed with a fertile mind to the younger generation and thus, we can see a good generation after 20 years. Otherwise this society will grow without any other style of this society and nothing can be done. There are many temples, but nobody uses them to realise the blessings of our forefathers, by which we can live very effectively. Those who are wishing to live till death, without any miseries, they must bow before their parents and then the whole world itself will salute our highness. This is pronounced by God Himself; the glory of yourself and through your service, you will be honoured and respected as the chief major. So all of us should live majestically without thieving, lieing and others may be, automatically, will change their mode of life and therefore, if one can modify his life, all others will follow this way as their motto as they are all willing to have peace, it is only through our righteousness and character wise oriented life. Thus, we had our life, we can exercise to do all our needs through our deeds with Pure knowledge, not by education. Now, many of us are educationists, but not up to date moral holders. These high people can elevate this world entirely to the pedestal of human (pure) plane of salutation. God, the common name is significant in their language, they call him ALLAH, that is all, there is no mistake or misunderstanding in this affair, if we are lovely ones, our bad events all are meant to be good when we come across those behaviors and through the mighty prayer, we can also solve and make him to escape from the clamps of sins. So, nothing to worry, people, we are all nothing but, His sons and daughters, thus, He has allotted our needs, some must request Him to donate us good thoughts and thus, we can do even in our out of time moods too; we can be divinely dipped jackfruits. Therefore, we should immensely captivate, such as, so to say, our performance through His mightiness. There is only one way, that is prayer, we pray now:- Oh Allah! silence, now he is concerned with our deeds and needs and He is willing to visit our residence, the heart, there from his operation, we will be good enough to describe our birth's secularism with full of details. Thus, we can come through the universal Truths of the mightiness of Him and His thorough abilities and disabilities. If she does these exercise regularly in course of time she will realise all our situations. Till then, by God's grace, be there silently and sleep. Amma called and she gets satisfaction. A few hours have gone, the sun rises, the next day dawns, all people and creatures with same sound of their own signals and their sounds full sound all the while. Thus, you should not have a thought in your heart at all. It is the first drop of poison which can have power to exhaust a whole family, that is why, they just tried a lot to get rid of and they must do some tricks with money.

Nothing is serious, but we have to win over our inner fear and thus, we must elevate ourselves to the highest pedestal of spirituality and we can have a permanent solution to all our uneasiness, agonies and structural, physical discomforts, but all these government servants are not doing their duties in a fabulous way and they are not adhering to the regulations of the municipal corporations. But when we are having a chance to deliver a lecture on any topic, they simply explore all their achievements and because of this, we should not compare and contrast with any others and articles are never moved here and there and such these inefficient activities are delayed by them but some wards are neat and gracious, because the servants are cleaning such places at the most with success, because their specific aspect of the contribution will be the distribution of blessings of the noble ones of other religions, because of the betterment of this universe. There are several political parties, but they are telling us, we are going to serve the society in all ways; when we see their actions, are they in action? No. Nil. They are speaking and having the remuneration in a cover with good tiffin and taxi travel to reach their house and be rested. What does he know about the welfare of the people, nothing, they are note educationists, cannot speak fluently in their mother tongue, cannot write a sentence boldly, they are willingly do the job of I.A.S. officials and the originals are blinking with desperation. Is it justice at all?

In early life, Gandhi had always been an angry and excited boy, but as he grew up, became full of santham. Thus, we got our freedom. So, we have to live like him, and he must hear about you, "Eai, what a superman your annan is! He had done developmental services in the middle of the village, but likewise, if we get to be like them, we are also on his side, this is a sathya pramanam". Just an excited Gandhi told them, "not only for your votes, earlier, they have elected me as the member of the state council, we will develop this area within a month." Thus, within 23 days, all works in the town, were done by Gandhi: it was through his God bhakthi, and national bhakthi which made him very strong to develop his constituency and thus, had finished all the works. "Very good congratulations, my son" thus, he praised his elder brother who was so much surprised and astonished. Lord chilkkanathar made him a Half dressed man; he teaches the value of simplicity and verily the diseaseless life to all beyond religions. His penance, Moun'a concepts are not at all common, at least I am doing all of these principles this is enough to realise the world, but, Saradha could not be......., silence. Like Gandhi, we should transform, it is a great welcome, but every single naya paise will be returned to him within time. See, then you will be affected by separation of his genius. That is all. Likewise, in this matter, "I handle peace including brahmin to pallan, the dharma is equal, if he does, why do I do it?" such kind of questions are not available from him. He has to be in mouna for several hours, and he then notices the subject, then all over India, the message will be spread out and whole India is in wake up position and they start to give slogans of their necessities. Likewise, he has attitude also a fabulous attitude of these two persons and where do we get money for working, thus, his eldest brother asked, Gandhi went into another room and was laughing for half an hour. All such types of characteristics are having a mixture, then, there may be, we can get good articles; because the owner is very much simple and a man of obedience. Every partner is together, they attacked him and these bloody nonsenses have gone on throughout the days. Thus, one good and great man's life ends. So, according to many of those gnanis, say the truth, will finally taste harmony, we do not like this harmony; they are on the basis of human blood in the name of rulership. It is kaliyuga, we have known very well about Kaliyuga's dharmas. Then, why do we unnecessarily fight with one another; nothing more to answer, he declared; they have awakened from the maya world into non stable, movable world and we are all now free; likewise our nation is also free from all types of agonies. We rule us for and of our unity. This is Republic Day. So, we have to celebrate our nation's auspicious days and thus, we must keep our mind's equilibrium at any cost. Now all should be released from all prisons and farmers should start to begin their trades; all the children should be educated, so they have to go to school without being absent. They should always be of smiling face and educate themselves and thus, we are very happy enough. Thereby we form new Indian systematic views, whosoever it may be anything which is said for the separation of anything in India, we should not allow it and we have to start taking battlewise action because we should maintain Unity or integration. Thus, our independence should be kept as an ever enlightening jyothi of India.

Independence day a very auspicious day for India, which gets and gives all rights to go forward towards the development of the nation, we are all nothing independently as they order and guide the ways for ourselves. Nothing to give and get policy is fully and completely erased from India. It will grow on its ownself and do whatever it needs, they develop their deeds. Today Independence day is celebrated, but are we living independently? If one can answer the question that they are living at their own will and pleasure, if you go and see a cinema, you can know how our country is going on. That is a shadow of 3 hours time but all the 24 hours duration, everyone and every second, all are in and out of our hands and wealthy people are leading a royal life through their earnings, but corruption is rampant, ready to earn and learn but they are enforcing others and also themselves to earn money in whatever way possible you should earn so that you can lead a jolly life and can enjoy contentment. All traders may earn something today, but penance holders cannot do so; this is the basis of their sanyasin life? In what correspondence, you are all struggling to earn. Just they do take risk, it is independence. Just we think of our own home's situation, then, come to realise what is the situation of the nation. So every body thinks of themselves as only man and woman, not a husband and wife. Crores and crores of rupees are given, they are not satisfied in their mind. They are living in a dreamy world and this part of life we have to suffer, Ok. It will be changed. God helps us surely, if we surrender and pray to Him, definitely we will get everything, the Vedas are not lying; they are sathyamitham. These births are the venomous creatures of nature, it is known then there is nothing more to know in the world. Money is the one and only hero of this world. If a man is having lots of money, no education no valour, body with full of diseases, ugly looking whether beautiful or handsome, many ladies and all will praise him because of his wealth; so education is the best among all our commodities, but we are giving importance only to the monitory status. May be kaliyuga's leela, very cruel thing it is. I personally have experience in this matter, in this regard, I am seriously affected to the bottom of my heart by these happenings. Is it family? Oh Goodmen, please say that: in this world, nothing, and nobody is independent, in this way, all departments are going on. Thus, how can we recognize and accept our Independence day celebrations, in name of this day, we are marching and lots of people are sitting and watching. Prime Minister speaks about independence day and praises our actions, then, sweets will be distributed; is this independence?

Please try to understand what is independence; it is a fine flowery favouring flavouring aspect and we have to systematically acknowledge this day as a Holy day. So, we the whole population of this nation should live with independence and then, we can accept that India is an Independent country. Except on this auspicious day, we are all working hard for the development of[1] the nation in all fields and departments and work for the country's elevation. We should respect first, ourselves then. Pure Love alone makes the task very easy in one day. There will be no necessity to improve the status of this nation by controlling our ego and greediness. We cannot satisfy our deeds and needs. We should pay the fine for that in due course of time. Then we curse our independent nation and ask what the nation does for us? This is what we should deeply think about in this independent nation of ours. So, we can assure ourselves that we are in the mood of construction. Independence should not be in words but it should be in our flesh and bones. Such, voice and words are not effective, we have to jump down into the deep well to sacrifice all and should cultivate our hearts towards the moral of Independence. All democratic system is nothing but to control the people with laws and orders and taxes which makes us very poor and the understanding of the public is very cheap. That is why our nation has beggars, they are ready to work and there is enough chance to do anything positively for their life for there is a big population of men and women here. Regarding this situation, it should be addressed at public meetings or in the zero hour. The minister should speak about his actions and turn the parliament towards his words. As such, this member spoke in the parliament and all the members silently heard and were silent and thus, what is the result or resolution, Nothing. All the mental fertile systems are not in their forms. The farmers do not wish to do farm work or a farmer's because they are meeting loss in their agricultural tradition and they have reaped profit due to agriculture. Lots of discomfort simply thrashed them, time is limited. These farmers are not considered as citizens of this nation. That is why they are trying to sell of all their lands for a good interest. So that is easy to run their materialistic life smoothly, So they do not like to continue this bloody agriculture.

Though we are completely independent, normally if we analyse our Independence is applicable for castes and creeds. There are always quarrels between two sections and we lose human tendencies and entries. Then how can we accept this is an independent nation. Go around the world, apart from India, they are not at all leading a restful life. In some aspects two groups involve in this kind of atrocities and they become disturbed socially. They, themselves fix some money and pay the cost of the panchayat's development. In this 2017th year too, we are afraid of man rather than the king cobra. These cobras come and go but men come and they will not leave the place even after one or two hours. They are thinking that they are the outstanding geniuses and nothing can be had from them. We are independent, there is no monitory support for us from anybody's assistance. By giving these slogans, they march past through the important ways of the town. Just boasting anything. Indians are the first and number one to achieve anything, because they are full-fledged without any other help or advantages, and thus, we live privately without others' assistance.

If it is said once, then why do they come to the door steps of each and every house, and have contact with one another, without this knowledge, in our heart beating hours, when we cannot call anyone for help. So independence for all must be present. We have missed our horses, and they are running here and there to find their horses. After a long period, they find out their own horses and continue on their journey; they entertain many more dreaming circumstances, and the assets are they original or is it our imagination? We have no knowledge about that and if we approach somebody, they are not ready to give money. That is why, we put all our packs on the back of this common ass, a miserable donkey. We have to be in Sanyasa bava; but our activities are going on the materialistic bavana, and how are we going to become and have the model of a Sanyasin.

So, do think my brothers and sisters, first, to the way of high position, is it ours, can we adjust to be careful and can win all subjects without arrears, in such a way, they select the lessons, there will not be anybody according to national level, but we are requiring to choose the subject and daily tuitions are very much essential to uplift themselves, this is not at all considered to be a good condition in education. Education comes out of ultimate natural phenomenon and thus, we score marks, and according to our marks, then, we pass or fail; this is the procedure which we follow for past several years. And many post graduates have gone through these colleges, they are put up in Higher jobs and are given good salaries, though they according to ourself we cannot believe the fact, so, you have to give confidence to study and its profits in which way they can be digested. Therefore, we must discharge our duties without any personal expectation, if we do all things, in due course of time, everyone, separately, gain or loss, they should be obtained from those people; So, we should submit all our allegations to the Feet of God, if it is true in action, we can reap all the inner and outer reflections at all times. At all time, in all circumstances whatever is being done is known well to Himself than anyone else. We can suggest, to be referred to the profit of the creatures. Thus, we should prohibit and avoid and stop all evil occurrences all of a sudden, therefore they are identified to the society by God as Gnanasidhan.

Besides talking, first we should have confidence upon ourselves and we must accept and follow His mighty gunabavas altogether, ever, for the development of our consciousness. Thus, we can easily manage our development and have a financial lift due to our honourable work rendered to the customers, if it is possible. We among all nations can win victory; it can be theirs due to tolerance and one pointed mind. These surely will make us to develop our self confidence and respect without doubt. Therefore, we must lead our life with concentration, dedication and sacrifice to all beings; watchful in life in order not to get gains from these outer happenings, if it is possible, we can surely have mental valour and physically, we will be associated with focusing righteousness and sathyagraha; these are the weapons Gandhi handed over to us and got freedom. These are powerful weapons without any battle field situations, no blood and no killing, automatically, we have to develop ourselves to the manhood episode of human life. Due to heavy tapas, we have got from God this human birth, it is not considered to be any value fixed for this body, it is the apparatus through which we must realise our inner consciousness, that is nothing but God. Who is He? where is He? He is in your heart! simple answer, if you want to realise it, do penance and take food materials timely and do not cheat yourselves by doing some unnecessary rituals of life, and thus, we fall into failure, So our motto should be normal and effective from first breath to last one. This is because we are divinely blessed and we can get it and do achievements through self-realisation. If you think of Him deeply with oneness of mind, without any deviation, you can realise the Almighty.

If we wish to elevate ourselves to God's abode, first we have to be humble, this is the only temperament which uplifts us to the highest pedestal in God's memory. Then, discipline, this is said to be calmness in any situation but we have to be speedy to recover the job which we taken on. Next is patience; if we are all doing our duties patiently, the final success will be ours. We can easily win the winning post in a quiet time. And what time we have, sathsangam is important, God's Kalayana Gunas should be chanted by blood and with bone's marrow as per our bhakthi should be glittering in the premises of Himself. If it sparkles thus, Lord Hari Himself will run towards us and do whatever we require, such child like swapa, that He has; all bakthimans try to attain this stage, this can be very easy without any special support, because of this human body and through which we can do service to Him alone sufficient to entertain Himself and at the same time, He will fulfill all our needs ever. Our deeds are perfectly done in the premises of God's Lotus feet, that is, the Heart of the bhakthiman, with full of confidence and dedication, we surrender to Him. He is nowhere; He is now here, mind it. Actually, we are all nothing but bony and fleshy materials but the soul which operates this body in a controlled path to make us to attain eternal liberation. This process is quite possible. So chanting manthras always with the remembrance of His mighty deeds, will enable us to achieve what we wish and give us its value of attainment. Thus, Bhagavan literally, comes and uses Himself to do service to the Bakthimans. After this manual life, we are encircled by His mighty hands and embraced chest to chest and gives us all the qualities of His heirship. If we decide to attain this Godly presentation, we should represent first as we are the first servant among the bhakavathas' service and be ready to recollect His deeds and do all our deeds perfectly because He Himself should satisfy with our/His satisfaction. He must be always satisfied in all dimensions and thus, we can attain the Vaikundam with these naked eyes; such bliss will be dispensed at the time of penance if submitted to His feet. So, we must chant manthra Japam bathing in the sacred rivers and chanting His names without numerical counting, visiting all His devasthanams, serving for the uplift of our grade to higher position and these make us so divine, and be blessed with the Eternal Bliss and royally we also become divine.

According to the human laws, the divine laws are very, very much different from each other. We consider dharma as humanity has, divine laws are entirely different from human laws. Thus, we misunderstand God's device when we go on analyzing the fact of this monitory world. Accordingly each and every Jeevan has the right to have education and of all the donations, Annadhanam (food distribution) is the foremost hospitality of Indians. Only this service can make us divine and saturate with divinity without further karma yoga's involvement, As we are training us to become a saint or a sage due to our doings, apart from time, we shall not be benefitted by God's mercy; when will we have the prosperity of His holy dharsan? Thus, vairgya rises in one's mind and he struggles to attain the liberation, so he has as many trials, and he becomes the disciple, his own son, as considered to be a true guru and begins trials for him. They are equally ranged in yoga and thus, they cannot attain the Bramha Gnanam, so they test all with Gnana yoga like this he tries to be an expert of all yogas; but in kaliyuga only bhakthi yoga is suitable to attain God Himself without any special care and intention. If we have some signs, physically and intellectually, then we can realise that we have Athma Gnana and we are considered to be an Athyathmic Gurumoorthy by the spiritual world. These gnana gurumars are ever travelling everywhere as they wish, as God furnishes their path and in between the journey they teach philosophies to the public and keep all from various mishappenings and diseases and keep going with pitcha as their meals and don't consider this is mine; no this mine that is mine, such controversies will never be seen. Between themselves they have a sense of brotherhood and they render duties to the whole creatures of the world, to make them fit to live in good health and sowbhagya path. That is why, they are ever doing penance not for themselves but for the welfare of the whole society; and hence they are saluted by all. These Gnanagurumars are very few in number and they have enlightened wisdom because of their Gurus and they dedicate their ownselves to the betterment of humanity. Such secret penance, they are probably vegetarians and they seem to be as if nothing is done by them, but they are doing all during their mouna by which the whole universe is getting benefits in all directions. By seeing and having some words from these rare sanyasins, our entire life will be changed and we can live a full-fledged life with honour and respect - self cognition. So, the called mouna (silence) gives us enormous strength to our outer and inner organs too and we can achieve anything by God's grace. So, you all must be ready to have a journey to God's abode and death, this valiant journey is quite impossible; so do finish as early as we can. Lord Thiyagarajar will assist us to pronounce in this career and victory will be the course of success.

Our era is not over and population of all creatures is as for the contents of the world. That is why, this process is introduced by God Himself. But, we now are ready to shoot cinemas with copulation scenes and make money. Does this come under Dharma? No; in due course of time, they will be sentenced by Him, also we have to be ready to experience the bitter experience. So, we should always be with good thoughts and deeds. If it is running life, He will be honoured by all creatures and they too will follow our life without any shuffles and difficulties. Nothing sorrowful incidents will happen in our homes. So, our ancestors stressed to do penance and chant mantras and do poojas and discharge our duties. One of these is pithurkarma (rites done for those who passed away). So our homes will be privately and particularly not in vain, profitable objects will be the nature throughout our life. So we should discharge good sketches without failures and have the Eternal rest and we will be out of births and deaths, i.e., Liberation means oneness with God Himself, this presentation can be dispensed by God only. Nobody can dispense this type of encouragement to be done. God, parents, the eldest brother and his wife, Guru and guru's wife are apart from our commentaries; we never should culminate them in any circumstances. Gurus should provide their Dharma and repel against nature. With our natural phenomena, we cannot do or succeed with anything, that is why, we are ready to install us in the best righteous way of life and therefore it is not enough to be a wise man. Oh we must be the one and only man among crores and crores of mankind. Thus, if we are honoured by the society, God will automatically shine before us; we have come to the world to rebuild and re-establish dharma and a clean and clear consciousness. What our mind thinks, it can be realised through our eyes, that is why the proverb is to be noted "Eyes are the index of the mind". We should classically adhere to these words as our duty and live with God's rules and regulations. God will gradually make us as a part and parcel of Dharma and dispense the soul with saturation. This is the human birth's privilege to investigate Him and whatever His name is, if you call Him, He will at once shower his blessings and make us clear and nearby to Him. Therefore, we should be always in Tapas not for the materialistic needs to be fulfilled, but for Eternal ecstasy and saturation with Him without failure. So, we should live abroad from five wrong actions for the welfare of humanity. Then it will be Rama Rajyam. As, such, we hereby declare in front of God's sannidhi, not to do five panchamapathagankal hereafter, if we do these, please do forgive us and give goodness in all our activities, and in this way, I adore Him with ease and attain the Lotus Feet of the Almighty very soon. This type of belief makes us pure and clear and clean thus, we too are divine and therefore, we know the purpose of our human birth and death, and the ways to get rid of all the unrestful trials and saturate with Eternity. This is our so called primary duty to attain God.

We may be crorepathis but, without divine will, we cannot taste anything; nothing can be gotten, by our money. This world rotates only on the axis of dharma, not by machines. The machine is our karma's significances. I do not try to take moral class, but no school is ready to do that and that is why, we are suffering with different diseases and so on. If we want to lead a life with divine support, we should be blessed by our parents (after death too), devas, and God too. He alone will, and serve you in your son/daughter's issue, form and roopam. It is a truthful word (devaprachnam). Every action has its own reaction; likewise, we have to face good happenings in old age and that is why, I wish to caution you, oh, young children, sow good thoughts you can reap good materials, if you sow bad ones you have to get their reciprocal happenings. This is the Universal fact at all times and by all means. So, do good things and have good thoughts, some golden vibrations will be round us, these rays give us enormous strength and valour to face anybody's enemity, and finally you will succeed in your life. Thus, you will be satisfied always. If we worship God, this is enough, we finish our duty as per our thoughts, God is ever, omnipresent and even makes stone into Gold. He gives and forgives and gives everything, if He does not, nothing can be got from ether and five elements. So, do bear in mind oh, younger generations, we have to bear all things to gain the support of mental ability, and thus, we can set up our life as He wills and hence we will be guarded and guided by all means, God. Thus, man becomes Almighty with His blessings. Sri, Ramakrishna Pramahamsar, Vivekanandar, Yesupiran all are worshipped by us as Godly organisms, why? They had never met a war and acquired others wealth, but they won their senses and activities, without doubt, they are worshipped and I am glad to meet their santum sanctorum.

All our needs are given by God and our well shaped body without defects all our organ systems work well. How is it possible? Do Athmavisara with yourself, you will get an answer and that makes us blissful and we will be in oneness with God soon. Time is an important factor, through which we can furnish our needs through deeds, mind's operation will be realised too. So, therefore, do worship God by all means.

Though this human life has been dispensed, we should utilize it only for the purpose of attaining Almighty. Most probably, we can get human birth without defects like dumb, deaf, handicapped and blindness. These are cursed ones by their poorvakarmic consequences, and this karma in human life is to be suffering for a very long time, and so, we should be careful of our metabolism of each and every organ. The whole organic systems are controlled by the mighty Parasakthi, which is in ten forms and makes us hale and healthy. Thus, God prepares a human body with spiritual intellect, confidence, health, words, character and so on. These are monitored by Him and there is no substitute for hard work, this is the mighty creation among all births. So, in this manual body, Athma can sign at all times, situations and doing things according to our karmas. So, our ancestors revealed as much as possible, man should live with dynamism, education according to his karma; we are given both health and wealth during this precious life; so, we should have fear in the presence of the Almighty, all else, will load and puzzle the mind, this is why, they have suffered very much and we are now free of all bondage and get birth as a divine boon by which we can attain His mighty kingdom. So, even in our sleeping state, we should be very careful, what are the unauthorised happenings throughout our mundane life. If we adhere to the priniciples, what Lord Krishna imprints through Srimad Bhagavad Gita, we can easily be out of rebirth and countless deaths, an immortal life will be given to each and everyone as their name in the order of the alphabet.

That is why, if we enter into new concerns, we should submit our desires. Like all creatures, man lives, is it acceptable to live like an animal; our life has no attestation that his/her life is divine; so, this jeeva, is properly suitable to be in my Lotus feet, just he will not attain the ambition and duty of human life. If we wish to have a divine life throughout, we have to be ready to render service to all in all places, circumstances and ever. This is the primary duty organised by Him and our whole life will be with full of fragrances ever. We will be well enough with all necessities fulfilled by glory of God. This is attainable by us if He declares and we request you to bless to be a part and parcel of our productive, present human birth itself. All are emphasised to do Dharma/alms to the poor, present Joyful celebrations to all, thus, you can attain Eternal salvation in your life. If we are in the form of God, it should be a surprise that he also has good beings and thus, they are brought to have this sensible man's blessings and other things. Therefore, if we wish to do annadhanam to all, its reaction will be enormous and time being it is not working in today's life; if we do it once and taste the inner nectar, the ambrosia, we will keenly adhere to the proper benefit of charity.

Whatever may be the celebrations in our surroundings and themselves, if we do, annadhanam it will eradicate all the sins and give mukthi certainly. So, we have to be beneficial economically, then this aspect will be eradicated without a single mistake, in the present and future, because God has all the responsibilities for our sake. We have to discharge our duties properly with intensive remembrance of Him ever. So, earlier I insisted on this life's meaningful situation and its greatness, will lift us towards God. I know very well about the owner; He is oneness and you are all blessed and myself too. Our life will be a beneficial one, because His introduction dispenses us with a divine life. This is not explicable.

If we dedicate our whole life to Godliness, certainly, we can attain Liberation with ecstasy, certain-beyond all doubts, we can have a solitary provision in God's Dharbar, and we majestically sit and watch God's style of rulership and giving judgements ever. This is positive; never by our exercises, but by the grace and glory of God, we got this golden opportunity. So, it is emphasised once more, do Annadhanam when you have time. God is great and likewise, we will be dispensed by all aspects because His servant will be another servant, and we can be beneficial and our names will be in the personal diary of His own. Thus, we are divinely blessed. Before this kind of divine experience, nothing in this world is equal to God's mighty dispensation. Therefore, we must pray repeatedly to allow us to attain a seat in the holy kingdom of Himself.

This father mother bondage is only for this birth. Only that kind of affection and love is there at least for the time being. But, Ambal-Swami are ever our truthful parents, and created us and to this universe, for things to be done by us and the goal of life will be revealed elaborately in the next chapters. Please wait; their quality of love has measures but, our ancestral, ever being our parents love and care can be compared to nothing; so, be bold, we must believe in God's mercy. Those pains and agonies will be charged on us only upto the mark. Do not worry, be happy, Every pain, it has remedy, it is not at all known at this moment, whenever, it is got, we cure you by grace of Himself. One thing, is there anything which has happened during our lives on the earth, which is truth and which is bad? Try to differentiate the two concepts. Please do it. No answer will be drawn from the sky. So, for no reason, you should bother about anything. Nothing more. He gives and forgives at all times, and so, be happy, do not worry you are to be going on praying Him for the sake of worshipping Him too. There should not be any needs unfulfilled with this belief, we can approach Him, but, He certainly responds only on such strength of our visit because, we undergo pilgrimage in the meaning. It is full of Lord Iyyappa's Holy dharsan. If you think like this, you can say, what are the Gods doing? If anybody asks, others will not be able to tell but you can have the answer and able to tell, that it is Iyappa's doing, then only, you have elevated to the highest pedestal of ecstasy.

Such kind of noble qualities, that Iyappa had, just do think in this way; you can come to have a decision, but your foolishness does not operate you to the highest level. So just trust God. If He does not come that is our mistake. He is always there, but we have no sakthi to witness that moment, this is the answer, but somebody can answer the question. Such a grand prayer that we should offer towards Him. If it is easy, then all questions have an answer. Do believe this concept, we are all, at our level best, try to pronounce His Name and Fame but, we cannot do it fully. If it is happening from the bottom of our heart, it will be answered. Do have belief, if there is a question, there is always an answer. Do not have frustration, today some thing cannot be understood, on the very next day, you may know it very well. Do ask her? She will teach the certainty of Truth. Truths are always abnormal and ever-living; so, do not lose your consciousness and victory over the senses will be your own within this short period, you fill your heart with full of ignorance and Ego, if you are free from these two you can understand all. Likewise, you should have your eyes opened through Gnana and your perception will be abnormal, and thus, you can know all. Do think of the Lord, He will heal and help you to be resolved whatever happens around you just watch it as a witness as a chemical catalyst. All are in His hands; why so you mind them and keep worrying about it? keep quite and all will end with full satisfaction and it will be very much appreciable. It is very simple to consider the matter we can resolve all things because it is in His hands. He will resolve all, do believe it.

Ok, go on, everything is fine and keep it up. We do our duty to save the nation at such a struggling period, we can give it with pure acceptance. If intellect appeals, we should be ready to give dhanam because it is nothing but a conscious concept. Thus, in those days, our ancestors wrote what they had grasped, for the future's welfare, they because of grace and mercy, they imprinted those words, and after several years, our fore-fathers had cleanly seen them that they were purely literature and they were interested in knowing about their wisdom and most of them became as much as educationalists and book writers. Thus, the whole world had the chance to introduce new authors, they wished to publish their own. Their names are in the literary fields. Whether literal or spiritual fields they are considered to be part and parcel of the spiritual field. Our ancient authors considered all Tamil literal fields, they are mainly considered to be the spiritual field. Spirituality means, which signifies the rules and regulations to lead this materialistic life; lines should be kept in a straight way as they are considered to be spiritual and literal. Our cultural books are having a notable end, they are considered to be the spiritual world through which the human race is educated to lead an entitled life to spiritual elevation and thereby, we can own an independence, ever-free from any burdens, is considered to be spiritualism. It means that our entire literal and materialistic lives should be full of truth, faithfulness confidence throughout and human life can be divided or classified to many, countless races. They totally emphasise the one and only spiritual bond of embodiment of spiritualism. From there, all truths, universal facts are cultivaled for the top most peak of life. The entire human life is not at all counted by human years, time table etc; but, it is counted through our inhalation and exhalation. Thus, we classified our whole life, and the astrologers are notable public who calculate our life span, counting only through the respiratony system. So, our spiritual journey of this universal voyage is upto the mark. They did no calculate as life span cannot be calculated; our counting of respiration keeps most inspiration in calculating our life span.

Throughout our lifespan, we would stay here with education, job earning, comfortable life, eating, bringing children to a good position. Then only, our mind will be finally filled with satisfaction. Such idealogy can be achieved only through adhering to our principles throughout our entire life. We will be proud enough that we have fulfilled our life's duties, thus, contented life attains and finally goes to God with the intention of Bhagavan without any doubts and we are very much contented by cardial and mental metabolisms to be in oneness with saturation.

From the childhood, if we tie the plait of a girl with regulation, it will have a good form as it can grow up straight. Otherwise, it will grow as per its circumstances and look very ugly. So, instead of straightening the fruit, we take care from the beginning of its growth that is why our plait should be brought into a straight snake, we must take care of it, likewise, human life should be in our direct care and control, otherwise, it will be spoiled. If we want to grow a fruit, we plan deed wise, we are planning and in deed also this kind of effort should be taken. Thus, our life should be taken care of, and must educate our children, from the beginning itself, taking special care to process their healthy life, we have to enlighten the life in a full-fledged angle. Thus, we should plan the route, we should drive the life, we can attain the goal and ambition within stipulated time. Therefore, we have to forward us as an optimal example and model of our parents. So, teachers mind our life, and that is why, we should respect them without a mistake. If the teacher blesses us full heartedly, we can thrive upto the mark of life.

Here, we got several degrees and one nation's prime momento, but it is not equal to those, and will never be considered to be the companion of, such truthfulness. We are all gifted with stones, metals and we call them precious, but there is no fixed price for it that is why, mankind is always searching these metals and stones, and synthetically produces some chemical composition and makes something, which is branded and gone to the market, where they are in demand. But we think deeply about these, there is nothing divine power and intellectual sakthi, but we are doing malpractice with these things by man to man for a wonderful price and thus, we are cheating among us. One person sells it for 100 Rs. another it is valid up to 1000 another is 50000 in such a way we tell others "I am a diamond jeweller" very proudly, but if it is given to a child or a 100 years old grandmother, they simply ignore our application; there is no matter to have knowledge about this and there is value of the child's age problem, in between these ages, we are trumpeting that we are doing such and such and earning, and own a building as my house, next week I am going to buy an audi car, costs about Rs. 2. crores, thus, we are boasting ourselves to the outer world and as such we cheat ourselves, because, nothing will be sent along with us after the last breath. If the truth is realised then life is very smooth. This is Mukthi.

People should have knowledge through their own sadhanas(yoga) for the good maintenance of physical body and do good exercise guided by a Guru, is success in their trials thus, they can teach others at that time, they must undergo some physical nervous system's progressiveness. One should try to understand oneself will be the mediator, through this can undergo these functions, this is called Athyathmigha sadhanas. You can realise the inner self, 'I' which is pronounced certainly in our own world in between all these doings, we mention us as 'I' and 'I' can be explained in over 1000 times in different angles and this 'I' is nothing, but realised as the supreme of all beings, then will be the scanner of others, and you will maintain the same equilibrium under these classifications and clarifications; if one realises the fact then the nucleolus of the nucleus can be easily realised and thus, a Gnani whoever may be no ordinary person can identify him and they pass him without knowing the Diamond from other precious metals or stones and thus, he can earn some money abundantly and his life will be happily settled without our own nature.

Mankind has some salient features, the main point is to feel the existence of God, which is always crossing us, but our modes of thoughts first give us failure, when our steps are right royally put forward with confidence and care we can attain glory of God. For this point of achievement, we are writing so many tests in our day-to-day life. Then, we are dispensed during our span of life, we can feel the importance and significance of this birth. We are having so many, innumerable formulae in our physical, chemical, mathematical sciences, but God's dispensation is this life. Nothing can be done by recommendation. Everything is passed as a regulatory significance and on the whole metabolism of us and others may differ, like our thumb's impression is not the same with another, what a geometrical calculation! It is the first, foremost significance of the All-pervading Being, we and all others should love life, this mentality, which is expected from us and thus, our whole life will be a meaningful one and these duties, discharged by us which make us happy and automatically all of this Universe will be satisfied in noting the nucleus of human life. There may be several or innumerable Sidhars and Rishis in this Universe; they are acknowledged by God's kingdom.

We are very much interested to earn money and gain fame forever but the qualifications are not at all suitable for us. So, firstly we should love our mode of life, we must do aradhana before our lively activities. We should not live a life with full of miseries, and unsupportable happenings; if it is possible, we can win the race day by day. One day, all shall have the qualification to have our Dharshan. This is the significance of our human birth and its proceedings. Whether we are not upto the mark of His willingness, we cannot have the Holiest Dharshan. Thus, life's ambition is granted by God Himself. Those who live a life of quarrels and misunderstandings, we, never get the concern of the Supreme Being.

Every path of this mighty creation should be swallowed up through the ear not by mind. Our soul contains several sheaths and they prepare us to do good things to the betterment of this whole universe. Not only we are rich, we should be human beings, example to others and thus, our life should be taken as an example for good-looking lively activities. All others created by Him also, eating, sleeping reproducing generations and finally they die. Is this allotted to the human race too? Certainly not. God expects our thankfulness to be created as a man/woman having life in India, because it is the only karmic land where, we can attain peace without any expenditure. Our sundry karmas are deleted by Him and always inducing to do good and all will live a full-fledged life. This is the Goal and aim and ambition of human beings, but very few can reach the pedestal of ecstasy. All others fail in their attempts, why they are not having such kind of marvelous livelihood in their day-to-day life.

We may have crores and crores of American dollars and luxurious banglows of our own, marrying a lovely lady, giving birth to some children, but, these are having some limitations, Is it ever pouring Anandham to all? Certainly not. Mankind should realise the fact and be ready to be with Him alone. Whenever we have time, or we have to set aside some time to do prayer and thank Him for giving food, dress materials and knowledge; then it is very easy to live a full-fledged human life. Otherwise, our lives will be full of sorrows and miseries and burdens. Apart from our analysis and Power, we cannot even trace the significance of His doings. He is merciful and so, we will be pulled off from all untoward happenings, otherwise we lose our peace and while living, hell is in the form of life. All happiness is from outer objects but when we penetrate ourselves into the basement of sensory organs, overall control of mind, if it is gained through Athma exercises, in due course of time, we realise that we are equal to God. Then Astamasidhis and all treasures of spirituality can be had from Ether. (Solar Dance) If this is possible to an Athma sadhahan, then he realises the importance of Truth, value and omniscience of Truth. Everything is due to Dharma (sathyam). This is the greatness of sathyam (Ever living sathyam or promise-Universal) Then he transforms himself as part and parcel of Godliness.

Bhagavan Krishnan in His Bhagavad Gita, He impresses in several places, time, He impresses and insists to do our duties, (save the life of all) try to have mercy and graceful heart, where gratefulness should be in full form and through which you must do your duties to the entire satisfaction of all beings; thus, god will recreate you with might and grace of Himself. Whether you are doing good of bad, you will be especially admitted into Heaven with my personal recommendation and there you will be an ever glorious enlightened soul; and you can have dharsan of myself at all times. This is a very much boostful enforcement and presentation to a disciple in the public. So, we must discharge all our abilities and thus, we can attain the enlightenment of the supreme soul. Therefore, we have to be free, when we are free, we should leisurely do the japa countless times of our teacher's upadesh and its strength is immense and the value of those manthras will give us a place in Heaven and the seat is ever preserved for you, whenever you visit this place, the holiest place. So, try to build a permanent building in His residence, where there is no tax and so once if we enter into this system, we never return to our place; there is no place in this earth and other stars even so. Our permanent place where we are, we have the power of operation of the ashtamasidhis. We can do whatever God decides and thus, we can achieve those things with the profit or loss of differenciations. Thus, we could have a fellowship life with what we have, this will give contentment and satisfaction for our soul. If our soul is accompanied by Divinity this is the state where God resides. We can identify from other particles very clearly and so we can live a solitary and solitude life. Then we can expel our spiritual Enlightened rays throughout the places, wherever we are, with full of enlightenment. Wherever we are, there, all will be showered by the most vibrating circuit of the spiritual world and such we can pass these vibrations towards others and thereby enlightenment will be theirs in their course of life. So, the saints and sages are doing ever for the benefit of this universe and this is confidential truth, which we should take into consideration, as such we can elevate ourselves and others to the magnanimous state of the highest ecstatic pedestal of Supremacy.

We are human beings, in this situation, if we serve people and God, will be the target of mankind to generate current and it will be used automatically, we can be in light ever and there is every necessity to educate ourselves at any age, we can educate us and eradicate our evil thoughts and be proud of our civilisation and harmlessness. All people will think that we are all free from conjury, this should be erased from our life and thus, we can spell whatever the manthra it will boost us to good health and wealth. We can live with such contentment throughout our life span very confidently. We are dispensed by god, the natural and special namavali, so we can invite God as a resemblance once again and He registers our good fortune at all times.

Sri Sivajiganesan had dharsan of Mahaswamiji of kanchi mutt, at that time, swami questioned him, what he was doing, business or occupation. Sivajiganesan was stunned. There are some who do not know about him, Sivaji. He was astonished! Then his companion and neighbor replied that Sivajiganesan was the finest artist he had enough experience in dramas and cinemas then only he came out of this unexpected situation. So, all are not knowing well about everything. That is why, there is a proverb in our language, Education is educated to Goddess Saraswathi through her Guru Lord Hayagriva. So, we have to be contented very well through our egoistic moods' eradications. When we are sitting alone, we have to chant any mantra, and its Devatha will dispense what is necessary to us. So, our aged are leading a very simple, calm life and such a way, they always pray for liberation. The eternal salvation is the goal of everyone, and thus, we will be filled with divine nectar and such life is divine and we become dear and near to Him. Though we are all good educationalists, even a single child can cheat with his/her mere LKG education. How do you identify a child as male or female? Please, explain, the child is interrogated, what shall be our answer. That is IQ. So, today our children are very much aware of education and its application. So. we have to deal with them strongly and smoothly and they will earn and learn money making methods. They will live a contented life through which they can attain Eternal fulfillment.

Such education is called super education, this mode of education should be encouraged amongst our students and teachers. In due course of time, we have to educate ourselves to the highest pedestal of Education; that is why, our ancestral proverb is suitable here; our ancestral penance is converted into our educational status which is primarily high; and we did not do enough penance, so education will not be possible. So, if we do penance in this birth, in the forthcoming births, we will be surely high class educational geniuses. So from this our motto and goal and aim should be to get rid of this births and deaths. This is the neutral state, where all seem to be ecstatic, permanent ownership.

Our education in our mother tongue and how many languages we learn, then we will be in the numbers of manlihood. So, we have to know it is a versatile universal boon to us, thus, we should educate ourselves to live our status of education. Each and everyone has the primary concern to be an educationalist in this way, we can stand tall among other nations. If we are illiterates we have to be in fearful mood, how to run our day -to-day life; such kind of negative thoughts make us weak and we are not eligible to be covered by the deity of Education.

Our daily performances are on the basis of correct character, all things will automatically accumulate and our life, will be a meaningful one. Such a man is supposed to be worshipped like God. His Character orientation will shower us with devathas' blessings irrespective of sects, creeds, and religions. So, we have to be careful to keep our chastity then we will be owned the ONER of the universe. Our motto should not be accumulating money because, idiotically, if we have enormous money, we will be the watchman to keep it safe. If wealth is earned in royal and loyal ways, there is no difficulty to be nervous and cowardish for all the government officials. Whenever, He invites, we should be ready to leave this materialistic world to God, along with Him. Because, the one and only acquisition is to note down our deeds when we are old, and our young age deeds should encourage ourselves, not corrupting between the tongue and throat, in such a way ,our ancestors kept themselves to be proud of those needs and deeds.

Whenever we think about the past deeds, they must give peace and we should continue to serve the poor, eradicating poverty, illiteracy. Thus, if we spend our valuable time in our young age, we will be the noble mankind through which we can attain Moksha without doubt. Dharmar is the best, who is keeping his prediction not to speak or tell lies, thus, he is an outstanding Eldest brother the first one who has followed moral matters carefully; all will be alright without doubt, so, we should not lie, not indulge in corruption, or steal these primary qualities lead us without nobody's recommendation until we attain Eternal Ecstasy. This is our life's goal and ambition, to achieve, mankind is dispensed by god, and we win the race.

He relieved us from births and deaths chain network of many more births. So, we have to march in the straight path.

If we wish to lead a peaceful and calm life, we have to do good deeds from our childhood days. Then only, we can continue our deeds in a perfect way. If there is no evil doing, egoism is not found in our day-to-day level, it will give us divine dispensation, then it will be easy to guide and guard others and make ourself as His representative; so he is a prophet or Annonist; if he orders, the sea waves will stand still and the actions will be pure and clean, and thereby we can reach the goal of life; thus, we must be full of divinity always, our mind should concentrate and pronounce God's name and fame; such things, if we follow them, automatically ours are divine issues. So keeping character, is worth; and it is enough to attain Godliness; he is while living in this materialistic world, he can be pronounced by the Almighty, and he can heal those who are bothering from serious diseases, the words he gives, will be purely attainable in day-to-day life. So, to attain divinity, characterwise we should do divine activities and orientation. Thus, we shall be ready to reach and reserve for us a seat in God's kingdom; God will be pleased when he hears about us and He will shower His mighty blessings on all of us. Now, people are going to temples, mosques, churches etc., but if we worship god with expectations, our worship and prayers are useless. We are such beggars going only to satisfy our needs and our intensive prayer is to have money, education and good family. God does not wish to see these cowardish people, He wants all to be free from bondage and alms. He knows very well about us and hence, through money, nothing can be fulfilled, and then we can realise this universal fact, those who are free of wants do not want, symbolised by Him and they alone are entered into His holy kingdom. His palace doors are always opened; but God gives entrance signal to those who lived in this mundane world without doing harm to all. He gives a stipulated time, whether it is short or long He does not bother about it. But, He examines us and then the Entrance will open to those who are noble only. Their character and conduct should be pure as a plain sheet, no remarks or mistakes should be there.

The salient feature of God is nothing but, to heal us whenever we are struggling with disease and mental depressions. If they are disturbing us not to have allegations of Swamiji and Ambal, we have a nice chance to hear and see the Almighty's presence and His workmanship, thus, all are with clean and pure soul. But it is sheer manual timing in which we have to get rid of these feelings of taking food materials and then assimilating and gain calories and strength to our bodies and as a result, the human beings are getting this kind of knowledge, by which we can cross the innings troublesome activities. Finally we are not having enough knowledge but they earn to learn or learn to earn the true wisdom, have to raise the settings of the stadium, from where He is acting as an antibiotic civilian and thus, all the citizens are noble. We should earn money and fame because fame alone can make us colourful and our negative thoughts will be thoroughly not entertained. So, do try to learn and earn social sambath, as soon then your savings money is essential to be the capita amount, and throughout we can earn something it will keep us very safe and thus, do not worry about our coming outside, it is side focusing about not the materialistic life but purely Divine charity. The leader of all nations, through their lectures stress the magnificence of pilot, majestic gesture of avoiding anger, makes the universe with Shanthi and peace, whosoever, we should be very aware of human life without fire, anger and instead of these bad qualities, we dictate and self educate with all the languages and thus, we are proof of all citizens and all peoples, wherever you are, as Christ's children we well propose to grow up these little angles into the Temple of God. That is the one and only reason we love them and they themselves love us; this universal love. It has the abundance of brain power and controlling power of sensual and sense organs. We can attain the light of all lights through the chief priest Christ through the other priests also. Thus, belief makes us unorthodox people, and if we call or pray intensively, we may get Him without fear and shyness. Such men are called for the welfare of all beings and I live without anybody; but God is always with us, to guide and guard myself, in all accords. So, I am nothing in front of these temples of God; if you seek Him to see, touch and embrace with brotherhood, it will be possible and there are no fixed comments and commitments to do so, thus, they finalise their good place and shelter and dress, they guard and guide those people to good, they live a solitary life style and thus, they will pass you the wild vibrant waves and tides, which reach you by means of water stream just as they go, if it is possible to atleast one of us. He is called the master or gnani.

If we have development in scientific field it is also applicable to one nation's pride and therefore, we should try hard to finish and furnish this world entirely and excellently, if we do not try our level best for the betterment of nation, why? the whole world must be benefitted and this class and level of development is also permanent and the forthcoming generations should be satisfied through our achievements and our colourful life which we had, if they know them they will be very much happy, and if they analyse our live's mode, they should try to furnish those comforts and further they should try to do the Best in all of their achievements and triumphs. In this matter, we should have no jealousy and no more bad qualities, we should not have to assimilate and if it is done, that will not be useful towards construction, and if it is not the case, it will be destructive to whom? No one but ourselves. If we want to be a superforce in the world, first, we must be characteristically wise and should be without bad happenings and underground marketing, and we should not be with disappointment because of all those immoral qualifications and activities. If such personalities are together, then this kind of forceful and truthful INDIA is possible; what our ancestors have demonstrated, we should be in human trace of journey and thus, we can ever possess such kind of noble qualities into Best qualities. We can briefly be known to and by the world; because of these noble qualities we will ever be blessed by the Almighty itself. We are the superiors and the reflections of their footpaths will also guide and guard us too. In all circumstances, we should stand erect as straight posts, we should not bend by any means, and that is why, our forefathers gave us the thalaiatti doll, given to our children to play with.

The theme of this play, is in any circumstances, we should not by any means bend and not associate ourselves to anything; ever stand straight and be calm till our activities are finalised and we should ever have only one suggestion, that is we have no result or delay to work and earn everything; if we have notice of our death, we would not be covered by bad habits and the children of today will be the masters of several subjects, should accompany with all, no one hand can alone raise any form of sound, there should be two it is easy to clap and sound is produced. We are living in this world, the maya's turbulent keys, if they hold us, never get rid of, because we shall stay here and that creature will make its glorious status and then it will not put its hands down or loosen its grip, then it will not be easy to be subjected towards construction in caliber education. Without Education, mere courtesy will not remain separately. If these two are assembled together, we can to do so many activities through which we can become characterwisely the best. Thus, our minds are kept very normal, we may be having so much of lands and wealth may be 22 crores. But at our funeral nothing is kept with us by any means; when we come to this world what is brought at that time, likewise, when we are also going, there is nothing to be taken ever. If we understand this truth, universal, we will be awakening from dark to bright sunshine. Therefore, you all should be with nutritious growth to the earth and wish all should be with good character and enough money to lead the life with satisafaction, that is all;

this is the mundane life. Nothing more is available to those who are living, while living, we should have an awareness in this matter, it will make you Divine.

We are cheating ourselves that we are knowing everything but, when we go deeply into education, nothing is grasped from schools and universities. We are aged, but civilisation and hospitality should be cultivated from the root and then stem; then only, we can get flowers, seeds and fruits. Nobody is willing to work simply, our secret lockers are filled with gold coins, and sophisticated buildings with all facilities spring up all over the world, unlimited savings in all types of banks, alas! What a man has is only this type of mentality. Then in which way is he going to elevate towards the pedestal of Ecstasy; nothing doing; we should be satisfied with what we have been given as a boon by the mighty grace of the Almighty. Then only, we can live a full-fledged human life.

Our ancestors saw God and they spoke with Him and He with them, and asked Him to sing a song such rescue and mercy is represented only to those who are dispensed, and thus, they lived a competent life. But we what do we do; Nothing, No satisfaction at all. We are seeming to be patient and characterwise nice, but we know our mistakes, and right royal activities so, we should not act, people may believe but God is the sole witness, and thus, we are rewarded with good health and wealth may be as great boons; There are many more crorepathies, we think, they are living a very calm, peaceful life. Not at all; our education emphasizes us not to follow the human regulations and rules, this is the main reason for our troubles and agonies; if we try to live a humanitarian life, God, Himself will assist us by all means.

Whatever is present in this World, it is found in the Earth. This simple science has to be realised by us, this is one of our aims and regulations. Our life's motto is not at all accumulation of wealth, sophistic finest life, prevention of disease, all are exaggerating us as a noble man; but our life's aim is to secure a place in the Holy kingdom of God, in which God should note us as a 'man' is only sufficient and He recognizes us as the supreme soul, from all the souls, we can lead a peaceful life. Whatever is wished, God can dispense it to us. But He can not give only one thing, that is, 'satisfaction' this is only because of one's mental integration and such mind alone rejoices with the Eternity. Today, there are many preachers present, and do they lead a satisfied life? Doubt only is the answer. If an Athma sathagan walks on the road, there he finds a piece of gold and silver, whether he looks at it or not and without taking it he proceeds on his pathway or he may take gold and silver along with him. May be, very few men and women have left the place, otherwise, they too would take it and try to find the owner of these things to hand it over. Many will take it along with them. In such a world, we are compressed to live an unsatisfied life. Everything is stolen and people keep on lying and there is nobody who tries to find out the path to get rid of births and deaths. Our familiar divine poets emphasise this as the nucleus, reciting so many poems. Life, teenage, our wealth will vanish away or we will not bear them in mind; so they are impermanent and everybody is knowing about death, after that sense of awakening, we are not able to come out of this worldly maya-sakthi. Whatever happens to the world, we are not egoless due to our education, wealth, youth we are having self-pride and hence when we come to lose it stage by stage, we do not think about their impermanence, and it takes away to get rid of maya, then we can manage to lead our life with calmness and peace. Today, we are seeing so many Lord Iyappa's bhakthimans and but they say that are adhering to fast, but if they are stimulated by somebody, they are ready to show their strength by quarrelling each other, and they do not eat non-vegetarian food, in this aspect, they show their egoism, one thing, we have to think overleaf our this fleshy, bony body is comprised of 81 percent water and bones, nerves, lungs, spleen, pancreas and our whole structure is made up of flesh and bones. In what respect we trumpet that we are only vegetarians. This kind of egoism should be withdrawn, and thus, we can awaken from this subject.

Those who are ornamentally dressed in black and with a small towel, on their forehead, pure yellowish chemical in the name of sandal paste, and put some kumkum dot show themselves as Iyappa's devotees. Is there anyone, show me who is a pure vegetarian food consumer, without any pronunciation of violent words and pure shanthi and peace. Not at all. They are cheating themselves; what is the use of saying this yathra to sabarimalai is my 48th year. But, when we go to Pamba shore, there are many asses climbing up the mountain by loading some articles on their backs.

These horses and asses are climbing with load of articles and they return empty and then climb up again the mountain with loads; if a horse or an ass speaks with egostic voice, we are climbing up to the sabarimalai, this is our 4000 th trip, is there any approval to them to their statements, not at all. Such position is to our pilgrimage, we are always chanting, 'Sarnam Iyappa' but we start to sabarimalai with food materials, alms from others, sustenances and some money, along with cell phone. In the midst of our pilgrimage, we call others by cell and some conversation will be going on. The trips conveniences and disturbances are spent in speaking to somebody, and we proudy say that we are in such and such place and we will reach sabarimalai within some time and come down, from there we start to our native place. Is this pilgrimage?' Swamiye Saranam Ayyapa 'is their manthra but nobody is having total confidence and unconditional surrender through their activities and they never have dharshan of Lord Ayyapa ever, whatever we sow, that we will reap. This is the universal fact and so, we have to grow with bhakthi and pious heart then only, we can be accepted by Ayyapa swamy. Such a person is wanted to be given dharsan, swamy is ready at all times, but He has never met such truthful personalities.

We must deliver our works without delay, and with perfection and adjustment; these narrow ways do not enable us to do the same as they pronounce, so we should be very careful in our efforts and we have to awaken our eyes, can achieve all things. Do believe God and trust in Him, everything will be given as a boon when time ripens, as many more great statesmen win their race, in this manner due to their patience, they finally won the series. So, should be prepared well for our interviews that we had, before the night hours in Puducherry, what a good type of Deepavali is going on otherwise, we do not mention its status hereafter. We should not encourage to give bribe at all times to finish everything with success, in order to have speedy recovery we are willing to give anything and that is why they are facing hurdles and doubtful methods of situations as per rules and regulations. Therefore, we do not reveal the things that happen in our working places, just time comes, she will attack by her words and we get into dejected mood and our whole ability is forgotten we have doubt over our confidence and desirelessness. Self confidence is stressed first and then all can be attained without any failures. If we wish all success, time factor is most important and our habits may differ one to another so, that we came from Bengaluru and going to do first aid touch in Madurai and finalize the result to be well supported by means of liberation; this word is not mentioned often because it has come out of Bhakthi towards God, mere spelling, this word liberation means just for the time factor we are prepared to be stable, calm and patient enough, these are called in the name of liberation, so try to know the differenciation at all. Our life is dispensed out of God's will and punyabhava salutations of sidhars, they recommend to God to start the path way for salvation and we can easily come out of the hurdles and be free from bondage and commitments. In our human birth and death, between that space of time is called living dates are here mentioned due to our karmas and may be by the path too. Our mentalities should be charged with our attitudes truly. If we become a truthful man and we pronounced as a saint, holy man, punithan those undoing things vanish and our life will have no illusionary notes either physically or intellectually, and they are spread over the universe and render their earnest services to all.

All edible fruits are from the trees and these are the food materials for very numerous saints and they take it, but some thus, take one and only privilege of food that is a few fruits and milk. Some or a few take fruits only once in a day and hunger sensations should not be usual. Such people are trying to do penance, for about crores of births, we can be granted such type of immense birth which is dispensible towards God, and as a result, we can penetrate the hardest bottom of earth, and stand still with science and botanical spiritual threads make it to twist and thus, they are the parents of all creations, such grade is communicated by birth, that is the source of all creatures, and so, they have non-vegetarian food and is truly recommended for the welfare of health and body structure. Some people are carnivorous and omnivorous because they are brought up in this style, and the style is processed with calamities of meat or beef, then the child automatically opens his mouth and takes the (non-vegetable) flesh materials, like this they taste the food and they are very much fond of mutton etc, but each and every individual should be choosing vegetable food, for, they are common to operate only through vegetable foods. In science and body care science, we can understand the stamina, which the body can get from it. We can understand implicity our mode of life is nothing but only vegetarian food materials, Non-vegetarian is edible through our ancestors' science which stands only on taste for the valourous.

We are expecting our children to go to school, thereby they must take sustenance thoroughly and they believe that the food materials will give them full of nutrients and they will be hale and healthy but, we do not go at lunch time to inspect what they are distributing and what ingredients they are using and so on. But this is our mistake; so we should take care of all things. Then only, we can be aware of good children we send the pupils to the schools not only for studying lessons but mainly we wish them to be the forthcoming all developed young generation and moreover they should be able to take care of the entire profits to the nation; if it is true, we should render our fullest service to the entire universe; thus, the Almighty ordered and that is why, He dispenses good wealth and health; if we do not utilize them for His benefits, He alone will simply pull us to the created hell. Then our original destination cannot be allotted even, it makes crores and crores or human years; now we are suspended for several years; so, the fear of God is the beginning of knowledge if we imprint these words, we should be aware of having such a good education. Only through language, we can eradicate our sects, religions and all differences.

Up to this date, we are all men of speech, but men of action are needed. We are all speaking, irrespective of places, sites, temples but we are not ready to become men of work and action. This is why we do not come forward in any field at the international level. To prevent this, Prevention is better than cure; we should educate ourselves thoroughly without deviation of mind, concentration on studies and full of dedication should be on lessons, we should read well for good marks, Marks are not the exhibition of our talents. Our ancestors, poets, sidhars and so on did not choose universities, their culmination of examination depends upon their mind and action. They concentrated only on studies and as well as service. They were educated on the practical side with practical knowledge too. By this method of education, they came forward without so much defects. They loved education, but now, our pupils are going to schools, then tuitions, there is no schedule for games and sports, that is why, many unidentified diseases make them very weak and illnesses come to them. And our food is not filled with full of vitamins and nutrients, That is why, our children cannot come forward with progression in many authoritative fields, Study, Study, Study, chorously parents are crying, this is not the proper approach to make our children to study. Some years, before, parents concentration was on nutritional sustenances and healthy body, secondarily, education will automatically make our children prospective with name and fame.

If our entire concentration is on the Almighty we can rejoice about His mightiest control over us, we can survive with sincerity, obedience, giving respect to the aged, Such good features, if one cultivates in himself, it will make him, a full-fledged disciplined disciple, selected by God Himself, and He teaches the lessons through various preachers, may be by tress, flowers, earth, fire etc. We can recognize the preachings which are grasped by ourselves, which will be the first, more most natural lessons, through them we can grasp patience, tolerance, non-violence etc., these kinds of sathvic Gunas, if one practices in his daily life, he will be praised by God Himself and more lessons will be taught in due course of time and then he becomes a fully fledged man, a spiritualist, who will be honoured even by Devas, Rishis, Munies and so on. These outstanding personalities cannot be seen or recognised by all of us, they are considered to be the most capable persons to preach what they acquire from the Universal University, He teaches them and gives practices to them through physical and intellectual experiences and they become Annonists. Thus, Christianity selects the noble persons of their religionwise, and gives sainthood convocational authorisation and these also have a sanctum sanctorium for themselves in many places, they are worshipped as God and they perform activities for the betterment of this world by all means. Here in Christianity, the Guru authorizes everyone and crores of people, will be honoured as Annonists. They have some identification by their divineliness, they must do some extraordinary happenings among all people, they should be honoured, and they govern them and lastly they are honoured by their people, the most sacred man, who is head of all of their institutions and councils, the one who gives the convocation as saint that is St. Mary, St. Joseph, St. John and so on. But in Hinduism there is no single institution which can call anybody as saint or confer sainthood on them, if someone is acknowledged and allured, grasped by them, they will call that person honourably 'swamiji' and no more customs are adhered to by Hinduism. Here everybody is equal and giving full freedom to all. In Hinduism anyone can worship in any way, thus, which thereby insists on Bhakthi and confidence in God which in the long run should be improved day by day, but there is no religion oriented authorisation. Respectfully, we call one who is doing or performing poojas in a small Sri Vinayagar temple 'Acharya' all the people call him 'Samy'. But there is no selection or election to promote them in religion wisely. It permits, everyone to perform poojas as they wish, whether you visit temples, or not, no compulsion to go to temples, those who have faith and confidence, alone have the permission of God, and thus, they can have the dharsan. There are Non believing people, in Hinduism also, but they are not at all condemned, and it also permits their discussions and respects them. Like, Ravana, Hriniyan, Sisubalan they were abusing God and even then they attained Mukthi for they too have the pure love upon Him, God's. It permits each and every custom of humanity and it never ignores anybody, but it also makes them, cultivated, and thus, they one day turn the table towards God. This is the Speciality of Hinduism. It gives all freedom to perform poojas to various deities, as the people wish, and vedic manthras are equal to all, and it permits various types of worshipping and offerings to Him. Thus, it reveals that if one can be able to show his bhakthi through purity of mind, there is nothing, expected from him and "I am always ready to show the entire Visaroopa Dharsanam to him. But he should be full of Bhakthi, oneness of mind, these are the expectations, I wish there is no necessity to enchant my Holy Manthras, whether he is educated or not, I will not bother about it. I expect only their confidence and total surrender. If they entrust, themselves within me, I shall look after them, and thus, we are ready to dispense them, what is suitable at the very suitable time. It is the best among all the best. This kind of mind, the sadhaka should cultivate through, by himself and myself is ready to saturate them within my Akandakra Jyothi. I am the one, who is residing in everybody's heart, dwells and does everything what they wish or not, according to good or bad, they are considering some as good and some are bad, but my perusal is not equal to them, thus, they must realise the truth entirely, there is no necessity for anxiety or self-pride, then they will get rid of all types of Egos. 'I' should be demolished from his heart, even thoughts too, then, he/she can realise all are mine not theirs and having this type of clarity wide perception in the heart, the oriental study of Guru can be compared to the perception of pure Gnanies. Therefore, they should be always ready to sense my arrival to them so that they can enlightern their whole life within my perception".

We are all having houses with all the comforts; otherwise, we can take up various types of occupations and learn to earn money and spend it in the right way and thus, live a full-fledged life. Since our birth, till this moment, we should try to think about our earnings of mentally and worldly survivals. It will be quite astonishing without imagination, apart from all types of our expectations, we have been given by Him, His grace as a boon because He is our creator according to our karmas. 40 students are taught by one master, but some fail, even secure -0- mark in a subject a few, secure 100% what is the reason, if we analyse this fact, we can come to know His glory and capacity of Divinity. According to our past and present karmas, our total present situations are erected without any kind of errors, because the Mightiest is controlling us, ever, our thoughts arise in our heart only according His will. We are all dependents on Himself. If we realise the secret of creation, we will be wonderful Gnanies. Such people are rare and they do not wish to exhibit the glory of God externally there is no need of His deeds, there is no need to write and paste them. If He punishes us, each and every minute we will be out of shanthi and contentment; even, we cannot have a deep sleep without dreams and disturbances. If one is dispensed, his remarks are such as follows; He, is out of sorrow and joy; He loves all this Universe; doing good for others; there will be no partition in His whole life and He lives with the guidance of God. His mode of these styles of lives will be out of reach by ordinary people, not even, can they think of Him too. That is out of reach of all. He has full realisation of God's presence in each and every atomic oscillation of this Universe hence, He keeps silence and is Anandhamaye. This position is otherwise called Sachithanantham (sat- chith - Aanandham). Thus, the holy people are doing their perception will be on not only their home, but their perception will be on the whole universe, because they love each and very creation of this Universe, they sacrifice themselves to do duties given by God, and so they are to be saluted and we should bow our heads in front of them, such density of penance is done and Godliness attained and they realise the present, past and future; this type of nobility cannot be even exhibited by the people. Therefore, such Godly personalities arise in this whole world once in 1000 years. Such annonists are capable of maintaining peace in this world, but now kalyuga is going on; and that is why, they do not want to exhibit themselves to the outer world thoroughly - those who have realised them, lives will blossom and be blessed by them.

Now, we are all with chastity and one concentration in our thoughts, this is because, some one starts a yoga centre through which many more masters, in the name yoga master, yogi, yogic structural beings start many more such centers and in these centers several people gather together and in the name of yoga, physical and body maintenance, in this meaning only they are doing some exercises and they say "I feel such and such, I am very happy enough because of this yoga". But there they are not struggling or inclined to know what yoga is? That is why, we are out of focus and doing our earnest in this birth to elevate us to the upper level, that is Enlightenment... thus, we have very much come out of the shackles of wealth. Ordinarily when we go elsewhere, we say something and it comes true, and thus, we are honoured by TVs., Radios and many public oriented accessories. Therefore, we should be doing our favorite happenings, our physical health is standardised without any falsehood. The centre, heads are usually called 'swamiji' and they are the yoga masters but they never see to or concentrate on their development in exercises and functions both physically and mentally. So, some of these students, within a few days, become mentally depressed and they are examined and upto their life span, they have to take these medicines. Such unfortunate actions and situations are on the flow. In the future if this condition is duly developed, we will be very much unusual beings and this life's meaning will vanish and all will have to pay huge amount of penalty and health. So, oh! public people of the universe, do take care of your father and mother without any customs and they should be enriched in all departments in all angles. We have to look after them in their particular age. If one is furnished by both of them, our life should be automatically, through performing poojas and rituals their consequences will be coming as its own nature. Almighty, Himself, operates one's ill-health and gives proper medicine, we can live luxuriously.

So, if you are enriched with, all subjected needs, will be settled by His Almighty power. So, we need not give any importance to sensual response to be developed; this is not at all the Goal of humanity.

All those, who chant His holy manthra throughout when time is had, he will will benefit benefit in and outer world's welfare. Thus, if we implant some beneficial doings done by us, those trees go and recommend for quick welfare, and, we come out of our burdens with an easy mentality. So, in Tamil they are called Thavaram', then, trees pray to God, to dispense us with good health and wealth. Thus, trees are rendering service to us by all means. Hence, we are very much fond of growing virtchas all over the world. Therefore, we should plant only young saplings which grow as trees, and they pray The Almighty, when we are with diseases, and have the chance to have rescue from illness, and they pray sincerely and myself is in front of them. It is asking God, that He is our father, because of planting us, we have grown up as trees, so our Appa should be alright, thus, trees planned my soul turns into my body, because the trees have a chance and hence they are praying intensively and now I am standing before you. Varam means in Tamil 'Give me a boon', thus, they save us, so, their prayer is called upon and for this reason, we are living, and trees also do penance in order to get boons from God. Thus, each and every temple has its own proper tree and they are worshipped as God, we worship God and they are ever living and scientific miracles can be done in due course of time. So, they are jeevandi of all creatures with the blessings of God and, they are to be governed and grown and name and fame will automatically come to us.

THE HIGHEST LEARNING IS THAT BY WHICH WE KNOW GOD; ALL ELSE ONLY LOAD AND PUZZLE THE MIND:- Therefore, we just study but the so many doctorates are not knowing about the immense value of human birth; but, the main goal and ambition is that by which we know God. If God is before us, nothing is impossible. In this way, our human system is created, to help the poor and therefore we should be ready to do Dhana and Dharma to all; whatever we can, it will come back to us when we are in a hectic situation; therefore, Dharma is basically education to all is emphasised to do Dhanam and Dharmam. Both it may seem as one and the same, they have differentiations. Dhanam is without expectation, we help others, Dharmam means we do with expectation, and if these are adhered to strictly, one can be helped by God in their hectic situations. Therefore, we have no need to think about their profits and benefits. Whatever and whichever way we can do our level best and thus, God, Himself will come towards us to rescue us from our untoward situations.

So, Education can be emphasised among those who are not having knowledge.

Those, who are illiterate, may find if difficult to lead their life. Most of the people cheat them and rob their money a lot and soon after they cheat them they swallow their whole wealth. Not only for this happening, we are saying that Education is very important. Saint Thiruvalluvar emphasised the value of Education thus, those who illiterate are nothing they have no eyes, they are blind. How much, indeed, he has emphasised Education's worth and its need over all; our wealth, when giving to others, they, immediately go from them. Then we also are beggars; our whole things may fire and we may have nothing; water washes away all our things in one cyclone; but, Education is day by day, if we give it, it will boost us up and we are sharpening our Education. Nobody can steal our Education; nobody can be a thief and he cannot steel from others. Education does not fire into ashes, it cannot vanish through water; shortly, when Education is allowed to grow at one stage, we shall become a genius, it cannot be stolen, it cannot be fired; such an excellent asset, that is why, we insist you to have the basics of education and you can face any body without firey fears; If you are in a mood of fear our enemies may kill us. So, we can emphasise about Education thus:— whoever you may be, irrespective of sects and creeds and religions, you will be respected and honoured by all people. Today, Government itself comes forward to educate in the morning or evening hours. Apart from your daily routine, you can write examination, you can pass with distinction; then after release from jail, you will get a job and thus, there is no necessity to work anywhere and poverty will be eradicated by the help of Education. So, make all to educate themselves; make others to become a genius in a subject, thus, all our people will have got education. So do turn over to the side of EDUCATION.

If, we are educated ones, we would be honoured as a collector or a philosopher or a saint and thus, the whole world will come around us and we can earn money, and live a comfortable life. Please do think of this Education.

If we are educated, then we can know the value of silence, and we can achieve all in this universe. An illiterate or an uneducated man who makes several crores of money, will not be an equal fellow like an Educationist. So, those who are not having proper elementary education please approach us, we shall show the way. If we educate ourselves, we can rule all over the universe. Therefore, please try to concentrate on this factor, and call no single person an illiterate. This is the most valuable service to the nation, we can idiotically say, that India is having no single person who is an illiterate. Most probably and truly all educationists are in India. Thus, we can win the world by all means, and wherever we go, there is no possibility to be with fear complex. We can meet with courage and fearlessly, telling our ideas and our concepts because of education, we have to encourage Hindi, English, Kannada, Sanskrit and so on; if these languages can be written and spoken, we will be contented with peace and joy.

Apart from education, nothing will spoil a whole nation. If there is knowledge and strength, we can win over all, in all directions. Indians are not illiterates but they are wisdom wise very great as ancient Indians, in any one of the fields, Indians are fore runners, this kind of name and fame should be kept with INDIA. For this, it may take several years, if we do our level best, one day, this goal can be achieved; in this divine confidence, we pressurize the media to give life to our illiterate people. Illiteracy, easily, whomever he is, transfers him as a fool. If we are educated, we can earn some money and we can take food materials with prestige. All will appreciate us as the best.

That is why, so push off religions, sects, and creeds. Education is the best and solitary way which can unite all under one roof, make us to be able to grasp Languages. Then, it will be very easy to be full of wisdom. Most probably, the Annonists are from India, is the forerunner of all and they realised the supernatural power and they discussed with God and made Him to give darsan of Himself to all the people. Education is a good leader and ladder to climb up to the mark of responsibility to bring our own children to the highest pedestal of Ecstasy. Our ancestral society was full of wisdom and they lived a superlative degree of trade, education, and self oriented businesses, and they did not complain to the Government to give subsidy when naturally something happens...! So, this kind of foolishness will be eradicated by the growth of education. Sirs, please do eradicate illiteracy and make India a super powerful nation.

He, who simply expresses his ideas on a simple topic, all will admire to hear and so, his eminence will spread to all places and all will listen and automatically admire his words, and he will occupy others' hearts without carelessness. So, our speech should be peace-oriented and in very simple language. Then we will be by regarded all. Wherever we speak all will come and gather to give their ears and a new renaissance will arise and it leads us to a pleasant and happy mood which grows at all times. THESE REGARDS ARE VERY MUCH RICH than our vote of thanks, such as we should and listen like book worms, but, the men of experience are today needed and as such mankind would thrive long generations, and the whole world will be benefited. This is the classical duty of all to create good-blooded experts, and they will manifest everything to the utmost elevation and thus, they make India, as a super powerful nation among all nations. If one is having weapons, it is symbolic that they are fearing so much because of their enemies, from this, we can understand them, their weaknesses and fear of being single, so they can be ruined because of mental depression alone.

Our ancestors gave their lives, even to keep their tongue, pronouncing and they tried their level best, to keep their tongue, that is why, have been dispensed, beyond doubt, and they were morally dispensed with all health and wealth. Such a life is a divine one. Therefore, we have to be over cautions, when we give promise to others. If some money should come from one person, expecting this, we should not sign any recommended forms. Even that man cannot give the money, what will we do? So, when we give promising words, we should be very careful, and then, we can fulfill our words and thus, both of us will be confidential for ever. Whatever education we had all will exhibit through this kind of dias, we have to live to keep our words, then, our fame will be spread all over, the people will talk about us and call us a sathyakeerthi, so, if we try to pronounce one word, we have to confirm about its receptive possibility, and then, we can give assurance beyond any doubts.

We should give respect and honour our thoughts and deeds, then we will be respected as God's pronunciation. So, in Tamil there is a proverb, 'your honour and respect are in the tip of your tongue' - Such valuable words are in Tamil literature. So, it is considered to be divine Tamil and in the name of others. If one well versed in Tamil scriptures, all are mentioned, all will be in poetic form and we have to educate us beyond doubts, and then, our lives will be sanctioned once more, thus, we can attain a divine life. May be, it is a tiny substance, but when it comes into consideration, we can realise its value and respect, those who are giving honour. The coins of money are also called 'Nanayam' means the metal rounded coins made of Gold, silver, or platinum, it has immense importance according to the money, we pay which our tongue propells. So, there is necessity to keep our economical status, then, only we should give words as declaration to others. So, our words are significant in day-to-day life. As such, when we give promises, we should be ready, to keep them without delay. If it is possible, then, we will be honoured in all ways in the world. May be, our nation has so many debts, but, our Scientists, Economists give assurances to the government, that, we have debts, and it can be refundable with interest as soon as possible; in this way our words will be respected and heard at the same time, all others will give honour to mere money; it has finished several deeds successfully, and therefore, our wealth is a boon from God, which is dispensed with mercy and glory. So, we have to be very careful to keep our words, one word can give livelihood and at the same time, a word may make us to end our own and another's life also. So, we should tell others, 1000 times, even after thinking so, then we realise our words through the tongue. So, our tongue is used to hear and it is helpful to speak also. As such, the tongue keeps ourselves both in the mode of speaking and telling some matter to us elaborately.

Whether one is interested in Vedic principles or not, if they know the values of living activities, then, their life will blossom with divine nature and our words are everliving ever and ever. So, we have to go through thoroughly whenever we have time, Vedic principles are living with siranjeevis' presence. Therefore, they are to be worshipped and read in a right Guru's existence. Thus, we can obtain divine basement, and our life will be quotable in all dimensions without omission at all; so, these concepts are insisted upon to who is very fond and has gratitude to God. Thus, we realise their values are innumerous and uncountable and there is nothing which is equal and incomparable motives of human life. A muslim, A Christian, A Hindu, A zen can follow any one of these Vedas; because they are stressing these Universal concepts. But, the model of expression will be modified according to their ages and customs, but they reveal and make us sincere to God. And so, we all have a beneficial life, which is to be synthetically, not transferable through all ages. So, if we adhere to these rules and regulations, our life will be filled with the very best constitutional truths, and they will have very good contentment in all ages ever and ever.

To those who are in the happiest modes, those who are full of agonies are to be drawn under and they will make us automatically, by nature, can obtain these truths which are Universal, and that is why, they are considered profitable. If there is a word-profit, then there is a word in the sense of opposition. That sorrow-which will not come in our life, so, boldly we can set our life's quotations and therefore, we have to believe first, and then try to uphold and adhere to them in our daily happenings. Then we can realise the omnipotentiality of the concepts. It is for all beyond religions, sects and cherishable races, All the Vedas are common to all, Christians only should follow Christian principles, thus, there is no note at all in the Bible and that no one should follow Gita's principles, thus, Brasthanathriyam, the holiest creation which is a boon to Hindus, so, all are well suited to all of us. The most, interesting thing is to adhere to them, then, we can realise their concepts, one concept is said to be in various styles. They are living because, they are Eternal..

If we need concentration and peace, we. have to have most patience whether we are religious or not. That is not the question we ask; can all of us have confidence and admiration for all by all in the Universe. May be.. But according to time and mode of living, the very best treasures are given in various styles, but the inner hidden truths are one and the same; thus, we must console them and live throughtout our life with all presence. God boosts and dispenses them, so their value is immeasurable - so, with full confidence of one's life, one should practice them in the midst of problems. Others have to take notes, anything from our words, I am getting failures so many times. Because, you had come to India, from the U.K., and that is why, you cannot understand our concepts and triumphs. If they win in the race, there is no necessity to follow our holiest vedic principles, so the everliving sathyam should be succeeded. Thus, you should lead life with the witness of shasthras and customs. We can be loyal living beings, according to the concepts of these sects and situation.

Through this book, we are assisting and proclaiming to you the noble qualities of human life and if we adhere to these facts, the universal eminent experiences and exercises throughout our lives, we will have heard a lot of good words; if these are not beneficial because of having heard the man's words, there is no chance to speak like him. All organs will be paining throughout daily and such, we should listen to whoever speaks; it is explained by Thiruvallur, it is nothing but the Gem of knowledge for the ears. So it is described as golden ears. As such we have to listen to many lectures to cultivate many rich conclusions, phrases, proverbs etc., they will help us to reassemble our duties throughout our life sketches. All the illness especially, dysentery, non-stop watery substance is due to food consumption. We should take proper food materials to stop it, thus, Athma will experience santhi and peace. Only if there is hunger we should consume food otherwise, this stage will be the cause of all diseases. To stop this we should consult a doctor and take medicine. This is the proper way to stop the disease, otherwise, we have to maintain this kind of stomach and become worried due to the inconveniences. All diseases are caused because of indigestion, food consumption when not hungry that is without sensation of hunger the time is important to take food; if this is the situation, we leave it. That is all. May be the heavy pain of hunger; do not take water, it is not at all enough it is essential we intake food filling ¾ of the stomach, remaining 50% is for water and 50% is with air; if this condition is kept on, nothing comes and attacks as diseases and we will be living at rest with crest. We should not take anything only for taste even if it is ambrosia. This is the easiest way not to take food. Hunger also acts as medicine, for all illnesses, and disorderly taking food materials, we would be affected by diseases. Only if there is hunger, we must think of food and eat it in silence and finishing it, we can speak to others. Our hungry sensation if not at all found, if the time is 4 pm, don't think of eating food materials and edibles; if we adhere to this rule, there will be no device of illness. Like this method nothing to worry take this decision; take breakfast as a king midday food like an ordinary man, then supper should be as a beggar; these are the common formulae for those who do not follow the rules and regulations and are suffering from serious diseases; we have to pray God and fast. If one is sleeping, he should not be awakened. If this is not done he/she will be affected by ulcer. So we should eat at the proper time and eating fruits will give good health. A male or a female, he/she must live with full health; then he/she is a millionaire. Then if he/she loses character everything is lost, most probably, if she/he loses her/his health, then the whole of life is nothing. There is no sense of living and he is not loyal to himself and others. So, we should give importance for studying various subjects, and a budhiful bhakhta, will be blessed by God and will be endowed everything by God; a chapter is closed, that is all.

Chapter - 7

Why Life and Death Occur

Do think like this:— if we are foretold that there are 144 years of life span that has been given as a boon by God, to oneself, will he rejoice or not, certainly, now 144 years will be a long period, periodically the heart should beat throughout 24 hours for 144 years. There should be no diseases and for food materials, somebody will cook good food and supply water for him. Approximately at the age of 77 years, his relations, neighbors, friends, wife and even our contemporaries will die, in the year of 110 years there will be no one as kith and kin, will he not be survived with this rate of friendship or such another form. After a few years, they will be settled elsewhere and he will feel that all are gone, why should I live for 144 years. For welfare of our brain, I added this chapter herewith. DEATH is a noble happening to a soul, which has a time to refresh and be ready to hold the next birth's preparation, thus, and therefore, we have to meet death. This is a certain needful one, without death, each one of us will quarrel and even evil habits like killing will be even settled in this earth. Is there any necessity for these happenings? If soul releases from a body, according to karmic? reflections of oneself, the skeleton and some kilos of fleshy substance from a womb of a lady, comes to this mundane earth, where we have to work hard in searching food and water and ego of livelihood too, otherwise, our mode of life will be ever changing and will get rid of God's ordnances.

There will be no justice no just judgement for the weaker sections, and they will live by their smallest income and with poverty, they will be, if induced, they kill you like Shree Narashimmamurthy samharmed Hiranyakasibu, such mental depressions they have to incur, so, we have to live freely without fear of intolerant activities, and enough rain will make our lives meaningful to those who do not lead this martial life. Leisure and pleasurable activities are necessary to hold materialistic life as a meaningful one, otherwise, morality will not be seen everywhere. He, who has body sakthi, or brain power can live a sophisticated life, when others will end with selfish deaths. So, Therefore, we have to pray Him to enable us to live peacefully and in this way our worldly visit should be fruitful and profitable. So, Thank you, God bless you by all means.

When birth is determined, at the same second itself, the very second our death is seconded by Sri Chithra Gupta, the secretary of Lord Esan, who is capable of snatching the soul from the body, i.e., death. If there is no death at all, if death is not available, everyone of us will be with crooked mind, as birth is an important one, Death is also a must to oneself.

Whether a man is rich or not, we want to show ourselves as rich as possible; we are believing that money can solve all the principles and give contentment by all means; but, upto the mark, we should be flourishing we cannot convince us by means of accumulating money, thus, we are ruining ourselves. Is it true, can we derive peace from money, or shanthi in mind? how is it easy to provide all provisions, it cannot solve our problems. Our life is a divine boon, through which we can be somewhat contented in an angle; Rest Assured is the fundamental conclusion of human birth. Death is not a final solution, we can attain Eternal peace.

Every single second, we are getting old and expecting death; this valuable human birth is not sure to be dispensed once again to us with sense of bhakthi and Athma Vichara. If this is possible, the only way, He must dispense Himself to us wholeheartedly approve of us as His Bhakthas; otherwise, we cannot even have a single thought of Him whether He is present or not; and we cannot be able to have a permanent solution for this puzzle, and thus, we plan this life for about 365 days (it is not at all sure that we can have 100 years of life) So within this stipulated period, we have to overcome all of our materialistic worries, miseries and loses. We have to be obedient, sincere and polite and patiently search our own selves. Thus, we can identify us and can realise our inner self is full of His own and nothing else. These are nothing but mere words; it is all dispensed by Him not our own imagination or money making efforts. It is sathyam on Himself. So, have belief upon these holy words. They are universal truths, they cannot be changed in any circumstance by these materialistic creatures. We should have such brain and mind to realise, then only we can be known by ourselves first and then by others as a true Gnani. He Himself comes to show His full infrastructural phenomenon of deeds and thoughts to us. He is ever ready to contact us, but we have not the thinking about the Holiest Paramathma to the entire upliftment of our materialistic and spiritual lives.

Chastity is very much important to all for liberation from this mundane world. This sentence is for all. If one adheres to the rules, they will live happily and contentedly with much support in their lives; if man is ready to live as a man, all the other creatures will automatically come and take the work and finish it with ease. Just for this privilege, we have to work; next do not tell advice unless asked, this is the essence of this human life. As such all other fears will go through our sensual organs, will be controlled by themselves and we will finish this human birth and saturate with one another, the Almighty. All are willing to live with wealth and health for a long time, but we have to know our fate. For all of us our time of death is mentioned herewith when we come to this earth. God fixed it, each respiration is counting in and out and how many respirations are to him, that is his span of life. We are thinking that through astrology, we can come to know all about our life and date of death. This is not known by anybody even Yamadharma Rajan does not know it, it is the intuition by Sivam at that time, the incident will happen and the soul will be free from all worthless life. If one lives up to 500 years, and on that day, his 501th birthday comes how will he be? and what will be his position? He may live, but all will come to note and they will not at all even care about his existence for this time. All of his ten fore-generations have gone and now he is living, what is the use? He is of no use to himself and to others. He is having life that is why he is living, in the sense there is nobody to take care of him. Even though some one says something it will not be taken into consideration by others and all others will seek his death only. This is the sad situation for the longest life. So, everything is having one and only, stage of rest, each and every being needs rest of mind and body, otherwise the whole body will be easily decayed to the bottom of the heart and become diffused, in a sense we become mad and nothing can be done forever. So, death is nothing but, an interval pattern for the passage of mind and soul. So, we have to live wholeheartedly and earn and learn each and everything. We should be alert to keenly notice the matter about what is being spoken. We should respond like that and appropriately listen to the cycle of births and deaths, we have to learn to be full of valor and face anything which is from this earth, but, something may come from these actions. So, our well being and keeping all situations of this mundane customs, we have to accomplish all customs of these systems to the entire calmness and bright future. If we wish to have peaceful life, then everything is waste and we have to simply worry about all, why? This is not at all the way of foaming circumferences to all dimensions of this life and world's seekings are only towards Loba and kama, if these are erased from our mind itself, God will be seated at the next second and we become the divineful Purushas. So do come and know from her and ask to make her to know, this is the philosophy. We are all taking risk and tasks of our mere life. This is all our duty and primarily this should be given education without this, all are growing like some creatures we live like our mind is going on its way. Your liberation should liberate all to sense of awareness, if this situation permits everything will be I in your heart, God will be seated ever.

Think once again, how many births we have to represent and how many deaths we have to face, to have this golden opportunity, not to lose our penance, we have to do penance always and chant His glorious names, nothing equal to this in this world. God's glorious names should be chanted without counting by which we can attain the goal of human life, that is saturation with the divine nectar of His virtues. If this state is maintained by us, there will be no chance to fall down from that position and possession, it is the Golden throne of God; and we also, got a small bit of place for us, it is only dispensed by His grace and mercy. Therefore, do try to attain His abode and thus, we will be honoured by people as saints and sidhars and sages and annonists. But some one may realise our original position to be the descendence of God Himself. Rightly, our life should be a meaningful one and it should be followed by many disciples and therefore we have to be the Aadharsa Purusha, meaning Incarnation, among all the people. So we should retain our tapas, without losing even 0.1 mg of it, grow up in spiritual strength and it should be used for the betterment of this universe. If it is spent, thus, nothing will be lost; it is always growing and growing and we can maintain our spiritual sakthi without any doubt. Man sets roots for upgrading himself by his selfish efforts and his personal identification of workload and finally he must find only money in the palms of his hands and he should be happy enough to recognize himself first. Then we can solve whatever the problem is, we can solve it and come out of it and we can resolve the problems, whether it is monitory or domestic, we can win the race. We are having the super most VIth sense and by God's grace, we can win the race whatever may be the woes and understand about ourselves first and then our self-confidence and divine guidance will lead us towards final victory. We can be the victors and successors of our own. So, let us pray God intensively to give us good health and knowledge to earn money and how to lead our knowledge in our processes and thus, we can be blessed by His majestic look and we can win money for this world is always a slave to money only. That is why, I am getting afraid and nervous but after all, when God's grace is with us, what can others do to us? Nothing. With this confidence, I step down into this world and He must dispense us to have victory over all our efforts, thus, we can be free from all of our failure in our life only success will be fed by God's mercy and grace. This kind of belief and behavior gives us normal and abnormal success in whatever effort we step in, and because of His will and pleasure we can win the race and get success with money and fame. So, never get tired ...! Go on. Everything will be ours, finally success will be our own by all means and we can earn money and good name and fame in all of our activities. Therefore, be bold and behave as you think, and try to withdraw anything for the sake of others, do not think about failures, never will you face failures in whichever subject of your activity or activation. God is with you. So do not be frightened and go through your straight path and succeed with success and money and gain by all means. Lord knows all, and whatever He gives to us is so familiar and favourable for us, belief in this golden phrase. God is loyal and quite royal, so His mercy and grace are unstoppable, thus, you must go and go never get tired and succeed in all your actions. You must be obliged to all your successors processes too. Therefore, our winning post is very close from our spot, and step up quickly gigantically. Oh, you have crossed the post now the medal is yours, and rejoice at this moment, we are all here to encourage you. Thereafter everything will not be false, finally you win with your own efforts.

Then there is no way to escape from Vaikundam itself. Ever you will be out of births and deaths and you are called a Nithyasoori. This is the motto of a human life. Now we have to understand the answer of this life and thus, we, ourself and all should have verily spiritual knowledge and by this we must serve the society by all means of our service. Bhagavan is the one and only master. We are always the serving authorities, we must consider us like this and discharge our duties. God will be pleased and anugraha will be our own priceless birth. Externally, we are doing many activities in an orthodox manner and nothing can give others dissatisfaction, they should see us with Dwesha, why this bhava arises? because of pride and ego, these Gunas should be completely erased from the bottom of our heart, and we must be as a just born baby. If it is possible, then everything will be easy to light all lights. Eternal light lights all of the other lights and those are blessed fully. Thus, the karunamoorthy sri Hari Himself ties us with Him and we will be with the tie as a bondage, no, it is embracing bavana. He is making His organs and physical amenities to be saturated with Sri Hari only. We are all telling ourselves and others, but, when problem rises in any account, our real colour that is sorrow, ego, anger.... which are all sleeping within ourselves and when time comes, all come outside with their natural nature. It will make us not to be fit to remain in vaikundam, and that is why, we must be sincerely, having hope upon us and others; this is the simple piece to maintain our knowledge and wisdom. Therefore, we must submit all our actions and deeds to the natural orals of Hari only and no touch or connection to anything, nothing. This bavana clearly makes us to deliver our duties with full of Eswararppanam. It is the final stage of human life to attain His Holy Feet with all good fortunes. Wherever we are, whatever we are doing, our whole heart should be in bondage with Sri Hari, taste this fragrance and taste the inner divine ambrosia of Thiruparkkadal. You all are not eligible to travel with God's personal, private tour to places, they are nothing but the pure hearts of the purest, original bhakthimans. Whatever you achieve, have done, wealth, health, name, fame everything is Himself, nothing is ours; if this is understood by us then our natural calamity filled heart alone comes and sits in our nucleolus of atom. So, we should be always aware of our thoughts and Hari's Divya Namam.

Those who are merging always into the depth of this materialistic life, it means, pressure from children, wife, friends, outsiders, neighbors, thickest relations who come to our house usually, but who is having or giving money to manage these sundry expenses? This to be analyzed and then, come to a conclusion and it should be suited to practical life. So, whenever we are getting confused, we have to think by brain not by mind; our mind itself for about 40% is false and that is why we do not give full acknowledgement to it, we have to give the first seat to our brain. It never misjudges or misleads us, confidently. When we are between 40 to 55 years, man is not able to come to a decision in all subjects because of many reasons like our parents' demise or kith and kin end, certain friend's illness or death and because of these actions, we also think about death and without proper understanding about death, we lose courage, valour etc, and become very weak. They never take food properly and they will not be in need of inspiration or respiration, and because of these many reasons, they are coming to a conclusion that death is coming to pick them within a second. This type of thought makes us not to do our duties properly. Brain thinking so will attack and make our life short; so, to get rid of these evil habits, we can lead a pretty handsome life and all will be happy and the society is always searching like us, persons, who are the Gems. This type of life should be our custom; all scripts emphasise us to live and keep them as life's model to have a moralised life. Whoever has fear of God, it is the beginning of knowledge; thus, they will be educated by Himself with high level education. Education means this mundane not apart from our knowledge, it is pure wisdom. Which is our mind or subconscious mind? This is because it alone induces us to do good things only. That is why our consciousness is called Satyam.

If we live in the custody of our consciousness, we will be as bright as the Sun. He or she has the tongue power especially apart from being a teacher she has some very fine qualities, it is very much a pride.

If India is to be kept going, we should work hard and shelter, food and water should be supplied to all. If we trust in God alone with full of. confidence and surrenderness, He will keep us from all evils. It is because God is ever merciful and without rest, He does His duties and many more activitists are created by Lord Brahma; and Esan declares them as Gnanis. These Gnanis have energy and boons to activate what He declares. Our knowledge, degrees, doctorates are nothing before the Almighty and, He is the best educationalist among all the learned. But He though learned has changed Himself earnestly to do service to mankind. Likewise, you should have some positiveness, and a straight heart. Forbearance should be cultivated and you must transfer yourself as these Gunas, and that is why, do not be afraid of anything, and finally you can be saturated with the Almighty. Thus, the role of human cycle is going on; that is why, copulation between all animals are different in modes, moods are explained through puranas and Athyathmic small stories and a lot of statues on the primary or main Gopurams of the temples. Thus, the couple understand and birth cycle situation is nothing but an awakening and thus, creation is without break, is running on.

When our prosperous, fruitful period comes we can live as our mind operates, everything will be possible for us and profit will be gotten very easily. But, when God's turn comes, these elements will vanish without any trace. The Universal Truth, i.e., DEATH., after this, there will be a discussion in the court of the Almighty and there we have to prove all our sins and its reactions, then only we can live calmly with peace. Otherwise the same births and deaths cycle will prolong without an End. If we realise this Truth, we will stop all of our atrocities and do good for others and thus, God will be ready to make us His own. We become Himself. This embodiment is wished by all. But we should make our habits and activities in our day-to-day life pleasing to Him. We must draw a budget according to our income and lead our life, in a peaceful manner as there is no stop for the acceleration of our human wants; but if we control it, then it will be like a dog and come under ourselves showing its gratitude by all means; thus, we should bring our mind under our control; not to go along in its control, if it is controlled, we will be the master of all actions in this birth and forthcoming births. All kinds of misfortunes are set up after God's judgment, He will count from the very base one, two, three.......then all these types of materialistic burdens will be around him and he can never come apart from these bondages very easily. So we caution them about the best and the worst beings of this human birth and death, for to come outside from this impact is not at all an easy task. Our entire life span should be to win over our selves with God, our Creator and thus, we can entrust ourselves with His elements and His gracious look. Apart from this, this kind of materialistic thoughts and deeds will make us have a grip with the earthly activities and we can never raise ourselves up to the pedestal of Heavenly abode. The attainment of this abode is the symbolic point of our life and therefore we have to struggle with all the obstacles, riddles, and puzzles, because these are the breaks throughout our life mode; we have to free ourselves from the grips of these troubles. So to say, these are very fine characteristics, if we emerge with these laws, we can have liberation and thus, this entire life will be beyond our imagination. Everything is illusionary and that is why, we have to entrust ourselves to the prosperity and saintliness of Divinity. Nothing is comparable to this godly life of Divine valuation. This is the readymade boon given by God, but we do not realise the point of attainment. As of now, we are very clear about the point of attainment by us. But, the Maya extremely distracts and pulls us away from the saturation with divinity towards hell. Because, so to say, hell is very much better than Heaven. In this manner we educate ourselves because of the massive illusionary happenings that befall us. We don't like to come out of this illusion easily. Our epics and puranas emphasise us to get rid of all illusions and come out of this Maya and try to attain the incomparable, unparallel point of ecstasy which is the END POINT of all these negotiations of this world. This worldly happenings are nothing but impermanent, but according to our Maya our thoughts, residence in this world and mergence, with the worldliness we believe these are permanent, and we can have no other conclusion apart from this, but if we are thinking about death at least once in a day, the illustrations of Maya will clearly be shown to us and we will be out of this operation and attain mukthi.

Each and every organism is blessed, because it has such good skeleton, the most blessed, dispensed aspect of our life. If we hold on to this grip, we can be elevated towards Him beyond suspicion. This is the repulsion of our ancestral mood of human life. The attainment of God is emphasised so much, because, our ancestral embodiment and metabolism come along with us because our original residence is Bahavan's residence. This Mighty abode should not be forgotten and we should go there. We can go elsewhere, but to live, we have to return to our Home. The HOME means kailash where Sri Umamaheswari is present.

Our prime duty is to enter into the stipulated place, because it is our permanent abode. Due to trials we, just come here; when time comes, we have to give up our materialistic body, should be withered and the soul, alone goes towards our natural abode to take rest; otherwise the soul will be taken by Yama gingarars that will be very much brutal in trial. So, the gnanis, whenever, time comes, should willingly submit us to the divine abode. This is the utmost benefit to the soul that is Moksha. Our duty is to submit ourselves before God. At the time of materialistic departure towards Eternal solution, we have to perform penance. (Mouna) silence, limited food will enable us to know our time and when the time of departure comes, He will send sivaganas to remind us of the time. Accordingly, when the time comes, the jeevan mukthas, naturally start to lead their journey towards the divine abode of Almighty, God. According to our past karmas and future, we have to reside in the stars and Grahas, then, we again come to uphold the humanity and chant the glorious kalyanaguna celebrations of God, will be written and shown to all, they start their journey and attain sivasayuiya, where there is no pain and sorrow, no gain or loss, simply living along with only one sadhana. God, has to shower and those are recorded word by word, when He comes to this universe, they repeatedly chant in various temples, before God, and the Almighty gives His Holiest Darshan and uplifts from evil to noble thus, our trials will willingly be on the circle of life mode willingly.

Then, the Gnani comes by birth into a royal, loyal family, at the time of birth, He will not have loss of memories, He will catch up with the past birth's concepts then and He will start to do His divine work, to elevate all towards His holy abode; just as we travel to several places on tour, and then getting back to our own Home. In this way, He finishes his life span, likewise all will undergo this process, the whole life circle is systematically governed by the Almighty. After the period of several years, we are once again kept with Divine Unity, we return to any one of the stars and render our duties capably. We reunite with each other, but there will be no effect in our reunion with sensitive unions; thus, the trial is a never ending process and with body process and it is ever pervading, process will be going on and on, since then, they are body and for several reasons, they will be as an astral body and distribute the best service to all beings and then, they return again to reach their natural abodes. Just as per divine concepts, the births and deaths are occuring in one's real life. Of course, they, themselves are responsible for their own richness and poverty. If they want a luxurious life, from this birth at all, they will be living the noblest life and thus, they can be seated in the row of divine personalities and after all rituals, all will say something as commentary; they will not attend any function and without telling about the goodness what facilities we have, to elevate to the highest pedestal of Human rejoicement. All irrespective of sects and creeds and religions, they give notes very clearly to adhere to be free from passion and non-durabilities. Just like this, our sole control of 10000 Andams are purely and neatly being controlled and beyond these partials, they are honoured as divine Annonists. Such a good life, which is preferable during all times record. These Annonists work for us apart from money, they show their gratitude, they live alone, such a way the whole universe is functioning without any mystic nature, they are so divine and they rule the nations with the best direction of their Rajaguru and He is considered to be part and parcel of our present world.

MUKTHI can be explained in words in our day-to-day life; it is an implicit feeling at all. It has some wide and rangeful worth of births. Then, we can receive the vibration of those feelings and their presence at all. Those who are an interesting soul which is ever thirsting for fellowship of life entirely, he may come across these voyages and thus, one can definitely elevate to the higher state or plane of ecstasy. Thus, we can explain mukthi in words but, in practical side, if we analyse the presence of Him and God, we should come across the set of soul and dawn of soul. In other words, Death and Birth, Therefore, everybody is trying to attain the independence custom of Mukthi, from where we visit any kind of choice coverage over mukthi, it is not at all Mukthi. We can describe our proceedings of the possession through which we cannot go elsewhere, because, we are in the earth, so, wherever, we go, this is nothing but inside the earth only. So, we are within this universe, struggling along for food, shelter and dress, besides mukthi. Mukthi should be the aim and ambition of one and thus, he can liberate himself from the cycle of deaths and births. After death, for a gap, of sometime we descend to this earth that is called birth, after finishing this body's work fully or partially, we return to means of custom is called birth. Births and deaths are confirmed, and pre-determined during our life span each minute by minute. Therefore, we should not waste a second in this life, but love and like it to a well furnished heartfully solemn humility and in this manner we can have some good marks to enter the ladder steps of mukthi stage. So, everything is pre-determined, therefore nothing can be done as we wish and pleasurable moments cannot be used by humanity throughout their whole livelihood. Nobody likes births and deaths and remaining like this in the valuable body and worthful soul. Thus, we are worrying for all, will not live at all, but perish, we need wealth and one day, perish, within this period, with the help of wealth, we try to live the happiest life thus, we are wishful creatures and whatever we have, at his level we have spent our tongue and sakthi to recover ourselves to the Almighty. Therefore, everyone is solemnly struggling to enter the path of Mukthi whether it is right or wrong; but all are saying that they are living completely, with constant belief upon God and He will cherish everything and we shall meet in Mukthi. But, it is doubtful, that all are going to meet out Mukthi. It is the state of this stage, in which our mind if it is the master, we can control all the sensual organs and bring them in our control, and even our eyelids are always pressurised, it is not in our control. If this simple periodology is understood, there will be no ego of fanaticism in our daily life. Everybody wishes to win all the competitions in the world but the soulful man tries his level best, one and only thing through which we can attain Mukthi is by liberation from this sensual world. Thus, senses will be under control, and we can win the race, between materialistic and spiritual paths. So, we should be always aware of these sensual reflections, and so, we should be doing soul searching and questioning thus, therefore we can easily win the race by God and Guru's grace and mercy. These two can do the same, otherwise, nobody can save us from the crucial happenings and this is beyond doubt, if senses go beyond these, these will not reintroduce them in any way. Such a stubborn heart must be efficient to win over all the senses. Then we will be yogis and thus, yogis are honoured by the people very much, if they are simple in their life, then they are equal to God without kama and lopa.

Outstanding characteristics of human life; all creatures born search their food, recreate, reproduce and one day they perish; this is the normal situation of the materialist world of a human being. But this situation of standing VIth sense of man is rare. He has the ability to laugh with its meaning herewith other than our humans, animals are also walking with legs, all are named kalnadai, but man does not come under this title, because he has his own writing, exercises, procreation, eating and recreation and so on. When compared to other creatures, man has a lot of differences of role model of mankind. So, we should be born as human beings; like other beings, he should not take the production of all creatures. He should be differentiated from others, especially brain working, thinking in several aspects and angles, these differentiate him from other beings. So, if we try to keep the discipline of mankind, it will be a divine life. That is why, this immense value of human life is dispensed by God to the soul and hence it exercises as an individual, goes to the proper place where it comes from; it is moksha. It should be the goal of mankind to reach it. Wherever we go, we must return home to live, is a proverb in English. For this example we should lead our human life without any hesitation, try our best to saturate with Mukthi. This is the goal and ambition of human life and therefore we should be ready to leave anything in respect of attaining it. This is the perfect goal which is meant for mankind. That is why his VIth sense is individually governed by God Himself, and as a result this materialistic life is full of maya (illusion) for maya, we must be aware of all things, irrespective of soul binding bondage. There are so many innumerous countable bondage binding himself to this worldly characteristics and these are to be cut off. Thus, if we cut and cut these bondage, the last precipitation is nothing from Brahmam. That is Tat Vam Asi Aham Brahmasmi this is said to be advaithic principle which is to be realised and experienced in day-to-day life and hence, he lives while he is living in this world. Then, he gets eternal salvation and thus, he can cut off bondage and, can go through with the chain of births and re-births. For this saturation, we are given a body with five elements and they are controlled through mind, and we should control our own mind and all must be cautious if the reign is withdrawn in turn we have to find the origin of this maya world once again and we never come out of this Maya because it is quite interesting to lead this life, which means we believe this life is with full of happiness.

No. Not at all; there is not an iota of happiness in this worldly life, we are searching for our mental peace and harmony by indulging in the mundane characteristics, and all the creatures, one day we also perish as such, our life ends. Are we ready for this kind of day-to-day life, No. Nil.. We have to rise up and raise ourselves to the pedestal of Ecstacy which was furnished by our forefathers, and their whole experiences are they are attaining the spot and note and quote the memories of this life's surroundings, is nothing but illusionary. Nothing more to convey because this type of life should be transferred into today's lively true life. When we think about our causes and projects, nothing is in it and we are quarrelling each other in order to fulfill our desires and this Desire, is the root of births and so, we grow this little, nothing but zero pointed life is ahead of our maya, life, it is controlled by divine maya and we are ready to sacrifice our life towards maya plus this life; what is life? It is a mixture of all aspects of this materialistic life, and never can we try to escape from this current world. So, we have to be afraid of death and birth. Death is very easy when compared to birth, the configuration of death is one second but birth takes 65 days approximately and in this way we had this rented body through which we are operated with full of miseries, mistakes misunderstandings and so on. God gives us the supreme power to lead this life with truth and full of confidence upon

Him alone. But we are not ready to be controlled by divine sakthi. We are always under the sense of hurry. Whatever strikes us in this life before my eyes, I do not believe this and they are not understood by wisdom, we do not have confidence upon anyone, and we also lose our confidence upon us first and then, we have to have true wisdom in our intelligence. Our intelligence is controlled by Wisdom, then only, our life will be blossomed by virtue of other matters. Our sincere art in our whole life is to erect our freedom flag without delay, this time, this second is worthful to hoist it to the peak of the pole and therefore, we can satisfy ourselves and our Creator. If there is one, which is existing is nothing but a creator should be in the background to make it and operate with rules and regulations, then only we can light the Inner Enlightening force which is even present in human deeds as well.

For passing our time, we should not live, we should have a mind to realise the importance of human life and therefore we have silence doing rigourous penance in order to achieve everything, and more over, our life should be taken as an example to others and our whole life should be full of confidence and cultural phenomenal circumferences. Circumstances never come alone, they are imposed on us to do good and earn name and fame. This concept is a maya or illusion, we just neglect this happening and be ready to saturate with Eternal solution. We are all very much fond of climbing on the back of an elephant, but if he lacks concentration how is it possible to achieve this goal. So, from our childhood itself, we should be trained and inculcated in good nature and character. Thus, we attain the supremacy over all beings. Human birth is not at all given by Him very easily, Bear it in mind; by doing rigourous penance in several births, we come forward and due to God's pleasurable mood, this creation of the soul is happening. So, we have to be happy. Do not worry about anything. We never have anything when we come to this universe. Moreover, several habitats and habits are adhered to by us. In this stipulated time (years of life) we are educated and in search of a job through which, we earn something and learn to be satisfied. But, it is not at all in custom. Lastly within a few seconds this invaluable birth, suddenly dies and the bearing body starts to decompose and nobody will even touch our body. Such changes are normal and quite natural at the time of leaving this Universe. Whenever, we lead a good life, all forms of deities will help us to attain jeevanmukthi. Jeevanmukthas are not at all produced, it is a divine convocation which is given to those who satisfy God through their mind, body and soul. So, we have to be alert always to gain victory over our senses and we should be the masters of our mind, then He will be pleased and give us a title Mahathma.

The cycle of births and deaths are unavoidable, because this birth is an unstable one, one who comes from the almighty, is always trembling to saturate with the Almighty, because it is the holiest place from where we come. Whatever a child is given either milk, toys, chocolates it plays for a stipulated time, after that it will search its original mother, likewise, we succeeded with anxiety of reaching God, because we are the descendent feature of the Almighty, and that is why, from birth the baby tries to attain its original refuge is God, and thus, it begins to saturate with the natural aspect irrespective of maya. Education, wealth, white coloured job, a V.I.P and having several duties of a village, whoever may be, all are submerged with the Almighty, and have the celestial form of God. Because of this, is our original state, from which according to our three kinds of karma, He gives birth and death and thus, if karmas without jeevan, then that stage is called nirvana of mukthi parapthi, where we are going between birth and births. We are inducing to do good morals and throughout our karmendriyas and Gnanendhriyas, we enlarge huge amount not bad habits; we develop from our spiritual ways, we acknowleged with the footage of God; He is always ready to grasp from it to its coverage, but, we due to maya's amusements, we remain, not to go to our natural own place, when time comes, this is the boring life and time will not pass, cannot eat and unable to read and concentrate on holy thoughts and deeds, these are the symptoms of, we are inch by inch, reaching steps of His lotus feet and thus, our birth without death saturates in such a form of mokasha and in this manner, there will be yamapasa only. If Yamadharma Raja's pasam is in front of us, we are the jeevan mukthas while living in this world.

Human beings have the privilege to get rid of births and deaths ?How? this is elaborately discussed. I and You; what does it mean? If these questions are to be answered, we will be ready to renounce and speak about this chapter very easily; we have type written several sentences, but, we can show anything with relation to the subject. That is why, we have analysis of our own; no discussions can conclude anything to furnish these typical manhood worlds, it should be thought of and thought of under the goal of life and thus, we can invite and discover the natural and manual answers of these typical questions throughout our birth and death; we have to identify I and You what do they mean? This is a favourite question. Daily, more and more discoveries are going on, but these questions in this field will not be answered. If we realise these answers, it cannot be told; if it is not discovered, we can speak about these phrases or one and only word, if we know the meaning and the goal of life then, quietly, slowly and steadily we are marching towards the medical and intellectual fields beyond doubt.

Approximately, the time of the creation is not known(earth) but we sincerely analyse our brain completely, we have still not found the exact structure of these words. The topmost inner hidden meaning of these words, if it is without doubt clearly absorbed by them, they will be benefited. In science and any other field, we should not make others to contest the meaning, what does birth and death denote; everybody will not know the answers of the immense truthfulness of this co-incidence of science and spiritual worlds. These are no two subjects; they are blended one with another, like an electric wire. If we consider this meaning, it is quite right to inspire ourselves and in this way we can go abroad and go beyond the limitations of mankind. Apart from manhood we cannot sign for this proposal and it will be easy to break out the chain of meaningful theories. The oneness of the Almighty will be realised through five elements properly and we have to return to mankind, in order to thrive it gradually. We shall go beyond mathematical theorems, will help us a lot to make survival of any time, it is beyond time and any synthetical and natural commitments. Mr. Ramanujam's remaining 11112 theorems are kept cool and nobody can solve and know their results. This Ramanujam is an Indian, as well as a Tamilian. In this angle, we are all very proud of him and praise him, if he were alive.

We already know that if there is a birth, definitely death is also fixed by the Almighty and why do they blabber by means of virtue that Tamil Nadu CM, who expired yesterday night, today, all pay their homage in several ways. They praise her to the skies; like her, no one can be given such a birth this is one of the statements, the commentators exclaimed about her, Had she faced any problems, like. shri. K. Kamaraj, no. She is the king and she is the servant also, likewise, she dictatorially, awkwardly and obstinately spoiled Tamilnadu's civilisation. According to Divine will, still 4 years has to be completed for her, and then pass away. But, He called her, why? Her service and means of rendering service to all was not satisfactory as recommended by the Almighty, and that is why, she had been pulled away at this junction, characteristically what human resources, were with her or from her. She is dead and that is why, all are praising like her; but, according to thought she is nothing but one among the creations. She should be a Vethala for 4 years. That is why, we are commenting about her like this. Who is man? truthfulness, selflessness, freedom and no expectation from others. She is a multi millionaire; how had she attained these assets. All are by corruption! Doing mischievous doings cannot come under God's rules. He gave us some syllabus and thus, we have to attain supreme ecstasy and what is the way to attain it? Nobody is here to enrole their names in the diary of God. Beware of these bloody idiots. According to them, there is no necessity to be a nobleman but we should act like a noble person. He is the mightiest Actor among all; so, we should be aware of these creatures. Do bear in mind if you have to rejoice the divine nectar, that is only because of His grace and dispensation. Nothing is permanent and pure, everything is illusionary. So hereafter we should be afraid of God and Death, be alert not to fall a prey to these kind of wicked and evil thoughts and deeds.

India is the biggest democratic country and it is honoured by all nations because of its holy principle, unity, may be, diversity between Religions, creeds, sects and languages, they are all together, when nation wide thought arises this nation is the karmic Boomi where God, Himself descended to the plane of earth and lived according to the mundane principles and regulations and they emphasised what is Dharma. How it is operating all and itself. Thus, crores and crores of Munis and Rishis were given birth on various sects, creeds, and religions and they preached the philosophy of human life and its immense value and what is the cause of births and rebirths, the cycle of births and deaths are happening throughout the universe, but only through mankind's birth one can lift himself to the highest pedestal of life. Thus, geographically and spiritually, INDIA is standing up to the mark of development, whether this nation emphatically stands among others in various fields it is the topmost country, by which all nations are deducting what is civilisation and unity in diversity but on the whole, which represents Godliness.

If we have a fine sketch of life's value and its cultural steadiness, our life will be the media of our human birth. Whenever our, wisdom and intellect merge together, at that particular time, we have Holy Dharsan of God, why? because the wisdom is our experience and it is the symbol of God, which is the seed, in which a strong, broad tree's fullscape of map is inhidden; likewise, this Universal map is hidden in the wisdom, that is why, we are struggling, in search of God. We fail by going here and there and therefore, we cannot attain God or our utilisation of our full wisdom. The scientific world, accepts, that our brain is utilised only 3% of its capacity. Nobody uses it as per its 100% to the mark of utilisation; if 100% is utilised, he will be a versatile genius among all the creatures, so to say, he is equal to God. We are using our mind and intellect just for a few accounts in search of needful money, and that is why, our human life has no value in God's kingdom. Because He does not appreciate or authorize us in order to have an awakened state of Divineness, and that is why, even nature, never considers us, and we are dependants of nature but nobody is independent in nature. So, no supplementary respect is given by all to this human birth.

We give so much respect and honour to this birth but, naturally it is an honourable birth, in God's view, but Mankind does not realise its value and how to lead a meaningful life. All are born, grow and are earning money in any way, reproduce and perish, they do not at all realise the mighty power of the human beings which is dispensed by the Almighty. If we realise truly, we will not waste even a single second without doing our karmas in appropriate ways. If we consider the value of time, that we have consumed and forthcoming time, we will not dream and regret about the past as well as we will work hard, and discharge our duties prescribed in this earth. For this reason, we can live a full-fledged life by which, Mukthi will be honoured by God at an earliest date in a Holy way. This excellent opportunity, as a human birth is a great boon by God's will and pleasure. We have to lead life which is appropriately accepted by the Almighty and useful for us and thus, it must be honoured henceforth.

As scheduled by the Almighty every single second of time can be utilised in a proper manner by which we can attain the abode of God. Whatever we earn whatever we learn, whatever we accumulate whether it is gold or platinum etc., our honours and convocation certificates, we will be got rid of. Nothing can be done, after death occurs. So, daily we have to spend a single second to think about death; here in this world all and everything is impermanent, what we see and study, are one and only due to MAYA illusionary, because of maya, it seems to be real and permanent, so we have to realise the full truthfulness and illusions and the courses between these two patterns in this way, we should realise that which is permanent is God alone; nothing is permanent other than Him, we must realise our truthfulness and destruction and we are day by day, marching towards destruction of this body, but nobody can even touch the soul, this is the supremacy of the supreme Truth. We have to adhere to the Dharmic rules and regulations, and live a rightful mode of life which will definitely give us the permanent bliss that is Eternity. That is why, we have to do our karmas without any kind of expectations and thereby we can elevate ourselves to the state as Arjuna, in the holy epic, Mahabharatha. He is a karma yogi and he attained Mukthi. Without the knowledge of all this karnan battled with all the woes and kept his honourable friend, Dhuriyodhana by the last second of time, he. got God's Viswaroopa Dharsan and attained Mukthi, by God's grace we are also eligible to have dharsan of the Lord too. Therefore, we have to make efforts towards getting the holy dharsan of God by this human birth in this very human birth. We should do and discharge our karmic duties without any expectations, but we have to spend atleast a minute of our time daily to be concentrated with God. Thus, the accumulated time in bulk, will keep us from sinful activities and we also have the wisdom of God's world. Otherwise, we should, not worry about anything of His abode and His presence. Thus, we are running our whole and entire life.

We may have the sixth sense, what is the use of this? Do we utilise this with sense in our day-to-day life, for elevating us to the pedestal of Godliness. Thirukkural describes, though we are so much educated, what is the benefit, we should salute and be grateful to God. Thus, the question arises, what is the value of our education our graduations and learning and earnings, without saluting Him gratefully; nothing. The Thirukkural emphasizes a great truth to us in 10 dimensions, if we are well versed with Thirukkural and Naaladiyar, then there is nothing more to be learnt to lead life successfully and yield good fortunes without sense of honour. Therefore, we have education, we are educating ourselves. Today's trend is to earn money by finding white collar jobs in Air conditioned rooms, but they do not wish to work hard for searching the soul and do difficult works; they are modernised, they believe, in this manner, we are not very much civilised and marching towards development. Everybody wishes to work in this manner to earn money. There are several works, by which, we cannot earn five digital money as remuneration, and now no pension at all. That is why, our younger generation is deeply afraid to seek a permanent job. What is meant by permanent? If you have a job, that is permanent, how many years, does it last till our life ends? If our age is 58 completed, they put up a farewell meeting very soon and send us to our homes. Up to this date, of retirement we have to be permanent, is there any guarantee for our life as a permanent one. Nobody can say that I am always permanent, the poor become the richest, the rich become poor. So, there is no permanent and impermanent, these two are mixtures that is life. So, everything getting permanent, seems to be true. For example take a just born baby. It has no knowledge, wisdom, efforts and so on. But it knows, in the mother's breast our food is there, it automatically, without anybody's instigation it feeds itself milk from the breast and it is satisfied and free from hunger and thirst. Likewise, when we grow and grow, the situations, our mode of life, our style of life, changes, everything is impermanent and nothing in this Universe is permanent. So everything will undergo sudden change like anything, naturally. We and everything is impermanent but we believe that we are going to live a long, healthy and wealthy life; that is our dream also; but they go through only as dreams and do not come into action at all. They, ask which is permanent? and what is impermanent? This kind of foolishness spoils the aim of education, it is only to come out with wisdom, with presence of mind, living with what we are dispensed with by the

Almighty up to time of leaving the world, we have to live with or without permanent, or impermanent things, then only our entire life will be a beneficial one....! Is there anybody who gives guarantee to others, or even himself, of the permanent feature of his own living period, if, impermanent is clear, then we realise our inefficiency to prolong even a second of our breathing without the permanent prospect of God. Therefore, if death is happening here, we should have belief in God, whether we believe or not, no loss to God, we lose something; the God believers may have the mentality of freedom that He dispenses them to do something better than nothing, non-believers live as blind cats jumping into a well. So, we have to have faith in God, He, Himself is the Mighty Creator of the Universe; He gives us the freedom to do what is wanted of us and He controls our status, whenever it is required. He governs always our doings and even our thoughts. We will be given as a boon with a pitiable look as - May God be upon us...thus, we will not face any major failures and impossibilities, He promotes all things, in order to change our fate, and gives us peace of mind and strength and energy to the fleshy body and purity to the soul. If we have belief in the existence of Himself, the ordinary people will have fear to do illegal activities to themselves and others. Generally, everybody will be fearing to do wrong to others and try to do good with finest thoughts and deeds, and thus, they will become wise in due course of time. Perhaps, the wise will have faith upon God's existence, they will entertain very good thoughts and show the right path, to be followed and like this, all will be with good thoughts. If we do any sinful activity, there will be severe punishment. It will be kept and when our turn comes, it will affect us. From, these clips, we cannot escape. Those alone who do think, will do services without any kind of expectations, the essence of Bhagavad Gita. In due course of time, all will be Rama Rajya's control and rulership. Then, there is no poverty and theft and no wrong ideas will even rise from the minds of all the people. God Himself descends to us as a human being, and Deva too, to enlighten the whole Universe with Eternal peace and shanthi. There will be no one with greed, ego, possessiveness. All these vanish from the minds of the people, because fear of God is the highest embodiment among the principles and therefore, the God fearing will be alright through their thoughts, deeds and so on therefore, God's concept will grow in this universe with peace beyond creeds and sects etc.

Human beings are born, consuming their food, flourish with bones and tissues, with all organs, reproducing their generation, one day, they perish, most of the people are living in this mood only. If Mankind also do these activities what is the particular difference between mankind and the animals. Man is dispensed with VIth sense and he/she should have some difference in the mode of set up of his/her life style. Man alone can laugh with meaning and having anxiety with his desire having conscious mind to show pity and hunger, thirst, etc., but animals cannot express their feelings, but they are also having their languages by which they reproduce their caste without destruction. They also have sense but not at the rate of mankind. Mankind is separately given birth to realise himself, and thus, he can know and realise the Creator. Therefore, we should cultivate ourselves to the plane of Mankind's living conditions, altogether without any symbolic presentations with animals. Whatever the animal is, it is pet to all, sometimes, it exhibits its natural quality by which we realise its cruelty and softness, so we, must be careful to prevent us from their cruelty and their consequences. But man also, often they show their animalhood's representations, but not realisation of their own personal efficiencies. Of all creations, man is considered to be next to God. Godliness, with the sense of caliber, he/she is given birth on this earth but circumstances and situations, make them not to allow them to exhibit their mankind's specialities to himself and others. That is why man is suffering from so may illusions, desires, unsatisfied life all his whole life. He is searching peace in many ways and from many ways, but he cannot attain it through his efforts. It is a boon to him, this life of course, we should cultivate our mind and consciousness with full of honesty, discipline, regularity and give respect to our livelihood and we should realise the importance of and value of human life, and thus, we can elevate ourselves to the plane, equal to Godliness. It is quite simple, but he is troubling himself and the whole mankind by illusionary thoughts and their consequences.

Whatever our efforts, we should face them with valor and fearlessness, then the final victory is ours. This is the natural fate for all our efforts. Many attempts fail in the end, but the final attempt. In all our dimensions, we try very much to achieve so many things, but, according to the final decision of Almighty will be the final result. We are given very modern noble body and flesh and particularly, we are created with sense, if we apply this in our up to date life, we will be free from ego. Destruction of ourselves through bodily ruining, and mentally praising us and expecting others bonafide certificates, we are cheating us in our day-to-day life. So we should at all times, ever arise, and awake to recharge us and through this exercise, we can elevate ourselves because of our spiritual sadhanas by our Guru and God's grace and mercy. Our human voyage is in the midst of not sophisticated moods, but in the midst of quarrels, and peace will be blossomed thus, our life is situated and operated by God, we should respect those regulations and rules, then final success will be ours ... that is attaining mukthi, no more births and deaths, free from this mundane circumstances agonies and unexpected diseases and mis-calculations. We simply be silent and keep our equilibrium with normal mood from birth to death. So, we should consider us to be His sons and daughters, then He has the responsibility to feed us and He has to impress and insist to feed us and giving clothes and residence. But, He is ever present in our Heart. His location is nothing but our Heart, if we do not know this truth, we simply do ceremonies and rituals that our knowledge insists, and the result is nothing but zero. So, we have to pray God not for wealth and so on, because He knows everything ,at what time, we have to give this in His time and what time, we have to pull out our worldly burdens, He is the Mightest among all the mighty ones. So, we should not pray for worldly matters, we have to pray Him without any expectation, and is not known and expressed the connection between us and God is the most successful yoga in this Universe, such people attain the qualification to attain mukthi in one attempt. God alone searches to His earnest to discover such unexpected and he is having the eligibility to realise himself and the creator of the Universe, God.

Every custom of all religions have their own symbolic recognition to the betterment of mankind. Therefore, we should be always alert to avoid mischievious actions and not to involve in innocent and foolishness's activities, if it is not, our whole and entire life will be meaningless. We should give an End to this life with our contentment and satisfaction and thereby, we attain Godliness beyond doubts. It is quite sure, achievable, so, oh, mankind! be alert to receive the light of Glory from God; we have to receive His plenty of mercy related things, it will establish us with peace and shanthi. All of our wealth and actions are in His mighty hands; if it is recognised and realised thoroughly we easily attain Himself, so, we should always be ready to live and ready to leave this world. One aspect is, nothing but, our efforts are for education and through education, jobs and it is because to accumulate wealth as a result we fall into the deepest well and are not at all able to return to the surface. Therefore, we are drowned in the water of worldly maya illusions, and so, to prevent these illusionary activities, we have always to be 'Rest Assured' is insisted. Whatever the action there will be a reaction, if we bear it in our mind, our life will blossom with flavour of Godliness. Such life is meaningful ever and an example for others to adhere to the rules and regulations. Of course, we have come to this earth from the abode of Almighty, so should have the resemblences according to God's will; He expects such development consciously from every human being. But, we do not know the value of human birth because its invaluable, we cannot measure it's magnanimity. May be, crores of words are sufficient to describe only one reflection of God's will so, we should be ready ever to saturate ourselves to the lotus feet of Paramathma. Everybody, apart from castes, sects, creeds, every human being is having worthful opportunity to make life with full of strength and resistance to recover us from sins, and poured and cleaned, and thus, we get rid of this worldly births and return to death. In this world, nothing is stable, so, we have to face all happy full moments and sorrowful events equally. Thus, we should elevate us to the pedestal of God; He also wishes to make us as a suitable man to attain and be given such a boon to her/him. He decides through our thoughts and deeds, hence nothing horrible will happen, and these events may be seen so easily, when we apply them in practical world, it is too difficult to adhere to and attain the Holiest feet of Himself. For this type of thoughts that we must have, we have to cultivate ourselves and as a Guru, we should show the way to others and thus, they can get salvation, live contentedly and satisfactorily. If it is realised by the Ever Pervading Soul, Paramthama, He will come to our residence, and bestow us with His mightiest blessings and then we can be either a saintful sidhar or Godly loaded human being and return to this world to serve for the betterment of this whole universe. God, Himself descends to the world and leads a human ordinary life and thus, He teaches us the value of human birth and how to tolerate our agonies and obstacles, as such, mankind get clarification for their doubts. The epics and puranas are not imaginary but they have truth and that is why still they are living and in every dimension of our day-to-day life, they cross our lives. Do take The Ramayana, it crosses in several ways of our daily life. If we feel this Universal truth we can realise the value of this life, and how it is spoiled by our innocence and ego. There is no loss for God and Ramayana, if we ignore them, if we apply them in our life, we will be living a full-fledged life and it is the gain to us.

In this stage, we have to realise that it is only maya or illusionary scenes and there is no particular importance that should be given in such a way to the scenes. We have to fight against whatever the burden is. It is the sole way to get rid of all inconveniences and from maya too. From birth until death, Maya that is, illusion, and imaginary doubts cross over our life and such things bring doubts in ourselves and in some illusionary experiences that should be of great help to us in our life in all circumstances. This is our motto and that is why, we have to try hard to prevent fear for anything because everything is controlled by our Creator, God and He will solve our problems and give way to live a right royal life. This kind of belief gives us confidence and regulates our life in such a way, that we can have contentment in our actions. Whenever death occurs, up to that moment, we should have faith upon God. God believers and non believers are going into death, but, there is a major difference as the God believers submit their souls to the Almighty, but the non believers' souls are picked by Yama's substitute. When we analyse it, the first is a pleasing experience, but the latter is very cruel so, there are lots of differences, when death occurs. In medical science, so many ways are illustrated in so many methods about death which occurs. Likewise, spiritually, there are so many differentiations in capturing or submitting their soul to the feet of God. This is entitled as MAHASAMADHI, from the time of the release of the soul, from the body there are 16 divine rays that are out and these spread throughout this universe and are stimulating the earth.. It is an embodiment of only one and only ray which is always in this Samadhi state, and it exhibits its full strength and is the cause of all the best to the human society. Thus, we are grasping so many good particles through their emission, in this way, the whole Universe, is still in some what a good way to attain the path of the Godly kingdom. Whether we have belief in God's existence or not, we are controlled by His rays only. The whole 11000 Brahmandas are controlled by the Almighty's good will, and we humans are having power to exhale and inhale, and in this way, by our breathing(breath) our lively years are calculated. If we have belief in the existence of God, our Good will be brightened, otherwise, we will be the losers of the magnanimous situations. Therefore, the society particularly, Hinduism gives the option of having belief upon God or not; it does not worry about the conclusion. Whether it is a river, or a sea or a flow of water fall, lastly it will submerge with the sea; likewise, the believers and non believers merge with the Almighty whether they wish or not. This is a life which can attain mukthi very easily and make others to enter and succeed in this way of attaining Mukthi. This person is also among us, but we cannot identify Him because our motto is working hard, earn money, do kitchen work, make our diet, then eat and thus, we are free from thirst and hunger and reproduce our generation, and one day we simply perish. Apart from this custom, there is an entire satisfied life, no one is interested in hearing about it too. This range of people are countable and abundant, then what shall we do? They are even ready to give their ears to listen to the news about the existence of other worlds and be contented only through their mode of daily living. To such people, God is not at all ready to open their eyes and ears to the voice of truth and He does not wish to pull them towards the attainment of Himself. How can one man who is worried by mental agony taste the honey. Everything will seem to be bitter in taste to such people. After their agony disappears they can taste the honey which is very tasty like jaggery. Therefore, those people are to wait when God will dispense them to the inducement to realise such phenomenal courtesy of life and it has its own rules and regulations. If we adhere to those strictly alone we can also be dispensed by God and Mukthi can be attained. This type of awakening may come after crores and crores of births, may be just one can attain it in this birth or after this birth. Let us wait, we cannot do anything for them. From birth to birth, there is no surety to have the next birth as a human being, there is no surety thus, we have to wait to have this human birth, then only we can get the gracious look upon us and we can estimate our birth's value and its importance, and then, we will surely entertain so much to attain liberation from this cycle of births and deaths and get Eternity. This is the most dispensed boon which is to be gotten from the Almighty and it should be enlightened by God, Himself, otherwise, we cannot even think of these kind of thoughts.

The laws of Godliness are entirely different from the laws and regulations of mankind. He, the man of Godliness has realised the supreme truth. He punishes or forgives them and dispenses them with some prizes. Those who are punishable, without any grace and mercy, the quality and quantity of punishment will be severe so that soul should realise its sinful density of sins, and they will be forgiven by any kind of aspects. Those who are involving in sinful activities, are to suffer with their consequences: this is the law and order of the Almighty. Here it will be applied without any mercy or gracious look at all. God is, no doubt, most gracious, but sins are most sinful then what shall I do? Punishment is the only way to make the person as a remarkable one to turn him into the right pathway of Dharma. Jail is not at all a slaughter shop, where the prisoners will think and regret about their cruel situation of the consequences of their faults, and they have to be changed as much as the wise, and this should come into action. They should realise the consequences of their cruel and unmindful action that they had done, as such, in course of time, they should realise the truth and know that because of their action, how many people are suffering; thus, he realises his cruel action and moderates himself and changes from such faults. This is the motto of jails. If we are self conditioned and disciplined through the regulations and principles of God, there is no necessity to go to jail for further treatment. All will be managed into normal custody. But sometimes the fault is beyond our control imprisonment is necessary. Hence, jail is another school for the wicked and these people will transform themselves as normal human beings and rightly, the whole human society will be hale and healthy. Thus, everyone has the right to Him first and their own relatives and neighbours and even so the whole human society. We have to live and make others to live as our own neighbors is the best concept of humanitarian aspect and in this way we can entertain ourselves and others. This is the vast planning, and this shows our wide ranged mentality and therefore, many years, once and one birth has to be furnished and given as a boon by God Himself, otherwise, this type of birth will not be bestowed by the Almighty. Therefore, we have to endorse a separate birth which is to be got only through doing penance; the birthful soul, and its parents too would do heavy penance and so it becomes fruitful. Today, may be, such birth has been given as a boon to us and such a birth may happen may be once in a crore of years. These Annonists may have the right and energy to promote the human birth to the supremacy of Godliness and perform Astamasidhis. They can run through the whole humanity towards constructive mode of life.

Each and everyone is willing eagerly to live a good, healthy and most probably wealthy life; and it should be a long one. Nobody wants to die; if one comes to realise about "DEATH' it is so sweet, sweeter than any other of these mundane Honey experiences. If death is not for creatures, who can feed all of these organisms? giving shelter and guarding them all. So, as our dresses are dirty, we wash them and make dry and iron them, then we wear it comfortably. Likewise, death is nothing but an interval between our long process of human life. So, forgetfullness and death if they are not in day-to-day life, nothing will be achieved by mankind. Do try to realise the importance of death. How long a period can one work and how long a time can one remember all things? So, these two processes are ever wishable and most necessary for not only mankind but for all creatures too. Naturally, whether we sin or not it comes and occupies at a certain age, it is not at all an End. Birth and death are never ending process, so birth and death occurs as a custom in daily life. Death has no particular time or minute to be present; so it is foolishness of rejoicing when a baby's born, and it is utter ignorance, if somebody dies, all are weeping and crying; naturally these two are one for reproductional process, and another is to equalize the world's Equilibrium. Therefore, we should not go into birth and death, because they are the best processes of God only and thus, we realise by our spiritual upliftness, we should not lose our mental balance at any cost of time. May be, birth cannot be placed in homes; but like that death is common it has no particular place and time, He only determines and as per schedule, it occurs and at the interval time, the Athma experiences the results of its fore births life's karmas. Ultimately they are experiencing their good and bad results for that and then, they return to lead a life in this Universe. But, there is no surety, in our next birth, we can be gotten this human birth, upper handly, there is not at all any surety given by God. As His will and pleasure, He gives skelton and structural looks and creates the shristi (creation). He nourishes them and when, time comes, He pulls them to Him. This process is in the day- to-day life of all mankind, for about so many crores of years. Nobody can predict the birth and the death. It is a very complicated one, no astrologer can calculate the cosmic science, he cannot predict the hours, minutes and seconds from and to, and as per death. But we can fix and as per God's calculation, if something happens it is a clue given to us by God, the VIth sense is in action. Within this space between death time, we should think and thank and chant His Holiest Namavali (Namas) throughout our lifetime, So we can attain Moksha, which is the supremacy, equal to Godliness.

Chapter 8

Rest Assured

"Rest Assured" means nothing but Tolerance, which is held by anyone, he will always be happy and, he will not effectively bother about anything. Be Bold we can execute and exercises can uplift us to the highest pedestal of Eternity. Often, we are stressing, this is the human birth's sole motto. As, we have to reveal what is relevant to those who are...! Otherwise, you will lose your shanthi and peace, then, you cannot be proud and self-confident. This type of enchanting words are innumerous; but what is the fact, it will be coming according to our fate. This world saw so many emperors and they fought with others and kept the land as an acquisition and thus, we are proudly (INDIA) trumpeting, that we have not fought any kind of war with any other nation for the past 25000 years. But we are affectionately quarrelling each other, they do not put us to sleep. So, we have to be alert, and then how can we solicit peace and a harmonious life. Nothing doing..!

The word violence means it is the basement of our temperaments of our culture and civilisation. If we think with more concentration, Tolerance is not at all omitted from daily life about which is we speak and speak but if we adhere to it in our daily life, then, it is a development for our ever living culture. Tolerance should be developed. As such we are speaking more and more, but we never try to build up the basement of this non-equaled philosophy, but by which we can achieve anything through our sakthi of tolerance. Whatever happens in our life and surroundings, we should not reject tolerance. Whatever happens throughout our mental strength we should keep tolerance in all froms of departments, as much as we say and act throughout our life, everywhere we can taste the harmony of sakthi forever. But outwardly we are acting as a fully new and tolerant man but inside of that gentleman, every man is with full of evil, as such, we cannot move up towards our own generation to be firm and trying to know the exact meaning of this word, Tolerance, we can easily construct and establish everywhere the peace and shanthi. If we really withstand these two qualities, we should act according to the situations and thus, we must progress to the peculiar and smoothful life of which we can interestingly live our life with harmony and honour. Such life is wished by all, but we do not implant its seeds in the minds of the public. If we need fruits, we have to. implant a sample of this heirship and thus, we can have ever tasting fruits without failure. If we implant some other tasty saplings, we cannot get such a good fruit from the trees which were implanted some years before. Thus, we should calculate and compromise with them the weakness of our inability to coincide with each other and there by, we lose the progress of our development from our consciousness. If tolerance is in the innermost layer of our heart, then tolerance can be pasted and it will not come out of that pasting; such unselfish service is needed by all and therefore we should be alert to adhere to tolerance and this is also a yogic exercise, and thus, we can enter into the mark of the pedestal of peace and real ecstasy. Therefore, we have to lead life with full of tolerance and satisfaction and dedication. The pure meaning of tolerance and its invaluable Prosperity can be understood by all means.

Sometimes when we return home from outside, we may have lost temperament, at this time, we should keep the officials' order, they keep quiet and if he does puzzle their tolerance, we have to handle the dharma of police and then, we can have the truth of immense explanations; we can easily understand our life's unsteadiness, and its impermance is also not stable. If these are applicable in our daily life, our life will be a divine one. So, we should have education from our happenings and thus, we can acquire huge experiences from the world. If we have the activities from outside, will not be compromised with inner circumstances; we should choose which is having the sakthi to do whatsoever. In all circumstances, we should be in actual organic system should not be under taken when we are in a solitary mood. At that time, we have to go through a book, we can have a huge task of wisdom to be furnished and such pure wisdom is not at all covering the materialistic world and thus, we should tolerate our do's and don'ts. This policy should be applied and thus, we can attain the center point i.e the oneness of mind should be considered to be the center point to take practice for our human qualities and so, we should perform all our needs and our deeds, which should be pure and clear, then our needs will be achievements to be brought into consideration and these will give us the tolerance needed. This in other words, one of the modifications or tolerance is an unworried subject which can be pertinently brought to the supremacy of all beings in this world. If we win over ourselves, the whole world can be under our control without any doubt. Therefore, we can do our duties as we expect at that time, if it is done by time, then He will be pleased.

If we sow good seeds, we can reap good results. If we sow unnecessary seeds, then how can we expect the best result? So, the basic need is that by which we know God, this is always through the inhalation and exhalation too. Our prana gas should be metabolised to realise us and the sole creator of this Universe who controls all the rotations. Such kind of mentality should be instilled day-by-day; we have to grow up with our soul, and thereby, reach the pedestal of God, certainly. We are going to temples, churches, mosques, gurudwaras etc., in order to beg something. It is a shame to us because He is our creator and He knows all; whenever time comes, He certainly dispenses our needs without our expectations. But we foolishly beg, in the name of prayer we bargain with Him, if you do this, I will donate something as alms. This shows our utter foolishness. Wherever, we are, He knows our thoughts and according to our needs, beyond these aspects, He gives the best for us, because He has the sole responsibility to feed us and give shelter and clothes. In the name of prayer, in these holy places, we simply waste our time, because, we beg to fulfill our needs, may be our prayer is not suitable for us, He simply ignores our needs, because without begging, He gives good health and wealth and so on. Apart from these materialistic needs, we have to thank Him at all times, as He has created our inner organs and outer significant activities are all by His grace. If He does not permit, nothing can be done by us. So, we should be grateful and each and every time we must show our gratitude for creating these bodily actions, and controlling our inner organs and their metabolism. If He begins to punish us, for whatever we do with and without our knowledge, deeds and thoughts, we cannot even survive with these sophistications. Whenever time permits, we should chant His holy manthra and see His form as per our civilisation and culture. Then we should be grateful for His entire contributions. When we measure them, it is out of reach of our thoughts, such great dispensations have been and will be given to us in due course of time. God gives and forgives, Man gets and forgets this is what we do nowadays in the name of cultivation of our mental capacity and most probably we are trumpeting that we are so much civilised, have all freedom to do things. Nothing can be done without His order only by His order, whatever man thinks, will be granted by Him.

REST ASSURED:-------The embodiment of Divinity is nothing but this existing materialistic life and its strength and basement of everliving (illusion-Pure) ever, without non-stopping process is due to its existential course of its impermanent nature. So, this whole materialistic life is not at all lapsed from the base of mind and so, we enquired ourselves, but we have no solution, to establish Divinity everywhere. If it is successfully established in a point of subconscious state, there will be no divinity or materialism. Every aspect is right royal and there is no distinction between the permanent and impermanent aspects, we cannot differentiate the difference between these two, because there is no permanent and impermanent, because illusions are getting vanished from this Universe. It is so to say SATHYAYUGA. Of course among the four yuga's, the sathya yuga is the very first of all yuga's and it has a lot of human years. In this yuga the descendence of God and Godly avatars here lead a materialistic life with divine perception. Thus, after Sathya, Dhvaba, Dhiraetha and now Kaliyuga is in progress. Kaliyuga is considered to be the very miserable yuga, with all the evils, all destructions, and very difficult to live according to Dharma. Adharma will be demolished by God, thus, He, Himself comes as the Mightiest man and destroys all the evils to construct the pillar of Dharma. We are expecting the descendence of God, but several lacs of years are to be awaited to welcome Kalki, the IVth avatar of God. He is the One, who can destruct the density of the Earth and establish and construct Dharma all over the Universe.

Up to this day, all illusions, unbelievable, unexpectable happenings will happen and thus, the whole universe will be in the grip of Adharma. Those who are leading a shanthi and peaceful life will suffer a lot, but illegal persons will be crowned as the First class men and women in this Kaliyuga. The pure Educationalists will not be honoured, but the wicked unpleasant creatures, will live the happiest and contended life. These seem to be the signs of Kaliyuga. The rulers and their rulership modes are not honoured and accepted by God, but according to the yuga Dharma, they also acknowledge the happenings and this Kaliyuga honours each and every rowdy element. Destructive people live with total success and they are given medals and crores and crores of money. The good and personally self oriented people suffer a lot and these people will be honoured with the crown of divinity. In the temples, nothing divine is to be adhered to. Everything is being done only on the prospectus of money, money is the chief in Kaliyuga; and thus, the good are very poor and the rowdies reregulate and standardise the world and they have most of the blackmoney and they boldly do illegally oriented actions and customs. The rulers and their rulership is personally satisfied and they are like owners of grocery shops and they will be ready to go along the motto of learn to earn most of the money. They have no education and their education is nothing but, they spend a lot to get a degree and in the name of a degree, our youngsters choose only subjects not worthful and due to their foolishness and these subjects and they are not fully worthwhile. Even the educationalists too are the slaves of money and they give ideas to the wicked to earn money and they make them to be the major donors to construct temples and the welfare of the normal people. These wicked and money minded people construct many universities, schools in order to acquire more and more money. With this money they shoot films and lose all the money then again they will try to become prosperous, by their illegal and irresponsible deeds. Such people will be wanted by the Police and they will be arrested. These elements without any worry of mind, they go to jail with a pleasurable mood, all the illegal elements will not be reasonably and legally punished for they are encouraged to do actions opposite to the political, legal opinions, just in order to earn money and that is why, they are ever ready to do many immoral activities. They fix a rate for their illegal businesses and they, one day, some of them, are imprisoned and several others escape because of the loop holes in our political and lawful systems. Those who are convicted by the Court do not bother about their conviction, they think they are martyrs, going to jail and waving and saluting the near by people enter the jail. Inside the jail, may be, they live a contented life and when released from it, they come with ease, they do not worry about anything. They continue doing their atrocities very regularly. But God is the witness; whenever His turns comes, these bloody rascals will be out of the frame; if they realise this truth the world itself will be very fine as God dispenses all.

REST ASSURED:- The prayers and thankful adorations are coming out of the navel point not from tears. We are all weeping in order to get the sympathy of others, but not God's. If their prayer is out from their hearts, they will be pulling out from the miseries and troubles. But these do not at all happen, why? Because our weeping is not from our heart and it is from our eyes and there is no jeevan in our tears. That is why He does not pardon our sins and hereby we undergo the consequences of bad symbols in our life continuously. Whenever we pray for our mistakes and sins and heartfully renounce them, we will be pulled off from the place and have a normal disciplined, dispensed heart and life. Thus, after getting an equilibrium in life, we have to put our heart at the feet of God, and thank Him for yielding these things due to His mighty grace and mercy. Thus, we have to pray and thank Him. Oh! Mankind...one day, there will be an end in our life, on that day, we should merge with death, if this thought is emerged with our blood and thoughts, we will get rid of our sorrows, happiness, ego and 'I' and thus, become a gnani and these worldly aspects begin to disappear from our inner sight, eye sight and, have a new perception, through which we can witness Brahma's mightiest creation of this whole Universe. This is nothing but a mere scenery but it determines our whole materialistic world, through which if we awake from the illusionary world, we can raise ourself to the topmost pedestal of Ecstatic finalisation of births and deaths. If it is nothing, we have to return again and back again to rebirths and deaths, there will no more END for this encircling and encycling process, as a result, our whole life will be nothing but only useless. We may imagine the highest point of ecstatic point, through which we can attain our perfection, but if we are not co-operative with our attempts, nothing will be of use to the whole of mankind and other creatures too. In such a way, all men and women and children too have interest to know the spiritual embodiments even from their childhood and thus, when they grow up they can elevate to the highest position that is GURU Sthanam (status).

It can be said that everyone is a guru, the whole Universe is full of Athmic Gurus and nothing there is or no job for God; we are His messengers, and we get entangled in this betterment of world very much, in such a way we can overrule the regulations of this universe and thus, we can attain Godliness very easily. Therefore, we should consider it as our life's goal and aim and ambition, without for any reason, that this manual life is dispensed by God. This kind of belief should be our one and only thought for all. It will enhance us to attain the ever flowing nectarful world and therefore in order to taste the divine nectar are we ready to taste mere water? This is our question to the universal creatures? If there is life of creatures of all kinds, water is the most essential element among all..! Thus, we experience its worth, but we have no interest to give orders to have heavy rain. If rains comes, only most of catastrophe happens. But if there is no water, it is painful to the creatures to get even a mouth of water. Whenever we are thirsty, we can buy and drink so many sophisticated drinks but the thirst will not be equalised with mental peace. Only water is the source taken inside will quench our thirst. So, whatever we do, we are in need of rain water. There are a lot of sources to have water, but mankind is not willing to grasp all by all means and now our lands are nothing, lands not fit to cultivate anything. On another side, Man has become lazy, and they are unwilling to cultivate our food materials, they are fond of seeing cult of money in papers and that is why, they come to a conclusion to sell their lands, in so many ways. For about 100 years hence, there will be a lot of houses and areas of industries and man has to take tablets for his hunger and another tablet for his thirst. Just like that, we transform this earth without water in such a way, we are towards our destruction and we are continuously blaming one another, but, we all are responsible for this mistake of lack of water of the earth. But as per the broadness of the seas is as the same and there is nothing to do, because of its saltish nature; if it is transformed, man will not stand by the seas simply. He will also pollute it within an hour and make it useless. We are all, on the march towards development, we are all ruining our civilisation and culture, we trumpet loudly we are marching towards developments in all fields and in all the ways, but it is not at all true today. They are false statements that the politicians and general people are advertising to us, that we are contended with all of our needs and living most satisfactorily. It is not at all true, first of all we are not having much water to quench our thirst. Even though, we are in such a situation, we are trumpeting that we are self-sufficient, self-determined and self- realised. It is a false concept by which we are cheating us in naked eyes.

REST ASSURED.... In this book, we are illustrating what is soul? What is Paramathma? What is the connection between the two aspects and why are we separately enhancing their services and duties, and why does the soul remerge with Paramathma and its reasons. These concepts are illustrated and even the readers can easily and deeply remember the feature of their co-relation from birth to birth.Thus, these major and supplementary subjects are clarified and verified with the fullest screen to the readers. If this subject is known by the readers, if they also be a part and parcel of spiritual believers, then their all kinds of doubts and sins disappear and they get crystal clear clarification of His manifestation of this Universe and what His duty is and so on. After the cycle of birth and death, what happens? And what do we have to do? With the awareness of this knowledge, we are simply knowing full knowledgeably about the causes of all activities. We question why some are not punished for their bloody mistakes for so many times, but at one time they may be, even severely, punished, and through this punishment, they are made to recover from their doubts and enlightened with pure divine scenes. This is so to say illusionary scenes and Maya simply. After, through our continuous and rigorous sadhanas, we can merge with the Almighty. Then our exaggerations and illusions will disappear from us. As and when we do not consult our Gurumars, it is a bulky mistake, we have to have dharsan of our Acharya and Acharyas. It is only by the look or sight of these purified souls we can change our mistakes in our sadhanas, our imaginations and our natural phenomena. Thus, we come outside of these maya, thoroughly, then, we can enter the materialistic life, the illusionary maya will be getting off away from us, thereby, we become one and character- oriented as God's representatives. Those who are spreading Esan's prosperities with the permission of God, are known as the uncrowned Gods and they with the same sakthi within themselves can overrule and even rule over us and because their godly gracious and merciful look will not permit us to see them even though we are standing before them. This is divine Vairagya, determination. This Vairagya for others comes through dejection, at the same time it is attained by a not fulfilled mind of desires; this is cheating ourselves. This type of vaigraya is not at all taken into divine custom. It has basement but it has arisen and stands for some hours, and then it falls down, likewise it is going through towards its own way. This type of sadhana is wasting his human life and thus, they cannot persevere and preserve anything in their own endorsement of spirituality. These kinds of people may seem to be Gnanies and yogis but they are not able to control their outer and inner organic systems and their evolutions, they fail in their proceedings. Finally they realise that they had failed in this Spiritualistic life by suffering from many agonies and diseases. True yogis are up and up in the elevation point of Mukthi, thus, their Vairayga stimulates day-by-day, they surely attain the lotus feet of God and whenever we see them, they will be normal, like other humans quiet and ever blissful in all aspects.

They are well experienced with all types of Gurus and project the Universe towards solution. This is the noble symbol of true sadhanic disciples. By merely saying Thank you, Majesty is not at all appropriate and a suitable phrase to glorify God. He is far away from such words and sentences, we are murmuring some words by the tip of our tongue, just saying chorously that they are significantly thanking the Almighty. It is not at all standardized by Him, because He is the all knowing, all pervading, omnipresent One. He knows very, very well all our mental thoughts and is intruding with our own thoughts. He knows what is going on and where we are going and what we are thinking. He is the Mightiest knower of everything, we are cheating ourselves by saying that we pray and thank Him. It is nothing but our intellectual cheating; we cannot cheat Him, we do cheat ourselves and thus, we cannot get from Him. If our prayer is strong enough we can live with full of determination, satisfaction and contentment, beyond all our fears. He will save us and in due course of time, His glory itself, chanting His names simply cure all of our mental sufferings and their reflections and refractions suddenly and we will be free as birds. But we have not at all reached this stage, why? Our prayer is one to show off as a big mass in the halls for all to see and who is looking at them admiring others saree and jewels, but this kind of prayer is not taken into consideration by God at all. He realises the good faith upon Him and He rectifies all and frees them.

REST ASSURED-------The supremacy of the mightiest Paramathma cannot be measured by us, because it is outside us and always within us, this is seeming to be a puzzle. We have discovered the co-rrelation between Jeevathma and Paramathma through intensive Spiritual sadhanas and through our spiritual straight cut life. We too can realise the oneness and the everlasting Being and we too become a part and parcel of the Paramathma which is considered to be ZERO POINT. Within this mortality we always are struggling to find out solutions for our day-to-day problems, but Gnanis, through this method, they are wishing to entertain themselves and others, entertaining to make others to be enlightened souls. There are obstacles and riddles in the midst of true spiritual life, but, we should do our spiritual sadhanas through right royal ways, Paramathma will pull us through to its true level. Our human birth is said and considered to be the most valuable one among all species of human beings. We have to do spiritual sadhans, taught by our spiritual Guru, and Upadesha manthra, by chanting this oneness of manthra, we become one with the point of the everliving concept of God. Therefore, if we wish to attain the salvation of human births we have to run through our right way of spiritual sadhanas, without any mistakes and wrong doings; then only, we can make others to know by wisdom and interact with wisdom, thus, we become the Greatness's posture of Mukthi. Of all our spiritual sadhanas, oneness of pure soul with the Supreme can be known without any puzzles and doubts. Therefore, we have to experience our spiritual oriented life, we have to be one among all and every creature in myself that is 'I' Thus, we are concerned with spiritual phenomenon of the human life, we can easily enter into the Holy Kingdom of God. Whenever, we realise the greatness of our human life, we are pushing towards its End, that is realising the supremacy of our own soul, which is the most important one by which we can do spiritual sadhanas without any puzzles or losses, therefore, we merge with spiritual elevation. So many Gnanies and savants are emphasizing this point, but the other ordinary people do not at all bother even, they have no awareness of this point, which is ecstatic, they alone live and perish. But, if we are masters of this study, with vast and thorough knowledge we will realise the value of human birth, that is enormous, thus, we can realise the invaluable and immeasurable goodwill of our Athman. If this is totally clarified and known by wisdom, our life if we have a fine will be meaningful and truthful for us and also for others too.

REST ASSURED:- Our strength of various births, accumulated, is the cause of this human body without any default accessories. We are here, to sophisticatedly live with all the satisfaction of our needs. Thus, we have this bony and fleshy body, why? To saturate our soul with the Eternal point. If this body is not at all given to us as a boon each and everyone, without any proper reason, has to realise the value of this human birth. Many of the children are orphans, maybe affected by so many diseases and also disabled in some parts of the metabolism of the body, but, we are fortunate to be one of those good creations (few exemptions) we are here to establish the greatness of Himself, and as a result, the forthcoming generations will follow the right paths to convert our idealogical life into livelihood. Otherwise there is no other gain for mankind, and the human birth is an utter waste, and so they cannot have the sense of spiritualism and its awakening to attain the embodiment of the Godly status. Therefore, we should not waste a single second of our stipulated life, and we have to utilize the valuable time, by which we should live a contented life through which, we must be ready to attain the spiritualised elevation at the highest level and we should use this birth only for this purpose, aim. We should never waste our life time without any action, karma, we cannot escape without doing our karmas, if there is no state of not doing karmas, stipulated by the Almighty, we have to be concentrated and construct a new era of our life only through spiritualism. Our efforts are mere nothings. In this materialistic world, in the midst of our daily activities some percentage of time should be spent to thank and pray the Almighty, otherwise there is nothing more valuable for us than our human birth.

REST ASSURED:---------An attempt to attain Mukthi, that is saturating with the Almighty is a Himalayan task, and we have to adhere to the rules and regulations of mankind strictly and He Himself well help us to form such thought will be transformed, into deeds and thus, our whole life should be with the flavour of Divineness. Maybe some mistakes may happen in our daily materialistic life, but there, is no sin according to the divine rulership. He will cause any kind of consequences in the Divine Path, the hurdles are purified, therefore, we can withdraw anything in this materialistic life, then only Ekagakrasidha is possible; that is why, the puzzles of today's worldly life led by us is not at all a sin, and the beholders of this life will vanish from our mind itself, then the divine life will be applied in our day-to-day life. There is no sin at all in Divine life. Nothing, is considered to be sin, if we wish to prolong in the path of spiritual life, the hurdles, and all the ties will cut off in the name of God, so they do not come under the title of sins and no consequences, will be wrongfully considered. So, we can boldly live together, even with others, not with passion, but only out divine will that is, 'Ready to live and Ready to leave' this is an excellent prologue of the human life. If it is dispensed by God, we can be successful in divine life and mukthi is certainly possible. In the Mahabharatha, the war was declared at Gurukshethra, two opponent ranges stood ready to fight, but Arjuna had a thought that if there was any necessity to battle with grandfather Bhisma, Guru Dhoronar, Krupar and so on, what shall we do with the victory and Lord Krishna preached Srimad Bhagavad Gita to him in 18 chapters, but he had no conviction at all, but karnan, a birth between the reunion of Rajamatha Kunthi with Sun God; she was afraid of the society, and she put him in a box and left it afloat in the Ganga. He has step parents and now he is the Karma Gnani who fights with the Gowravas without any mental oscillation. He had no Bhagavad Gita, he had no puzzles and though he knew very well, that those five men were his younger brothers, he never put down his bow and arrow as there was no oscillating mind. He had no Acharya to give upadesh such as Bhagavad Gita. But he stood like a rock and fought with all and he attained Mukthi. Take down this example of the Karma yoga's finest authorisation. In such a way we have to live in this world, and so this is an epic, since then, up till today it is having the finest seat to Aaradhana, our mind is still not at rest with anything, more and more thoughts are mixed with doubts, and we cannot be restful or peaceful even half a minute with pure patience and silence. If this is possible, then we can easily exhibit the way to attain Mukthi in due course of time. Whether we realise or not we are doing our activities only through mukthi, maybe in this numerical code of his life span, somebody may attain his 416th birth, some may have birth after crores of years but finally we have to attain and finish with Mukthi. This is the Universal Truth, if this Eternal Truth is realised, we will minimize our sinful activities and for this reason make us suitable for saturation with the Lord. Until this we will do our earnest whether it is sin or virtue. Everybody's karma is fulfilled with the aim of attaining mukthi, by virtue of knowingly or unknowingly mukthi is the our final finishing point of whole life circle. Thus, the births and deaths are coming to an End point, at that time, this is very finely illustrated by Swami Sri Vivekanandha himself to his disciple, Niveditha, from kings to all citizens efforts are knowingly or unknowingly directed towards liberation and these will all be diminished one day, and each will attain finally Mukthi, may be, the time of point of saturation may differ. Therefore, with this confidence, if we do our daily duties (karmas) the consequences will not affect us severely and thus, we attain shanthi and peace of mind. Our Generation is to be with oneness of God, and therefore, we are aiming towards that final point, we are doing our materialistic or spiritual prayer for our welfare first and others secondarily; we should begin only to worry about all ours neighbours, those who are all in this whole Universe's welfare. In this manner we develop towards Eternal saturation, free from all anxieties and disabilities, and attain God's feet, in fact, this is the satchitananda. Apart from this, nothing is to be attained, because there is nothing though everything seems to be truthful.

In this Universe, there is no such as miserable things and joyful things, we mistakenly in our ignorance make division of categories ,we ignorantly consider that this is fortunate, and that is unfortunate; like our divisions are econsidered to be an imaginative mood, some things are the happiest somethings are the unhappiest is what we apply in our day-to-day life. So, this imagination has to disappear from our mind itself. Whatever happens, it is symbolic of God's maya which is going on and whenever some unfortunate, illustrations occur in day-to-day life, that is also an illustration done by God's maya, thus, we should consider and tolerate them with our will power, then, God, will assist us and guard us to the right path way to stabilize our site of learning and understanding the phenomenon of cultural feelings which is taught by Himself. So, we have to face boldly whatever happens. There is nothing more than birth, growth and destruction, these three are happenings and within these 3 dimensions, our whole life is withheld. Whoever we are, whatever we are, He is ready to sanction us the best, dispensed by God, and He is ready to forgive all of our sins, and make us pure and hale and healthy both body and mind. Then, why do we have to fear about anything ? there is nothing to worry about, nothing horrible will happen. The guide lines of our guardian, are pulling us away from anxieties and egos, hence we will happily remain as the purest souls, in the Dharbar of God. He Himself is ready to make us His disciples, but what can others do in unfavourable things and activities towards catastrophe. God, will act as a catalyst and make us saturated with His Almighty power, and thus, our whole life's schedule is going on. These kinds of thoughts will provide us a good, possible life and with the leading processes of possessions with leading our efforts towards victory. So REST ASSURED--------is emphasised throughout this book and hence we have to be ready to make us the best disciples throughout our life. We should trust our soul towards His holy feet and thus, we can live and lead the happiest life, therefore, we should be emphatically filled with the marvelous things. Also we have to do things in our own favor and in favor of others this chance is given in this life; it is a rare chance, which is gotten through our punya karmas in so many lives, and thus, we have such and enlarged, eminent human life which is dispensed. It should not be wasted through our illusions. Every second is allotted to pay our tributes and salutations, and be grateful for the fine engineered construction of our body; likewise nothing is equal to our human body. No two bodies are same in shape, habits, mental attitude, habitats and so on. One may be soft and peaceful in character, another may be cruel and murderous. Such wicked people have Government punishments, though these happen, they will not return to normal life. Two children born from one mother, are different from one another and such qualities and infrastructural metamorphosis is entirely different from one another. This is the Excellent and Unequalled creation which is done by God, not at all by Man's science or by his VI or X sense.

REST ASSURED:------All are willing to have a fulfilled life of happiness, riches, food, good dresses and to appear very much beautiful, handsome, always with sufficient wealth, nobody intends to die soon, they wish to lead a long life, without diseases, for this each and everyone, should undertake God's rules and regulations and adhere to it in day-to-day life. If we adhere to those restrictions, we surely can accommodate these things very easily, A life without disease, is booned by God only, likewise, our good will is in the hands of God; so, if we are good enough, we will be blessed with all things by God. He is Almighty, and He is capable of giving everything that is good to us. We pray to demand so many things, but, He will dispense the best ones. He gives; so that our life will be Eternal. Therefore, some percentage of honesty, obedience, sincerity, humbleness, controlling the senses, we must possess to lead the best mode of life style. He gives surely, and fulfills our best needs with His deeds. When we undergo the tests which are given us, we should behave not like a coward, we should access them with bold mind full of valour. Therefore, REST ASSURED is necessary for those who wish to attain the abode of the Almighty. God knows our needs and deeds, and thoughts. If we realise the fact, we can win over any kind of torture at any moment. If anything comes before or behind us, we can win the final victory; victorious in the riddle of this hurdle of life. Whatever thought we have, should be entrusted with the Almighty then, see, automatically it is sanctioned and the fruitful results will come throughout life; and nothing horrible, will happen besides God's will and pleasure. He is apart from sorrows and happiness. He is like a weighing machine, and He dispenses both good and bad, they are according to our karmas, to those, who are loved by Him(Habibullah) can escape from the clippings of the bad happenings. Therefore, fear is the beginning of knowledge, and thus, we certainly attain the Holy spirit that is distilled soul without Kama, krotha, Madha, Maacharya. These are the four bad qualities that make us illusive in nature and so, we think we are the one and only person who can do anything. This type of mind, will surely ruin and take us from the path of supremacy of Truth.

Now, we must cultivate our mental and will power than our physical power to face the force of the Athman, that is our inner strength of our soul, supremacy, then there is nothing to be solved; within some minutes, we can win over our senses and mind, thus, we can operate our body and mind, if this state is attained by oneself, he will realise the importance and the features of his ownself. For, it is very much beneficial to proceed on our spiritual journey and therefore, our mental strength is the mostly needed factor. Every Athmasadhaka should be ready to face any kind of obstacles, that come through the spiritual journey, and as stated above, if we treat them smoothly; we will win the race between Maya and Truth. Maya illustrates itself through various forms and exhibits like so many ideals therefore, it seems to be in the highest, position and possession of the Universe. Hence, this illusionary scene should be burnt by our self-confidence, and bhakthi towards worshipping God. This has nothing better than or nothing more like yagnas and spiritual rituals and yoga exercises. If the soul is realised, everything in this universe seems to be considered not as the truths. Therefore, we should confidently go through the right path towards saturation with God, and this is to be understood with proper guidance of our mightest Guru who has descended as God, Guru is Brahma, Guru is Vishnu, Guru is Maheshwara and He is all and Universal. So, we should cultivate ourself to the entire satisfaction and contentment of our mind before the knowledge and recognition of others. If we recognize ourselves, God, alone, His grace and guidance will be possible very easily. Thus, our spiritual life should be constructed over the basement of confidence and will. In the midst of our day-to-day life, we should have some seconds of the thought of God and because of His dispensations, we have to thank Him, because such a life given by Him is a wonderful one, by which we can attain mental equilibrium to a certain extent and maybe, according to our karmas, our fate, will remunerate us with the solution of Eternity though it will be late, but one day, all will be saturated with the Holiest Divinity. This is the end of Kaliyuga era. Then, Sathya yuga will start, it will run through for several thousands of years, as such the world meets the deepest and the highest point of the Universe.

REST ASSURED-----The whole universal beings are created by the Almighty, fed by him, governed by Him and finally makes them to get rid of this universe and is made of nothing by itself. Man has confidence, due to Maya and illusions thinks that he has no death and end to life. The Almighty, only proposes, and He also disposes of all. Therefore, we must realise the inhidden universal truth, that is, everything is operated by the Almighty and we are only like puppets, As a playback singer and speaker, we are making to oscilate our tongue and lips according to His languages, thus, we live for some days or years only, and those years, half will be gone in sleeping and the other half will be spent in our efforts to make money in order to face our materialistic life comfortably. So, if we have a life time of 200 years, 50 years are spent in sleeping, with the other 50 years some years are gone for our education and some years go into earning money for daily expenses, and a certain percentage for our savings, and some percentage for our medical expenses and so on, ok. Within the stipulated period of time how many hours do we spend in thinking of and thanking God for His innumerable dispensations given by His grace, of course, may be only a few countable minutes will be the result. In this type of life, we egoistically say, that we are always thinking and thanking Him through our intensive prayers throughout the night time and day time. Is it a truthful statement? We are cheating ourselves and others. By this we cannot elevate even a millimeter of attitude after our death, our soul cannot penetrate even the gravitational force's lightened level. The soul, when released from this body, must have so much of Dharma Sakthi to go beyond the limitation of all planets and it gets its own proper residence, like Jupiter, Mercury and so on. Therefore, Saint Awwai tells that if one does Dhanam and Penance in this birth and his previous births Dharmic reflections will be abundant in measure to attain the Holy places, to extensively do service to all kinds of consequences, whether they are sufficient or insufficient, they should under go the natural phenomena. In this way, after death, there is no full stop for the soul itself. It has to under go so many experiences to attain final saturation with the Almighty, for that, in our various births we should have enhanced our penance's sakthi through soul, which enlightens us in the darkness of the whole universe. And according to our past and present karmas, we are admitted into any one of the planets or stars by which the whole Universal Universe has light and they continue their duties, this is Brahma secret, for the benefit of all, we reveal this truth and it should be confidently preserved in our mind and we should be afraid of God, as a result we can earn a good sign, significant mode of life's goal. Whether we have belief in God or not, all beings have to in some birth travel through this one and only path, we attain our creator and remain with this Eternal belief, saturation, that is, the birthless and deathless principle state and this principle is common to all creatures to attain our sole and own abode. That is why, we are bounded by this principle by all epics and vedas repeatedly.

REST ASSURED------This human life dispensed by God to us, through which, we have to render our efficient service to others, and thereby we get purified mental awareness, by this factor, we can easily merge with the

Almighty, and our life will be a meaningful one. It is only that we have to climb up to the pedestal of humanity and reach up to the mark of whole divinity. For this, we have to minimize our needs and the money can be utilised for those who are in need of money and for the welfare of the needful men and women. Thus, we can feed them and keep them from starving. Then God gladly blesses us to the entire satisfaction and His blessings make us more pure and gives better clarity to some extent. We have to climb up the topmost branch of the Dharmic Tree, so that we can touch our goal of our entire life. This life is a boon to us, to realise our creator and about His creation and creatures. If we realise ourselves we can realise the whole philosophy of God. Such, boon is not given easily. Most of the people are pious minded because of fear. Others are accumulating wealth and so on, and some others do survive for the development and betterment of others. Such Dharmic attitude is dispensed only by God, so we should continue our dharmic thoughts and daily actions by following of dharmic attitudes. Such kind of human life is expected by Divinity and such lives are dispensed mukthi very easily. There should be no interruption between our deeds and our thoughts, they should have the same principles of Godliness, for the sake of others one such person lives a divine life which is the salient feature of God only. Others if they have such quality, can win the race very easily and fulfill their lives with contentment and satisfaction. So, we have to provide the chance of human birth to put an end to births and deaths that can be avoided by the grace of God. Thus, we can attain the Rest Assured status. It is necessary we must be with full of love and affection towards all first, then we can spread it over the world, therefore, we have to have a broad minded mentality and our penance should be with the first classical relationship with some Annonists. It is not easy at all, but if God likes, He will give His co-operation of the prophets and our life will blossom with divine flavour and our entire life will be with full of love and thus, REST ASSURED-------state can be a standardized one, so we can be easily satisfied with our deeds and if we are satisfied, God will dispense us to have a holy seat in His dharbar, council. Our entire life is dedicated normally to accumulate money and name and fame, but we do not know the uncertainity of these factors, we will be free from life circle. Thus, we attain Mukthi and it is considered to be karma yoga and when it ripens, it will have no end at all. Therefore, we will be ever siranjeevi(ever living) By this we can help other creatures to attain the betterment stage, we can uplift them without distinctions of sects, creeds and religions.

REST ASSURED-------A man with the complex of fear will not become an ardent follower of God, and the complex of fear will be rectified in this manner, we should make God as an efficient doctor, accordingly not explainable, implicitly felt vibrations make us as His disciples and by which, when His namas are chanted, whenever we speak about His Holiness, automatically our tongue will be slipped into its normal position and pure mouna (non- speaking) stage is reached which is final. Then, we know the efficiency of a disciple and these children are divine births. Thus, Sri Ramakrishna Paramahamsar states in His golden voice. If these deeds are happening, nothing to be Rest Assured, by which we can meet any incident or accident, we will lose our self confidence it is nothing but out of our confidence should be born trust to entrust ourselves to Him. In this way, we are running our life's race, nothing horrible, will happen, this is 100% the words of sathyam or truth. When we are in any position or possession, we should fear Him in our mind, if it is done, regularly without any mistake, chanting maha manthras gotten through a Guru, will dispense the position of a GURU. Therefore, we can attain everything by doing this kind of recitation on God, it is not at all that these words are unreal or untruthful. These are Universal truths, so we should keep this in our mind, and proceed in our own path, in searching God, He is dwelling within us, and there is no necessity to do rituals but go deeply in our Athma, we can realise the presence of God inside us. This cannot be understood or realised only through our organic systems, it is only through our soul, so our soul should be ever conscious, purity that is to nothing and the cleanliness without any traces of thoughts. Therefore, if we chant the holy manthras of God, it will take us to reach the abode of God without doubts. So, pure surrender and trust in Him is essential. Therefore, we have to live a manly life and thus, we will be getting purification to make us divinely oriented souls.

There is no value of this celestial body, if the soul is out of reach, this body is useless, but in kaliyuga only, whenever this body is alive, we can survive in this world. So, to have a healthy body condition we have to intake more nutrious sakthiful food materials, and thus, this fleshy body will survive a long period and we can lead life with full fate. So, it is necessary to take energy giving food materials at the suitable time with full of confidence. There will be contentment enough, the food will be saturated and transformed into blood and so, our sakthi (energy) will increase to an extent. And with energetic food materials, good sleep and good rest are the necessary things for our long life without any damage. We should not avoid our good breakfast, for it is very much essential that it should be full of calories and such food only can give us enough energy for our work and intellectual thoughts. There is a version in English - In the morning take your breakfast as an Emperor, in the afternoon, take your meal like an ordinary man, in the night hours take your food as a beggar should. Therefore, if we apply these conditions, we can survive with full media of life and be energetic, to do our work with full of satisfaction and contentment. All our activities are concentrated only on one thing for earning money. Why? In order to have good food, dress and shelter, these three things are most necessary to all. If we wish for these three aspects we have to work hard, then only, we can live a fully fledged human life. We should not cheat ourselves by any means. These three matters are very necessary for a human life, if we get it with parental care itself it is natural(ancestral) boon for us.

The minimum duty in this world is to discover the existence of God. Otherwise our duties are from the oneness of the pathway, we consequently have to face its ill-factors, so we must bear in mind, about cultural and civilisational encroachment is to attain God, with our entire efforts of any yoga which will help us, if it is taught by a Holy Guru, it will be so easy to attain this embodiment without failure, as Sri Ramakrishna Paramahamsar got his enlightenment from his Guru Bairavi Bramani within 3 days. She also told him that if these sadhanas, were grasped by any other person other than himself would have taken more than 12 years. But you have grasped them within 3 days, and felicitating him, she vanished. Thus, our Dharmic deeds are enormous, we can practice these sadhanas, without any mistakes and get enlightenment. Without the most difficult ways or manners, we can be masters of those sadhanas within 12 hours. So, Athymic sadhanas through various births, if the sadhaka is accumulating spiritual strength, the victory depends upon those sadhaka's exercises of spirituality. Therefore, we should grow up with spiritual sadhanas with a grasping mentality and one must believe that these are our respiration mode. Thus, we can practise and win over our spiritual sadhanas very easily and attain our goal of life without much difficulties. Therefore, physical efforts and mental strength are enough to have salvation of spiritual embodiment. We can learn to earn the Adhyathmic sakthi and thereby we can attain Mukthi very easily. Our entire life should be dedicated to Parasakthi and for this reason, thus, in the various forthcoming births, we have to enrich ourselves with spirituality with full of concentration and total trust in Him who only can give us the fruit as a result. Thus, we can taste the nectar of Ambrosia of our spiritual elevations and the oneness of a standstill mentality. This is the most necessary factor of our liberation.

REST ASUURED------All are having equal right to search God, and it is our human birth's goal, that is why, this human birth is considered to be the best birth among all creations. Nothing is equal to human metabolisms of mind and organ's systems, it is quite apart from our brain power, because the brain is also being operated by our birth, that is Pranan(Not Oxygen). If we study and realise our human body's scientific miracles, we will be astonished by all means. So, man alone has the extra-ordianary power to think and take decisions over our and others, problems. Therefore, by Human birth alone we can attain the Supreme Truth, and thus, he/she can merge with the divine Ecstatic Saturation. There is no other bother in any mannerisms. Whether we are educated or not, wealthy or not and so on, this life is the Mightiest boon to the soul and with our soul that is Paramathma, we are part and parcel of human/divine life. The allurement towards ladies and the allurement towards gents is for some period only, and then, there is no necessity for that attraction for both of them, as husband and wife; this is considered to be a divine life. Till the time of females marriage we are virgins and males are Bramacharya, and for them the conjugal life is going on for some years and it is stopped after a stage or age. Up to their life time, there is nobody in this universe who has fulfilled all his desires, if this concept is realised thoroughly by us we can live without any particular desire; if it has happened there is nothing to give so much importance in our life. Therefore, all things will meet their own change their codes at their particular ages. So, this kind of realisation and illustration, if we enter into the spiritual mood of life with the mode of inspiration, which is insisted by the Almighty, then, what is this? It is considered to be the Deva stage, that is the fore birth of human beings, without any desires, if we worship God, without chanting His Holy manthras, it will be the finest experience, felt by both soul and this body too. Thus, our rishis and sages and saints achieved their goal of Paramathma's grace and in due course of time, they too became God. Thus, our Kulatheivams are formed and worshipped by us in each and every family there is only one need, is to concentrate ourselves on a particular atomic stage of this life, in nothing but the Divinity within us, which is dwelling in our mind, we are all searching outwardly, but He is dwelling in our ownselves, if this supreme truth is realised and recognised by us, we will be honoured by all.

Such Gnanies are born once in 10000 years only, they are enlightened souls for this reason they are having even in their jeevasamadhi, the power to correct their disciples and the whole universe by their divine vibrations. Even today when somebody dies, their body is buried and, a Samadhi is built. They establish a sivalingam there and they say that it is jeevasamadhi, these are not well versed in the vedic principles, they do rituals on Pradhosa days, (we should not perform rituals or any celebrations on Pradhosa days in samadhis), only on the eve of Amasavai (New moon) and Power-nami(full moon), we consider these 2 days per month as monthly Sivarathri, and it is permitted to do rituals and ceremonies; so say our vedic principles and the 10th Thirumurai (Tamil) that is Agni Veda, Thirumanthiram, teaches us the principles, but we are not showing any kind of response or responsibility to those verses, that is why, Nature gets frustrated and thereby, we are all suffering from various diseases and become helpless people. If we wish to live a complete, comfortable life, we should adhere to the principles from the Vedas and Agamas, otherwise, nature will not give rain and without water, there will be no natural fertility of Human beings. Therefore, planted by our ancestors in each and every temple, there is a sthala virutchaham and it is also worshipped by the people, and nature dispenses all. Thus, they lived a full-fledged life, and contentment was attained by them.

REST ASSURED....Each and every creature has its own woes that is why, they are afraid of the many happenings that occur at any time they hope to prevent such bad happenings not to come into their, life. To prevent this fear, we have to proceed with God fearness, if one who is having fear upon God, then he will not involve in illusionary things and will be free from all agonies and bad happenings. Such fearless life alone gives us shanthi and peace. If in the corner of our heart, there is some percentage of fear there will be no peace of mind. It affects each and every organ from its metabolism, and we have to bear the responsibilities of our diseases. Whichever may be the habitat of everyone and whatever may be their habits, we have to adhere to some rules and regulations, from our undertaking to get food materials up to our daily consumption of our energy. This has become a custom. At this time, we should not be late or early in keeping up the time schedule. At the particular time we should consume our food keep up punctuality in doing our duties and thus, we can keep our body healthy. If we have fear about any aspect, we should not work hard in the memorandum of our daily prosperities and perfections. We have to have fear upon such illnesses and over our habits. So, we have to regularize ourselves in all our habits and in choosing our friends, neighbours and relationships. Our relationships too, God has given us as a boon. We should maintain the relation always but due to some unavoidable reasons we have to get rid of these relations, we should live solitarily, there is a proverb 'if one door is shut down, another will be opened', such universal truth will come in action in our day-to-day life. Therefore, we have to cultivate our civilisation and modernisation along with the ancestral customs, and nothing should go over the limitations set by our experienced ancestors. Such belief and regulated life will get rid of fear over unauthorised happenings, because they are the images of illusionary maya only.

REST ASSURED:-------EVERYBODY IN THIS FIELD, they always have fear about ANYTHING and EVERYTHING. BUT IN OUR LIFE, we must not have FEAR COMPLEX, it should be eradicated. BUT FEAR OF GOD IS THE BEGINNING OF KNOWLEDGE. Therefore, we have to be out of fear complex, and thus, we can boldly face any kind of problems throughout our entire life. By virtue of this, our ancestors led their whole life with trust in their relations and most probably God. He is the Mighty Creator of this Universe, all of His words and deeds are ever living; that is we honour Thirukkural which is told to mankind by a man himself, Thiruvalluvar. As such, Thiruvasagham which written by Saint Manickavasaghar, was told by a man to God; 12 - Geethas are emphasised by the Lord's intuition and this was told by God to man, they keep us calm ever in case of all our deeds and thoughts and therefore, we hold honour first for ourselves, and then others, as you expect honour from others, as per schedule you should be ready, and firstly give honour to others; this is the way of attaining all goodness in our entire Universal life. Then our entire life will be meaningful, and we should be very cautious in our thoughts first, and have the blessings by God. It is enough only, to up lift our life and also for the betterment of others' lives through us. All are in His Mighty Hands. If we please Him we can very easily attain Eternal solution and salvation throughout our life in all circumstances and time and ever. FEAR COMPLEX IS ALWAYS A DANGEROUS ONE, AND IT SHOULD BE ERASED by heart itself from the sapling's stage; if it grows, it will uproot us without any kind of worthfulness and value of our whole dispensed life. If we have fear upon God, it will always keeps us to lead a beautiful life which is registered and He will dispense Himself through Himself; thus, our ancestors like Karaikalammaiar, Theresa, Kamarajar lived a very calm life; without name and fame, and today we are trying to live that kind of life. This is Tapas and penance. This is the one and only way to attain His grace and mercy, by which we can set up our self betterment life very easily; so, we also emphasise that if we have belief upon God Himself, He is ready at all times and circumstances to come to our assistance throughout life span. If we also are ready to trust Himself, to entertain our life with fullest satisfaction and contentment, He will fulfill all our needs.

If we wish to have an educational degree from an University, from L.K.G. we have to spend 15 to 20 years with concentration and with oneness of mentality. We can attain and achieve all in this whole Universe. God will

Guard and Guide us by all means. He must fulfill all our needs, that is His responsibility of the Mightiest Lord, Himself. Firstly we should be grateful to Him to dispense this whole world with very beautiful goodnesses and all needs are fulfilled by Himself only to entertain ourselves, nothing is expected from us, from other fellow live holders. We, ourselves, can run our life quite satisfactorily, such a good, life, if it is only blessed by Lord Himself. So, in God we must trust and be with fear, bhakthi and confidence, then only we can live very satisfactorily, and therefore we have to lead our life with regulations and rules, which are proposed by God Himself through Epics and Puranas. Every Tharmasasthra is emphasising us to lead a truthful life. Honesty will automatically give both mental and physical strength, though there are more ways to keep our body's strength and mental attitude in a plane surface. Everything can be kept for some years, then, it is predetermined, this perishable body will not have such strength, and mind has richness of stubbornness; both will lose their valour in due course of time; everything, and every minute, the energy and the infrastructure will be transformed according to age and our habits. So, whatever we take as food or snacks, in the name food, now-a-days, we take some food materials irrelevant to our body and mind; thus, should be rejected by us; it is possible, we can be healthy and wealthy for some years only; after that stipulated time we have to lose all our temperaments; it is natural and one day, we are going to die; Whether the body will be buried or cremated, we all know this truth beyond doubts; but, we are very eager to do rituals and ceremonies to various deities and fulfill our desire. Whether we do or not, time will automatically change our temperament and make us to live life. This is can be understood by a very few people only; and this perishable body has so called diseases and medication and control on food, prevention is better than cure; such philosophical words may give us mental awareness, but in our old age, we need nothing, in due course of time, our organs will not respond like in our young age; that is why, everything is impermanent, everything, one day, they will be destructible; such Universal truth is saturated with our blood and feelings (micro). But we do not think about this concept, this so called life will be up to endless time and our wealth will not be decreased by any means; like these thoughts, we are extending our desires beyond limitations; these should be stopped, likewise, our Manual scripts educate us and impulses us directly or indirectly once in a day; if we assume this truth, we can live with ego, self pride and self prestige (Maya structure to everyone), will get off from us and we will be ready to attain our final goal of solution and saturation with the Almighty.

If one is travelling along in this path, nothing miserable will happen, it is surely taken as an oath. Thus, we can realise our possibilities and impossibilities in all dimensions and angles of our whole life, if this is pronounced by one self, He will be a Gnani (Brahma) ever which is apart from time and happenings. Therefore, nothing in this Universe is real, everything is unreal; so, we have to understand our possibilities and impossibilities very well and thus, we can attain self contentment, if it is attained, nothing more to attain, everything is in the limit of this only and our entire life should be in search of God, because He had given us to our parents, they are only receivers not creators, we cannot shape a single piece of grace, this is human strength; if thinking like this, we are quietly leading our lives, then, everything will be possible. If we have had such a fate already by our Guru or Lord, we can win the race. Otherwise, everything and all our efforts only end in vain. So, first, realise that we are reliable and He is the Creator and Controller of this Universe, and feeds us, controls organs systems and metabolism. When death occurs, nothing of this fleshy and bony body remains. If we realise this Universal fact, we can simply live with contentment and peace. Those who come nearby to us, the golden, divine vibrations can make them Ecstatic and have repulsion of others vibes too. Such Divine souls are with and without this skeleton body, they are called Sidhars and they help humanity and organisms of this Universe to the satisfaction of ourselves of our own sense of activation and they make us, how to control or erase it from the bottom of our inner tissue of the heart. Thus, we can be glorified to restore the Almighty's worthful Vibrations, through which He/ She can maintain peace and harmonious life. Therefore, probably, our ancient Rishis, Munis, and Saints were normaly calm and quiet and they bless us with full of Heart, we can have all the Best, throughout our life span. Therefore, we should be very much careful to choose such Highest souls for identification; this will make us Divine, and we can merge with Godliness and His duty will be fulfilled according to the Human regulations. He is always without any gap, but ourselves, say that we have no time to think of Him. Our time is, most probably, spent to accumulate wealth and in these days, MONEY is the base of all and also somewhat truthful, with money, we can do and fulfill anything as we wish. It is a must one; but it is not all; it is very much essential to lead our life peacefully (domestic) and without any quarrels. Otherwise, the House will not change as a Home at all.

Though all human beings are seeming to be one by only infrastructural appearance, there are crores and crores of Gunas (habits) and all in all they are all having many more differences, that is God's mighty creation.

One parent has 4 children 2 sons and 2 daughters, they are differing in their outer structure and taste of accumulation of things, standard of education, accumulation of wealth, mode of whole life, their desires, dressing and all habits, even twins are not at all having resemblances between them, we can imagine the Tech-constructional Engineering of God. Therefore, we pray Him, when He is satisfied with our penance, He will show His form and so, all can change into divine. Thus, everybody should elevate themselves to the life's eternal plane of Divinity. Their grasping, understanding, mode of feeding, style of speaking, some are left handed by birth, some are deaf and dumb, some are not dumb, but deaf, some are deaf but not dumb, some are handicapped even while they are being given birth to on this earth. One teacher educates all, some will secure centum, most pupils pass with average marks and some may have 'O' mark, after all the full one year education. Why these kinds of many more differences are seen in this mankind. I am not going into all other organisms, if it is quoted, it will prolong up to many pages, that is why I take only mankind. Oh! Human beings, Born Geniuses, please do analyse about yourselves, and we can know, clearly have an idea about our possibilities and impossibilities. If we realise our strength and minus points, weaknesses, we can live without bowing to others or in front of anybody and also we can spread out throughout our area full of shanthi and peace. These Holy men/women are very necessary in this juncture to uplift us, it is only due to God's grace only. Therefore, we have to become divine, and hence we have to perform rituals, righteous life, politeness and always be ever grateful to Him. First, we must be ready to be grateful to our parents, and then we can spread it throughout all creatures and creations. In those days, in all of our King's Darbar, very good personalities were garlanded in the darbar, as ministers and RajaGurus and Military Majors; such persons, were living only for the development and betterment of their own kingdoms, their patriotism cannot be told and written, is not easy. Apart from our imagination, they sacrificed themselves to their nations' pride and development. Now, Nothing to write; all know very, very well.

As according to those kingdoms, if our Bharat or India constructs itself over sense and third eye's divine perception, it will stand still up to many ages. So, we are all ready to sacrifice ourselves to the betterment of the nation. Now, in the name of developing and serving the nation, we, ourselves construct our own, others and neighbors and relatives lives very well, and some are punished by the court too. Through the small gaps, they are able to escape from punishment also. But, God alone, knows all and everything; when time, comes, He will reap all and place them in hell ever. Poverty, diseases, inescapable diseases will suddenly attack them and they cannot be cured by medicine and meet death instantly. Their name/fame will disappear, nobody to remember them even by words and thoughts. So, we should lead a justified divinely life, at all times. Then, we can be ever with Shanthi and Peace. Such opportunity is given to all of us, but we are not ready to adhere to those rules and regulations. Because of our Ego, wealth, we are ignoring our vedic concepts, we are living as we wish; then, the result will be also 'o'. They themselves are responsible for this pitiable result. Nobody will be responsible for this kind of treatment, which is directly done by God Himself. In His kingdom, our wealth, recommendation and so called fraudulent things will not be even heard by Him. He does not take our possessions into consideration at all. So, like a just born tender child, if we surrender to Him, without the sense of 'I', He, Himself puts an eye ray upon us ever and thus, we can live in this world up to our last breath quite contentedly, otherwise, nothing will be possible. Therefore, He should be imprinted into our heart and for this reason, we also can attain Himself and by time when itself ripens, we will saturate with the bliss of full Ecstasy beyond any kind of doubt. All of our thoughts, deeds and their consequences are always known by us earlier. He makes us to play (like toys) in this world in order to return to the originality, i.e. Divinity. We are nothing but God Himself, His will and pressure pushes through curses, boons and dispensations, we are here to resolve all of our credits. If there is no income and expenses, automatically, He will definitely release us from this births and deaths' cycle. This is the juice of all Religions' epics', puranas' and whole spiritualism's goal and will. We should co-operate with Him, then, He alone comes to rescue us to make us to attain His feet without any kind of discomfortable situations. We are born of our parents ecstatic situation of mood. So, we should take rest, until death occurs, and there is no gain because of our anger and jealously. He watches at all times, we must have this concept by heart; if we do it, He will walk along with us by all means of circumstances and His assistance, guidance will guard us in all situations, the one and only thing, we have to develop towards Him is to trust us in the feet of Him, totally surrender to Him, He will do all the rest. It is an ever. Universal, self realised TRUTH.

REST ASSURED:- If one is in an angry mood, he is supposed to be an animal; if he discusses whether it is correct or not, he is in a manual mood; if he is in the mood of speaking and thinking about God's prosperity and values, he is considered to be in a divine mood. Thus, we must identify and in this way, we should live our own life. If it is possible, God will come to us without any rituals and ceremonies. He is the utter slave for Bhakthi only. Do bear this in mind. Whichever and whatever may be our life style and occupation, relationship, neighbourhoods, relatives and friends, they and these are having certain limitations. Apart from that, they cannot enter into the barrier of God. Thus, we can realise ourselves' value of life on our own. There is nobody's or Rishis's perceptional words, are unnecessary. They may make a calculation, everything will be collapsed and their words do not have 100% universal truths. If we realise ourselves, everything can be realised through the grace of Divinity. Because, such ability will be bestowed as a boon by God to those, like true Bhakthimans—Also, this is the time of Kaliyuga, no rituals and ceremonies are yielding such sakthi as in Sathyayuga. So, if we chant (Namasmarana) His Mightiest Holy names, will keep us safe and give all what we need in our run through of our day-to-day life. In these circumstances, total surrender is unavoidable, and such confidence makes us, divine both physically and mentally and therefore, always, we must be with this Namasmarana, in the midst of our daily duties and works. If we follow this simplest way only, we can be Devathas and know Tri-period happenings and we can cure all diseases and problems of the common, innocent people; there is no necessity to make fraudulent deeds, no need to get bribe and money has no value at all. All will work hard with sincerity, thus, our Nation will become the 1st in all fields and we can help the poor people by giving good education to all.

Whoever may be as per our good and bad perception, whether we seem to be fit or not, we have to approach any problem with natural eyes; it needs EYES to be wisdom oriented and thus, we can come to a conclusion whether this life is miserable or eternal. No one can know our Vedanta or spiritual eyes, cannot be viewed by others. It means our exercises and optic systematic witness through our sensual organs thus, we have to come to a conclusion whether life is miserable or is it optimistic, to all at all times, it cannot seem to be miserable; likewise at all times, life cannot be impressed and imprinted with full of happiness; day and night, short and tall are naturals of His marvelous creations all over the universe. Whatever the problem, if the members sit together and discuss, they should believe there is a final solution, will be gotten in the name of justice; with this confidential heart and intellect, all problems will vanish and a remarkable result will be had.

Our politicians and leaders are all trumpeting on the daises that they are struggling to take risks to develop our nation as the super power. Already, it is the one and only super power country itself, up to this second, we are having belief in this stage. If we believe, it is OK. otherwise, if others certify only, we can believe that we are also a Super Power. Super Power is meant as what? For battles, killing all, atomic bombs and rocket ejection is not only meant as super power. Humanity, humanitarianism, humility, character oriented, chastity, etc, these are the truthful traits or characteristics of a super power. Already we are adhering to these qualities from the beginning of human life on this earth itself. We mean something, and hold it, without dropping it, do drop it and hold what is meant as super power. According to Myself and the world, all should have good food, shelter, clothes and the best Education only. It is dispensed by God, without any special prayer of us. His creation, this is not thrown into the pyre. He remakes according to the time and circumstances and so, we are always having good friendship because of this Super Power only. Of all nations, India attained this natural super power stage verily beginning of this whole Universe. Therefore, no need to take quotations from scientists and savants. They may be savants, but they know only hand wise. Universe is incalculable, these discoveries will one day perish. So, there is no necessity to give more value to their words and preachings. Daily, through radios and televisions, today heavy rain fall will be in and throughout night time, take caution, this is their news to the public. But, at that night, nothing will happen, this is our savants' contribution to mankind. Mere foolishness that we are having, if our Dhobi asked us Rs. 1000/- as debt we will not give it to him. But, we give him lots of dirty clothes, new and old, may be the cost of several thousand rupees. A pure kancheepuram sari was given to wash and iron its cost may be about Rs. 1,20,000/- but, we are not ready to give him Rs. 1000/-. Are we educated? We are ashamed, and we should cultivate and educate ourselves as to what is meant by civilisation and broadmindedness then everything will be REST ASSURED.

"They should never bother about anything else whether they are favorable, or unfavorable, happenings, they can win the final victory, that is eternal realisation, by which I and him /her are equal. But they are within the skeleton body and myself is bodiless. So, whenever it requires, Myself will come as skeleton with fleshy body to keep my disciples, for safety, guard and guide them. Thus, all Annonists are Myself only. If they have the mighty truth, they will honour each other and through all types of preachings and modes of lives, they go forward in their life without failures. So, they should not even think about the miserable happenings in their dream too. Of course, there are many conditions and regulations to attain me, perhaps, I am the beginning and the end of all the universal aspects as we respect or disrespect them, they are ever living concepts. Of all the population of this Universe, few can think of me, and maybe a very few or someone will think and try to attain me, but, because of the hectic situations of this worldly circumstances, the percentage will be very merge of course, maybe one among 10 crores of the people, who try to overcome all hurdles and puzzles, then win maya, and finally saturate with my so called Eternal Bliss". For some beings, they reserve with planets, give their harmonious rays to the betterment of all people and creatures, and then may be 900 years of Sri Raghavendhra, their divine power is measurable according to their Tapas, they remain in the planet and return to this earth as a dispensed child, whether male or female, they grow up and at a particular age, they awake within themselves and they themselves live a moderate life, which is the example to all, they live and leave the world and finally they get into Eternity. Then, birthless and deathless life in God ever is possible. It is measurable only through their sinful and dispensable actions and thoughts too, therefore, everybody will attain the greatness of this birth's in various planets, but this earthly life is so dispensable for enlightening one among all births, they can make the souls ever lightened with the glory of itself, because it is from, and its form is nothing but God. According to their culture, place of living and circumstances and languages, their mode of perception of preachings may differ, but the final goal or victory is to get the grip of God's Mightiest hands and climb up His shoulders. So thus, we are lifted by Himself, to have full stop for this our materialistic life. Only we should be endlessly having the awareness to attain the goal of life through our own customs, through the grace of God, and the remarkable, significant point should be the End of our Eternal saturation.

I am not at all writing this book for name and fame and particularly not for money. He insists and gives "REST ASSURED" — and He, Himself imprints all the words, so, it is not my work. He makes me an instrument and this is delivering as His wish and pleasure. So, I may be popular or not, but, He gave the job, now I am doing it. Rest will be His will and pleasure. This kind of simple English fluency is His and He, Himself does the work, and those who can grasp it and swallow it throughout his/her life, he can attain Mukthi. whoever may be, if one, who is having gone through this book, it will alone give Mukthi, these are not my words; it is His comments. So, try to realise the value of the book. 30% of the people write books, 20% of the people are singing, 15% of the people are playing their musical instruments, and on the whole they are all Bhakthimans, but up to date, after saint Thiagarajar, nobody can see Rama Dharsan in their life. They live comfortably and are trying to have chances to sing in sabhas and collect money and with enormous wealth and diseases, they are struggling, and how can they see the Holiest Dharsan of Sri Rama. Nobody is ready to even, believe, we can have Rama Dharsan, they are singing Panchahrathna

Krithis in His Aarathana, but, nothing happens, day-by-day, they increase their sampavanai/mite for singing and if it is thus, how can Sri Rama come before them? IT is impossible; only singing His krithis, we cannot attain Ramamoorthy, through pure bhakthi and dedication, only, we can attain Him, He, Himself comes before us along with His family members and Hanuman. This is my personal experience. I am not lieing at all. If you behold this principle, and at all times, if you try to have Himself as your own, He is ready to be into your bundle of depthful pure love and affection. His love, should be won by our purity of LOVE. Thus, we can definitely have Sri Rama Dharsan. Sathyam.

Conclusion

In our attempt to discover the miraculous sakthi which is managing this whole show we find our attention arrested by a residential building which we see before us. It is found to have a big entrance by which we can enter the house. It also contains a number of windows and ventilators at various points to admit air and light. The interior of the house has many huge pillars and arches. It is also provided with roofs and balconies to protect the inmates from the sun and showers. Every device has been employed to minister to the comfort of the inmates in every room and apartment. Drains have been constructed to allow water and waste to flow into the sides of the house. Every device, the house has been so designed to provide comfort to the inmates during every season. By seeing this house a skilled architect has designed it in such a way as to provide every comfort to the inmates. Although we have not seen the architect, who built the house, and that it is or was a clever and intelligent man. Now let us examine the machine of our structural body. It has got a mouth by which we are eating and drinking, teeth and jaws with which we masticate our food and a passage in our throat, known as the alimentary canal, through which we pass the food on to the stomach. Adjoining this there is another passage by which we inhale and exhale. The stomach has got a separate compartment in which the food which we eat is stored and undergoes the process of digestion and assimilation. The food, when digested is transformed into blood, which accumulates in the heart, and from there it is conveyed through the numerous arteries to all parts of the body and sustains, invigorates, enlivens and rejuvenates the whole an outlet for passing the superfluous element of the food, which is not necessary for the nourishment of the body, in the form excreta and another canal called urethra, for pumping out the refund part of milk, water and other liquids that were taken, which is nor required for the nutrition of the whole body. We have also been provided with a pair of nostrils to take smell, a pair of ears of arms and legs with which to work and walk along respectively, and a generative organ for procreation. We now wonder as whether this most wonderful mechanism has come into being merely as a result of concatenation of particles of matter or whether it has been moulded and fashioned by some architect similar to the one who built the house referred to above though infinitely more skillful, intelligent and powerful than the latter. As we turn to our mind and, while engaged in these thoughts, we find that our mind, too, is a wonderful specimen of divine skill. The diverse faculties, of our mind; such as the cogitative and cognitive faculties, the constructive faculty, retentive power of imagination are all such that faculty, leaves us in bewilderment. It is by exercising these faculties that so many books have been written, so many sciences have been made and are also marvelous, we find this purposiveness working everywhere in this universe. Moreover, we do not find the beginning or the end of this creation. The various limbs of the different species of living beings have been fashioned and assorted in such a symmetrical way that the whole creation appears full of charm. We, thus, see that ever since the beginning of creation some miraculous power has been at work in every clime and at every age and that it will continue to work for ever. Our intellect forces upon us the conclusion that this purposive creation has a premodial, eternal, unborn, imperishable, and ubiquitous, efficient cause who is the infinite power and is all existence, all intelligent, and all blissful. That one indescribable power is called by thousands of names such as Esa, Eswra, Narayana, Brahma, Sun, Govinda, God, Kartha and Allah and so on. There is only one God, one without a second, Who is called by the wise by various names, although He is one, people have different notions about Him. The Vishnu Sahashranama and Sivasaha-shranama are a striking illustration to this truth. Yudhistra asked Grandfather Bhisma to name the deity who is one without a second, who is the greatest refuge of all living beings, and whose worship and eulogy brings everlasting happiness to man. To the above query Bhisma gave the following reply:— "That is to say, every morning quitting one's bed, one should extol God Vishnu, who is the Lord of the whole Universe, the Supreme Deity, the Eternal and ideal Being. One who always eulogies Him as the Supreme Ruler (LORD) of the whole universe and who is all-pervading, unformed and imperishable, is free of all troubles. He is the brightest of all effulgent beings and the most austere of all beings and the most imperishable and the most austere of all penances. He is the greatest of all the greats and the most hospitable refuge of all creatures. He is the purest of the pure, the most sacrosanct of all that is holy, the most auspicious of all that is sacred, the most preferable, the godliest of all Gods and the undying father of all created beings." The above excerpts should suffice to show that the Vishnusahashramanam and Sivasahashranamam and all other laudatory contemplations of that type are that there is one God and no other is the object of their praise. It, therefore, behoves us all to worship Him. This one God is known in three names Brahma, Vishnu, Siva. The Vishnupurana denotes:—"Lord Janardhana, though essentially one, assumes the name of Brahma at the time of creation of this Universe, that of Vishnu while maintaining it and that of, Siva while destroying it." We find the same idea echoed in the Brahatharaya Purana:- "Narayana is imperishable, infinite, omnipresent and untainted by maya. He pervades the whole creation, consisting of sentient and insentient beings. That ever young, primeval deity is called by some by the name of Lord-Shiva. By others the name is Vishnu, and by still others by the name of Brahma." Lord shiva says thus, in Sivapurana, OH Vishnu, although in reality I am always undifferentiated, I have to assume three different appellations, viz., Brahma, Vishnu, Shiva, while discharging the functions of creation, maintenance and dissolution (Universe) respectively. Yourself, Brahma who is with us at present, Myself and Rudra who is still to come, are all one. There is no difference between us all, differentiation entails bondage. In Gita, Paramathma tells;- Vrahma, Sarva and myself are the ultimate cause of this Universe. We are the Universal soul, the Lord of all, the Spectator, Self-seeing, and Unqualified. Oh, Brahman, after penetrating My own Maya, which consists of the three gunas (attributions), I assume three different epithets accordingly as I create, maintain or dissolve the Universe. Hence it is a mistake to regard Brahma, Vishnu, and Shiva as different from one another. They are the appellations of the one and the same God. Also, Sivapuranam tells;- Shiva, Maheswara, Rudra, Vishnu, Pitamaha, Healer of the word SAVAGYA and Paramathma (the supreme soul) these Eight names particularly refer to Lord Shiva Himself. The Vedas describe Him as Srimad Bhagavadha, which describes Him as Rudra — Lord is the really one God, is real; He has always existed and shall exist for ever. He is all-knowledge, all-intelligence and all-bliss. Having no separate body, He is existing in this drama of the universe through the various perishable bodies. He is absolutely pure, consisting of nothing but knowledge and self-sufficient. He has no beginning and no end. He is ever Eternal and Peerless. Though one, He manifests Himself in various forms. In another context;— Entering the various bodies as their very self that Eternal Being and peerless, though one, He manifests Himself in various forms. The Paramathma who is ever self-luminous and unborn who is the supreme Lord and who is known by the names of Narayana, Bhagvan and Vasudeva, is illuminating every form created by Himself by dint of His MAYA. King Jana describes like this;- The 3rd chapter of Skanda, 11th of Srimad Bhagavatha contains a full and most illuminous exposition of God, who is the main theme of the Vedas, the Upanishads and the Puranas.

Saint Janaka describes like this:- Oh, viewers, you are the very cream of those who are well-versed in theology. Be pleased to give me an accurate idea of that Supreme Being, the Ultimate Reality who is called by the name of Holy Narayana. The saint Pippalayana gave the following answer:— Oh king! Know that Ultimate Reality to be Narayana who is responsible for the creation, maintenance, and destruction, of this Universe though Himself attributable to no cause; who persists, within as well as without, in all the three stages of dream, waking life and sound sleep and who inspires and stirs the body along with its various sense-organs, the respiratory organs and heart to their respective functions. Just as sparkles organs and sense organs are incapable of comprehending that ultimate Principle; nay. they cannot even approach it, much less describe it. He was never born and shall never die; He does not grow, nor does He ever diminish in size; but is only a witness of all changing conditions; He is everywhere and at everytime and consists of knowledge and knowledge alone. Just as vitality is one, although it functions differently through different organs and thus, appears differentiated similarly, the soul, though one, appears as differentiated, because of its oneness appears differentiated, because of its differentiation-in the whole creation - alike in mammals, such as the whole creation alike.

The Holy Vedas, which affirm the existence of such a God, also say that we cannot perceive Him with our eyes:— 'True no one can see Him with his eyes; but everyone of us can realise Him with the help of his purified intellect after purging his mind of evil propensities'. Accordingly, those who seek to have a vision of God with their mind's eye (intellect) should cleanse their body and mind and purify their intellect, and then commence their search for God. From the day we are born, this Universe and till we leave this tabernacle of our body we see grand and wonderful sights which excite a great curiosity in our mind to know how they come into being and how they disappear. We daily observe that the bright orb of the sun with its wreath of thousands of rays appears in the eastern horizon early in the morning and journeying through the heavens and transmitting light, heat and vitality to the whole world disappears in the west in the evening. By arithmetic calculation, all the scientists come to a conclusion that the sun is 92830000 miles away from this earth. What a wonder that from such a long distance The Almighty Sun is light, and heat. So, it is considered to be vital project of all creations in habiting this globe! It sucks up the moisture of this earth during every season through its myriad rays, sends it up to the Ether, transforming it as clouds and discharges it again as water and thereby revitalizes it again over all the planets and thereby revitalizes the creatures and infuses life and new life cycle is formed as living beings. Astronomy trumpets, tells us that there are innumerous millions of suns much larger than the one which we see, but which appear to us like tiny stars element of the female's body. This combination of the male and female elements is known as the JIVA, it is only out of His desire. (LIVING ORGANISM). Divide the extreme end of a hair into hundred parts and take the hundredth part of one of these parts; this jiva grows in the form of an organism from the moment of its conception. Students of medical science have been able to discover with the help of microscope that a single drop of our seminal fluid contains hundreds of thousands of living germs, and that only one of such germs, finds its way into the uterus where it persists and grows to be a foetus. The organism of a female's body is so constructed as to enable the jiva from the time of conception onwards to draw its nourishment through something which is shaped like a pipe. As the foetus grows in size there forms round it inside the uterus a sort of membraneous bag full of fluid, which protects the foetus from injury. Wherefrom does this minutest and subtlest substance, as nice as the ten-thousandth part of the point of a hair, derive the capacity to assume gradually the features, the complexion and the shape of its parents? What is the power which sustains it and helps its growth in the mother's womb? How do you account for the strange phenomenon that milk begins to ooze from the mother's breasts shortly before the child's birth? What sakthi is there which supports numberless living creatures, including men, animals and birds, worms and insects, nay, even trees and plants, and provides them with nourishment in time? what is the power which enables the ant to ascend in a steep wall during the day-time, as well as at night? What plant power enables birds of every size, and small, to soar high in the limitless expanse of the sky without any guide or support? How are innumerable varieties of forms such as males and females, human beings, cows, lions, tigers, elephants, birds and insects, created? How is it that only human beings are born of human beings, lions of lions, tigers of tigers, elephants of elephants, horses of horses, a true copy of their parents in every respect. From tiny seeds spring up numberless big and small trees, reared with the help of some unknown power and serve the living creatures for many years with their foliage, flowers, juice, oil, bark, and wood, nourish and feed them with hundreds of thousands of their rich, juicy and delicious fruits, breath and clean the air, suck the moisture and draw their nourishment from the earth and the atmosphere, and wave and dance majestically in the air and they bred by sweat and refuse in the body etc., and the vegetables which spring up from the soil; in short, whatever there is vitality is functioning in some from of another. That which is seen abiding in us as a constant witnessing factor even when all our senses lie dormant, nay, when even the EGO as expressed by the words 'I' "am" is merged for the time being, and which we recall to our mind, on waking by using such expressions as we had a good sleep we saw him, this dream and so on, which is Paramathma (Lord). What is the abode of the Lord? There is one and only God who is hidden within us all, nay, who is pervading everything, everywhere, who is the inner self of all living beings and is the Controller of all that is going on in this universe. He is the indweller of all creatures, the disinterested witness of all the activities of the world, the one Intelligent principle without a compere, and untainted by attributes. The most sacred Vedas, the smirities and the puranas are all unanimous in declaring that this Supreme Deity is immanent in fire, in water, in the air and in the whole Universe, in all who feel the holy presence of this Great Being in their hearts with their purified minds become immortal. He owes allegiance to none in this world, nor is He amenable to anyone's authority or control. He has no distinguishing mark either. He has no origin, no originator, and protector. We have come to know that paramount Lord of all those who are in power or authority the presiding Deity of all the deities, the Master of all the three worlds, the most adorable of all. According to Sri Goswami Tulasidas's description;—Verily Rama is that God who is all existence all intelligence and all bliss, who is unborn, who has knowledge as His very essence, and is a great reservoir of strength; He is the embodiment of all unfilling unfailing power and the Lord of all; He is unqualified; vast, unapproachable by speech and other senses, impartial, faultless, invincible, blotless, formless, free from ignorance, eternal and untainted by maya. He is a mass of happiness He is beyond the reach of prakrithi, the master, the indweller of every heart, free from desire and attachment, and imperishable. Infatuation cannot prevail over Him. Can darkness ever appear before the Sun? The aforementioned God dwells is the heart of every living organism, metobolism in the form of the spirit. 'God dwells in the hearts of all living beings', oh Bhagavan says to Arjuna, thus..! The saint Yagyavalkiya has put if in a nutshell the viewpoint of the Vedas on this subject as follows one hundred and forty four thousand positive and negative arteries branch out from the heart of every human being and are spread throughout the body. In the midst there is an orb, as luminous as the disc of the moon, and in the core of this orb shines the soul, emitting a steady light like that of a lamp. That is the only object worth knowing as its knowledge frees one from the cycle of births and deaths. The Paramathma is present alike in all forms of life, big and small, from the human being down to meanest insect, ney, even in trees and plants. Sri Vedavyasa tells:-------God's light dwells within us; it shines alike in every living being. One can see it with the mind's eye after one has fully composed and steadied the mind. Through Srimad Gita, Bhagavan, Himself, stresses, 'Verily He is the seer who sees the lord installed in the heart of every living body—being as the only imperishable substance among all perishable things. Every human being ought to do homage to that one God who dwells in every heart with unalloyed devotion. One should love every creature, taking it to be His abode. One should be friendly to every living being. Blessed are they who have been initiated into this sacred and philanthropic creed: My devote prayer is that, guided by this divine light, all religious-minded persons, after refining and solidifying their knowledge and replenishing the store of their vigour and zeal, may propagate the truths underlying this creed and convince the whole world that God is one and only one, that in his vigour and zeal, lies His essence. He is present not only in all human beings but in all other animals, and plants, in other words, in human beings, beasts, birds and insects, moths, trees, herbs, shrubs, alike, and that the best mode of worshipping Him is to feel the divine presence in all creatures, to be friendly with all and to wish all well. Let us all consolidate and propagate the divine energy by preaching the cult of universal love and diffusing this true knowledge, and that is why we should not have fear over anything in this Universe, because the Lord is the mighty creator, preceptor and destructor, He is our parents and why do we fear about anything? Let us drive ignorance out of this world, eliminate wrong and injustice and promote mutual good-will, happiness and peace among men by preaching truthfulness righteousness and compassion. REST ASSURED.

SRI KRISHNARPPANAM